MW01708735

Solutions Manual

Adair Dingle

C++

An Introduction to DATA STRUCTURES

Larry Nyhoff

PRENTICE HALL, Upper Saddle River, NJ 07458

Publisher: Alan Apt
Supplement Editor: Jake Warde
Special Projects Manager: Barbara A. Murray
Production Editor: Meaghan Forbes
Supplement Cover Manager: Paul Gourhan
Supplement Cover Designer: Liz Nemeth
Manufacturing Buyer: Pat Brown

Printed in the United States of America

10 9 8 7 6 5 4 3 2

ISBN 0-02-388727-3

Prentice-Hall International (UK) Limited, London
Prentice-Hall of Australia Pty. Limited, Sydney
Prentice-Hall Canada, Inc., Toronto
Prentice-Hall Hispanoamericana, S.A., Mexico
Prentice-Hall of India Private Limited, New Delhi
Prentice-Hall (Singapore) Pte. Ltd.
Prentice-Hall of Japan, Inc., Tokyo
Editora Prentice-Hall do Brazil, Ltda., Rio de Janeiro

C++: An Introduction to Data Structures (Nyhoff, 1999)
Solutions Manual

Chapter Six: Templates & Containers

Chapter Seven: Recursion & Algorithms

Chapter Eight: Lists

Chapter Nine: Other Linked Structures

COMMENTS

C++ is a very powerful and complex language, affording the freedom to use different constructs to solve the same problem. Experienced C++ programmers are usually aware of common stylistic differences. Such knowledge is particularly useful when debugging and when manipulating legacy code.

C (C++) can interpret every variable of a pointer or fundamental type as a boolean value: zero is false, non-zero is true. Hence, traditionally, comparing a variable's value to 0 was frequently skipped when the variable's value as zero (or nonzero) controlled the path taken in an if statement or conditional loop. The recent addition of `bool` to the C++ language has encouraged the explicit use of boolean variables and expressions, a style that makes code more readable. However, this use, as with many features, is completely optional. Like the text, the solution manual uses boolean expressions explicitly.

<u>Variable interpretated as `bool`</u>

```
int p;
cin >> p;
while (p)
{
        ...
}
```

<u>Boolean expression</u>

```
int p;
cin >> p;
while (p !=0 )
{
        ...
}
```

Note that the same stylistic difference applies to the use of pointers because pointer variables are frequently assigned the value of zero when they no longer hold a valid address. A caveat here: when comparing a variable to zero, e.g. `while (p == 0)`, if the second = symbol is missing, yielding `while (p=0)`, the variable p is assigned the value 0, resulting in an expression of value zero, and the while loop is never executed. This type of bug is especially difficult for novices to catch.

In the same vein, standard data structures come in different forms. In this manual, as in the text, stacks and queues are developed with lookahead features. Hence, we have `top()` and `pop()` functions for a stack and `front()` and `removeQ()` for a queue. Since the `pop()` and `removeQ()` functions do not return values, they must be used in conjunction with `top()` and `front()`, respectively, if one wants to use the value taken out of the container. It is worth noting that stacks and queues can be developed with `pop()` and `removeQ()` methods that return values.

Chapter One: Software Engineering

1.5 Exercises

1. A. *Problem analysis and specification* involves determining:
- output required to solve problem
- input given
- other info, such as software usage, feasibility of computer solution

B. *System design* involves
- selecting appropriate data structures to organize the input data
- designing algorithms needed to process the data efficiently

C. *Coding and integration* involves
- selecting appropriate programming language
- translating algorithms into well-structured, well-documented, readable code

D. *Verification and validation* may involve
- "walking through the code" or, possibly proving correctness of algorithms
- executing the software and correcting errors
- modifying algorithms

E. *System maintenance* may involve
- fixing possibly obscure bugs
- modifying software to improve performance
- adding new features, etc.

2. A. *Identify* the objects in the problem specification and determine their type

B. Identify operations needed to solve the problem

C. Arrange the operations in a sequence of steps

3. Introductory programming problems are usually: well-defined, simple, clearly stated and solvable, Real world problems are generally: not well-defined, may be complex, may not have an obvious method of solution.

4. Structured data types are user-defined structures used to collectively organize data in a given problem. Typical examples include arrays, files, stacks, etc.

5. An algorithm is a procedure that can be executed by a computer. It must be:

1. unambiguous (clear what each instruction is intended to do)
2. simple enough to be done by a computer
3. finite (definite termination)

6. Pseudocode is shorthand notation for representing programs in texts, articles and design phases. It is a mixture of natural language (English) and features and syntax common to high-level languages.

7. Three control structures:

1. *sequential* -- steps performed serially, one after another in established sequence
2. *selection* -- one of several alternative actions is selected and executed
3. *repetition* -- one or more steps is performed repeatedly

8. Students programs are typically: small (< 1000 lines), exercised infrequently, correct (easily found bugs), standalone, and maintenance-free.

Real-world programs are typically: large, exercised frequently, intolerant of bugs (which may not be easily found), integrated with other software, and maintained (possibly indefinitely if legacy code -- expensive!)

9. Programming errors

A. Syntax errors: misspelled words, incorrect syntax, missing declarations, misplaced or missing semicolons, etc.. The compiler generates error messages identify source and type of error.

B. Run-time errors: integer overflow, missing files, divide by zero, illegal memory access, etc. Execution of the program will be terminated with an error message.

C. Logical errors: improper initialization, aliases, incorrect or misplaced instructions, etc. Incorrect results may be produced, but possibly only for extreme (unusual) cases.

10. Program maintenance is required to fix bugs, accommodate new uses of software (changes in environment), improve performance, or incorporate new features.

Programming Problems

1.
```
int row = 0;
bool found = false;
while (!found && row < n)
{
      row++;
      int col =0;
      while (!found && col < n)
      {
            col++;
            if (mat[row][col] == item)
                  found = true;
      }
}
if (found)
      cout << "item found" << endl;
else
      cout << "item not found" << endl;
```

2. The else clause resets the boolean found with each pass of the inner for loop. Hence, the boolean found is always false unless the last element, mat[n][n], contains the item sought.

3. The matrix is searched completely, regardless of where item is found (inefficient!).

4. Poor format (inadequate spacing, indentation, multiple statements per line).
Not readable (insufficient comments, nondescriptive variable names)
Not structured (gotos and use of global variables)

```
boolean LinearSearch(int List[], int length, int item)
/*    Input: list List, its length and item sought
      Function: linear (sequential) search of List for item
      Return:  true returned, if item found; false, otherwise
*/
{
  int index = 0;
  boolean found = false;
  while (!found && index < length)
  {
    index++;
    if (list[index] == item)
        found = true;
  }
  return found;
}
```

Chapter Two: ADTs – C-Style types

2.2 Exercises

1.	a) true	b) FT	c) FFFF FFFF FTFF FFFF
2.	a) true	b) TT	c) FTTF TTTF FTTF TTTT
3.	a) true	b) TT	c) TFTT TTTT TTTT TTTF
4.	a) true	b) TT	c) TTFF FFFF FFFF FFFT
5.	a) true	b) TT	c) TFFT TFFT TFFT TFFT
6.	a) true	b) TT	c) TFTF TFTF TFTF TFTF

7. null @
8. no

9. 64
10. 28271
11. -16382
12. -16385
13. -6553
14. -10922

15. 64
16. 28271
17. -16386
18. -16383
19. -26215
20. -21846

21. -32704
22. -4497
23. 16382
24. 16385
25. 6553
26. 10922

27. 0.5
28. 6
29. 252
30. 0.25
31. 170×2^{34}
32. -0.6875

33. 0000 0000 0110 0011
34. 0001 0100 1010 0000
35. 0000 0000 1111 1111
36. 1111 1111 0000 0001
37. 0000 0100 0000 0000
38. 1111 1100 0000 0000

39. a) 0011 1111 0010 0000	0000000000000000	b) same
40. a) 0100 0001 1100 1101	0000000000000000	b) same
41. a) 0100 0001 0110 1100	1000000000000000	b) same
42. a) 0011 1100 1100 0001	0000000000000000	b) same
43. a) 0011 1111 0000 1011	1111111111111111	b) 0011 1111 0000 1100 0000 0000 0000 0000
44. a) 0100 0000 0000 0101	1111111111111111	b) 0100 0000 0000 0110 0000 0000 0000 0000

45. 01000010 01000101
46. 01100010 01100101
47. 01000001 01000010 01001100 01000101
48. 01001101 01110010 00101110 00100000 01000100 01101111 01100101
49. 00110001 00110010 00110011 00110100
50. 00110001 00110010 00101110 00110011 00110100

2.3 Exercises

1. 10
2. 80
3. 70
4. 104
5. 28

6. a[3]: base + 3	a[9]: base + 9
7. a[3]: base + 24	a[9]: base + 72
8. a[4]: base + 40	a[9]: base + 60
9. a[1]: base + 4	a[2]: base + 8
10. a[2]: base + 8	a[6]: base + 24

11. a[i] = base + i
12. a[i] = base + 8*i
13. a[i] = base + 10*i
14. a[i] = base + 4*i
15. a[i] = base + 4*i, where i = ord(day)

16. 108, 112
17. 164, 356
18. 192, 152
19. 250, 420

20. 116,112
21. 740, 284
22. 168, 272
23. 300, 270

24. a) base + w*i*N2 + w*j   b) base + w*i + w*N1*j, where N1 and N2 are dimensions of 2D array

25. base + w*i*N2*N3 + w*j*N3 + w*k, where N1, N2 and N3 are dimensions of 3-D array

26. base + 8*i*N2*N3*N4 +8*j*N3*N4 +8*k*N4 +8*l

27. Generalize the formulae above to derive a series (sum of terms from 1 to q)

28. b + 8*(i(i+1)/2) + j), (based on summing (1 through i))

29. same idea as above but sum decreasing terms from N1 downto N1-i from

30. If the tridiagonal matrix has N1 rows, you effectively have a 3*N1 matrix, where m[0][0] and m[N1-1][2] are empty cells.

2.4 Exercises

1.
```
struct CivTime
{
   int      hour, min, sec;
   bool     am;
};
```

2.
```
struct MilTime
{
   int            hour;
   int            min;
};
```

3.
```
struct Length
{
   int            yards, feet, inches;
};
```

4.
```
struct Angle
{
   int            degrees, min, sec;
};
```

5.
```
enum Suit_t     {CLUBS, SPADES, HEARTS, DIAMONDS};

struct Cards
{
  Suit_t        suit;
  int           value;
};
```

6.
```
struct Listing
{
  string  name, address, number;
};
```

7.
```
enum CarStyle  {SUV, SEDAN, MINIVAN, LIMO};
enum Color     {RED, BLUE, YELLOW, GREEN, CHAMPAGNE_SILVER};

struct Car
{
  string        model, make;
  CarStyle      style;
  Color         color;
};
```

8.
```
struct Book
{
  string        author, publisher, title;
  int           num_pages;
};
```

9.
```
struct TeamRec
{
  string        name, manager, owner;
  int           wins, losses;
};
```

10.
```
struct Checker
{
  int           row, col;
};
```

11.
```
struct Civ
{
     int  sec;
     bool am;
};

struct Time
{
  int     hour, min;
  char    tag;

  union
  {
     Civ  civilian;
  };
};
```

12.
```
enum MaritalStatus  {MARRIED, SINGLE};

struct Person
{
  string       name, birthday, ss_no;

  Length       height;            //use struct from #3
  Color        hair, eye;         //use enum from  #7

  int               age, weight;
  MaritalStatus     status;

  union
  {
     int  num_child;
  };
};
```

13.
```
enum Position_t     {PITCHER, CATCHER, INFIELDER, OUTFIELDER};
enum Pitcher_t {STARTING, RELIEF};
enum Swing_t   {LEFT, RIGHT, SWING};

struct Pitcher
{
 int      wins, losses, strikeouts, walks;
 double   earned_run;
 Pitcher_t     tag;
 union
 {
  int      games;
  struct   {int innings, saves;};
 };
};



struct Player
{
 double   bat_avg, slug_avg, field_percent;
 Swing_t  bats;
 Position_t position;
 union
 {
  Pitcher      pitcher;
  Position_t   infielder;
  bool         catch_knuckle;
 };
};
```

14. same idea as above.

Programming Problems

1.

```
/*  Functions to add and multiply nonnegative numbers in base two
      Input:     two bit strings
      Output:    display corresponding sum and product
      Note:      If the bit strings are stored as arrays, and
                 of a set size (or right-justified), one may proceed
                 with right to left addition, carrying any overflow.

      Reference:     This program is very much like #4 and of
                 relatively the same degree of complexity.
*/
```

2.

```
/*  Program to compute letter grades
      Input:     at most N real numbers, where N is a predefined value
      Process:   Calculate mean and standard deviation
                 Assign letter grade based on formula given in book
      Output:    Mean, standard deviation, each real input with
      associated grade
*/

#include <iostream>
using namespace std;

double Mean(double score[], int  num)
{
      double sum = 0.0;

      for (int n = 0; n < num; n++)
            sum += score[n];

      return sum/n;
}


double StdDev(double score[], int  num, double mean)
{
      double sum = 0.0;

      for (int n = 0; n < num; n++)
            sum += (score[n]- mean)*(score[n] - mean);

      return sqrt(sum/num);
}
```

```
void AssignGrades(double score[], int  num,
                                    double mean, double stdev)
{
     double DF  = mean - 1.5 *stdev;
     double CD  = mean - 0.5 *stdev;
     double BC  = mean + 0.5 *stdev;
     double AB  = mean + 1.5 *stdev;

     for (int n = 0; n < num; n++)
          if ( score[n] < DF)
               cout << score[n] <<  "   = F" << endl;

          else if ( score[n] < CD)
               cout << score[n] <<  "   = D" << endl;

          else if ( score[n] < BC)
               cout << score[n] <<  "   = C" << endl;

          else if ( score[n] < AB)
               cout << score[n] <<  "   = B" << endl;

          else
               cout << score[n] <<  "   = A" << endl;

     return;
}

const int N = some_value;     // a positive integer, e.g. 50

int main()
{
     int input[N];
     cout << "Enter scores (-1 to stop): ";
     cin >> input[0];
     int index = 0;
     while (input[index] != -1 && index < N)
     {
          index++;
          cin >> input[index];
     }
     double mean = Mean(input, index);
     double stdvar = StdDev(input, index, mean);
     cout << "The mean is : " << mean <<
               " and the standard deviation is : "
          << stdvar << endl;

     AssignGrades();
     return 0;
}
```

3. Use the boolean values of true and false to model open and shut, respectively. Represent the state of the 150 mailboxes by a 151 element boolean array (ignore the 0th element).

   Then the problem becomes one of simply toggling the boolean value (that represents the state of the mailbox) when going through the process of opening or shutting.

   If all boxes are initially open, i.e. all values initially false, the boxes left closed at the end will be those indexed by squares of integers: 1, 4, 9, 16, etc.

```
for (int index = 2; index < numboxes; index++)
      {
       int j = index;

       while (j < numboxes)
       {
           mailbox[j] = ! mailbox[j];
           j += index;
       }
      }
```

4.

```
/*  Program to add two large integers

        Input:     nonnegative integers

        Process:   Store digits of each number in a separate array,
                   Remember to right-justify the number and add leading
                   zeroes,
                   Add corresponding elements of the array, carrying any
                   overflow.

        Output:    Output sum computed above
        NOTE:          The underlying approach here is the same whether
                   the digits are stored individually in the array, or in
                   groups of three.

                   The grouping into sets of 3 supports the user's input
                   of numbers where thousands are separated by commas,
                   e.g. 1,0001 versus 1001.
*/

#include <iostream>
using namespace std;

const int MAXLGTH = some_value;

typedef int Number[MAXLGTH];          // for readability
```

```
void InitNum(Number x)
{
     cout << "Enter an integer, separated by commas into groups
               of three digits (e.g. 12,465,321):  "<< endl;

     int lgth = 0;

     Number reversed;

     char comma;

     // NOTE: NO ERROR CHECKING ON INPUT VALUES
     while (cin >> reversed[lgth])
     {
          lgth++;
          cin >> comma;
     }

     for (int index = 0; index < lgth; index++)
          x[index] = reversed[lgth - index];

     return;
}


Number Add(Number x, Number y, int& lgth)
{
     int carry = 0;
     Number result;

     for (int index = 0; index < lgth; index++)
     {
          result[index] = x[index] + y[index] + carry;
          carry = result[index] % 1000;
          result[index] %= 1000;
     }

     if (carry)
     {
          lgth++;
          result[lgth] = carry;
     }

     return result;
}
```

```
void PrintNum(Number result, int lgth)
{
     cout << "/n/n/n/The sum of your input is:  ";

     for (int index = lgth-1; index >= 0; index--)
     {
       if (result[index] < 10)
          cout << "0";
       if (result[index] < 100)
          cout << "0";
       cout << result[index];

       cout << ",";
     }

     if (result[0] < 10)
          cout << "0";
     if (result[0] < 100)
          cout << "0";
     cout << result[0];

     return;
}

int main()
{
   Number add1, add2;

   InitNum(add1);

   InitNum(add2);

   cout << "Please input 2 positive numbers, up to "
     << 3*MAXLGTH << "digits" << endl;

   int lgth1 = GetNum(add1);
   int lgth2 = GetNum(add2);

   if (lgth1 < lgth2)
     int length = lgth2;
   else
     int length = lgth1;

   Number sum = Add(add1, add2, length);

   PrintNum(sum, length);

   return 0;
}
```

5. **Although similar to #4, this problem is more difficult.**

6.

```
/*  Program to track demographic changes due to population migration
     Input:    canned, initial population figures for urban,
               suburban, rural
     Process:  Calculate successive population changes in 10 year
               increments according to given percentages
     Output:   population for urban, suburban and rural regions
     NOTE:     The trick here is to realize that 2 population arrays
               are needed because of the dependencies between
               elements in the calculations
*/

#include <iostream>
using namespace std;

int main()
{
   enum        Region_t  {URBAN, SUBURBAN, RURAL};

   double Migration[][] = new double[Region_t][Region_t];

   double Population[] = new double[Region_t];

   double New_Pop[] = new double[Region_t];

   cout<< "Please input migration percentages (table on p. 80)"
          << endl;

   for (Region_t row = urban; row < rural; row++)
     for (Region_t col = urban; col < rural; col++)
        cout << Migration[row][col];

   cout<< "Please input population figures (given on p. 81)" << endl;

   for (Region_t index = urban; index < rural; index++)
   {
     cout << Population[index];
     New_Pop[index]= Population[index];
   }
```

```
    // clear screen and headers go here
    for (int rep = 0; rep < 5; rep++)      // better to use constants!
    {
      for (int year = 0; year < 10; year++)
      {
         for (Region_t row = urban; row < rural; row++)
           for (Region_t col = urban; col < rural; col++)
              New_Pop[row]+=Migration[row][col]/100 * Population[col];

         for (Region_t index = urban; index < rural; index++)
             New_Pop[index]= Population[index];
       }

      for (Region_t index = urban; index < rural; index++)
         cout << Population[index];

      cout << endl;
  }

  return 0;
 }
```

7.
```
/*  A straight-forward assignment.  The students may get caught on
passing multi-dimensional arrays.  Since pointers have not been covered
yet, use typedef.
*/

#include <iostream>
using namespace std;

typedef double TwoDArray[m][n];        // m & n given

void SumDisplayMatrix(TwoDArray A, TwoDArray B, int m, int n)
  {
// no need to store sum but can easily
   for (int row =0; row < m; row++)
   {
    for (int col = 0; col < n; col++)
       cout << A[row][col] + B[row][col];

    cout << endl;
   }
   return;
  }
```

8. This problem is similar to #6 but slightly more difficult.

9.
```
/*  Magic square -- an excellent program to reinforce 2D structures
*/

#include <iostream>
using namespace std;

const int DIM = 21;
int square[DIM][DIM];          // global avoids passing array
                               // see above for passing 2D
int size;

void init_Sq()
{
 bool size_ok = false;

 while (!size_ok)
 {
     cout << "/n/n/n/Please enter an odd integer for the dimension
               of the magic square (between 3 and" << DIM << "): ";
     cout.flush();

     cin >> size;
     if (3 <= size && size <= DIM && size % 2 == 0 )
          size_ok = true;
 }

 for (int row = 0; row < size;  row++)
     for (int col = 0; col < size; col++)
          square[row][col] = 0;

  return;
}
```

```
void CreateSq();
{
  int row = 0;
  int col = size % 2;

  square[row][col] = 1;              // 1 in top row, middle column

  int num = 2;
  while (num <= size)
  {
     int nextrow = row - 1;
     int nextcol = col + 1;

     if (nextrow < 0)
          nextrow = size - 1;

     if (nextcol == size)
          nextcol = 0;

     if (square[nextrow][nextcol])        // position already filled
     {
          row++;
          if (row == size)
               row = 0;
     }
     else
     {
          row = nextrow;
          col = nextcol;
     }

     square[row][col] = num;
     num++;
   }  // end while

   return;
}

void PrintSq()
{
  for (int row = 0; row < size;  row++)
  {
     for (int col = 0; col < size; col++)
          cout << "/t" << square[row][col];
     cout << endl;
  }
  return;
}
```

```
int main()
{
      init_Sq();
      CreateSq();
      PrintSq();

      return 0;
}
```

10.
```
      /* Program that demonstrates initialization of 2D array and its
               manipulation in successive refinements

      Input: Four edge temperatures; tolerance
      Process: Guess temperature of interior nodes, repeated averaging
               of interior nodes relative to four neighbors.
      Output: Temperatures of entire array and number of iterations to
               achieve steady state.

      Assume size n of matrix has been given

      */

#include <iostream>
using namespace std;

const int n = some_value;            // a positive integer, e.g. 50
typedef double TwoDArray[n][n];           // n given above

double initialize(TwoDArray A, int n)
{
      cout << "Please input the tolerance" << endl;
      cin >> threshold;

      cout << "Please input the four (constant) edge
               temperatures" << endl;

      cin >> A[0][0] >> A[0][n-1] >> A[n-1][0] >> A[n-1][n-1];

      for (int index = 1; index < n-1; index++)
                           //set edge temperature
      {
            A[0][index] = A[0][0];
            A[n-1][index] = A[n-1][0];
            A[index][0] = A[0][n-1];
            A[index][n-1] = A[n-1][n-1];
      }
```

```
for (int row = 1; index < n-1; row++)    // guess interior temperature
     for (int col = 1; col < n-1; col++)

          A[row][col] = (A[0][0] + A[0][n-1] + A[n-1][0]
                                             + A[n-1][n-1])/4;

     return threshold;
}


bool steadyState(TwoDArray A, TwoDArray B, int n, double lmt)
{
     bool steady = true;
     int row =0;

     while (steady && row < n)
     {
       int col = 0;

       while (steady && col < n)
       {
          if (B[row][col] - A[row][col] > lmt)
               steady = false;
          col++;
       }

       row++;
     }

     return steady;
}


void Average(TwoDArray A, TwoDArray B, int n)
{
  for(int row = 1; row < n-1; row++)
    for (int col = 1; col < n-1; col++)

       B[row][col]=(A[row-1][col]+ A[row+1][col] + A[row][col-1]
                                             + A[row][col+1])/4;

  return;
}
```

```
void display(TwoDArray A, int n, int reps)
{
      cout << "Steadystate was achieved in    "
           << reps << "repetitions" << endl;

      for(int row = 1; row < n-1; row++)
      {
        for (int col = 1; col < n-1; col++)
           cout << A[row][col];

        cout << endl;
      }
      return;
}


int main()
{
  const int N = 100;

  double  T[N][N];

  double tolerance = initialize(T, N);

  int iter = 0;

  while (!steadyState(T, newT, N, tolerance))
  {
     Average(T, newT, N);
     iter++;
  }

  display(T, N, iter);

  return 0;
}
```

11. This problem is similar to #10.

As in the preceding problem, one needs two matrices so that the new state of a cell does not affect the state of cells to be processed subsequently.

Each matrix contains boolean values, true representing alive, false representing dead. For any given cell, the number of neighbors can be calculated from the matrix coordinates. The number of alive neighbors can then be simply counted and the appropriate action taken.

12.

```
/*  File input program */
#include <iostream>
using namespace std;

int main
{
    const double WarningThreshold = 0.9;

    cout << "Please enter today's date (mm dd yy): " << endl;
    int month, day, year;
    cin >> month >> day >> year;

    cout << "Please enter data filename" << endl;
    string file_name;
    cin >> file_name;

    ifstream inFile(file_name.c_str());
    if (!inFile)
    {
          cerr << "Unable to open file " << file_name << endl;
          return 1;
    }

    cout << "User Accounts: " << month << "/" << day << "/"
              << year << endl;
    cout << "/tUserName/t/tUser-ID/t/t/Resource Limit/t/tResources Used"
              << endl;

    string    name;
    int       id;
    int       resourceLmt;
    double    resourceUsed;

    while (inFile >> id)
    {
          inFile >> name;
          inFile >> resourceLmt;
          inFile >> resourceUsed;

          cout << "/t" << name << "/t/t" << id << "/t/t" << resourceLmt;
          cout << "/t/t" << resourceUsed;

          if (resourceLmt * WarningThreshold < resourceUsed)
                cout << "***";
          cout << endl;
    }
    return 0;
}
```

13. This problem is similar to #12.

14. This problem is a straight-forward application of the union data structure as described in the text. One needs only to set up the data structure and process the character denoting the type with an if-else control structure.

Chapter Three: ADTs – C++-Style types

3.2 Exercises

1.
```
class Time
{ …
  public:
      …
      void Read(istream& in);
      …
};

istream& operator>>(istream& in, const Time& t)
{
      t.Read(in);
      return in;
}
```

2.
```
class Time
{ …
  public:
      friend bool operator<(const Time&, const Time&)
      …
};

bool operator<(const Time& t1, const Time& t2)
{
      return t1.myMilTime < t2.myMilTime;
}
```

3.
```
class Time
{ …
  public:
      …
      bool operator==(const Time& t) const;
      …
};

inline bool Time::operator==(const Time& t) const
{
      return myMilTime == t.myMiltime;
}
```

4.
```
class Date
{ …
  private:
      int  month, day, year;
};
```

5. same idea as #4

6.
```
class Checker
{ ...
  private:
      int  row, col;
};
```

7.
```
class CartesianCoor
{ ...
  private:
      int  x,y;
};
```

8. same idea as #7

9.
```
enum Suit {Heart, Spade, Diamond, Club};
class Card
{
  private:
      Suit suit;
      int  face;
};
```

10.
```
class Date
{
public:
      Date();
      Date(unsigned, unsigned, unsigned);

      void Display();
      int getMonth(){ return month;}
      int getDay() {return day;}
      int getYear() ( return year;}

      void setMonth(unsigned m){ month = m;}
      void setDay(unsigned d)  { day = d;}
      void setYear(unsigned y) (year = y;}

  private:
      int  month, day, year;
};
```

```
Date::Date()
{
      month = 1;
      day = 1;
      year = 1990;
}

Date::Date(unsigned m, unsigned d, unsigned y)
{
      month = m;
      day = d;
      year = y;
}

void Date::Display()
{
      cout << "The date (month, day, year) is: ";
      cout << month << "  " << day << ", " << year << endl;
}
```

11. same idea as #10

12.

```
class Checker
{
  public:
      void move(int, int);
      int whatCol(){return col; }    //inline for efficiency
      int whatRow(){return row; }
...
  private:
      int  row, col;
};

void Checker::move(int r, int c);
{
      row = r;
      col = c;
}
```

13.
```
class CartesianCoor
{
  public:
     // use constructor if want to set Point only once!
     void moveXY(int X, int Y) {x = X; y = Y;}
     void setX(int v) {x = v;}      //inline for efficiency
     void setY(int v) {y = v;}
     int whereX() {return x;}
     int whereY() {return y;}
...
  private:
     int  x,y;
};
```

14. same idea as #13

15.
```
class Card
{
  public:
     Card(Suit, int);
     Suit whatSuit() {return suit; }
     int  whatValue() { return face; }
private:
     Suit suit;
     int  face;
};

Card::Card(Suit s, int v)
{
     suit = s;
     face = v;
}
```

16. see #12 in 2.4, `class` contains data for persons (as in `struct`) but with functionality encapsulated

17. see #13 in 2.4, `class` contains data for player (as in `struct`) but with functionality encapsulated

18. see #14 in 2.4, `class` contains data for weather (as in `struct`) but with functionality encapsulated

3.3 Exercises

1. /* Compares strings A and B, returning true if the same, false otherwise

```
        NOTE: the receiver, A, is not modified by this action
*/
bool Strings:: Compare(const Strings & s)
{
        int lgth = s.Length();
        int mylgth = Length();

        bool same = lgth == mylgth;

        int index = 0;
        while (same && index < mylgth && index < lgth)
        {
                same = myStorage[index] == s.myStorage[index];
                index++;
        }

        return same;
}
```

2. /* Concatenates strings A and B, returning AB, when message A.Concatenate(B) received. If AB is longer than STRING_LIMIT, the largest possible beginning portion of B is concatenated to A.

```
        NOTE: the receiver, A, is not modified by this action
        It is fairly simple to make this method destructive (i.e.
        replace A with AB)
*/
Strings Strings:: Concatenate(const Strings & s)
{
        int lgth = s.Length();
        int mylgth = Length();

        char con[mylgth];                   // copy data from A
        for (int index =0; index < mylgth; index++)
                con[index] = myStorage[index];

        int conLength = mylgth;             // append B (as much as possible)
        while (conLength < STRING_LIMIT && conLength <= lgth + mylgth)
        {
                con[conLength] = s.myStorage[conLength - mylgth];
                conLength++;
        }
        return Strings(con);          // construct Strings object to return
}
```

```
3. /* Copies a substring of B to A when message A.Copy(B, start, end)
   received.
        NOTE: the receiver, A, is modified by this action.
   */
   void Strings:: Copy(const Strings & s, int start, int end)
   {
        for (int index = start; index < end; index++)
             myStorage[index - start] = s.myStorage[index];

        myStorage[end] = '\0';          // null terminate string
        return;
   }


4. /*  Inserts string B into string A, at specified position, when
   message A.Insert(B, position) received. If the result is longer than
   STRING_LIMIT, the string is truncated.
        Assumes position is a valid index into string A.
        NOTE: the receiver, A, is modified by this action.
   */
   void Strings:: Insert(const Strings & s, int start)
   {
        int lgth = s.Length();
        int mylgth = Length();
        char backup[mylgth-start];          // store end of string A
        for (int index = start; index < mylgth; index++)
             backup[index] = myStorage[index];

        int index = 0;
                                     // insert B (all but terminating char)
        while (index+start < STRING_LIMIT && s.myStorage[index] != '\0')
        {
             myStorage[start + index] = s.myStorage[index];
             index++;
        }

        int newlgth = index + start;
        index = 0;
                                        // append rest of A
        while (newlgth  < STRING_LIMIT && backup[index] !='\0')
        {
             myStorage[newLength] = backup[index];
             newLength++;
             index++;
        }
        myStorage[newlgth] = '\0';
        return;
   }
```

5.
```
/*   Deletes the specified length of a string, at specified position,
when message A.Delete(size, position) received.
     Assumes size+position is within range of data
     NOTE: the receiver, A, is modified by this action.
*/
void Strings:: Delete(int length, int start)
{
     for (int index = start; index < mylgth; index++)
          myStorage[index] = myStorage[index+length];

     return;
}
```

6.
```
/* Replaces the specified portion of a string with another string
when message A.Replace(B, start, end) received.
     NOTE: the receiver, A, is modified by this action.
*/
void Strings::Replace(const Strings& s, int start, int end)
{
          Delete(start - end +1, start);
          Insert(B, start);
}
```

7.
```
class WorkSpace
{
  private:
     int start;
     int length;
};
```

8.
```
class WorkSpace                      // expanded class definition
{
  private:
     int start;
     int length;
  public:
     void display();
     void input(int);
     int  Length();
     bool Compare(Workspace);
     void Concatentate(Workspace);
     void Copy(Workspace);
     int  Find(Workspace);
     void Insert(Workspace, int);
     void Delete(int, int);
     void Replace(Workspace);
};
```

```
/* The actual buffer ("storage") is external to the class definition.
One could allocate an array outside the class definition to be of
some (large) predefined size.  The functionality associated with this
buffer must include some indication of the next available free space
(this would be the index passed into the Workspace constructor). */
```

9.
```
/* display:definition in .cpp file */

#include <iostream>
using namespace std;

void Workspace::display()
{
     for (int index = start; index < start + length - 1; index++)
          cout << storage[index];

     cout << endl;

     return;
}
```

10.
```
/* input:definition in .cpp file */

#include <iostream>
using namespace std;

void Workspace::input(int where)
{
     int index = where;

     while (cin >> storage[index])
          index++;

     length = index - where + 1;

     return;
}
```

11.
```
/* Length:definition in .h file; simple inline */
void Workspace::Length()
{
     return length;
}
```

12. /* Compare:definition in .cpp file */

```
bool Workspace:: Compare(const Workspace & s)
{
     int slgth = s.length();

     bool same = length == slgth;

     int index = 0;
     while (same && index < slgth && index < length)
     {
          same = storage[start + index] == storage[s.start + index];
          index++;
     }

     return same;
}
```

13. /* Concatenate:definition in .cpp file
    Alters string object invoked by appending passed string s */

```
void Workspace::Concatenate(const Workspace & s)
{
     int slgth = s.length();

     for (int index =0; index < slgth; index++)
          storage[start + length - 1 + index]
                              = storage[s.start = index];

     length += slgth;

     return;
}
```

14. /* Copy:definition in .cpp file */

```
void Workspace::Copy(const Workspace & s, int Sstart, int Send)
{
     for (int index = 0; index < Send - Sbegin + 1; index++)
          storage[index + start] = storage[index +Sstart];

     length = Send - Sbegin + 1;
     return;
}
```

15.
```
/* Find:definition in .cpp file */

int Workspace::Find(const Workspace& s)
{
     int slgth = s.length();

     int index = 0;
     while (index < length)
     {
          int where = 0;
          while(storage[start+where+index] == storage[s.start+index])
               where++;

          bool found = where == s.length();

          if (found)
               return index;
          else
               index++;
     }

     return -1;      //not found
}
```

16.
```
/* Insert:definition in .cpp file
     Inserts string B into string A, at specified position
     NOTE: setup of common storage makes it very easy to write over
     someone else's "string".
*/
void Workspace::Insert(const Workspace& w, int start)
{
     int wlgth = w.length();

     char backup[length-start];          // store end of string A
     for (int index = start; index < length; index++)
          backup[index] = storage[index];

     for (int index = 0; index < wlgth; index++)   //insert
          storage[start + index] = storage[w.start + index];

     // append rest of A
     for (int index = 0; index < length - start; index++)
          storage[start + index] = backup[index];

     length += wlgth;
     index = 0;
     return;
}
```

17.
```
/* delete:definition in .cpp file */

void Workspace:: Delete(int delLgth, int start)
{
     for (int index = start; index < start + length -1; index++)
          myStorage[index] = myStorage[index + delLgth];

     return;
}
```

18.
```
/* Replace:definition in .cpp file
     NOTE: setup of common storage makes it very easy to write over
   someone else's "string".  String object called here can expand if
   replacement is larger
*/
void Workspace::Replace(Workspace w, int begin, int end)
{
     char  backup[length - end];

     for (int index = end + 1; index < start + length -1; index++)
          backup[index - end -1] = storage[index];

     for (int index = 0; index < w.length ; index++)
          storage[index + begin] = storage[w.start + index];

     for (int index = 0; index < length - end; index++)
          storage[begin + w.length + index] = backup[index];

     length += w.length - begin + end +1;

     return;
}
```

3.4 Exercises

1.
```
/* Returns the number of times string s appears in string target
*/
int  NumHits(const string& s, const string& target)
{
     int  matches = 0;
     int position = target.find(s);
     while (position < target.size())
     {
          matches++;
          targer.find(s, position + 1);
     }
     return matches;
}
```

2.
```
/* Returns name of month
*/
string MonthName(int month)
{
     if (month == 1)
          return "January";
     else if (month == 2)
          return "February";
     else if (month == 3)
          return "March";
     else if (month == 4)
          return "April";
     else if (month == 5)
          return "May";
     else if (month == 6)
          return "June";
     else if (month == 7)
          return "July";
     else if (month == 8)
          return "August";
     else if (month == 9)
          return "September";
     else if (month == 10)
          return "October";
     else if (month == 11)
          return "November";
     else if (month == 12)
          return "December";
     else
          return "Invalid Number";

}
```

```
3. /* Returns number of month
   */
   int MonthName(string month)
   {
        if (month == "January")
             return 1;
        else if (month == February")
             return 2;
        else if (month == "March")
             return 3;
        else if (month == "April")
             return 4;
        else if (month == "May")
             return 5;
        else if (month == "June")
             return 6;
        else if (month == "July")
             return 7;
        else if (month == "August")
             return 8;
        else if (month == "September")
             return 9;
        else if (month == "October")
             return 10;
        else if (month == "November")
             return 11;
        else if (month == "December"
             return 12;
        else
             return -1;

   }
```

```
4. /* Using <cctype> function(s), return string first in all
             lowercase and then in all uppercase
   */
   #include <cctype>

   string    CopyUp(const String& s)
   {
        string copy = tolower(s);
        return copy;
   }

   string    CopyLow(const String& s)
   {
        return  toupper(s);
   }
```

5.
```
/* Replaces all occurrences of substring old with substring nnew in
       target string
*/
string replace_all(const string& source, string& old, string& nnew)
{
     string target = source;

     int position = target.find(old);

     while (position < target.size())
     {
          target.replace(position, old.size(), nnew);
          targer.find(old, position + 1);
     }

     return target;
}
```

6.
```
string FullName(const string& first, const string& mid,
                                        const string& last)

{
     string full = last;
     full.append(", ");
     full.append(first);
     full.append(" ");
     full.append(mid);

     return    full;
}
```

7.
```
string FullName2(const string& name)
{
     int  p1 = name.find(" ", 0);
     int  p2 = name.find(" ", p1);

     string full(name, p2+1, name.size() - p2); // last name

     full.append(", ");
     full.append(name, 0, p1);                //first name

     full.append{" ");
     full.append(name, p1+1, p2-p1+1);        //middle

     return full;
}
```

8. /* Convert string to integer. Caution: string may not be well-formed */

```
#include <cctype>
#include <cstdlib>

int  convert(const string& s, bool& success)
{
     success = true;
     char sign = "";

     string local = s;

     if (s[0] == '+')
     {    sign = '+';
          local.erase(0,1);              //strip sign
     }
     else if (s[0] == '-')
     {    sign = '-';
          local.erase(0,1);              //strip sign
     }

     bool digit = true;

     for (int index = 0; index < local.length(); index++)
          digit = isdigit(local[index]);

     if (digit)
     {
          int holder = atoi(local);
          if (sign == '+')
               return holder;
          else
               return -holder;
     }
     else
     {
          success = false;          //indicate poorly formed string
          return  -1;
     }
}
```

9.
```
/*  Convert string to real number.
               Caution: scientific or decimal format may be used */
#include <cctype>
#include <cstdlib>

double    convert(const string& s, bool& success)
{
     success = true;
     char sign = "";

     string local = s;

     if (s[0] == '+')
     {    sign = '+';
          local.erase(0,1);                //strip sign
     }
     else if (s[0] == '-')
     {    sign = '-';
          local.erase(0,1);                //strip sign
     }

     bool digit = true;
     int numE = 0;
     int numP = 0;

     for (int index = 0; index < local.length(); index++)
     {
          if (local[index] == '.')
               numP++;
          else if (local[index] == 'E' && !firstE)
               numE++;
          else
               digit = isdigit(local[index]);
     }
     if (digit && numP <= 1 && numE <= 1)
     {
          double holder = atof(local);
          if (sign == '+')
               return holder;
          else
               return -holder;
     }
     else
     {
          success = false;          //indicate poorly formed string
          return  -1;
     }
}
```

10.
```
/*  Determine if a string is a palindrome */
bool Palindrome(const string& s)
{
      bool pal = true;
      int  last = s.size();
      int  first = 0;
      while (first < last && pal)
      {
            pal = s[first]==s[last];
            first++;
            last--;
      }
      return pal;
}
```

11.
```
/*  Determine if a string is an anagram of another string */
bool Anagram(const String& s, const String& t)
{
      int  sizeS = s.size();
      int  sizeT = t.size();
      if (sizeT != sizeS)
            return false;
      bool anagram = true;
      bool cover[sizeT];
      for (int index =0; index < sizeT; index++)
            cover[index] = false;

      for (int indexT =0; indexT < sizeT; indexT++)
      {
            bool done = false;
            int position = 0;
            while (!done and position < sizeT)
            {
                  position = s.find(t[indexT], position);
                  if (position >= sizeT)          // char not in s
                        done = true;
                  else if (!cover[position]) // char in s,not counted
                  {
                        cover[position] = true;
                        done = true;
                  }
            }
      }
      for (int index =0; index < sizeT; index++)
            if (!cover[index])
                  anagram = false;
      return anagram;
}
```

3.6 Exercises

1. Examine all n-bit strings in which only one bit is 1. These n such strings can then be encrypted, and in so doing the permutation is uncovered. This permutation can be verified by examining the n n-bit strings that contain exactly one 0 bit. For example, 1000 -> 0100; 0100 -> 0001; 0010 -> 1000 and 0001 -> 0010 yields permutation (1 2 3 4) -> (3 2 4 1) where the number refers to the bit position (most significant is 1, least is 4).

2. The encrypted string is
   11101010 01101101 10110011 01000111 11100010 11101011 01100101 11010010

3. a) The ciphertext is 0554 1486 2112

   b) e*d % ((p-1)(q-1)) ==1 and the two prime factors of 2881 are 43 and 67
   so, 5 * 1109 % 42*66 ==1
   5545 % 2772 ==1

4. 2537 = 43*59 and we have e=13 so we need to find d
   13*d % (43-1)(59-1) ==1
   13*d % 2436 == 1
   13*d == 2436*k + 1, for some k. Try a few values of k and get, k=5, d=937

5. First calculate d=675 of Al's encryption key. Then H I, represented by char codes 07 08 gets encrypted first to 10 62 and then to 02 95

6.
```
string NumToBin(int x)
{
     string bin;            // empty string

     if (x / 2 != 0)
          bin = NumToBin(x/2);

     if (x % 2)
          bin.append("0");

     else
          bin.append("1");

     return bin;
}
```

```
/*  Compute y = x^k % n */
int ExpoMod (int x, int k, int n)
{
     string bin=NumToBin(k);

     int y = 1;
     for (int index = bin.size(); index > 0; index--)
     {
          y = (y*y) % n;
          if (bin[index] == "1")
               y = (y*x) % n;
     }

     return y;
}
```

3.7 Exercises

1. 01102020110
2. 00000
3. 01111111111
4. 0110110510
5. 01021040
6. 0101302
7. 01101322
8. 0110110110

9.

Instruction	k	i	NextValueComputed
Initially	0	1	Next[1]=0
2a	0	1	
2b	0	1	
2c	1	2	
2d	1	2	Next[2]=1
2a	1	2	
2b	0	2	
2c	1	3	
2d	1	3	Next[3]=1
2a	1	3	
2b	0	3	
2c	1	4	
2d	1	4	Next[4]=0
2a	1	4	
2b	1	4	
2c	2	5	
2d	2	5	Next[5]=2
2a	2	5	
2b	0	5	
2c	1	6	
2d	1	6	Next[6]=0
2a	1	6	
2b	1	6	
2c	2	7	
2d	2	7	Next[7]=2
2a	2	7	
2b	0	7	
2c	1	8	
2d	1	8	Next[8]=0
2a	1	8	
2b	1	8	
2c	2	9	
2d	2	9	Next[9]=1
2a	2	9	
2b	2	9	
2c	3	10	
2d	3	10	Next[10]=1
2a	3	10	
2b	3	10	
2c	4	11	
2d	4	11	Next[11]=0

10.

Instruction	k	j	NextValueComputed
Initially	0	1	Next[1]=0
2a	0	1	
2b	0	1	
2c	1	2	
2d	1	2	Next[2]=0
2a	1	2	
2b	1	2	
2c	2	3	
2d	2	3	Next[3]=0
2a	2	3	
2b	2	3	
2c	3	4	
2d	3	4	Next[4]=0
2a	3	4	
2b	3	4	
2c	4	5	
2d	4	5	Next[5]=0

11.

Instruction	k	j	NextValueComputed
Initially	0	1	Next[1]=0
2a	0	1	
2b	0	1	
2c	1	2	
2d	1	2	Next[2]=1
2a	1	2	
2b	0	2	
2c	1	3	
2d	1	3	Next[3]=1
2a	1	3	
2b	0	3	
2c	1	4	
2d	1	4	Next[4]=1
2a	1	4	
2b	0	4	
2c	1	5	
2d	1	5	Next[5]=1
2a	1	5	
2b	0	5	
2c	1	6	
2d	1	6	Next[6]=1
2a	1	6	
2b	0	6	
2c	1	7	
2d	1	7	Next[7]=1
2a	1	7	
2b	0	7	
2c	1	8	
2d	1	8	Next[8]=1
2a	1	8	
2b	0	8	
2c	1	9	
2d	1	9	Next[9]=1
2a	1	9	
2b	0	9	
2c	1	10	
2d	1	10	Next[10]=1
2a	1	10	
2b	0	10	
2c	1	11	
2d	1	11	Next[11]=1

12. Instruction	k	j	NextValueComputed
Initially	0	1	Next[1]=0
2a	0	1	
2b	0	1	
2c	1	2	
2d	1	2	Next[2]=1
2a	1	2	
2b	0	2	
2c	1	3	
2d	1	3	Next[3]=1
2a	1	3	
2b	0	3	
2c	1	4	
2d	1	4	Next[4]=0
2a	1	4	
2b	1	4	
2c	2	5	
2d	2	5	Next[5]=1
2a	2	5	
2b	2	5	
2c	3	6	
2d	3	6	Next[6]=1
2a	3	6	
2b	3	6	
2c	4	7	
2d	4	7	Next[7]=0
2a	4	7	
2b	4	7	
2c	5	8	
2d	5	8	Next[8]=5
2a	5	8	
2b	0	8	
2c	1	9	
2d	1	9	Next[9]=1
2a	1	9	
2b	0	9	
2c	1	10	
2d	1	10	Next[10]=0

13.

Instruction	k	i	NextValueComputed
Initially	0	1	Next[1]=0
2a	0	1	
2b	0	1	
2c	1	2	
2d	1	2	Next[2]=1
2a	1	2	
2b	0	2	
2c	1	3	
2d	1	3	Next[3]=0
2a	1	3	
2b	1	3	
2c	2	4	
2d	2	4	Next[4]=2
2a	2	4	
2b	1	4	
2c	2	5	
2d	2	5	Next[5]=1
2a	2	5	
2b	2	5	
2c	3	6	
2d	3	6	Next[6]=0
2a	3	6	
2b	3	6	
2c	4	7	
2d	4	7	Next[7]=4
2a	4	7	
2b	2	7	
2c	3	8	
2d	3	8	Next[8]=0

14.

Instruction	k	j	NextValueComputed
Initially	0	1	Next[1]=0
2a	0	1	
2b	0	1	
2c	1	2	
2d	1	2	Next[2]=1
2a	1	2	
2b	0	2	
2c	1	3	
2d	1	3	Next[3]=0
2a	1	3	
2b	1	3	
2c	2	4	
2d	2	4	Next[4]=1
2a	2	4	
2b	2	4	
2c	3	5	
2d	3	5	Next[5]=3
2a	3	5	
2b	0	5	
2c	1	6	
2d	1	6	Next[6]=0
2a	1	6	
2b	1	6	
2c	2	7	
2d	2	7	Next[7]=2

15.

Instruction	k	j	NextValueComputed
Initially	0	1	Next[1]=0
2a	0	1	
2b	0	1	
2c	1	2	
2d	1	2	Next[2]=1
2a	1	2	
2b	0	2	
2c	1	3	
2d	1	3	Next[3]=1
2a	1	3	
2b	0	3	
2c	1	4	
2d	1	4	Next[4]=0
2a	1	4	
2b	1	4	
2c	2	5	
2d	2	5	Next[5]=1
2a	2	5	
2b	2	5	
2c	3	6	
2d	3	6	Next[6]=3
2a	3	6	
2b	1	6	
2c	2	7	
2d	2	7	Next[7]=2
2a	2	7	
2b	1	7	
2c	2	8	
2d	2	8	Next[8]=2

16.

Instruction	k	j	NextValueComputed
Initially	0	1	Next[1]=0
2a	0	1	
2b	0	1	
2c	1	2	
2d	1	2	Next[2]=1
2a	1	2	
2b	0	2	
2c	1	3	
2d	1	3	Next[3]=1
2a	1	3	
2b	0	3	
2c	1	4	
2d	1	4	Next[4]=0
2a	1	4	
2b	1	4	
2c	2	5	
2d	2	5	Next[5]=1
2a	2	5	
2b	2	5	
2c	3	6	
2d	3	6	Next[6]=1
2a	3	6	
2b	3	6	
2c	4	7	
2d	4	7	Next[7]=0
2a	4	7	
2b	4	7	
2c	5	8	
2d	5	8	Next[8]=1
2a	5	8	
2b	5	8	
2c	6	9	
2d	6	9	Next[9]=1
2a	6	9	
2b	6	9	
2c	7	10	
2d	7	10	Next[10]=0

Programming Problems

1 - 3 are not difficult (and reinforce class concepts, especially if the student is familiar with geometric concepts). A class containing the necessary data members (CartesianPoints (from ex 7 in 3.2) and scalars for slope) and the given functions must be defined. Problem 2 follows. Problems 1 & 3 are of similar coding difficulty.

```
#include <iostream>
using namespace std;

class Line
(
   public:
     Line(double, double, double);
     void PointSlope();
     void SlopeIntercept();

   private:
     double    slope;
     double    x;
     double    y;
}

Line::Line(double m, double xcoord, double ycoord)
{
     slope = m;
     x = xcoord;
     y = ycoord;
}

void Line::PointSlope()
{
     cout       << "The point slope equation of the line is: "
          << "Y-" << y << " = " << slope << "(X-" << x << ")" << endl;

     return;
}

void SlopeIntercept()
{
     cout       << "The slope intercept equation of the line is: "
          << "Y = " << slope << "X+" << -slope*x + y << endl;

     return;
}
```

```
// in application program

#include "Line.h"
#include <iostream>

using namespace std;

int main()
{    cout << "please enter the slope and x, y coordinates of your line"
          << endl;

     double m, x, y;
     cin >> m;
     cin >> x;
     cin >> y;

     Line myLine(m, x, y);
     Line.SlopeIntercept();

     Line.PointSlope();
     return 0;
}
```

4. This problem is also straight-forward but a good exercise since the student must examine and analyze the structure of C++'s complex class. Once done, the problem is simply one of reading in a symbol for an operation and applying the appropriate predefined function.

5. This problem is an extensive, although not necessarily difficult, exercise. A sample class declaration follows. Operator overloading is the critical application here. The class definition would need to include an implementation of the class functionality. Once done, the application program needs to declare objects from this class to hold input, calling the appropriate function based upon the user's selection of operation.

   Note that the restriction that b cannot be zero must be enforced through the class methods (i.e. in the constructor).

```
Class Rational
{
  public:
     Rational(int, int); //may provide default constructors

     void input();         // read in rational in form "a/b"
     void display();
     Rational operator+(const Rational&);
     Rational operator*(const Rational&);
     Rational operator/(const Rational&);
     Rational operator-(const Rational&);
```

```
        bool operator<(const Rational&);
        bool operator<=(const Rational&);
        bool operator>(const Rational&);
        bool operator>=(const Rational&);

        Rational invert();
        void DisplayMixed();
        Rational reduce();
        int GCD();
        int LCD();
        Rational  LinearX(const Rational&);

     private:
        int  a;
        int  b;
};
```

6. /* A driver program is a program that is run primarily to exercise all the functionality of a given data structure (or class).

Instantiation of the class (i.e. declaration of objects) in all possible ways should be tested.

For classes that contain dynamically allocated data, such testing should include also passing objects into a function, returning an object from a function, and assigning one object to another.

Each method in the public interface should be exercised (invoked).

If any methods alter the state of the object (i.e. change one or more data members), different sequences of function invocations should be devised. In this manner, the consistency of an object can be insured.

It should thus be apparent that all the drivers in problems 6-14 are essentially the same. One needs to refer to the class definition in order to discern all that needs to be exercised.

The driver that follows can be used as a guide for the drivers in problems 7 - 14
*/

```
#include "Date.h"

int main()
{    Date d;
     Date now(5, 20, 1999);          // no Y2K here

     d.Display();
     now.Display();

     d.setMonth(11);
     d.Display();

     d.setYear(1823);
```

```
        d.Display();

        d.setDay(22);
        d.Display();

        int x = now.getMonth();
        int y = now.getDay();
        int z = now.getYear();

        Date future(++x, ++y, ++z);
        future.Display();

        return 0;
    }
```

```
7 - 14:  analogous
```

15.

/*
The drivers in problems 15-20 are essentially the same: each should be written to test the specified functionality of the string class as developed in section 3.3.

The driver that follows can be used as a guide for drivers 16 - 20.

The only difficulty here is that input was not one of the methods implemented as an exercise in 3.3. Here, we assume that a constructor, taking a char array, with a terminating 0, as input, accomplishes the task of initializing a String object */

```
    #include "String.h"
    #include <iostream>

    using namespace std;

    int main()
    {
         String One("Some test data");
         String Two("Different string");
         String Three("Different string");

         bool match = One.Compare(Two);

         if (match)
              cout << One.display() << " is same as: " << Two.display();
         else
              cout << One.display() << " is NOT the same as: "
                   << Two.display();

         match = Three.Compare(Two);
```

```
        if (match)
             cout << Three.display() << " is same as: "
                  << Two.display();
        else
             cout << Three.display() << " is NOT the same as: "
                  << Two.display();

        return 0;
   }
```

16 - 20: analogous

21.
/*
The drivers in problems 21 - 30 are essentially the same: each should be written to test the specified functionality of the second version of the string class as developed in exercises 7 & 8 of section 3.3.

The primary difficulty here is that the workspace is external to the Workplace-string class definition in exercises 7, i.e. the string objects contain only indices into the common buffer. The buffer is managed externally, as described in exercise 8.

The driver that follows can be used as a guide for drivers 22 - 30 */

```
   #include "Workplace.h"
   int main()
   {
        int freeSpot = GetIndexWP();
        Workplace s;

        s.input(freeSpot);          //string read in from user and stored

        s.output();

        return;
   }
```

22 - 30: analogous

31.
/*
The drivers in problems 31 - 41 are essentially the same: each should be written to test the specified functionality of C++ strings.

There are no difficulties associated with setup here since this string type is provided by the language.

The driver that follows can be used as a guide for drivers 32 - 41 */

```
#include <iostream>
#include <string>
using namespace std;

int main()
{
     string source = "Mississippi"
     string hit = "is";
     string nope = "Nope";

     cout << hit << "  was found " << NumHits(source, hit) <<
          << " times in " << source << endl;

     cout << nope << "  was found " << NumHits(source, nope) <<
          << " times in " << source << endl;

     return;

}
```

42. This program is straight-forward. One needs to define a word as a string of nonblank characters separated by blank characters or EOLN, and define a sentence as a group of words terminated by a period. Then, after opening a file, one simply processes the file contents, character by character, incrementing a counter for nonblanks. Tracking the number of words, characters and lines is also easy, making the computation of the averages at the end an easy task.

43. This program is easy. One simply reads in a string, stores it, and then line by line, processes lines of text input by the user to determine if the original string is contained in any subsequent lines. Use of the predefined string operations such as `getline` and `find` make these tasks trivial.

44. Like the previous two programs, this program is an easy application of strings. Marker strings need to be placed in the "personalized" text. Then the user's personalized strings are substituted for the marker strings.

45.
```
/* This simple program nicely illustrates the use of consts to make
code more self-documenting.  Some conversion constants like the
following should be defined.  Additional constants can be defined to
support a menu interface for conversion selection
*/

const int TEA_PER_TABLE = 3;
const int TABLE_PER_QCUP = 4;
const int CUP_PER_PINT = 2;
const int PINT_PER_QUART = 2;
```

46.
```
/* The main portion of this program is simplified by using the
predefined string functions.  The user enters a target string.  Then,
while the user has guesses remaining and he or she has not won yet,
the user enters a character.  A simple scan of the target string
determines if there is a match.

Some work can be done in jazzing up the user interface.  The
essential component is given below.
*/

#include <iostream>
#include <string>

using namespace std;

int main()
{
     string target;
     const int maxGuesses = 7;

     int numGuesses = 0;
     int numMatch = 0;
     bool won = false;

     cout << "Please input the word to guess "" << endl;
     cin >> target;

     int numCh = target.length();
     char ch;

     while (!won && numGuesses < maxGuesses)
     {
          cout << "Please input your character guess" << endl;
          cin >> ch;

          int start = 0;
          while (start < numCh)
          {
               start = target.find(ch, start);
               if (start < numCh)
                    numMatch++;
          }

          if (numMatch == numCh)
               won = true;
          else
               numGuesses++;
     }
```

```
        if (won)
             cout << "You won in " numGuesses << " guesses!!" << endl;
        else
             cout << "Sorry, try again" << endl;
   }
```

47. This program is straight-forward. Code up the given conversion into the `Day_of_the_Week()` function. All that remains then is to input several strings, parsing each so that the month, day and year are properly extracted, and then call the conversion function, outputting the result.

48. This program involves copying one file to another, suppressing identifiable lines. From the input file, copy to an output file until:

a) "//" encountered. At this point, throw away the rest of the input line and resume copying

b) "/*" encountered. At this point, throw away all text from the input file until a "*/" encountered, then resume copying.

49.
```
/* Text-formatting program: text is input from file; maximum line
length is input
     from keyboard.  Note there are many ways to process the file
     contents -- using strings, characters, or arrays.  The main
     difficulty here is not conceptual, it is just acquiring
     proficiency using C++ I/O
*/

#include <iostream>
#include <fstream>
#include <string>

using namespace std;

const int maxLgth = 72;

int getLgth()
{
 int LineLgth = -1;
 while (LineLgth < 1 || LineLgth > maxLgth)
 {
      cout << "Please enter maximum length of line
                (1- " << maxLgth << ")"<< endl;
      cin >> LineLgth;
 }
 return LineLgth;
}
```

```
int main()
{
 string filename;

 cout << "Please enter the name of the file
          containing unformatted text" << endl;
 cin >> filename;

 ifstream infile(filename.c_str());
 if (!infile)
 {
      cerr << "Error: unable to open file " << filename << endl;
      return 1;
 }

 cout << "Please enter the name of the file
          to contain formatted text" << endl;
 cin >> filename;

 ofstream outfile(filename.c_str());
 if (!outfile)
 {
      cout << "Error: unable to open file " << filename << endl;
      return 1;
 }

 int FormatWidth = getLgth();
 bool blank = false;
 string prevWord, word;

 while (infile >> word)
 {
      if (word.length + prevWord.length > FormatWidth)
      {
           outfile << prevWord;
           outfile << endl;
           prevWord = word;
      }
      else if (word.length() == 1 && word[0] == " " && !blank)
      {
           blank = true;
           prevWord.append(" ");
      )
 }

 infile.close();

 return 0;
}
```

50. This extension to program 49 is not trivial. An effective approach for distributing extra space must be constructed and applied. The approach of determining the number of words per line and distributing the extra spaces between works but possibly not as well as one that considers the length of the words and moving words from line to line to achieve more even spacing. A buffer for the words will have to be used. One can reuse some of the code used for program 42 and program 49.

51. This program is an extensive project. Formatting the different types of C++ constructs (comments, for loops, if statements, etc.) is not trivial, especially since no restrictions have been placed on the input file. Some restrictions (such as no more than one statement per line) may simplify the task somewhat. Still, one needs to be able to accommodate large compound boolean expressions, nested for loops, etc.

52.
```
/* Caesar cipher: straight-forward */

#include <iostream>
#include <string>
#include <cstdlib>

using namespace std;

int main()
{
     cout << "Please enter the message to be encoded,
                    followed by CR" << endl;
     string message;
     cin >> message;

     cout << "Please enter shift value"  << endl;
     int shift;
     cin >> shift;

     int index = 0;
     const int ALPHABASE = atoi("A");

     while (index < message.length())
     {
       int ordinal = (atoi(message[index]) - ALPHABASE + shift) % 26;
       message[index] = static_cast<char>(ordinal + ALPHABASE);
       index++;
     }

     cout << "Encoded message is:  " << message << endl;

     return 0;
}
```

53. /* Vignere cipher: straight-forward */

```
#include <iostream>
#include <cstdlib>
#include <string>

using namespace std;
int main()
{
     cout << "Please enter the message to be encoded,
               followed by CR" << endl;
     string message;
     cin >> message;

     cout << "Please enter keyword"  << endl;
     string keyword;
     cin >> keyword;

     int index = 0;
     const int ALPHABASE = atoi("A");

     while (index < message.length())
     {
          int k = 0;
          while (index < message.length() && k < keyword.length())
          {
               index++;
               k++;
               int shift = atoi(keyword[k] - ALPHABASE;
               int ordinal = (atoi(message[index]) - ALPHABASE
                                        + shift) % 26;
               message[index] = static_cast<char>
                                        (ordinal + ALPHABASE);
          }

     cout << "Encoded message is:  " << message << endl;

     return 0;
}
```

54. This program is a straight-forward implementation of the text's discussion.

55. This program is a straight-forward implementation of the text's discussion.

56. This program requires a fair amount of effort. Even though the algorithm is given in the text, there are many details that need to be taken care of properly.

57.

```
string NumToBin(int x)
{
     string bin;          // empty string
     if (x / 2 != 0)
          bin = NumToBin(x/2);
     if (x % 2)
          bin.append("0");
     else
          bin.append("1");
     return bin;
}

/*  Compute y = x^k % n */
int ExpoMod (int x, int k, int n)
{
     string bin=NumToBin(k);
     int y = 1;
     for (int index = bin.size(); index > 0; index--)
     {
          y = sqr(y) % n;
          if (bin[index] == "1")
               y = (y*x) % n;
     }
     return y;
}

#include <iostream>
#include <cstdlib>

using namespace std;
int main()
{
     int NumBlocks = 0;
     int  k, n;

     const int MaxBlocks = 50;
     int  Block[MaxBlocks];

     char ch;
     int ALPHABASE = atoi("A");

     cout << "Please enter the number of cipher block to encrypt"
          << endl;
     cin >> NumBlocks;

     cout << "Please enter message with even number of characters"
          << endl;
```

```
        for (int index = 0; index < NumBlocks; index++)
        {
             cin >> ch;
             Block[index] = (atoi(ch) - ALPHABASE) * 100;
             cin >> ch;
             Block[index] += (atoi(ch) - ALPHABASE);
        }

        cin >> ch;            //flush EOLN

        cout << "Enter e (or d) and Modulus" << endl;

        cin >> k;
        cin >> n;

        for (int index = 0; index < NumBlocks; index++)
             cout       << "Block #" << index << " = " <<
                  << ExpoMod(Block[index], k, n) << endl;

}
```

58. This program involves some effort but is fairly uncomplicated. A good exercise to familiarize oneself with the random number generator and the processes of tracking results: the programmer must keep track of values of x generated in order to use only new ones. A boolean array can be used to do so easily.

59.
```
/* KMP algorithm: input for the string to find and the text to find
it in can take many forms.  Here, for simplicity, we take both from
the keyboard.  Examples of file I/O can be taken from previous
programs */

#include <iostream>
#include <cstdlib>
#include <string>

const int STRINGLIMIT = some_value;

using namespace std;

int main()
{
     cout << "Please enter the text, followed by CR" << endl;
     string text;
     cin >> text;

     cout << "Please enter pattern to find"  << endl;
     string pattern;
     cin >> pattern;
```

```
        int next[STRINGLIMIT] = CreateNext(pattern);

        int where = KMP(string text, string pattern);

        if (where = -1)
             cout <<"Pattern " << pattern << " not found in text: "
                  << text << endl;
        else
             cout <<"Pattern " << pattern << " found, starting at
                  position " << where << " in text: " << text << endl;

        return 0;
}
```

60. The modification of the above code must accommodate multiple occurrences of a pattern in a given text. Care should be taken so that degenerate cases are satisfied (e.g. searching for a single character in a string of that character, or a small pattern that repeats itself).

61. This program involves a fair amount of effort since one must also code up the brute-force method. Then, some familiarity with the platform's system calls must be gained in order to credibly evaluate the running times. A theoretical analysis on paper would also yield a meaningful comparison between the two approaches.

Chapter Four: Stacks

4.2 Exercises

1. myTop = = 0; myArray contains 3 "set" elements: 10, 22, 37, ?, ? but note that only element 10 is considered to remain in the stack.

2. myTop = = -1; myArray contains 3 "set" elements: 10, 9, 8, ?, ? but note that none are visible since top= = -1 indicates that the stack is empty.

3. Error: attempt to push 6 elements onto a stack with a capacity of 5

4. myTop = = 0; myArray contains 1 "set" elements: 11,?,?, ?, ? but note that, as in #2, the stack is considered empty.

5.
```
bool Stack::full()
{
      return top == STACK_CAPACITY -1;
}
```

6.
```
int  Stack::bottom()
{
      return myArray[0];   // does not alter stack
}
```

7.
```
int  bottom(Stack s)       // destructive!! Alters stack.
{
      if (s.empty())
          cerr << "Stack empty: no bottom element"  << endl;

      int value = -1;

      while (!s.empty())
      {
          value = s.top();
          s.pop();
      }

      return value;        // stack now empty
}
```

```
8. int  Stack::nthElement(int n)
   {
        int elem = -1;
        int rep = 0;
        while (rep < n && myTop != -1)
        {
             rep++;
             elem = top();
             pop();
        }

        if (rep < n)
             cerr << "Fewer than " << n << " elements in stack" << endl;

        return elem;
   }
```

```
9. int  Stack::nthElement(int n)
   {
        if (myTop < (n-1) )
             cerr << "Fewer than " << n << " elements in stack" << endl;
        return myArray[n-1];
   }
```

10. a) n=3 Possible permutations:
123, 132, 213, 231, 321

Impossible permutations:
312

b) n=4 Possible permutations:
1234, 1243, 1324, 1342, 1432, 2134, 2143, 2314, 2341, 2431, 3214, 3241, 3421, 4321

Impossible permutations (10 out of 24):
1423, 2413, 3124, 3142, 3412, 4123, 4132, 4231, 4213, 4312

c) n=5 Possible permutations:
12345, 12354, 12543, 12435, 12453,
13245, 13254, 13452, 13425, 13542,
14325, 14352, 14532, 15432,

21345, 21354, 21435, 21453, 21543,
23145, 23154, 23451, 23415, 23541
24315, 24351, 24531, 25431

32154, 32145, 32451, 32415, 32541
34215, 34251, 34521, 35421

43215, 43251, 43521, 45321
54321

Impossible permutations (78 out of 120): those remaining

d) Possible permutations are those for which any digit d in the permutation, the digits to the right of d that are less than dare in reverse order.

For example, 21354 is valid
21534 is not valid because 34 lie to the right of 5 but are not in reverse order.

11. Proposed storage method assumes that the two stacks will always be of the same relative fullness. Not so. One stack could become full while the other remains empty.

12.
```
/*  two-stack class: hence two top members
    One stack operates in usual manner
         push increments top[0], pop decrements top[0]
     Second stack starts at high end of array,
         push decrements top[1], pop increments top[1],
ASSUMES that error checking is done outside class
*/

class DoubleStack
{
 public:
  DoubleStack() { top[0] = -1; top[1] = STACK_LIMIT;}

  bool empty(int);
  bool full(int);

  ElementType top(int);
  void pop(int);

  void push(int, ElementType);

 private:

  const int STACK_LIMIT = some_value;

  int          top[2];
  ElementType  data[STACK_LIMIT];

};
```

```
bool DoubleStack:: empty (int id)
{
     if (id == 1)
          return top[0] == -1;
     else
          return top[1] == STACK_LIMIT;
}


bool DoubleStack:: full (int id)
{
     return top[0]+1 == top[1];
}


ElementType DoubleStack:: top (int id)
{
     if (id == 1)
          return data[top[0]];
     else
          return data[top[1]];
}



void DoubleStack:: pop (int id)
{
     if (id == 1)
          top[0]--;
     else
          top[1]++;

     return;
}



void DoubleStack:: push (int id, ElementType item)
{
     if (id == 1)
     {    top[0]++;
          data[top[0]]= item;
     }
     else
     {    top[0]--;
          data[top[1]] = item;
     }
     return;
}
```

13. /* Multi-stack class
Each stack is initially given an equal portion of the storage area. **So, STACK_LIMIT is a multiple of n**

NOTE: Shifting elements is grossly inefficient (as noted in the text) and not a habit desirable for students to develop. If efficiency is desired, a different design should be used.
See Programming Problem #1

To implement shifting, one must decide whether to shift after an insertion fills a stack or before an insertion request is made on a full stack. The latter approach may save unneeded work but its effectiveness then depends on the user not checking for fullness before pushing. In either case, to hide implementation details from the user, shifting should be an auxiliary private (utility) function.
*/

```
const int n = some_value;

class MultiStack
{
 public:
  DoubleStack();

  bool empty(int);
  bool full(int);

  ElementType top(int);
  void pop(int);
  void push(int, ElementType);

 private:
  const int STACK_LIMIT = n*another_value;

  int              top[n];
  int              bottom[n];
  ElementType  data[STACK_LIMIT];

  void move_elem(int);
};

Multistack::Multistack()
{
     for (int index = 0; index < n; index++)
          {
               top[index] = n*index -1;
               bottom[index] = n*(index+1);
          }
}
```

```
bool MultiStack:: empty (int id)
{
     return top[id-1] == n*(id-1)-1;
}


bool MultiStack:: full (int id)
{
     return bottom[id-1] == top[id-1];
}


ElementType MultiStack:: top (int id)
{
     return data[top[id-1]];
}



void MultiStack:: pop (int id)
{
     top[id-1]--;
     return;
}


void MultiStack:: push (int id, ElementType item)
{
     top[id-1]++;
     data[top[id-1]] = item;
     if (top[id-1] == bottom[id-1])
          move_elem(id);
     return;
}
```

```
void MultiStack::move_elem(int id)
{
     bool hole = false;
     int where = id;

     while (!hole && where < n)     // look above for space
     {
          hole = top[where] == bottom[where];
          where++;
     }

     if (hole)                      // shift in stacks above
     {
          int upperl = bottom[where-1];
          int lowerl = bottom[id-1];
          for (index = upperl; index > lowerl; index--)
               data[index] = data[index-1];

          while (where >= id) // adjust pointers
          {
               top[where-1]++;
               bottom[where-1]++;
               where--;
          }
     }
     else                           // look below for hole
     {
          where = id-2;
          while(!hole && where > 0)
          {
               hole = top[where] == bottom[where];
               where--;
          }
          if (hole)                      // shift in stacks below
          {
               int lowerl = bottom[where-1];
               int upperl = top[id-1];
               for (index = lowerl; index < upperl ; index++)
                    data[index] = data[index+1];

               while (where <= id) // adjust pointers
               {
                    top[where-1]--;
                    bottom[where-1]--;
                    where++;
               }
     }    }
     return;
}
```

4.3 Exercises

1. -6
2. -2
3. 28
4. 12
5. 12
6. 12
7. 12
8. 2
9. 2
10. 8
11. 4

12. stack (top, rightmost): 8, 32 => 5, 4 => 20
13. stack (top, rightmost): 5, -15 => 3, -3 => -9
14. stack (top, rightmost): 5, 15, 7, 19 => 10, 7, 19 => -3, 19 => 22

15. ab*c+d-
16. abc/+d+
17. ab+c/d+
18. abcd+/+
19. ab+cd+/
20. ab-cde+-*
21. ab-c-d-e-
22. abcde----

23. accumulated output; stack (top, rightmost):
    ab; +,/ => abc;+, / => abc/+; - => abc/+d-

24. accumulated output; stack (top, rightmost):
    ab+; / => ab+c/: -=> ab+c/d-e+

25. accumulated output; stack (top, rightmost):
    abc; +,/ , (=> abcd-; +, / => abcd-/+; - => abcd-/+e

26. accumulated output; stack (top, rightmost):
    abc; +,/ , (=> abcd-; +, / => abcd-/; +, * => abcd-/e*+

27. accumulated output; stack (top, rightmost):
    abc; +,/ , (, (=> abcd-; +, /, (=> abcd-e*; +,/ => abccd-e*/+; - => abcd-e*/+f-

28. (a-(b+c))*d
29. (a+b)*(c+d)
30. a*(b-(c+d))
31. (a+b-c)/(e*d)
32. a/b/c/d
33. (a/b)/(c/d)

34. a/((b/c)/d)
35. a/(b/(c/d))

36. 1
37. 9
38. 5
39. 15
40. 1
41. -5

42. abc~+*
43. ab+cd-/~
44. a~b~*
45. ab~cd~+*-~
46. ab&& c||
47. abc! || &&
48. ab&& !
49. ab|| cde! && || &&
50. ab== cd== ||
51. a3<a9>&& a0>! ||
52. bb*4a*c*-0>= a0>a0<|| &&

53. +*ab-cd
54. +a+/bcd
55. +/+abcd
56. +a/b+cd
57. /+ab+cd
58. *-ab-c+de
59. ---abcd
60. -a-b-c-de
61. -24.5
62. -7.34
63. 8
64. -2
65. 4
66. 2
67. error: invalid prefix (a+b)*(c-d) has prefix expression *+ab-cd

68. 33
69. (a+b)*(c-d)
70. (a*b)+(c-d)
71. (a-b)-(c-d)
72. a-(b-c)-d
73. a-b-c-d
74. a*b+(c-d)/e
75. (a*b+c)/(d-e)
76. (a+b*c)/(d-e)

Programming Problems

1. /* Modification of Ex #13, 4.2. As before, assumes error-checking done outside class. For example, the user calls full before attempting to push */

```
class MultiStack
{
 public:
  DoubleStack();
  bool empty(int);
  bool full(int);

  ElementType top(int);
  void  pop(int);
  void  push(int, ElementType);

 private:
  const int STACK_LIMIT = some_value;
  const int LOWER_LIMIT = some_value2; //some_value2 < some_value

  int                  top[n];
  int                  bottom[n];
  ElementType          data[STACK_LIMIT];

};


Multistack::Multistack()
{
     for (int index =0; index < n; index++)
          {
               top[index] = n*index -1;
               bottom[index] = n*(index+1);
          }
}


bool MultiStack:: empty (int id)
{
     return top[id-1] == n*(id-1)-1;
}


bool MultiStack:: full (int id)
{
     return bottom[id-1] - top[id-1] <= LOWER_LIMIT;
}
```

```
ElementType MultiStack:: top (int id)
{
      return data[top[id-1]+1];
}


void MultiStack:: pop (int id)
{
      top[id-1]--;
      return;
}


void MultiStack:: push (int id, ElementType item)
{
   if (bottom[id-1] - top[id-1] > LOWER_LIMIT)
   {
      top[id-1]++;
      data[top[id-1]] = item;
   }
}
```

2. This program is an easy application of stacks. The underlying algorithm is:

   - Read a character
     a) if it is a "(", push on stack
     b) if it is a ")"
        ERROR if stack empty -- malformed expression
        ELSE (stack nonempty) pop off top value and discard
     c) discard all other characters

   - When input done, if stack empty, expression ok. If stack nonempty: ERROR

3. Upon reviewing the above algorithm, one should note that the values on the stack are not examined. Hence, one could easily use an integer count to implement a solution to checking balanced parentheses, viz.
   - Initialize COUNT = 0
   - Read a character
     a) if it is a "(", increment COUNT
     b) if it is a ")"
        ERROR if COUNT 0 -- malformed expression
        Otherwise, decrement COUNT
     c) discard all other characters
   - When input done, if COUNT ==0, expression ok. Otherwise, ERROR

4. This problem is another easy application of stacks. One applies the factorization algorithm, testing first if 2 is a multiple of n, and then all odd numbers starting with 3, until the value of the potential factor exceeds the square root of n. The trick here is noticing that the prime factors are output in the reverse order of how they are generated. Stacks are a natural way to acquire reversal. Hence, simply push the factors on a stack as they are generated. Then, when done factoring, pop them off for display.

5.

(a) The maze can be represented by a two-dimensional array. Use the integer values contained therein to represent whether a position is open, blocked by a wall, or traversed.

(b) A stack can be used to record the path taken through the maze and to "remember" where the path is when backtracking is required.

```
/* This program is rather challenging.

    A two-dimensonal matrix is needed to store the maze.   Also, we
  need to record where a path has been tried so that no path is tried
  twice (use a stack).

  The process of constructing a path is incremental.  When another step
  is taken in the path, its last position is pushed onto a stack.
  Thus, if a dead-end is reached, generation of a path can be resumed
  from a nonblocked position.  An (arbitrary) order of path selection
  needs to be established: 1) go West (inc col); 2) go North (dec row);
  3) go South (inc row); 4) go East (dec col).

  The stack records position objects (x-y coordinates).   Since
  templates have not been covered yet, the ElementType used in the
  above stack definitions should be replaced with the classname
  Position, where the Position class is defined below, and the class
  Stack recompiled.

  If backtracking is required, an object can be popped, yielding the
  position.

  To initialize the maze, use an input file that conforms to some
  predefined standard.  Here, we use 1 to indicate the starting point,
  9 the stopping point, 0 open point in maze, 8 blocking wall.
  Changing a 0 value indicates that that point has been traversed.
  */

  class Position                    // could also be struct
  {
    public:
       int  x;
       int  y;
  }
```

```
    ...        // recompile stack class with Position as ElementType

#include "Stack.h"
#include <iostream>

using namespace std;

const int OPEN = 0;
const int WALL = 8;
const int START = 1;
const int STOP = 9;
const int MAZE_HEIGHT = 40;
const int MAZE_WIDTH = 50;

typdef int  Maze[MAZE_HEIGHT][MAZE_WIDTH];

void  initMaze(Maze& maze, Position& start, Position& stop);
{
  string filename;

  cout << "Please enter the name of the file containing maze setup"
       << endl;
  cin >> filename;

  ifstream infile(filename.c_str());
  if (!infile)
  {
       cerr << "Error: unable to open file " << filename << endl;
       return 1;
  }

  for (int row = 0; row < MAZE_HEIGHT; row++)
    for (int col = 0; col < MAZE_WIDTH; col++)
    {
       infile >> maze[row][col];

       if (maze[row][col] == START )
       {
            start.x = row;
            start.y = col;
       }
       else if (maze[row][col] == STOP
       {
            stop.x = row;
            stop.y = col;
       }
   }
  return;
 }
```

```
void BackTrack(Stack& s, Maze& m, Position& p)
{
  while (m[p.x][p.y+1]!= OPEN && m[p.x+1][p.y]!=OPEN &&
         m[p.x-1][p.y]!= OPEN && m[p.x][p.y-1]!= OPEN)
                                                // no moves open
  {
       m[p.x][p.y]++;
       p = s.pop();              // backtrack
  }

  m[p.x][p.y]++;

  return;
}



int main()
{
  Maze      maze;
  Stack     path;           //path under construction
  Position  point, end;

  InitMaze(maze, point, end);

  while (point != end ||
       ( maze[p.x][p.y+1]!= OPEN && maze[p.x+1][p.y]!=OPEN
                && maze[p.x-1][p.y]!= OPEN && m[p.x][p.y-1]!= OPEN
                && path.empty()) )
  {
     maze[point.x][point.y]++;  // set as traversed

     if (maze[point.x][point.y + 1] == OPEN)   // move East
     {
       path.push(point);
       point.y++;
     }

     else if (maze[point.x-1][point.y] == OPEN)     // move North
     {
       path.push(point);
       point.x--;
     }

     else if (maze[point.x+1][point.y] == OPEN)     // move South
     {
       path.push(point);
       point.x++;
     }
```

```
    else if (maze[point.x][point.y - 1] == OPEN)    // move West
    {
      path.push(point);
      point.y--;
    }

    else
      backTrack(path, maze, point);
  }

  if (( maze[p.x][p.y+1]!= OPEN && maze[p.x+1][p.y]!=OPEN
          && maze[p.x-1][p.y]!= OPEN && m[p.x][p.y-1]!= OPEN
          && path.empty())

     cerr << "There is no path through this maze from the given
          starting position to the desired ending position" << endl;

  else
       PrintMaze();

  return 0;
}
```

6. A straight-forward modification of the given program. Adding trace to a program usually is.

7. An expression is malformed if:

   a) an ")" is encountered with an empty stack,

   b) there are leftover "("s when parsing is done, or

   c) there are an insufficient number of operands, e.g. `a + .`

   The first case is covered by the `assert` in Fig 4.12. Replace this assert with an identification of error.

   The second case is covered by the short output error message in Fig 412. May add more information to the error message by identifying the type of error.

   The third case requires the addition of a counter to track the number of operands relative to the number of operators. Initialize this counter to zero, increment with each operand encountered, decrement by 2 for each binary operator and by 1 for each unary operator encountered. If the counter == 0 at the end of processing, the expression is well formed.

8. The hint gives the answer: establish a priority ranking system. Then compare the priority of the token to the priority of the top symbol in the stack. Displaying exponentiation can then be suppressed until necessary.

9 - 11. All are relatively straight-forward modifications of the given code.

12 - 15. All involve using a stack to evaluate RPN expressions. #15 is given below, the remaining programs are similar.

```
/* As before the Stack class needs to be recompiled with string replacing
ElementType */

#include "Stack.h"
#include <iostream>
#include <cctype>

using namespace std;

int main()
{
  Stack S;
  string RPN;
  cout << "PLEASE enter the RPN expression to be evaluated " << endl;
  cin >> RPN;

  int temp = 1;

  for (int index= 0; index < RPN.length(); index++)
  {
       char token = RPN[index];

       if (isalpha(token))
            S.push(token);
       else
       {
            char op2 = S.top();
            char op1 = S.top();

            S.pop();
            S.pop();

            cout << "LOAD ";

            if (isalpha(op1))
                 cout << op1 << endl;
            else
                 cout << "TEMP " << op1 << endl;
```

```
            if (token == "+")
                 cout << "ADD " << endl;
            else if (token == "-")
                 cout << "SUB " << endl;
            else if (token == "*")
                 cout << "MULT " << endl;
            else if (token == "/")
                 cout << "DIV " << endl;

            if (isalpha(op2))
                 cout << op2 << endl;
            else
                 cout << "TEMP " << op2 << endl;

            cout << "STORE temp" << temp << endl;

            S.push(temp);
            temp++;
  }
  S.pop();

  if (!S.empty())
       cerr << "RPN expression  " << RPN << "was not well formed "
            << endl;

  return 0;
}
```

16. The essence of this program is an easy application of stacks. Use a stack of string objects to store the infix expression under construction. Read a postfix expression, and then based on the type of the token, manipulate the stack, viz:
    a) if token is an operand, push it onto the stack
    b) if the token is an operator, say operator $, pop two strings, X and Y, off the stack
        i) form the string (Y $ X)
        ii) push this string on the stack

For example, ab+cd-* is processed as follows:

Push a
Push b
Read +
Pop b, Pop a, form (a + b), Push (a + b)
Push c
Push d
Read -
    Pop d, Pop c, form (c-d), Push (c-d)
Read *
    Pop (c-d), Pop (a+b), Form ((a+b) * (c-d)), push onto stack
Parsing done, extract infix expression from top of stack

Chapter Five: Queues

5.2 Exercises

1. q.myArray: A, B, C, A, ? q.myFront = 1; q.myBack = 4;

2. q.myArray: X, Y, Z, ?, ? q.myFront = 3; q.myBack = 3; // queue empty

3. q.myArray: s, r, q, r, r q.myFront = 3; q.myBack = 1;

4. q.myArray: C, A, B, B, B q.myFront = 4; q.myBack = 3;// queue full

5.
```
/* Implementation of Queue class.
    Empty slot used to distinguish between empty and full
*/

#include <iostream>
using namespace std;

Queue::Queue()
{
  myFront = 0;
  myBack = 0;
}


bool Queue::empty()
{
  return myFront == myBack;
}


void Queue::addQ(int item)
{
  if ((myBack +1)% QUEUE_CAPACITY == myFront)
       cerr << "Queue is full: cannot add to queue.  Error!! " << endl;

  else
  {
       myArray[myBack] = item;
       myBack = (myBack+ 1) % QUEUE_CAPACITY;
  }
  return;
}
```

```
yBack)

ue is empty:Error!!" << endl;

ng::npos;          // should be invalid data item;


ray[myFront];



Q()

myBack)
ue is empty: cannot remove from queue.
Error!!" << endl;

myFront+ 1) % QUEUE_CAPACITY;





Full() function
.()

ront == (myBack + 1)% QUEUE_CAPACITY;







myBack)

   else if (myFront > myBack)
        return myBack - myFront + QUEUE_CAPACITY;

   else
        return myBack - myFront;
}
```

8.
```
/*  size() is neither a member function, nor a friend.
 */

int size(Queue  Q)
{
   Queue     temp;
   int       count = 0;

   while (!Q.empty())
   {
         temp.addQ(Q.front());
         Q.removeQ();
         count++;
   }

   while (!temp.empty())
   {
         Q.addQ(temp.front());
         temp.removeQ();
   }

   return count;
}
```

9.
```
/*  another public method: back()

  Notes:
  1)if back() is destructive, i.e. all elements are dequeued and the
        last one returned, look at the second version.  If back()is non-
        destructive, i.e. none of the elements except the last is
        dequeued, look at the first version.

     2) the result of modulus of negative numbers (go toward 0 or
        negative infinity ) is platform dependent.  Hence an if-else is
        used in the first version
  */

int Queue::back()
{
   int index_last;
   if (myBack == 0)
         index_last = QUEUE_CAPACITY;
   else
         index_last = myBack-1;

   return myArray[index_last];
}
```

```
int Queue::back()
{
   int last;

   while (!empty())
   {                  // assumes called with non-empty queue
        last = front();
        removeQ();
   }

   addQ(last);      // last element retrieved not dequeued.

   return last;
}
```

10.
```
/* nonmember function and nonfriend function.
        Only the non-destructive version provided here
   */

int back(Queue Q)
{
   Queue      temp;
   int        last;

   while (!Q.empty())
   {
        last = Q.front();
        temp.addQ(last);
        Q.removeQ();
   }

   while (!temp.empty())
   {
        Q.addQ(temp.front());
        temp.removeQ();
   }

   return last;
}
```

11. /* D[illegible]n */
```
int Que[illegible]t n)
{
   int e[illegible]
   while( n > 0 && !empty())
   {
         elem = front();
         removeQ();
   }
   if (n > 0)
   {
         cerr >> "Insufficient number of elements in the queue!" >> endl;
         return string::npos;      // return invalid data item
   }
   else
         return elem;
}
```

12. /* Nondestructive version */
```
int Queue::nthElement(int n)
{
   if (abs(myBack - myFront) < n)
   {
         cerr >> "Insufficient number of elements in the queue!" >> endl;
         return string::npos;      // return invalid data item
   }

   int index_n = (myFront + n - 1) % QUEUE_CAPACITY;
   return myArray[index_n];
}
```

13. The algorithm to reverse the elements in a queue uses the LIFO nature of a stack:

```
      a) Stack S;

      b) while (!Q.empty())
         {
            ElementType data = Q.front();
            Q.removeQ();
            S.push(data);
         }

      c) while (!S.empty())
         {
            ElementType data = S.pop();
            Q.addQ(data);
         }
```

14.

(a) For n = 3:

Possible Permutations	Impossible Permutations
123 132 213 231 312	321

(b) For n = 4:

1234 1324 1342 1423	1243
2134 2143 2314 2341 2413	2431
3124 3142 3412	3214 3241 3421
4123	4132 4312 4321 4213 4231

(c) For n = 5:

12345 12354 12435 12453 12534	12543
13245 13254 13425 13452 13524	13542
14235 14253 14523	14325 14352 14532
15234	15243 15324 15342 15423 15432
21345 21354 21435 21453 21534	21543
23145 23154 23415 23451 23514	23541
24135 24153 24513	24315 24351 24531
25134	25143 25314 25341 25413 25431
31245 31254 31425 31452 31524	31542
	32145 32154 32415 32451 32514 32541
34125 34152 34512	34215 34251 34521
35124	35142 35214 35241 35412 35421
41235 41253 41523	41325 41352 41532
	42135 42153 42315 42351 42513 42531
	43125 43152 43215 43251 43512 43521
45123	45132 45213 45231 45312 45321
51234	51243 51324 51342 51423 51432
	52134 52143 52314 52341 52413 52431
	53124 53142 53214 53241 53412 53421
	54123 54132 54213 54231 54312 54321

(d) The rule is: for each digit d in the number, the digits to the right of d that are less than d MUST be in ascending order.

15. /* NOTE: Our class implementation does NOT leave us an empty slot, allowing us to distinguish between empty and full states by virtue of the front and back pointers. Hence, we need to use an auxiliary data member to track fullness.

Below, we rely on a count integer, which is:
  1) initialized to zero in the constructor,
  2) decremented in removeQ() and
  3) incremented in addQ().

Another modification in the Queue class implementation would, of course, be the pre-test performed in the addQ() method, i.e. use the empty slot
*/

```
bool Queue::full()
{
   return count == QUEUE_CAPACITY;
}
```

16. /* NOTE: Our class implementation does NOT leave us an empty slot, allowing us to distinguish between empty and full states by virtue of the front and back pointers. Hence, we need to use an auxiliary data member to track fullness.

Below, we rely on a bool data member **full**, which is:
  1) initialized to false in the constructor,
  2) set to true in addQ()if myBack == myFront after addition,
  3) reset to false in removeQ() if full before the call.

*/

17. Similar to the use of one buffer for two stacks, place the two queues in the arrays so that each front is at the end of the array. Then each queue can grow toward the middle. If each queue size is fixed, then wraparound within each queue could be employed to avoid shifting elements.

18. /* A deque (double-ended queue) is similar to a queue but additions and deletions may be performed on either end. Hence, the implementation must now be given a directive (tag) indicating at what end, the operation is to be performed.
We assume a circular array implementation here. */

```
#include <iostream>
using namespace std;

enum where {front, rear};

Deque:: Deque ()
{
  myFront = 0;
  myBack = 0;
}


bool Deque::empty()
{
   return myFront == myBack;
}


void Deque::addQ(int item, where w)
{
 if (w == rear)              // regular enqueuing
 {
  if ((myBack +1)% QUEUE_CAPACITY == myFront)
       cerr << "Cannot add to rear of queue.  Error!! " << endl;

  else
  {
       myArray[myBack] = item;
       myBack = (myBack+ 1) % QUEUE_CAPACITY;
  }
 }

 else                        // enqueue at front
 {
  if ((myFront-1)% QUEUE_CAPACITY == myBack)
       cerr << "Cannot add to front of queue.  Error!! " << endl;

  else
  {
       myFront = (myFront - 1) % QUEUE_CAPACITY;
       myArray[myFront] = item;
  }
 }

 return;
}
```

```
int Deque::removeQ(where w)
{
      if (myFront == myBack)
      {
           cerr <<"Queue empty: Cannot remove from front or rear.
                     Error!!" << endl;

           return string::npos;  // should be invalid data item;
      }
      else if (w == front)                  // regular dequeuing
      {
           item = myArray[myFront];
           myFront= (myFront+ 1) % QUEUE_CAPACITY;

           return item;
      }

      else                          // dequeue from rear
      {
         myBack = (myBack - 1) % QUEUE_CAPACITY;
         item = myArray[myBack];

         return item;
      }
}
```

18.
```
/* A scroll removes (reads) from the front
             but adds or removes from the rear.
   Hence, a modification of the above hybrid
   where the ability to add to the front was proscribed would suffice.
   */

#include <iostream>
using namespace std;

enum where {front, rear};

Scroll:Scroll ()
{
   myFront = 0;
   myBack = 0;
}


bool Scroll::empty()
{
   return myFront == myBack;
}
```

```
void Scroll::addQ(int item)          // additions only to rear
{
   if ((myBack +1)% QUEUE_CAPACITY == myFront)
        cerr << "Full: cannot add to rear of scroll.  Error!! " << endl;

   else
   {
        myArray[myBack] = item;
        myBack = (myBack+ 1) % QUEUE_CAPACITY;
   }

    return;
 }


int Scroll::removeQ(where w)
{
   if (myFront == myBack)
   {
        cerr <<"Scroll empty: Cannot remove from front or rear.
             Error!!" << endl;

        return string::npos;          // should be invalid data item;
    }
    else if (w == front)              // regular dequeuing
    {
        item = myArray[myFront];
        myFront= (myFront+ 1) % QUEUE_CAPACITY;

        return item;
    }
    else                              // dequeue from rear
    {
        myBack = (myBack - 1) % QUEUE_CAPACITY;
        item = myArray[myBack];

        return item;
    }
  }
```

Programming Problems

1.
/* A driver program is a program that is run primarily to exercise all the functionality of a given function, data structure (or class).

Instantiation of the class (i.e. declaration) of objects in all possible ways should be tested.

For classes that contain dynamically allocated data, such testing should include also passing objects into a function, returning an object from a function, and assigning one object to another.

Each method in the public interface should be exercised (invoked). If any methods alter the state of the object (i.e. change one or more data members), different sequences of function invocations should be devised. In this manner, the consistency of an object can be insured.

The driver that follows can be used for exercises #1, #2, #9 and #10. These three exercises test the functionality of different implementations of the Queue ADT. Since our data structures have been defined with a placeholder, ElementType, the type of parameter targeted must replace ElementType and the class recompiled. Drivers for #11 and #12 are similar.

Construction of a queue, adding to a queue, deleting from a queue, testing for fullness and emptiness should be tested. To ensure consistency, different sequences of addition and deletion should be exercised.

*/

```
#include "Queue.h"
#include <iostream>

using namespace std;

int main()
{
      Queue     Q1, Q2;

      cout << "Please enter a sequence of integers,
                              terminated by a 0" << endl;
      int data;

      while (cin >> data)
      {
            if (!Q1.full())
                  Q1.addQ(data);

            if (data % 2 && !Q2.full())
                  Q2.addQ(data);
      }
```

```
    cout << "The following even numbers were entered " << endl;
    while (!Q2.empty())
    {
        cout << Q2.front();          //display item in queue
        Q2.removeQ();
        Q1.removeQ();          // remove "even count" of items in Q1
    }

    cout << endl;

    int count = 0;
    while (!Q1.empty())
    {
        count++;
        Q2.addQ(Q1.front());
        Q1.removeQ();
    }

    cout << count << "Odd numbers were entered " << endl;

    cout << "You should count " << count <<
            " leftover numbers below" << endl;

    while (!Q2.empty())
    {
        cout << Q2.front();
        Q2.removeQ();
    }

    return 0;
}
```

3. /* Drivers for problems #3-#10 test specific features of variations on Queue implementations.

For each, one needs to:

initialize the Queue object,
perform the desired functionality,
verify the result(s),
modify the Queue (by a sequence of deletions and additions)
perform the desired functionality again, and
verify the result(s).

The following driver satisfies #3, #4, #6, # 7 and #8. A recompilation of the Queue class with the ElementType of int is assumed. */

```
#include "Queue.h"
#include <iostream>

using namespace std;


int main()
{
     Queue Q;

     for (int index = 1; index <= 10; index++)
          Q.addQ(10*index);

     cout << Q.nthElement(7); << endl;            // should be 70

     while (Q.size())
     {
          cout << Q.front();
          Q.removeQ();
     }

     cout << " Above display will be 3 or 10 numbers,
               depending on implementation of nthElement as
               destructive or nondestructive" << endl;

     return 0;
}
```

13. /* This program is straightforward. An algorithm follows:

a) Store the random sequence in a queue, call it InputQ.

b) Using either a nondestructive nthElement() or a backupQ,
Display the contents of InputQ

c) Store user's input in a queue, call it TestQ

d) If the two queues are of unequal size, the user's memory is faulty

e) Else (Element by element) until both queues are empty,
Dequeue an element from each queue and compare

f) If any comparisons above fail, user's memory is faulty
Else, replication was fine.

14. /* The classic palindrome problem is solved effectively using a stack and a queue. We assume char as the ElementType */

```
#include "Queue.h"
#include <iostream>

using namespace std;

int main()
{
     Queue word;
     Stack reverse;

     cout << "Please input string to determine if
               it's a palindrome " << endl;

     char ch;

     while (cin >> ch)
     {
          word.addQ(ch);
          reverse.push(ch);
     }

     bool pal = true;

     while (pal && !reverse.empty())
     {
          pal = reverse.top() == word.frontQ();
          reverse.pop();
     }

     if (pal)
          cout << "You input a palindrome!" << endl;

     return 0;
}
```

15. A straightforward program. An algorithm sketch follows:

a) open input file, call it infile

b) open output file

c)
```
char ch;
while (infile >> ch)            // input file nonempty
if (ch == "{")
{
```

```
                enqueue "{";
                while (infile >> ch && ch != "}")
                      enqueue ch;
          }
          if (ch == '})
                enqueue ch;
    }
    else
          write ch to output file;
```

d) // input file now empty, empty contents of queue (footnotes) into output file

```
while (!Q.empty() )
    item = Q.front()
    Q.removeQ()
    write item to output file
    if item == "}},
          write end of line (separate footnotes in output file)
```

16. The average turn-around time is :

TotalTurnAroundTime / NumCalls,

where TotalTurnAroundTime is the sum of the turn-around times of all the calls. This calculation can be done in Simulate by adding the following statement:

```
TotalTurnAroundTime += CallCompletionTime - Call.TimeOfArrival
```

17. The average length of the queue is determined by monitoring the queue every time its length is changed. Thus, the queue length should be recorded each time addQ or removeQ is called. A variable LastTime records the Clock time whenever a change is made, so that the length of time between changes can be calculated. If the total sum of ((the length of the queue) times (the length of time since the last change)) is recorded in TotalQueueWeight, then the average queue length is:

```
AverageQueueLength = TotalQueueWeight / Clock;
```

18. This programming modification is rather complex as calls must now be distributed, presumably randomly, among several agents. Hence, a multiQ simulation is now employed.

19. Although less complicated than the previous problem, this modification requires the student to add monitoring to the queue, either internally or externally.

20. Like #19, this modification requires the internal or external monitoring as well as an additional queue (managerQueue) to which calls need to be shifted.

21. This problem is an extensive programming project.

Chapter Six: Templates and Containers

6.3 Exercises

1.
```
template <typename value>
value     average(value  a, value b)
{
     return (a+b)/2;
}
```

2.
```
template <typename value>
value     max(value  a, value b)
{
     value     local;
     if (a > b)
          return a;
     else
          return b;

     // don't use a>b?a:b;
}    // ternary operator cannot be overloaded
```

3.
```
template <typename value>
value     median (value  a, value b, value c)
{
     value     max;
     value min;

     if (a > b)
     {
          max = a;
          min = b;
     }
     else
     {
          max = b;
          min = a;
     }

     if (c > max)
          return max;
     else if (c < min)
          return min;
     else
          return c;
}
```

4.
```
template <typename element>
element   sum(element A[], int length)
{
     element sum = A[0]; // can't do sum = 0; A[] may not be numeric!

     for (int index = 1; index < length; index++)
          sum += A[index];

     return sum;
}
```

5.
```
template <typename element>
// selection sort, described in 11.1
void sort(element A[], int length)
{
     for (int index = 0; index < length; index++)
     {
          element min = A[index];
          int     index_min = index;

          for (int index2 = index + 1; index2 < length; index2++)
               if (min > A[index2])
               {
                    min = A[index2];
                    index_min = index2;
               }

          x[index_min] = x[index];
          x[index] = min;
     }
     return;
}
```

6.
```
template <typename element>
int  search(element A[], int length, element target)
{
     int target_index = -1;    // return -1 if target not in array

     // for loop returns last occurrence of target
     // use while loop if first occurrence desired
     for (int index = 0; index < length; index++)
          if (A[index] == target)
               target_index = index;

     return target_index;
}
```

7.
```
template <typename element>
class Queue
{
public:
     Queue();

     bool empty() const;
     void addQ(element);
     void removeQ();
     element front();

private:
     const int QUEUE_CAPACITY = 128;

     int myFront;
     int myBack;

     element myArray[QUEUE_CAPACITY];
};


template <typename element>
Queue<element>::Queue()
{
     myFront = 0;
     myBack = 0;
}


template <typename element>
bool Queue<element>::empty()
{
     return myFront == myBack;
}


template <typename element>
void Queue<element>::addQ(element item)
{
     if ((myBack +1)% QUEUE_CAPACITY == myFront)
          cerr << "Queue is full: cannot add to queue.
                    Error!! " << endl;
     else
     {
          myArray[myBack] = item;
          myBack = (myBack+ 1) % QUEUE_CAPACITY;
     }
}
```

```
template <typename element>
void Queue<element>::removeQ()
{
     if (myFront == myBack)
          cerr <<"Queue is empty: cannot remove from queue.
               Error!!" << endl;
     else
          myFront= (myFront+ 1) % QUEUE_CAPACITY;

     return;
}
```

```
template <typename element>
element Queue<element>::front()
{
     if (myFront == myBack)
     {
          cerr <<"Queue is empty: cannot remove from queue.
               Error!!" << endl;

          return myArray[0];        // should be invalid data item;
          //problem with templates: lack of access to invalid data
          // exceptions should really be used to signal error
     else
          return myArray[myFront];;
}
```

8.
```
template <typename element>
class Cartesian
{
     element   x, y;
};
```

Chapter 6

6.4 Exercises

1. 49, 16, 22, 44, 11, 5, 27, 33, 38, 0

2. 49, 16, 22, 44, 11, 5, 0, 0, 0, 0

3. 99, 33, 44, 88, 22, 11, 55, 66, 77

4. 0, 1, 2, 3, 0, 1, 2, 3, 4, 5

5. 33,33, 88, 88, 11, 11, 66, 66, 77

6. 99, 33, 44, 88, 22, 11, 55, 66, 99

7. 77, 33, 44, 88, 22, 11, 55, 66, 99

8. w: 0, 0, 0, 0, 0, 0, 0, 0, 0, 0, 119, 53, 64, 108, 42, 31, 75, 86, 97

9. v: 20, 20, 20, 20, 20; number: 11, 55, 66, 77

10. number: 22, 11, 55, 66, 77

11. w: 0, 0, 0, 0, 0, 0, 0, 0, 0, 0, 99, 33, 44, 88, 22, 11, 55, 66, 0

12.
```
vector<int>    seq;
for (int index = 1; index < 100; index++)
     seq.push_back(index);
```

13.
```
vector<int>    seq;
for (int index = 99; index > 0; index--)
     seq.push_back(index);
```

14.
```
vector<bool>   seq;
for (int index = 0; index < 50; index++)
     seq.push_back(index%2 == 0);
```

15.
```
template <typename T>
bool ascend(const vector<T> v)
{
    for (int index = 0; index < v.size(); index++)
        if (v[index] <= v[index+1])
            return false;

    return true;
}
```

16.
```
template <typename T>
//operators "=" "<" & "-" must be defined for T
T range(const vector<T> v)
{
    T  min = v[0];
    T  max = v[0];

    for (int index = 0; index < v.size(); index++)
        if (v[index] < min)
            min = v[index];
        else if (v[index] > max)
            max = v[index];

    return max - min;
}
```

17. see 6.2 ex #7

6.5 Exercises

```
1. // assumes vector non-empty so that table[row].size() has meaning
double sumRow(const vector< vector<double> > & table, int row)
{
   double sum = 0.0;
   for (int col = 0; col < table[row].size(); col++)
        sum += table[row][col];

   return sum;
}
```

```
2.
double sumCol(const vector< vector<double> > & table, int col)
{
   double sum = 0.0;
   for (int row = 0; row < table.size(); row++)
        sum += table[row][col];

   return sum;
}
```

```
3. // assumes vector non-empty so that table[row].size() has meaning
double avgRow(const vector< vector<double> > & table, int row)
{
   double sum = 0.0;
   for (int col = 0; col < table[row].size(); col++)
        sum += table[row][col];

   return sum/table[row].size ();
}
```

```
4.  // assumes vector non-empty so that table[row].size() has meaning
#include <cmath>
double stdDevRow(const vector< vector<double> > & table, int row)
{
   double mean = avgRow(table);
   double sum = 0.0;
   int num = table[row].size();

   for (int col = 0; col < num; col++)
        sum += sqr(table[row][col] - mean));

   return sqrt((1.0/num)*sum);
}
```

5.
```
double avgCol(const vector< vector<double> > & table, int col)
{
   double sum = 0.0;

   for (int row = 0; row < table.size(); row++)
        sum += table[row][col];

   return sum/table.size();
}
```

6.
```
#include <cmath>
double stdDevCol(const vector< vector<double> > & table, int col)
{
   double mean = avgCol(table);
   double sum = 0.0;

   int num = table.size();

   for (int row = 0; row < num; row++)
        sum += sqr(table[row][col] - mean));

   return sqrt((1.0/num)*sum);
}
```

7.
```
const int MatrixRow = some_value;
const int MatrixCol = some_value2;
const int default_value = some_value3;

class Matrix
{
 public:
   Matrix();
   Matrix(string);
   // since dynamically allocated data is not used here, the
   //         compiler-provided copy constructor will suffice

   void Display();
   Matrix operator+(const Matrix& B);
   vector<int> operator*(const Matrix& B);

 private:
   vector< vector<int> >  data(MatrixRow, vector<int>(MatrixCol));
};
```

```
Matrix::Matrix()
{
   for (int row = 0; row < MatrixRow; row++)
     for (int col = 0; col < MatrixCol; col++)
        data[row][col] = default_value;

}

Matrix::Matrix(string filename)
{
   int holder;

   // best to initialize large matrices is from a file
   ifstream infile(filename.c_str());
   if (!infile)
   {
        cerr << "Error: unable to open file. " << filename << endl;

        for (int row = 0; row < MatrixRow; row++)
             for (int col = 0; col < MatrixCol; col++)
                  data[row][col] = default_value;
   }
   else                    // assume file of correct size
       for (int row = 0; row < MatrixRow; row++)
        for (int col = 0; col < MatrixCol; col++)
             infile >> data[row][col];
}

void Matrix::Display()
{
   for (int row = 0; row < MatrixRow; row++)
   {
     for (int col = 0; col < MatrixCol; col++)
        cout << data[row][col] << "    ";
     cout << endl;
   }
   return;
}

Matrix Matrix::operator+(const Matrix& B)
{
   Matrix    temp;

   for (int row = 0; row < MatrixRow; row++)
     for (int col = 0; col < MatrixCol; col++)
        temp.data[row][col] = data[row][col] + B.data[row][col];

   return temp;
}
```

```
Matrix Matrix::operator*(const Matrix& B)
{
  Matrix temp;

  for (int row = 0; row < MatrixRow; row++)
   for (int rc = 0; rc < MatrixRow; rc++)
    {
     int sum = 0;
     for (int col = 0; col < MatrixCol; col++)
       sum += data[row][col] * B.data[col][rc];

     temp[row][rc] = sum;
    }

  return temp;
}
```

6.7 Exercises

1. 01010101010101010101

2. 00110101000101000101

3. 00100000000000000000

4. 01110101010101010101

5. 01000000010000010000

6. 01111111111111111111

7. 10000000000000000000

8. 001110000000

9. 000000000000

10. 000000001010

11. 111111111111

12.

```
#include <bitset>
const int SetRange = some_value;

class Set
{
 public:
   Set();
   Set(int);
   Set(string);

   Set Union(const Set& B);
   Set Intersection(const Set& B);
   Set Complement(const Set& A);

   void add(int);
   void remove(int);
   bool Member(int x);

 private:
   bitset<SetRange>    data;

   int cardinality;
};
```

```
Set::Set()
{
   data.set();           // all bits set to 1, indicating members 1..n
   cardinality = SetRange;
}


Set::Set(int num)
{
   data.set();

   for (int index = num; index < SetRange; index++)
        data.reset(index);

   cardinality = num;
}


Set::Set(string bitstring)
{
   data.reset();

   for (int index = 0; index < bitstring.size(); index++)
        if (bitstring[index])
             data.set(index, 1);

   cardinality = bitstring.size();
}


Set Set::Union(const Set& B);
{
   return Set(to_string(data | B.data));
}


Set Set::Intersection(const Set& B);
{
   return Set(to_string(data & B.data));
}


Set Set::Complement(const Set& A);
{
   return Set(to_string(data.flip() ));
}
```

```
bool Set::Member(int x)
{
   return data.test(x-1);
}


void Set::add(int x)
{
   data.set(x-1, 1);
}


void Set::remove(int x)
{
   data.set(x-1, 0);
}
```

6.8 Exercises

1.
```
#include <valarray>
void OutValArray(valarray<double> data)
{
   for (int index = 0; index < data.size(); index++)
        cout << data[index];
   cout << endl;
   return;
}
```

2.
```
#include <valarray>
void InitValArray(valarray<double>& data)
{
   cout << "please input your " << data.size()
             << "real numbers: " << endl;

   for (int index = 0; index < data.size(); index++)
        cin >> data[index];

   return data;
}
```

3.
```
#include <valarray>
#include <cmath>
double Magnitude(valarray<double> data)
{
   double sum = 0.0;
   for (int index = 0; index < data.size(); index++)
        sum += data[index]* data[index];
   return sqrt(sum);
}
```

4.
```
#include <valarray>
double DotProduct(valarray<double> A, valarray<double> B)
{
   double sum = 0.0;

   for (int index = 0; index < A.size(); index++)
        sum += A[index]* B[index];

   return sum;
}
```

Programming Problems

1 - 6.
/* A driver program is a program that is run primarily to exercise all the functionality of a given function, data structure (or class).

Instantiation of the class (i.e. declaration of objects) in all possible ways should be tested.

Hence, for a template definition, one should instantiate the template with all applicable types, including both primitive (int, double, char, etc.) types and user-defined types.

CAUTION: Most compilers recommend that you explicitly instantiate a template before use. Implicit instantiation is legal, according to the language definition but may not be supported well (or at all) by some compilers.

The driver that follows is of the form required for programs 1 - 6. It satisfies #1, the remaining problems are similar.
*/

```
#include "Template.h"
#include <iostream>

using namespace std;

int main()
{
     // function prototypes provide explicit instantiation of template
     int  average(int, int);
     float average(float, float);
     double average(double, double);

     int        a = 100, b = 200;
     float           p = 15.2, q = 13.4;
     double     t = -12.2, v = 22.8;

     cout << "The average of " << a  << " and " << b << " is: ";
     cout << average(a, b) << endl;

     cout << "The average of " << p  << " and " << q << " is: ";
     cout << average(p, q) << endl;

     cout << "The average of " << t  << " and " << v << " is: ";
     cout << average(t, v) << endl;

     return 0;
}
```

7.
/* See above for description of driver programs.

Recall that each method in the public interface of the class should be exercised (invoked). If any methods alter the state of the object (i.e. change one or more data members), different sequences of function invocations should be devised. In this manner, the consistency of an object can be insured.

The driver that follows can be used for problems #7 and #11. These two exercises test the functionality of the Queue ADT with different ElementTypes. The driver for #8 is similar; actually it's simpler since the class CartesianPoint is less complex. The driver for #26 is similar and roughly of the same complexity.

Construction of a queue, adding to a queue, deleting from a queue, testing for fullness and emptyness should be tested. To ensure consistency, different sequences of addition and deletion should be constructed.
*/

```
#include "QueueT.h"
#include <iostream>

using namespace std;

int main()
{
     Queue<int>        IntQ;
     Queue<float>      FloatQ;
     Queue<char>       CharQ;

     for (int index = 0; index < 10; index++)
     {
          IntQ.addQ(index);
          FloatQ.addQ(index/3.0);
          CharQ.addQ("Q");
     }

     for (int index = 0; index < 5; index++)
     {
        cout << "Front of intQ on pass " << index << " is " <<
                    IntQ.front()<< endl;

         cout << "Front of FltQ on pass " << index << " is " <<
                    FloatQ.front()<< endl;

         cout << "Front of charQ on pass " << index << " is " <<
                    CharQ.front()<< endl;

         IntQ.removeQ();
         FloatQ.removeQ();
         CharQ.removeQ();
     }
```

```
    int num = 0;

    while (!IntQ.full() && num < 21)
    {
         IntQ.addQ(num*100);
         FloatQ.addQ(num/3.0);
         CharQ.addQ("T");
    }

    while (!FltQ.empty())
    {
         cout << "IntQ dequeues " << IntQ. front () << endl;
         cout << "FloatQ dequeues " << FloatQ.front() << endl;
         cout << "CharQ dequeues " << CharQ.front() << endl;

         IntQ.removeQ();
         CharQ.removeQ();
         FloatQ.removeQ();
    }

    return 0;
}
```

9 - 10.

/*

The driver that follows can be used for problems #9 and #10. These two exercises test the functionality of template functions written for the vector type.

*/

```
#include "VectorT.h"
#include <iostream>

using namespace std;

int main()
{
    vector<int>     IntVector(10);
    vector<float>   FloatVector(15, 100);
    vector<char>    CharVector(26);


    for (int index = 0; index < IntVector.size(); index++)
    {
         IntVector[index] = index;
         FloatVector[index] -= index;
         CharVector[index] = "M";
    }
```

```
     for (int index = 0; index < FloatVector.size(); index++)
     {
          FloatVector[index] -= index;
          CharVector[index] = "Z";
     }

     bool ascend(vector<int>);            // explicit instantiation
     bool ascend(vector<float>);
     bool ascend(vector<char>);

     int range(vector<int>);              // explicit instantiation
     float range(vector<float>);
     char range(vector<char>);

     cout << "Verifying ascension "  << endl;

     if (ascend(IntVector))
          cout << "Integer Vector in ascending order!" << endl;

     if (ascend(FloatVector))
          cout << "Float Vector in ascending order!" << endl;

     if (ascend(CharVector))
          cout << "Character Vector in ascending order!" << endl;

     cout << "Determining range  " << endl;

     cout << "The range of values in the Integer vector is: ";
     cout << range(IntVector) << endl;

     cout << "The range of values in the Float vector is: ";
     cout << range(FloatVector) << endl;

     cout << "The range of values in the Character vector is: ";
     cout << range(CharVector) << endl;

     return 0;
}
```

11. See #7

12 - 17.
/* The driver that follows can be used for programs #12 through #17. These exercises test the functionality of functions defined earlier. These functions test the vector ADT with different base elements.
*/

```
#include "VFns.h"   // could also place function definitions here directly
```

```
#include <iostream>
using namespace std;

int main()
{
    vector<vector <double> > MyTable(10, vector<double>(20, 0.0));

    for (int row = 0; row < MyTable.size(); row++)
       for (int col = 0; col < MyTable[row].size(); col++)
            MyTable[row][col] = row*col;

    for (int row = 0; row < MyTable.size(); row++)
    {
        cout << "The average value in row " << row << "is: ";
        cout << avgRow(MyTable, row) << endl;

        cout << "The standard deviation in row " << row << "is: ";
        cout << stdDevRow(MyTable, row) << endl;

        cout << "The sum of values in row " << row << "is: ";
        cout << sumRow(MyTable, row) << endl;
    }


    for (int col = 0; col < MyTable[0].size(); col++)
    {
        cout << "The average value in col " << col << "is: ";
        cout << avgCol(MyTable, col) << endl;

        cout << "The standard deviation in col " << col << "is: ";
        cout << stdDevCol(MyTable, col) << endl;

        cout << "The sum of values in col " << col << "is: ";
        cout << sumCol(MyTable, col) << endl;
    }

    return 0;
}
```

18. This problem as well as #20 and #21 involving storing, retrieving and then formatting for output, data in two-dimensional form. Such applications are straight-forward implementations. The student must determine the size of the data structure used, and then implement for-loops for storage and retrieval where appropriate.

Two-dimensional arrays, or vectors, may be used. Actually, since each of these three problems involve fixed-sized tables, arrays would be appropriate. However, to test one's understanding of section 6.5, use two-dimensional vectors.

19. /* Pascal's triangle: the trick to computing the output is to realize that the first and last numbers in each row are 1; for all others **point(a, b) = point(a-1, b-1) + point(a-1, b);**

One does not need arrays to solve this problem. However, such a data structure may be used as a good illustration of the manipulation of triangular arrays (or 2-dimensional vectors).

Below, we construct and initialize Pascal's triangle row by row to illustrate the capability of increasing a `vector`'s size. Remember in C++, indexing starts from zero.
*/

```
#include <iostream>

using namespace std;

int main()
{
     vector< vector<int> >     pascal(1, vector<int> (1, 1));
                               // initially "1"

     for (int row = 1; row < 10; row++)
     {
          pascal.push_back(vector<int>(row+1, 1);
                                             // add next row
          for (int col = 1; col < row-1; col++)
               pascal[row][col]=pascal[row-1][col-1] + pascal[row-1][col];
     }

     //display need not be separate,
     // we separate it here to illustrate triangular
     // structure.  Formatting to center may be added.

     for (int row = 0; row < 10; row++)
     {
        for (int col = 0; col <= row; col++)
          cout << pascal[row][col];
        cout << endl;
     }

     return 0;
}
```

20. See #18

21. See #18.

22. - 25. These three exercises are straightforward substitutions of a two-dimensional vector for a two-dimensional array. Other than the type change, the modifications to the solution code for each of these problems should be minor. See named problems from chapter 2.

26. See #7

27 - 31. All of these exercises originate from earlier chapters on stacks and queues. Instead of using the student's own defined and implemented Stack or Queue class, one uses the ADTs provided by the STL. The effect on the application programs is minimal. Refer to references for each problem.

27. See chapter 4, #2

28. See Chapter 4, #4

29. Use the following algorithm:

```
a) While (!Q.empty())
       Stack.push(Q.front())
       Q.removeQ()

b) While (!Stack.empty())
       Queue.addQ(Stack.top())
       Stack.pop()
```

30. See chapter 5, #13

31. See chapter 5, #14

32. Exploit the two-ended nature of a deque to determine if a string is a palindrome. Use the following algorithm:

```
a) While (! end-of-string)
       Deque.push_back(character)

b) While (!Deque.empty() && !done && PALINDROME)

   i)     CharA = Deque.pop_front();

   ii)    if (Deque.empty())
              done = true             // is a palindrome
```

```
else
    CharB= Deque.pop_front();
    if (CharB != CharA)
            PALINDROME = false;
            done = true;
```

c) if (PALINDROME) give appropriate message.

33. As noted above, the capabilities of the Set class need to be exercised in any driver program. Construction of set objects, additions and deletions to such objects (in arbitrary sequences) need to be performed.

Problem 34 below exercises the class template for `ints`. Problem 35 can be constructed to use `ints` only or `ints` and `chars`.

34. /* A straight-forward application. One must instantiate a set object to represent the range of id numbers. Whenever, a number is read in from a file, reset the corresponding set member. Thus, it does not matter how many times an id-number is read in, the set is used just as a record of existence. When done reading the file, one identifies those id-numbers reset in the set object.

Without too much trouble, one could also identify those id numbers that were found in the file more than once, i.e. distinguish between distinct and unique*/

```
#include "Set.h"
#include <iostream>

using namespace std;

int main()
{

     const int range = some-value;        // legal range of id numbers
     Set idSet(range);

     string filename;
     cout << "Please enter the name of the file
               containing id numbers" << endl;
     cin >> filename;

     ifstream infile(filename.c_str());
     if (!infile)
     {
          cout << "Error: unable to open file " << filename << endl;
          return 1;
     }
```

```
     idSet.Complement();        //empty set initially

     int id;
     while (infile >> id)
          idSet.add(id);

     cout << "Distinct id numbers follow" << endl;
     for (int index = 0; index < range; index++)
          if (idSet.Member(index))
               cout << index << "  ";

     cout << endl;


     return 0;
}
```

35. This program is similar but more complicated than #34. Each city code number must be associated with a set of tour numbers (or vice versa). When the user enters the city he or she wishes to visit, one must find all tours that contain all of the named cities. (One could also identify those tours that contained, say, two or more of the named cities.)

One must instantiate multiple set objects here, say one for each city, then initialize each set object to contain the numbers of the tours that visit that city (retrieved from file).

User input then can be processed by taking the union of all named cities and identifies those tours that cover (are contained in the set of) the named cities.

36 - 39.

/* The driver that follows can be used for problems #36 through #39.
These exercises test the functionality of double valarrays.
*/

```
#include "VAFns.h"  //could place function definitions here directly
#include <valarray>
#include <iostream>

using namespace std;

int main()
{
     valarray<double>    InitV(12.5, 100);
     valarray<double>    NoInitV(100);

     OutValArray(InitV);
     OutValArray(NoInitV);
```

```
        InitValArray(NoInitV);

        OutValArray(InitV);
        OutValArray(NoInitV);

        cout << "Dot product of our 2 vectors is: "
             << DotProduct(InitV, NoInitV) << endl;

        cout << "Magnitude of pre-initialized vector is: "
             << Magnitude(InitV) << endl;

        cout << "Magnitude of user-initialized vector is: "
             << Magnitude(InitV) << endl;

        return 0;
}
```

Chapter Seven: Recursion, Algorithms

7.1 Exercises

1. ABC

2. ABCDEFG

3. Blank line output

4. HGFEDC

5. CBA

6. CBAABC

7. Two trace sketches follow
F('a', 'e') ->
F('b', 'd') ->
F('c', 'c') ->
F('d', 'b'), recursion terminates, 0 returned
0 + 2 = 2 returned
2 + 2 = 4 returned
4 + 2 = 6 returned

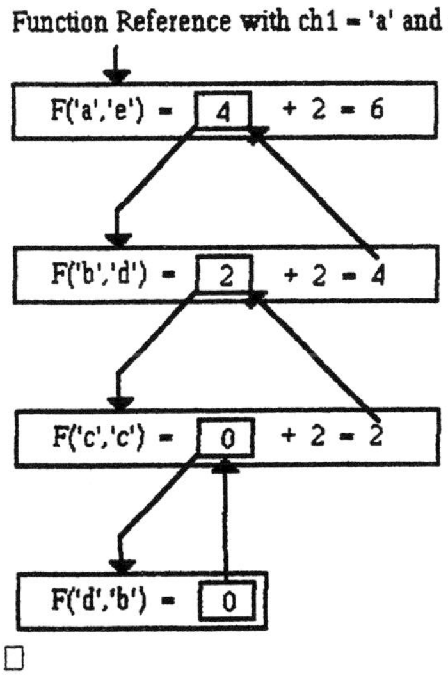

F('h', 'c') is trivial: recursion terminates, 0 returned

8. J
K
L
L
L
M
N
M
L
M
N
N
N
O
P

9. $2^{10}-1 = 1023$ letters

10. MLKJ

L

ML

N

NML

N
ON
P

11. 0

12. n(n+1)/2 (i.e. the sum of the integers 1 to n)

13. The floor (lower-bound, truncation) of $\log_2 n$

14. The sum of the digits of n, e.g. 1234 yields 10

15. The most significant digit of n

16.
```
int F(unsigned n)
{
      return 0;
}
```

17.
```
int F(unsigned n)
{
      int sum = 0;
      for (int num = 1; num < n+1; num++)
            sum += num;
      return sum;
}
```

18.
```
int F(unsigned n)
{
      int log = 0;
      while (n >= 2)
      {
            n = n/2;
            log++;
      }
      return log;
}
```

19.
```
/* corresponds to #14 */
int F(unsigned n)
{
      int sum = 0;
      while ( n>0)
      {
            sum += n % 10;
            n /= 10;
      }
      return sum;
}

/* corresponds to #15 */
int F(int n)
{
      if (n < 0)
            n = -n;
      while ( (n/10)>0)
            n /= 10;
      return n;
}
```

20.

/* recursive: count # digits in n */

```
int F(unsigned n)
{
     if (n < 10)
          return 1;
     else
          return 1 + F(n/10);
}
```

21.

/* nonrecursive version */

```
int F(unsigned n)
{
     int count = 1;

     while ( n >= 10)
     {
          count++
          n /= 10;
     }
     return count;
}
```

22.

/* recursive version: reverse integer's digits */

```
void PrintReverse (int n)
{
     if (n < 0)
          n = -n;

     if (n == 0)
          cout << endl;
     else if ( n < 10)
          cout << n << endl;
     else
     {
          cout << n/10;
          PrintReverse (n/10);
     }

     return;
}
```

23.

```
void PrintReverse (unsigned n)
{
     if (n < 0)
          cout << "-";

     while ( n >= 10)
     {
          cout << n% 10;
          n /= 10;
     }

     return;
}
```

24.

```
double Power(double x, int n)
{
     if (n==0)
          return 1;

     else if (n < 0)
          return Power(x, n+1)/x;

     else
          return Power(x, n-1) * x;
}
```

25.

/* very similar to #22 */

```
void PrintReverse (unsigned n)
{
     if (n == 0)
          cout << endl;
     else
     {
          cout << n%10;
          PrintReverse (n/10);
     }
     return;
}
```

26.

```
void ReverseArray(ArrayType A, int first, int last)
{
      if (first < last)
      {
            ElementType temp = A[first];
            A[first] = A[last];
            A[last] = A[first];
            ReverseArray(A, first+1, last-1);
      }
      return;
}
```

27.

```
int SumArray(ArrayType A, int n)
// NOTE: indexed from 1 to n (not 0 to n-1)!
{
      if (n ==1 )
            return A[1];
      else
            return A[n] + SumArray(A, n-1);
}
```

28.

```
int Location(ArrayType A, int first, int last, ElementType elm)
{
      if (first == last && elm != A[first])
            return 0;

      else if (elm == A[last])
            return last;

      else
            return Location(A, first, last-1, elm);
}
```

29.

```
string RecReverse(string word)
{
   if (word.length() == 1)
      return word;
   else
      return RecReverse(word.substr(1,word.length()-1))+ word[0];
}
```

30.
```
string Reverse(string word)
{
      string reverse;
      int length = word.length();
      for (int index = length; index > 0; index--)
            reverse[length - index] = word[index-1];

      return reverse;
}
```

31.
```
bool Palindrome (unsigned number, unsigned numDigits)
{
      if (numDigits <=1)
            return true;
      else
      {
            unsigned firstDigit = number;
            unsigned expNum = 1;
            for (int exp = 1; exp < numDigits; exp++)
                  expNum *= 10;
            firstDigit = number / expNum;
            unsigned lastDigit = number % 10;
            if (firstDigit != lastDigit)
                  return false;
            else
                  return Palindrome( firstDigit%expNum%10, numDigits-2);
}
```

32.
```
int GCD (int a, int b)
{
      if (a < 0)
            a = -a;

      if (b < 0)
            b = -b;

      if (b == 0)
            return a;

      else
            return GCD(b, a%b);
}
```

33.

```
int GCD (int a, int b)
{
      if (a < 0)
            a = -a;
      if (b < 0)
            b = -b;
      if (b == 0)
            return a;
      else
      {
            int r = a % b;
            while (r > 0)
            {
                  a = b;
                  b = r;
                  r = a % b;
            }
            return b;
}
```

34.

```
int BinCoeff(int n, int k)
{
      if (n==k || k==0)
            return 1;

      else
            return BinCoeff(n-1, k-1) + BinCoeff(n-1, k);
}
```

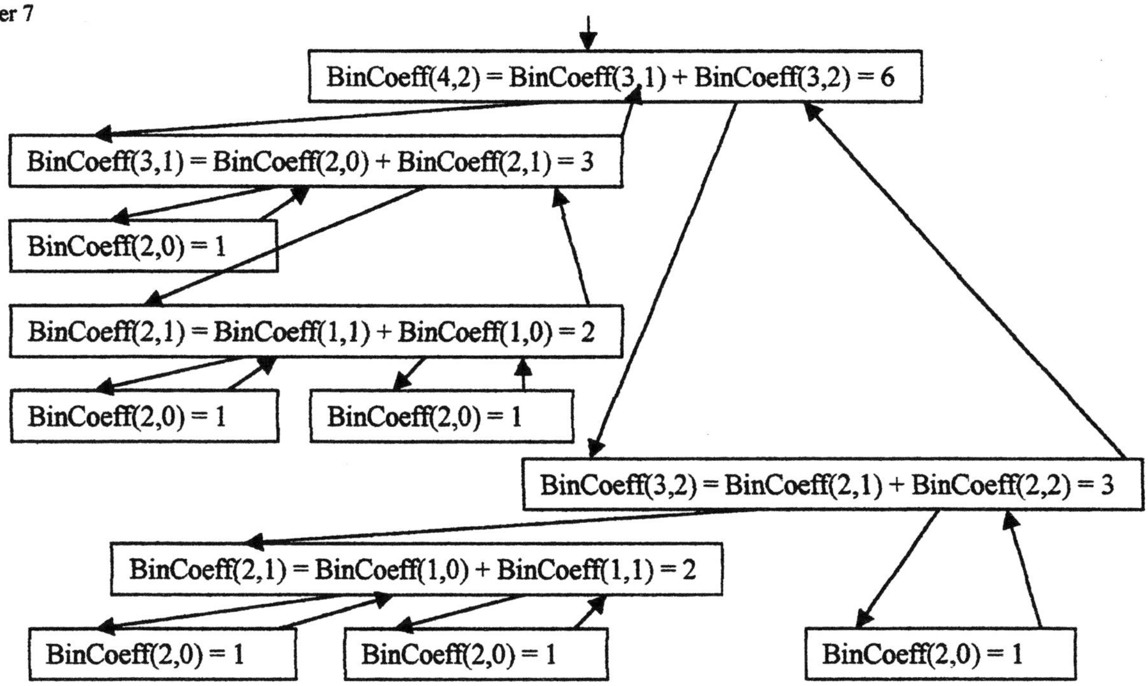

35.

```
int BinCoeff(int n, int k)
{
     if (n==k || k==0)
          return 1;
     else
          return    Factorial(n)/(Factorial(k)*Factorial(n-k));
}
```

7.2 Exercises

1. The instructions are executed in the following order.

Move (4, A, B, C)
Move (3, A, C, B)
Move (2, A, B, C)
Move (1, A, C, B)
Move disk from A to B.
Move (1, A, ,C)
Move disk from A to C.
Move (1, B, A, C)
Move disk from B to C.
Move (1, A, ,B)
Move disk from A to B.
Move (2, C, A, B)
Move (1, C, B, A)
Move disk from C to A

.
.
.

Similarly for Move (5, A, B, C)

2. A * B

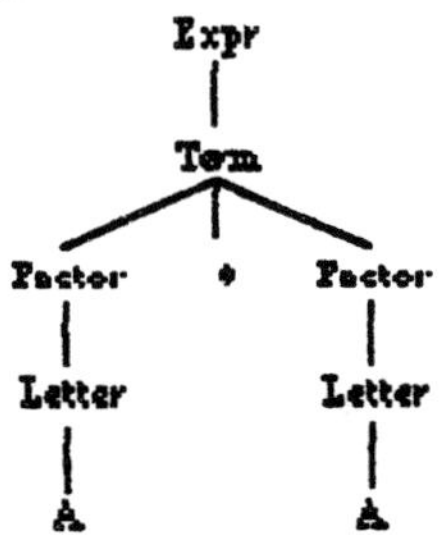

3. (A * B)

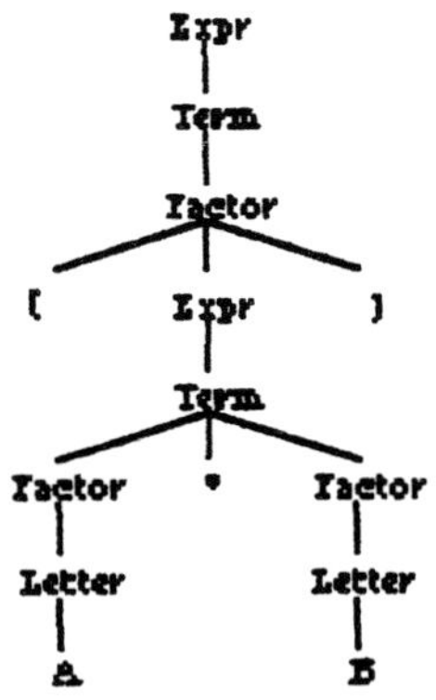

4. (((1)))

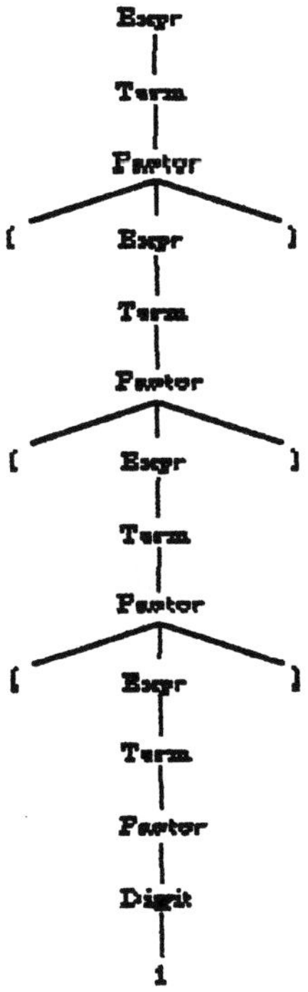
Expr
Term
Factor
(
Expr
)
Term
Factor
(
Expr
)
Term
Factor
(
Expr
)
Term
Factor
Digit
1

□

5. (A * B) * C

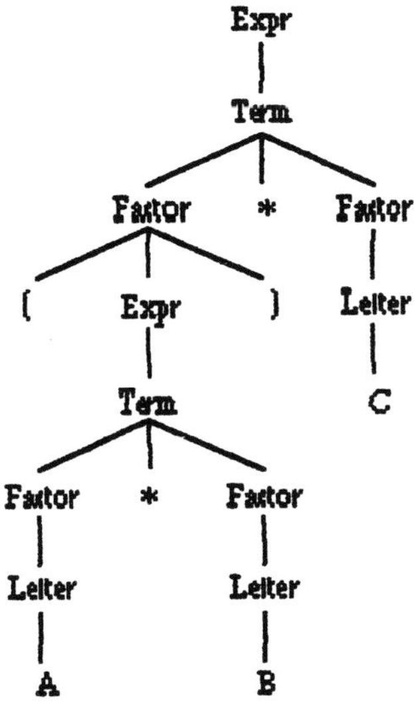
Expr
Term
Factor
*
Factor
(
Expr
)
Letter
Term
C
Factor
*
Factor
Letter
Letter
A
B

6. A * (B * C)

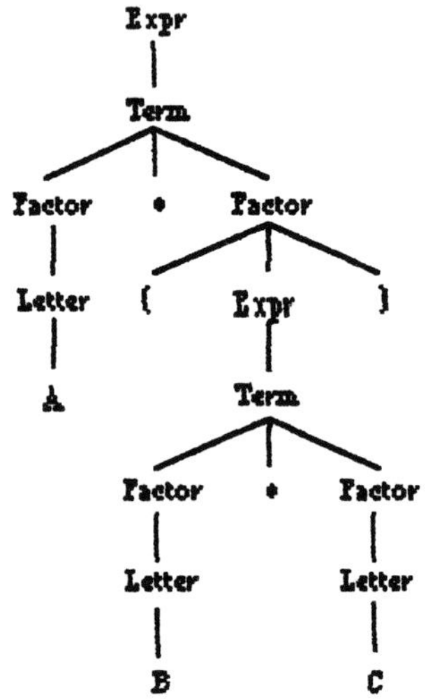

7. ((A + B) * 2) - (C * D)) * 5

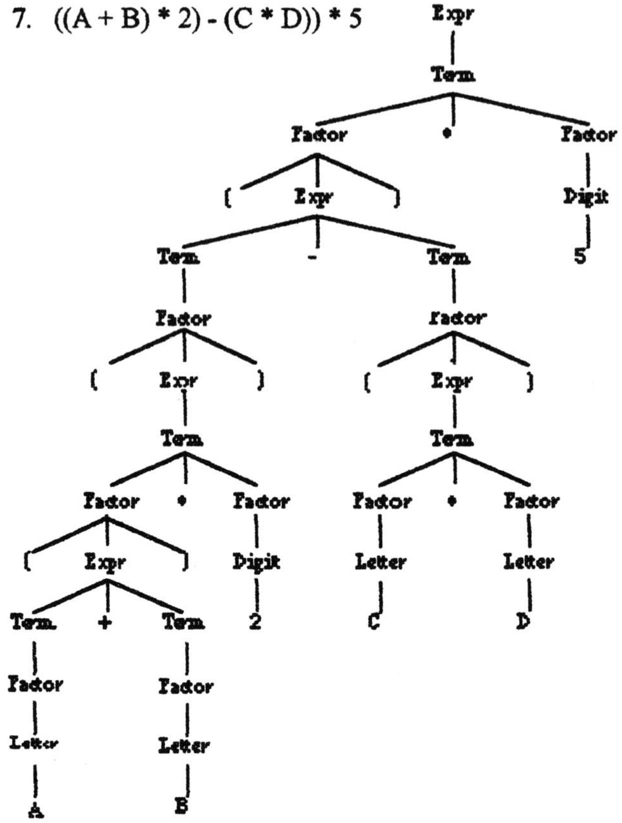

8. A*B

□

□

Main program	0			Call ValidExpression
ValidExpression	0			Call ValidTerm
ValidTerm	0			Call ValidFactor
ValidFactor	0			Call GetChar to get next symbol
	1	A		GetChar increments Pos and returns
	1	A	true	Valid set to true; return to ValidTerm
ValidTerm	1	A	true	Call GetChar to get next symbol
	2	*		GetChar increments Pos and returns
	2	*	true	Call ValidFactor
ValidFactor	2	*	true	Call GetChar to get next symbol
	3	B		GetChar increments Pos and returns
	3	B	true	Valid set to true; return to ValidExpression
ValidExpression	3	B	true	Call GetChar to get next symbol
	4	$		GetChar increments Pos and returns
	3	$	true	"Unget" a character
Main program	3			

9. (A*B)

Main program	0			Call ValidExpression
ValidExpression	0			Call ValidTerm
ValidTerm	0			Call ValidFactor
ValidFactor	0			Call GetChar to get next symbol
	1	(		GetChar increments Pos and returns
	1	(		Call ValidExpression
ValidExpression	1	(		Call ValidTerm
ValidTerm	1	(		Call ValidFactor
ValidFactor	1	(		Call GetChar to get next symbol
	2	A		GetChar increments Pos and returns
	2	A	true	Valid set to true; return to ValidTerm
ValidTerm	2	A	true	Call GetChar to get next symbol
	3	*		GetChar increments Pos and returns
	3	*	true	Call ValidFactor
ValidFactor	3	*	true	Call GetChar to get next symbol
	4	B		GetChar increments Pos and returns
	4	B	true	Valid set to true; return to ValidExpression
ValidExpression	4	B	true	Call GetChar to get next symbol
	5	)		GetChar increments Pos and returns
	4	)	true	"Unget" a character
ValidFactor	4	)	true	Call GetChar to get next symbol
	5	)		GetChar increments Pos and returns
ValidTerm	5	)	true	Call GetChar to get next symbol
	6	$		GetChar increments Pos and returns
	5	$	true	"Unget" symbol, return to ValidExpression
ValidExpression	5	$	true	Call GetChar to get next symbol
	6	$		GetChar increments Pos and returns
	5	$	true	"Unget" a character
Main program	5			

10. (A-B)-C

Main program □	0			Call ValidExpression
ValidExpression	0			Call ValidTerm
ValidTerm	0			Call ValidFactor
ValidFactor	0			Call GetChar to get next symbol
	1	(		GetChar increments Pos and returns
	1	(		Call ValidExpression
ValidExpression	1	(		Call ValidTerm
ValidTerm	1	(		Call ValidFactor
ValidFactor	1	(		Call GetChar to get next symbol
	2	A		GetChar increments Pos and returns
	2	A	true	Valid set to true; return to ValidTerm
ValidTerm	2	A	true	Call GetChar to get next symbol
	3	-		GetChar increments Pos and returns
	2	-	true	"Unget" symbol, return to ValidExpression
ValidExpression	2	-	true	Call GetChar to get next symbol
	3	-		GetChar increments Pos and returns
	3	-	true	Call ValidTerm
ValidTerm	3	-	true	Call ValidFactor
ValidFactor	3	B	true	Call GetChar to get next symbol
	4	B		GetChar increments Pos and returns
	4	B	true	Valid set to true; return to ValidTerm
ValidTerm	4	B	true	Call GetChar to get next symbol
	5	)		GetChar increments Pos and returns
	4	)	true	"Unget" symbol, return to ValidExpression
ValidExpression	4	)	true	Return to ValidFactor
ValidFactor	4	)	true	Call GetChar to get next symbol
	5	)		GetChar increments Pos and returns

ValidTerm	5	)	true	Call GetChar to get next symbol
	6	-		GetChar increments Pos and returns
	5	-	true	"Unget" symbol, return to ValidExpression
ValidExpression	5	-	true	Call GetChar to get next symbol
	6	-		GetChar increments Pos and returns
	6	-	true	Call ValidTerm
ValidTerm	6	-	true	Call ValidFactor
ValidFactor	6	-	true	Call GetChar to get next symbol
	7	C		GetChar increments Pos and returns
	7	C	true	Valid set to true; return to ValidTerm
ValidTerm	7	C	true	Call GetChar to get next symbol
	8	$		GetChar increments Pos and returns
	7	$	true	"Unget" symbol, return to ValidExpression
ValidExpression	7	$	true	Return to main program
Main program	7			

11. A-(B-C)

□

Main program	0			Call ValidExpression
ValidExpression	0			Call ValidTerm
ValidTerm	0			Call ValidFactor
ValidFactor	0			Call GetChar to get next symbol
	1	A		GetChar increments Pos and returns
	1	A	true	Valid set to true; return to ValidTerm
ValidTerm	1		true	Call GetChar to get next symbol
	2	-		GetChar increments Pos and returns
	1	-	true	"Unget" symbol, return to ValidExpression
ValidExpression	1		true	Call GetChar to get next symbol
	2	-		GetChar increments Pos and returns
	2	-	true	Call ValidTerm
ValidTerm	2	-	true	Call ValidFactor
ValidFactor	2	-	true	Call GetChar to get next symbol
	3	(		GetChar increments Pos and returns
	3	(	true	Call ValidExpression
ValidExpression	3	(	true	Call ValidTerm
ValidTerm	3	(	true	Call ValidFactor
ValidFactor	3	(	true	Call GetChar to get next symbol
	4	B		GetChar increments Pos and returns
	4	B	true	Valid set to true; return to ValidTerm
ValidTerm	4	B	true	Call GetChar to get next symbol
	5	-		GetChar increments Pos and returns
	4	-	true	"Unget" symbol, return to ValidExpression
ValidExpression	4	-	true	Call GetChar to get next symbol
	5	-		GetChar increments Pos and returns
	5	-	true	Call ValidTerm
ValidTerm	5	-	true	Call ValidFactor

ValidFactor	5	-	true	Call GetChar to get next symbol
	6	C		GetChar increments Pos and returns
	6	C	true	Valid set to true; return to ValidTerm
ValidTerm	6	C	true	Call GetChar to get next symbol
	7	)		GetChar increments Pos and returns
	6	)	true	"Unget" symbol, return to ValidExpression
ValidExpression	6	)	true	Return to ValidFactor
ValidFactor	6	)	true	Call GetChar to get next symbol
	7	)		GetChar increments Pos and returns
ValidTerm	7	)	true	Call GetChar to get next symbol
	8	$		GetChar increments Pos and returns
	7	$	true	"Unget" symbol, return to ValidExpression
ValidExpression	7	$	true	Return to main program
Main program	7	$		

12 - 15. Are straight-forward and similar to 16 - 18 below.

16 ()()()

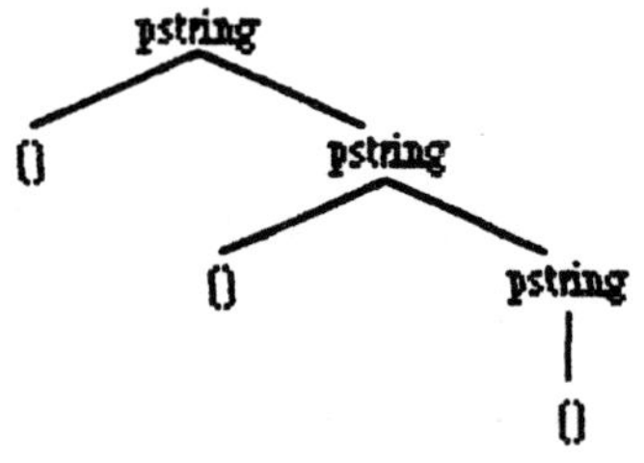

17 ((()))

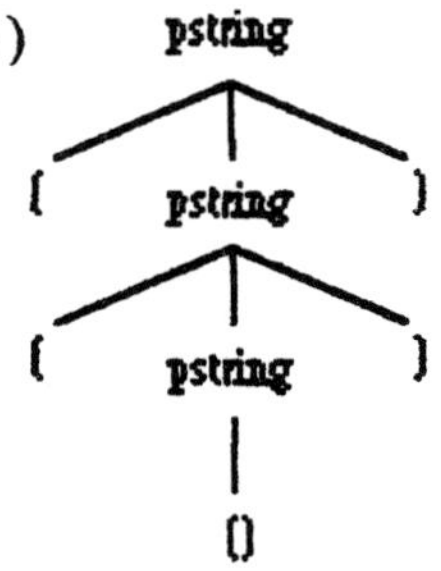

18. () (() ()) ()

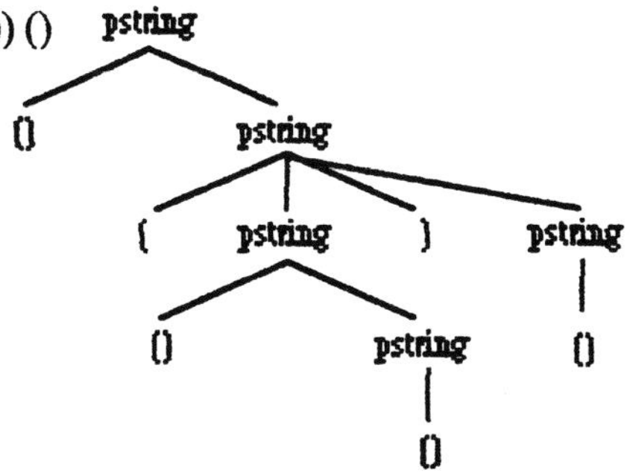

7.4 Exercises

1. $O(n^3)$

2. $O(2^n)$

3. $O(n)$

4. $O(2^n)$

5. Retrieving the xth element of any ordered collection, e.g second element of an array, fourth line of a file, third element in linked list, seventh element in stack, etc.

6. If $T(n)$ is less than or equal to Cn, then $T(n)$ is also less than or equal to Cn^2

7. $O(n)$

8. $O(n^2)$

9. $O(n^3)$

10. $O(n^2)$

11. $O(\log n)$

12. $O(2^n)$

13. $$\begin{aligned} T(n) &= 1 + T(n-1) + T(1) + T(n-1) \\ &= 1 + T(n-1) + 2 + T(n-1) \\ &= 3 + 2T(n-1) \\ &= 3 + 2\,(3 + 2T(n-2)) \\ &= 3(1+2) + 2^2T(n-2) \\ &= 3(1+2) + 2^2(3 + 2T(n-3)) \\ &= 3(1+2 + 2^2) + 2^3T(n-3) \\ &= \ldots \\ &= 3(1+2+ 2^2+ 2^3+\ldots+ 2^{n-2}) + 2^{n-1}T(1) \\ &= 3(2^{n-1}- 1) + 2^{n-1}2 \\ &= 3(2^{n-1}- 1) + 2^n \end{aligned}$$

7.6 Exercises

1. Let k = # of times execution has reached point A,
   i_k, $Count_k$ = values of i and Count, respectively, at this time.

We must prove that:

$i_k = k$, and

$Count_k$ = # of array elements among X[1], ..., X[k] greater than Cutoff.

Anchor step:

Suppose k = 1, i.e., execution reaches point A for first time. Then,

$i_1 = i_0 + 1$ (since only instruction 3a changes i)

$= 0 + 1 = k$ (since instruction 2 sets i_0 equal to 0)

If path 1, 2, 3, A is followed, $Count_1 = Count_0 = 0$, since instruction 1 initializes $Count_0$ to 0; thus, $Count_1$ is correct, since this path is followed only in case X[1] is not > Cutoff.

If path 1, 2, 3a, 3b, A is followed,

$Count_1 = Count_0 + 1$ (instruction 3b)

$= 0 + 1 = 1$ (instruction 1)

and this is correct since this occurs only in case X[1] > Cutoff.

Induction step:

Assume $i_k = k$ and $Count_k$ = # of first k items in array X that exceed Cutoff.

Then, $i_{k+1} = i_k + 1$ since only instruction 3a changes i

$= k + 1$ by the induction assumption.

If path A, 3, A is followed on (k+1)-st pass,

$Count_{k+1} = Count_k$

= # of X[1], ..., X[k] that are > Cutoff (induction assumption).

= # of X[1], ..., X[k], X[k+1] that are > Cutoff since this path implies that X[k+1] > Cutoff is false.

If path A, 3, 3a, 3b, A is followed on (k+1)-st pass,

$Count_{k+1} = Count_k + 1$

= (# of X[1], ..., X[k] that are > Cutoff) + 1

= # of X[1], ..., X[k], X[k+1] > Cutoff since this path implies that X[k+1] > Cutoff is true, so one more array element > Cutoff has been found.

This establishes that I implies A.

A implies O is now clear, since execution will eventually reach point A for the n-th time, so by assertion A, it will eventually attain the value n + 1, causing repetition to terminate, and again by A, at that time, Count will be the number of X[1], ..., X[n] that exceed Cutoff.

2. The proof is straight-forward. Refer to the chapter for the code.

3. The pseudo-code algorithm looks like:
(1) Largest = X[1].

(2) Do the following for k = 2 to n:
    If X[k] > Largest then:
        Largest = X[k].

The proof of this algorithm's correctness is very similar to that of exercise 1.

4.
```
int Factorial(int n)
/* Accepts:   A nonnegative integer n.
      Function:  Recursively calculates n!
      Returns:   Integer n!.
*/
{
    if (n)
        return n*Factorial(n-1);
    else
        return 1;
}
```

I : The input consists of a nonnegative integer n.
O : The function terminates and when it does the value of the function is n!.

Anchor: If n = 0, the anchor statement Factorial := 1 is executed immediately, so execution terminates and the correct value is returned for 0!.

Induction Step: Assume that for some nonnegative integer k the function terminates for n = k and returns the correct value for k!. When it is referenced with parameter n = k+1, the inductive statement Factorial := n * Factorial (n - 1) is executed. The value of n - 1 is k, so by the induction hypothesis the function reference Factorial (n - 1) terminates and returns the correct value for k!. Thus the function reference with parameter n = k + 1 terminates and returns the correct value (k + 1) * k! = (k + 1)! for n!. Thus in all cases the output assertion follows from the input assertion.

5. *Anchor* : If n = 1, then the number of moves made = 1 = 2 - 1.
Induction :
Assume for n = k, procedure Move(k) executes $2^k - 1$ moves.
Then, for n = k + 1, the statement Move(n - 1, ...) is executed.
But, n - 1 = k, so Move(k) is called, which executes $2^k - 1$ moves.
Then, Move(1) is called which executes 1 move.
Then, Move(n - 1, ...) is again called, which executes $2^k - 1$ moves.
So, the total number of moves executed = $2^k - 1 + 1 + 2^k - 1 = 2 * 2^k - 1 = 2^{k+1} - 1 = 2^n - 1$.

Programming Problems

1. - 18.
All of these programs are essentially drivers.

#17 and #18 demand that one adds trace output to the target functions.

There are several ways to implement this indentation. One common way is to add a second parameter which indicates, for each function call, the level of indentation required. Alternatively, you can set up a static or global variable which indicates the level of indentation at all times. Note that with the second method, you must increment the level at the beginning of the function and decrement it at the end.

The following illustrates the second method for the function in Exercise 13:

```
unsigned F(unsigned n)
{
   static level = 0;

   cout << setw(2*level) << "";   // indent

   if (n < 2)
   {
      cout << "F(" << n << ") returns 0\n";
      level--;
      return 0;
   }
   // else
      level++;
      cout << "F(" << n << ") = 1 + F(" << n/2 << ")\n";
      unsigned val = 1 + F(n/2);

      cout << setw(2*level) << "";   // indent
      cout << "F(" << n << ") returns " << val << endl;
      level--;
      return val;
}
```

#16 requires the comparison of the computing times of recursive and nonrecursive functions. To do this, one must use appropriate system calls (for example, one could use `clock()` to get the time before a function runs and then again after it finishes).

The remaining drivers are all straight-forward exercises.

19.

There are many ways that one could structure a recursive function to output the BINGO song. None are particularly elegant, primarily because this problem is most easily solved using iteration and strings: use a for loop to control output, each pass of the for loop corresponds to one verse. Some portion of BINGO is output, depending on the index of the for loop.

Whether or not recursion is used, one should define string constants, such as

```
string line1 = "There was a farmer had a dog"
```

to simplify the output process.

A sample recursive program follows:

```
#include <iostream>
#include <string>
#include <cctype>
using namespace std;

void Sing(string name, int numClaps)
{
  string line2andLast = "And " + name + " was his name-o";
  if (numClaps <= name.length())
  {
    cout << "There was a farmer had a dog.\n" << line2andLast << ".\n";

    for (int i = 0; i < 3; i++)
    {
      cout << "    ";
      for (int j = 1; j <= numClaps; j++)
      {
        cout << (j == 1 ? "(Clap" : "clap");
        cout << (j < numClaps ? ", " : ")");
      }
      if (0 < numClaps && numClaps < name.length())
        cout << '-';
      if (numClaps == name.length())
        cout << endl;

      for (int j = numClaps; j < name.length(); j++)
      {
        char letter = name[j];
        if (islower(letter))
          letter = toupper(letter);
        cout << letter << (j < name.length()-1 ? "-" : "!\n");

      }
    }
    cout << line2andLast << "!\n\n";
    Sing(name, numClaps + 1);
  }
}
```

```
int main()
{
  Sing("Bingo", 0);
}
```

20.

```
/* Recursive parsing of a nonegative integer in order to add commas.

   Note the use of a boolean value to distinguish the first recursive copy from the remaining ones.

   Such identification is necessary in order to properly print out 0, 9, 19, 1,010, etc.
*/

#include <iostream>
using namespace std;

void comma(unsigned n, bool start)
{
     int digits;

     if (n==0 && start)
          cout << n << endl;
     else
     {
          if (n > 0)
          {
               digits = n % 1000;


               if (n > 999)
               {
                    comma(n/1000, false);
                    cout << "," << endl;
               }
          }
          else
               digits = n;

          if (!digits)
               cout << "000";
          else if ( digits < 10 && !start)
               cout << "00" << digits;
          else if (digits < 100 && !start)
                    cout << "0" << digits;
               else
                    cout << digits;
          }
  }
```

21. /* Recursive examination of a 2D structure in order to determine the number of blobs (contiguous asterisks) in a grid.

This classic example rests on the notion of using the recursive structure to control searching in multiple directions. Linear evaluation is not sufficient because most grid points have neighbors to the north, south, east and west.

Care must be taken here to control recursive invocation in order to prevent infinite recursing. For example, one does not want to call one's south neighbor and then be called by one's south neighbor, etc. Typically, one alters the grid to indicate that a point has been visited.

*/

```
#include <iostream>
using namespace std;

const int maxRow = some_value;
const int maxCol = some_value;

typdef char Grid[maxRow][maxCol];

void initGrid(Grid& g)
{
      int rows = 0;
      int cols = 0;

      while (rows <=0 || rows > maxRow)
      {
            cout << "Please enter the number of rows, less than "
                  << maxRow << endl;
            cin >> rows;
      }


      while (cols <=0 || cols > maxcol)
      {
            cout << "Please enter the number of columns, less than "
                  << maxCol << endl;
            cin >> rows;
      }

      for (int row = 0; row < rows; row++)
         for (int col = 0; col < cols; col++)
           g[row][col] = " ";          // empty grid point


      for (int row = rows; row < maxRow; row++)
         for (int col = cols; col < maxCol; col++)
           g[row][col] = "?";          // invalid grid point

      cout << "Please enter the x,y coordinates of each asterisk";

      cout << "Input terminated by out-of-bounds value, e.g. "
            << maxRow + 1 << "for row value"  << endl;
```

```
    cout << "coordinates? " << endl;
    cin >> rows;
    cin >> cols;

    while (rows > 0 && rows <= maxRow && cols > 0 && cols <=maxCol)
    {
        g[rows-1][cols-1] = "*";

        cout << "coordinates? " << endl;
        cin >> rows;
        cin >> cols;
    }
    return;
}


void countBlob(Grid& g, int x, int y)
{
    if (g[x][y] == "*")
    {
        g[x][y] = "X";      // mark as visited, thus counted
        if (x < maxRow-1)
            countBlob(g, x+1, y);

        else if (x > 0)
            countBlob(g, x-1, y);

        else if (y < maxCol-1)
            countBlob(g, x, y+1);

        else if (y > 0)
            countBlob(g, x, y-1);
    }
    return;
}


int main()
{
    Grid grid;

    initGrid(grid);

    int count = 0;

    for (int row = 0; row < maxRow; row++)
      for (int col = 0; col < maxCol; col++)
         if (grid[row][col] == "*")
         {
              countBlob(grid, row, col);
              count++;
         }

    cout << "The number of blobs in your grids is " << count << endl;

    return 0;
}
```

22. /* Recursive examination of a 2D structure in order to determine the number of paths from one point to another.

This classic example is similar to the problem immediately above. One needs to establish a set order of examination, say visit one's north and then one's east neighbors. Then one simply recurses north until one falls off the grid. Recursion "automatically" takes care of backtracking to a legal grid point and then recursing to the east.

By restricting travel to only these two directions, one need not worry about creating cycles (and thus infinite recursion).
*/

```
/* Input:  location of B relative to A
 * Output: the number of northeast paths from A to B
 *****************************************************************/

#include <iostream>
using namespace std;

int NortheastPaths(int pointsNorth, int pointsEast);

int main()
{
   int pointsNorth,
       pointsEast;

   cout << "\nHow many points north of A is B? ";
   cin >> pointsNorth;

   cout << "How many points east of A is B? ";
   cin >> pointsEast;

   cout << "\nThere are " << NortheastPaths(pointsNorth, pointsEast)
        << " northeast paths between A and B.\n";

   return 0;
}

/* NortheastPaths returns the number of northeast paths from the current
 * point to the point pointsNorth north and pointsEast east of the
 * current point.
 *
 * Receive:  pointsNorth, the points north to the destination
 *           pointsEast, the point east to the destination
 * Return:   the number of northeast paths
 *****************************************************************/

int NortheastPaths(int pointsNorth, int pointsEast)
{
   if ( (pointsNorth < 0) || (pointsEast < 0) )
      return 0;

   else if ( (pointsNorth == 0) && (pointsEast == 0) )
```

```
      return 1;

   else
      return NortheastPaths(pointsNorth - 1, pointsEast) +
             NortheastPaths(pointsNorth , pointsEast - 1);
}
```

23. /* The LIFO structure of stacks gives one an "automatic" method for reversal, just as recursion does. Thus, there is a strong correlation between stack and recursive solutions.
*/

```
#include <iostream>
using namespace std;

void convert(int x)
{
     int rem = x % 2;
     if (x/2)
          convert(x/2);

     cout << rem;
     return;
}
```

24. /* The LIFO structure of stacks gives one an "automatic" method for reversal, just as recursion does. Thus, there is a strong correlation between stack and recursive solutions.
*/

```
#include <iostream>
using namespace std;

void primeFactor(int num, int divisor)
{
     if (num !=1)
          if (num % divisor)
               primeFactor(num, divisor + 1);
          else
          {
               primeFactor(num/divisor, divisor);
               cout << divisor;
          }

     return;
}
```

25. /* Permutation generation is another classic example of the power of recursion when used for backtracking. Again, the recursive structure is used to complete path generation (in this case permutations) from partial paths at all levels.

One could easily use characters here instead of integers, to view all permutations of a string for example.
*/

```
#include <iostream>
using namespace std;

const int maxValue = some_value;

void PrintPerm(int[] p)
{
      int index = 1;

      while (p[index])
      {
            cout << p[index];
            index = p[index];          //get next number in permutation
      }

      cout << endl;

      return;
}


void Permute(int[] p, int k, int n)
{
      int index = 0;
      do
      {
            p[k] = p[index];
            p[index] = k;
            if (k == n)
                  PrintPerm(p);
            else
                  Permute(p, k+1, n);
            p[index] = p[k];          // swap back
            index = p[index];
      }
      while (!p)

      return;
}


int main()
{
    int    Perm[maxValue];
    int    number = 0;
```

```
    while (number <=0 || number > maxValue)
    {
      cout << "Enter number of elements to permute, less than "
                << maxValue-1 << endl;
      cin >> number;
    }

    Perm[0] = 0;
    Permute(Perm, 1, number);

    return 0;
}
```

26. - 28. These problems are straight-forward extensions to programs given in the text.

29. This problem is not a natural, or efficient use of recursion.
The basic recursive structure would be used to read a line, character by character.

One must record (keep) all characters that precede "//" (C++'s end of line comment delimiter).

Recursion continues until a "/" is encountered.

The difficulty lies in distinguishing between "/" in, say, division, and "//" for a comment.

Since one cannot read ahead in the buffer, one must pass some information into the recursive call indicating whether a "/" has just been read. Passing the character just read will suffice.

Recursion terminates then when the EOLN is reached or the second consecutive "/" is read.

One last detail: each recursive call is responsible for printing the character received, if the character read and the character received both are not "/". This prevents a spurious "/" from being printed (stored).

30- 31. These two problems use recursion in place of a stack.
Use each copy of the recursive function to read in a character.

To determine if parentheses are balanced (and matched), one need only to store each left paren (say, concatenate a string while recursing) and then when a right paren is encountered, match it with the last stored paren. A match necessitates the removal of the matched left paren.

Recursion terminates at the end of the string or upon a mismatch (right paren read with no stored matching left paren). If the constructed (concatenated) string is empty when the input string has been parsed completely then the string contains correctly matched parentheses.

32 - 37. These problems use the STL for previously defined containers and algorithms.

Each problem can be solved with a variety of approaches, although the approach chosen affects the ease of solution.

All programs involve input of substantial test data. Some suggestions follow.

32.
The 15-day period is arbitrary. It could be 30, 20, or 102 (so use a constant). One needs to record the high, the low and the closing price for each day. Hence, one should use a struct with these three fields as the basic element stored. Unless stored in order of day examined, one needs also to record the day (or an index of the day in the range studied).

Any sequential container will do. One could use a priority queue, with the closing price as the key, and thus avoid the sorting step. However, doing so may complicate the scan required to find the daily high/low range.

When scanning to determine the daily high/low range, one can easily track the current trading range for final output. This scanning is most logically done if the items in the container are ordered by day.

33.
This problem is very much like the preceding one.

Now, however, one really should store the data, sorted by day.

Then it becomes easy to show the daily highs and lows(#b), display the cumulative (by day) production (#c), as well as compute the daily low, high and average (#c).

34 - 35. Use of a set simplifies the tasks of finding all product numbers common to both warehouses (#34) as well as the aggregrate set of product numbers (#35).

36.
This problem is the most extensive of the six in this section, primarily because it requires a lot of functionality.

The basic element stored in the container needs to be the price and product number, as above.
#a and #b require a scan of the container.
#c requires a modification of all matched elements after the first match.
#d is a sort.
#e is output.

As suggested, if one a `Product` class, one may overload == and < and thus use standard algorithms for the required functionality, drastically reducing the code needed.

37. This problem is simply a driver. The algorithms used in chapter 2 are not changed. Now, containers are used rather than arrays.

Chapter Eight: Lists

8.1 Exercises

1. Sequential storage, without links, is an inherently inefficient manner for storing a list, if the list is to be modified at all. Deletion requires shifting the elements in order to retain the sequential storage nature of the list, unless the deletion occurs at the end. In this **best** case, the cost is O(1). The **average** case requires shifting half the elements while the **worst** case is deleting the first element, requiring a shift of n elements. Both these cases require O(n).

2.
```
/*  Sequential list with holes, where a hole is marked by a special
value.

    We assume a list of integers here, as does the text, but the
  idea can be generalized to any type)
*/

double FindMean(int[]  myArray, int mysize, int marker)
{
      double sum = 0.0;
      int count = 0;

      for (int index = 0; index < mysize; index++)
            if (myArray[index] != marker)
            {
                  count++;
                  sum += myArray[index];
            }

      if (count == 0)
            return 0;
      else
            return sum/count;
}
```

3.
```
/* Since holes are allowed, deletion is O(1).  Simply replace
element with special marker value
*/

void Delete(int[]  myArray, int elemToDel, int& mysize, int marker)
{
      myArray[elemToDel] = marker;
      mysize--;
      return;
}
```

4.

```
    /*  Insertion requires a scan for a hole.  In the worst case, the
    scan may go through the entire list, hence the complexity is O(n)
    */
  int Insert(int[]  myArray, int element, int position, int& mysize,
                                                      int marker)
  {
      bool holeFound = false;
      int  index = position + 1;     // look to right for insertion

      while (!holeFound && index < mysize)
          if (myArray[index] == marker)
              holeFound = true;
          else
              index++;
      if (holeFound)
      {
          // shift elements right (up) to hole
          for (int shift = index-1; shift > position + 1; shift--)
              element[shift+1] = element[shift];

          element[position+1] = element;
          mysize++;
          return 0;       // element inserted!!
      }
      else        // find hole to the left and shift
      {
          index = position - 1;
          while (!holeFound && index >= 0)
          {
              if (myArray[index] == marker)
                  holeFound = true;
              else
                  index--;
          }
          if (holeFound)
          {
              // shift elements left (down) to hole
              for (int shift = index; shift < position; shift++)
                  element[shift] = element[shift+1];

              element[position] = element;
              mysize++;
              return 0;       // element inserted!!
          }
          else
              return 1;       // no holes found!
      }
  }
```

5. /* This implementation does not use operator overloading. Contrast to subsequent implementations */

```
const int maxDegree = some_value;

class Polynomial
{
   int  degree;
   int  coeff[maxDegree];          // generalizes to any type

public:
   Polynomial();
   Polynomial(int);

   void Input(istream& in);
   void Output(ostream& out);

   Polynomial  operator+(const Polynomial&);

   Polynomial  operator*(const Polynomial&);
};


Polynomial::Polynomial()
{
   degree = maxDegree;

   for (int index = 0; index < degree; index++)
        coeff[index] = 0;
}


Polynomial::Polynomial(int Degree)
{
   degree = Degree;
   for (int index = 0; index < degree; index++)
        coeff[index] = 0;
}

inline istream& operator>>(istream& in, Polynomial& p)
{
   p.Input(in);
   return in;
}


inline ostream& operator<<(ostream& out, Polynomial& p)
{
   p.Output(out);
   return out;
}
```

```
void Polynomial::Input(istream& in)
{
   in >> degree;   // the degree of this polynomial

   // the coefficients in ascending order
   for (int index = 0; index < degree; index++)
        in >> coeff[index];

   for (int index = degree; index < maxDegree; index++)
        coeff[index] = 0;
}

void Polynomial::Output(ostream& out)
{
   out << "The degree of this polynomial is " << degree << endl;
   out << "The coefficients in ascending order are " << endl;

   for (int index = 0; index < degree-1; index++)
        out << coeff[index] << "^" << index << " + ";

   out << coeff[degree-1] << "^" << degree-1 << endl;
}


Polynomial Polynomial::operator+(const Polynomial& B)
{                              // complexity is O(max{degree, B.degree})
   Polynomial  C;
   if (degree < B.degree)
   {
        for (int i = 0; i < degree; i++)
             C.coeff[i] = coeff[i] + B.coeff[i];

        for (int i = degree; i < B.degree; i++)
             C.coeff[i] = B.coeff[i];

        C.degree = B.degree;
   }
   else
   {
        for (int i = 0; i < B.degree; i++)
             C.coeff[i] = coeff[i] + B.coeff[i];

        for (int i = B.degree; i < degree; i++)
             C.coeff[i] = coeff[i];

        C.degree = degree;
   }
   return C;
}
```

```
Polynomial  Polynomial::operator*(const Polynomial& B)
// As the nested for loops below demonstrate, complexity is
//      O(degree * B.degree)
{
   Polynomial  C;

   for (int index = 0; index < C.degree; index++)
        coeff[index] = 0;

   for (int i = 0; i < degree; i++)
        for (int j = 0; index < B.degree; j++)
             C.coeff[i+j] += coeff[i]*B.coeff[j];

   C.degree = degree + B.degree;
   return C;
}
```

8.2 Exercises

1. Algorithm to count the nodes in a linked list

    1. Count = 0,
       CurrentPtr = first;

    2. While (CurrentPtr != null_value)
           Count++;
           CurrentPtr = CurrentPtr -> Next;

2. Algorithm to compute average value in a linked list of real numbers

    1. Total = 0.0,
       Count = 0,
       CurrentPtr = first;

    2. While (CurrentPtr != null_value)
           Count++;
           Total += CurrentPtr->Data;
           CurrentPtr = CurrentPtr

    3. If (Count ==0)
           average = 0;
       Else
           average = Total/Count;

3. Algorithm to append a node at the end of a linked list

    1. Get NewPtr.

    2. NewPtr -> Data = item,
       NewPtr-> Next = null_value;

    3. If (first == null_value)
               first = NewPtr
       Else
               CurrentPtr = first;
               While (CurrentPtr->Next != null_value)
                       CurrentPtr = CurrentPtr->Next;
               CurrentPtr->Next = NewPtr;

4. Algorithm to determine if the nodes in a linked list are in non-decreasing order.

```
1.      CurrentPtr = first;

2.      If (CurrentPtr == null_value || CurrentPtr->Next == null_value)  //note short-circuit eval
                return true;
        Else
                NextPtr = CurrentPtr->Next;
                While (inOrder && NextPtr != null_value)
                        If (CurrentPtr->Data > NextPtr-> Data)
                                Return false;
                        Else
                                CurrentPtr = NextPtr,
                                NextPtr = NextPtr-> Next;
                Return True;
```

5. All algorithms in exercises #1 - #4 require a scan of the entire linked list. Hence, they are O(n)

6. Algorithm to search a linked list for a given item.

```
1.      CurrentPtr = first;
        Found = false;
        PrevPtr = null_value

2.      While (CurrentPtr != null_value && !Found)
                If (CurrentPtr-> == item)
                        Found = true
                Else
                        PrevPtr = CurrentPtr;
                        CurrentPtr = CurrentPtr->Next;
```

7. Algorithm to insert a given NewNode after the nth node.

```
1.      CurrentPtr = first;
        num = 1;

2.      If (n==0)
                NewNode->Next = CurrentPtr;
                first = NewNode;
        Else
                While (CurrentPtr != null_value && num < n)
                        num++
                        CurrentPtr = CurrentPtr->Next;
```

```
If (CurrentPtr != null_value)
        NewNode->Next = CurrentPtr->Next;
        CurrentPtr = NewNode;
Else
        Error: fewer than n elements in list
```

8. Algorithm to delete the nth node in a linked list.

```
1.    CurrentPtr = first;
      num = 1;

2.    If (n==1)
              TempPtr = CurrentPtr;
              first = CurrentPtr->Next;
              Delete TempPtr;
      Else
              While (CurrentPtr != null_value && num < n-1)
                      num++
                      CurrentPtr = CurrentPtr->Next;

              If (CurrentPtr != null_value && CurrentPtr->Next != null_value)
                      TempPtr = CurrentPtr->Next;
                      CurrentPtr ->Next= TempPtr->Next;
                      Delete TempPtr;
              Else
                      Error: fewer than n elements in list
```

9. Algorithm to perform a shuffle-merge of two linked lists

```
1.  GetNode(MergedList).  /* temporary head node */

2.  Last = MergedList,
    Ptr1 = List1,
    Ptr2 = List2.

3.  While (Ptr1 != null_Value && Ptr2 != null_Value)

        a.  GetNode (TempPtr).
        b.  TempPtr->Data = Ptr1->Data
        c.  Last->Next = TempPtr.
        d.  Last = TempPtr,
        e.  Ptr1 = Ptr1->Next
        f.  GetNode (TempPtr).
        g.  TempPtr->Data = Ptr2->Data
        h.  Last->Next = TempPtr.
        i.  Last = TempPtr,
        j.  Ptr2 = Ptr2->Next
```

4. While (Ptr1 != null_Value)

   a. GetNode (TempPtr).
   b. TempPtr->Data = Ptr1->Data
   c. Last->Next = TempPtr.
   d. Last = TempPtr,
   e. Ptr1 = Ptr1->Next

   □

5. While (Ptr2 != null_Value)

□

   a. GetNode (TempPtr)
   b. TempPtr->Data = Ptr2->Data
   c. Last->Next = TempPtr.
   d. Last = TempPtr,
   e. Ptr2 = Ptr2->Next

   □

6. TempPtr = MergedList.

□

7. MergedList = MergedList->Next

8. Delete TempPtr.

10. Algorithm to perform a shuffle-merge without copying

    1. If (List1 = =null_Value)
       MergedList = List2
       Else
       1. MergedList = List1.

       2. Ptr1 = List1,
          Ptr2 = List2.

       3. While (Ptr1 != null_Value && Ptr2 != null_Value)

          a. TempPtr = Ptr1.
          b. Ptr1 = TempPtr->Next
          c. TempPtr->Next = Ptr2.
          d. If (Ptr2 != null_Value)
             TempPtr = Ptr2.
          e. Ptr2 = TempPtr->Next
          f. TempPtr->Next = Ptr1.

4. If (Ptr1 = null_Value)
   TempPtr->Next = Ptr2.

11. Algorithm to merge two non-decreasing lists

1. GetNode (MergedList).

2. Last = MergedList,
   Ptr1 = List1,
   Ptr2 = List2

3. While (Ptr1 != null_Value && Ptr2 != null_Value)

   a. GetNode (TempPtr).
   b. If (Ptr1->Data < Ptr2->Data)
      1. TempPtr->Data = Ptr1->Data
      2. Last->Next = TempPtr.
      3. Last = TempPtr
      4. Ptr1 = Ptr1->Next
   c. Else
      1. TempPtr->Data = Ptr2->Data
      2. Last->Next = TempPtr.
      3. Last = TempPtr
      4. Ptr2 = Ptr2->Next

4. While (Ptr1 != null_Value)

   a. GetNode (TempPtr).
   b. TempPtr->Data = Ptr1->Data
   c. Last->Next = TempPtr.
   d. Last = TempPtr
   e. Ptr1 = Ptr1->Next

5. While (Ptr2 != null_Value)

   a. GetNode (TempPtr).
   b. TempPtr->Data = Ptr2->Data
   c. Last->Next = TempPtr.
   d. Last = TempPtr
   e. Ptr2 = Ptr2->Next

6. TempPtr = MergedList.
7. MergedList = MergedList->Next

8. Delete TempPtr.

12. Algorithm to reverse a linked list without copying.

1. CurrentPtr = first;
   PrevPtr = null_value;

2. While (CurrentPtr != null_value)
   NextPtr = CurrentPtr->Next;
   CurrentPtr->Next = PrevPtr;
   PrevPtr = CurrentPtr;
   CurrentPtr = NextPtr;

3. first = PrevPtr

8.3 Exercises

1. a. List = B, C, J, P   b. Free M, Z, K, Q, ?, ?

2. first = 4; free = 1

node	data	next
0	J	3
1	Z	6
2	C	5
3	P	-1
4	B	2
5	F	0
6	K	7
7	Q	8
8	?	9
9	?	-1

3. first = 4; free = 0

node	data	next
0	J	5
1	Z	6
2	C	3
3	P	-1
4	B	2
5	M	1
6	K	7
7	Q	8
8	?	9
9	?	-1

4. first = -1; free = 4

node	data	next
0	J	5
1	Z	6
2	C	3
3	P	0
4	B	2
5	M	1
6	K	7
7	Q	8
8	?	9
9	?	-1

5. first = 5, free = 2

node	data	next
0	J	3
1	Z	7
2	C	1
3	K	-1
4	B	0
5	A	4
6	K	8
7	Q	9
8	?	10
9	?	0

6. /* nonrecursive *followed by a recursion version* to count the # of nodes in a linked list */

```
int  NumNodes(int first)
{
   int count = 0;
   int index = first;

   while (index != NULL_VALUE)
   {
         count++;
         index = node[index].next;
   }
   return count;
}


int  NumNodes(int where)
{
   if (where != NULL_VALUE)
         return 1 + NumNodes( node[where].next )
   else
         return 0;
}
```

7. /* nonrecursive and recursive functions to determine if list is sorted */

```
bool isSorted(int first)
{
  int currentP = first;

  int nextP;

  if (currentP != NULL_VALUE)
       nextP = node[currentP].next;
  else
       nextP = NULL_VALUE;

  bool inOrder = true;

  while (nextP != NULL_VALUE && inOrder)
  {
       if (node[currentP].data > node[nextP].data)
            inOrder = false;
       else
       {
            currentP = nextP;
            nextP = node[nextP].next;
       }
  }
  return inOrder;
}


bool isSorted(int first)
{
  if (first == NULL_VALUE)
       return true;

  else if (node[first].next == NULL_VALUE)
       return true;

  else if (node[first].data > node[node[first].next].data)
       return false;

  else
       return isSorted(node[first].next);
}
```

8. **/* nonrecursive and recursive functions to return pointer to last element in list */**

```
int     LastP(int first)
{
   int CurrentPtr = first;
   int LastPtr = first;

   while (CurrentPtr != NULL_VALUE)
   {
        LastPtr = CurrentPtr;
        CurrentPtr = node[CurrentPtr].next;
   }
   return LastPtr;
}


int     LastP(int first)
{
   if (first == NULL_VALUE || node[first].next == NULL_VALUE)
        return first
   else
        return LastP(node[first].next);
}
```

9. **/* Reverse a linked list */**

```
int     Reverse(int first)
{
   int Prev = NULL_VALUE;
   int CurrentP = first;

   while (CurrentP != NULL_VALUE)
   {
        int NextP = node[CurrentP].next;
        node[CurrentP].next = Prev;
        Prev = CurrentP;
        CurrentP = NextP;
   }
   return Prev;          // new head of (reversed) linked list
}
```

8.4 Exercises

1.
```
double    *p1, *p2;
```

2.
```
p1 = &d1;
```

3.
```
// NOT POSSIBLE i2 is an integer, p1 is typed to hold the address of
a double
```

4.
```
Point     *q;
```

5.
```
int  *ptr1 = &i1, *ptr2 = &i2;
```

6.
```
p1 = p2 = &d1;
```

7.
```
*ptr1 = *ptr2;
```

8.
```
cout << " x coordinate is: " << (*q).x()
     << " y coordinate is:  " << (*q).y() << endl;
```

9.
```
p1 = &d1; p2 = &d2; //given association
double temp;
temp = *p1;
*p1 = *p2;
*p2 = temp;
```

10 - 19 : machine dependent results

20.
```
typedef char* CharPointer;
```

21.
```
&anArray[0];
```

22.
```
//same as &anArray[0]
```

23. an array variable is a pointer to its first element, i.ee the address of its first element. Thus, arrays and pointers are viewed to be the same in C++

8.5 Exercises

1. `char*    charPtr;`

2. `charPtr = new char;`

3. `cin >> *charPtr;`

4. `cout << *charPtr << endl;`

5.
```
if (isupper(*charPtr))
      *charPtr = tolower(*charPtr);
else
      *charPtr = toupper(*charPtr);
```

6. `double* doublePtr;`

7. `doublePtr = new double[n];`

8.
```
for (int index = 0; index < n; index++)
      cin >> doublePtr[index];
```

9.
```
double avg = 0.0;
for (int index = 0; index < n; index++)
      avg += doublePtr[index];

cout << "AVERAGE of n doubles input is:  " << avg/n << endl;
```

10. `delete[] doublePtr;`

11. machine-dependent results

12.

```
1
1   3
4   3
5   5
7   7
9   9
```

13.

```
template <typename element>
class Queue                    /* $ indicates modification from ch 6 */

{

        element*  myArrayPtr;
        int   myFront;
        int   myBack;
        int   capacity;     //$

    public:
        Queue(int num = 128);                  //$ overloaded constructor
        Queue(const Queue<element>&);          //$ copy constructor
        ~Queue();                              //$ destructor

        Queue<element>& operator=( const Queue<element>&);
                                  //$ assignment
        bool empty() const;
        void addQ(element);
        element front();
        void removeQ();
   };


   template <typename element>
   Queue<element>::Queue(int num)
   {
        capacity = num;
        myFront = 0;
        myBack = 0;
        myArrayPtr = new element[capacity]; //allocate in constructor
 }


   template <typename element>
   Queue<element>::Queue(const Queue<element>& source)
                                       //copy constructor
   {
        capacity = source.capacity;
        myFront = source.myFront;
        myBack = source.myBack;
        myArrayPtr = new element[capacity]; // allocate in constructor

        for (int index = 0; index < capacity; index++)
             myArrayPtr[index] = source.myArrayPtr[index];
 }
```

```
template <typename element>
Queue<element>::~Queue()
{
     delete [] myArrayPtr;          // deallocate in destructor
}


template <typename element>
Queue<element>&
Queue<element>::operator=(const Queue<element>& source)
{
  if (this != &source)
  {
     delete [] myArrayPtr;

     capacity = source.capacity;

     myFront = source.myFront;
     myBack = source.myBack;

     myArrayPtr = new element[capacity]; // allocate in assignment

     for (int index = 0; index < capacity; index++)
          myArrayPtr[index] = source.myArrayPtr[index];
  }
  return *this;
}


template <typename element>
bool Queue<element>::empty()
{
     return myFront == myBack;
}


template <typename element>
void Queue<element>::addQ(element item)
{
     if ((myBack +1)% capacity == myFront)
          cout << "Queue is full: cannot add to queue.
                    Error!! " << endl;
     else
     {
          myArray[myBack] = item;
          myBack = (myBack+ 1) % capacity;
     }
}
```

```
template <typename element>
element Queue<element>::front()
{
     if (myFront == myBack)
     {
          cerr <<"Queue is empty: Error!!" << endl;

          return myArray[0];       // should be invalid data item;
          //problem with templates: undefined invalid data values
          // exceptions should really be used to signal error
     else
          return myArray[myFront];
}


template <typename element>
void Queue<element>::removeQ()
{
     if (myFront == myBack)
          cerr <<"Queue is empty: cannot remove from queue.
               Error!!" << endl;
     else
          myFront= (myFront+ 1) % capacity;

     return;
}
```

14. Simply add a `cout << "In` *`put_method_name_here`*`" << endl;` statement to each constructor as well as the overloaded assignment operator and destructor.

A very useful debugging trick, especially when used with a debug flag that can be turned off and on.

8.6 Exercises

1. 123 456

2. 34 34

3. 34 34

4. error because the next field of p2 does not contain a valid address

5.
```
12  34
34  34
34
34
```

6.
```
111  222
222
111
```

7.
```
34  34
34  34
```

8.

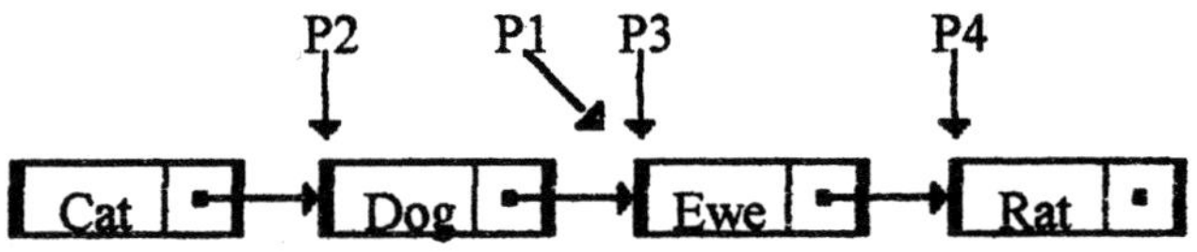

9.

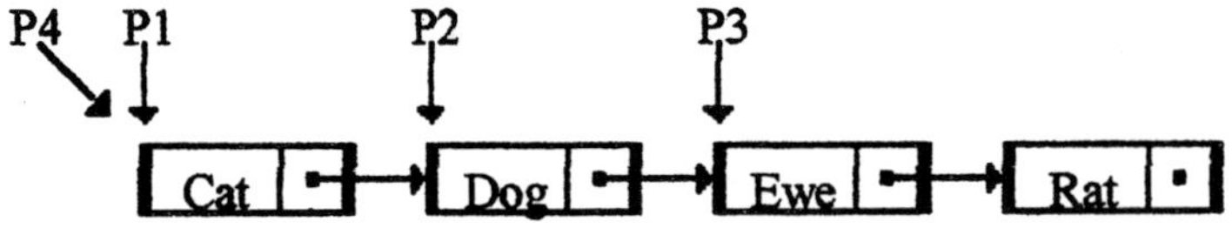

10.

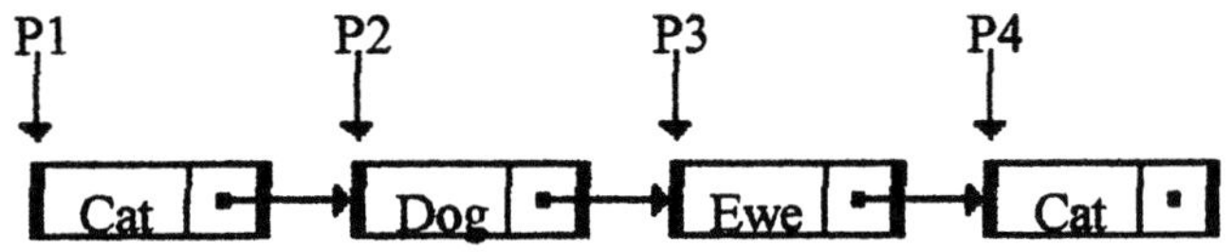

11.

```
p4->next== NULL!!
Therefore, p4->next->data UNDEFINED.
ERROR!!
```

12.

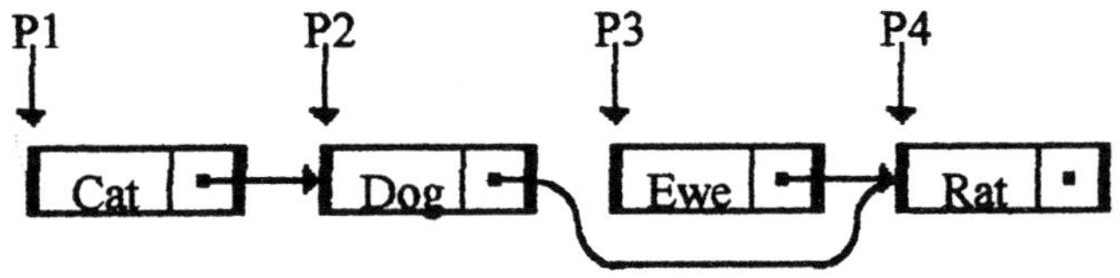

13.

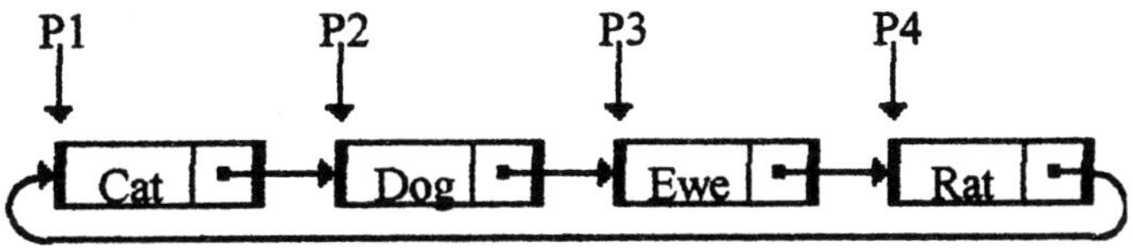

14.

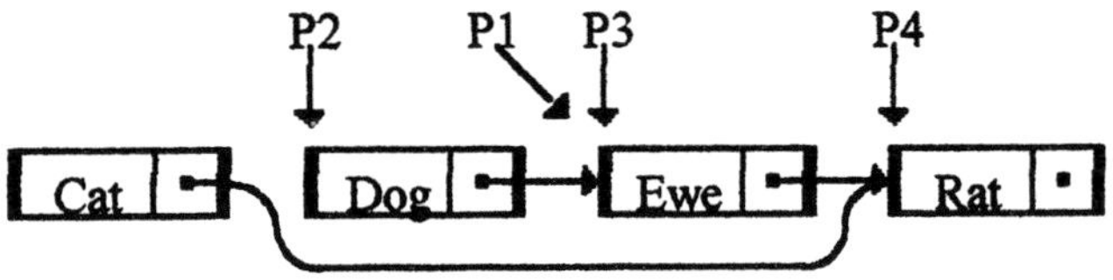

15.

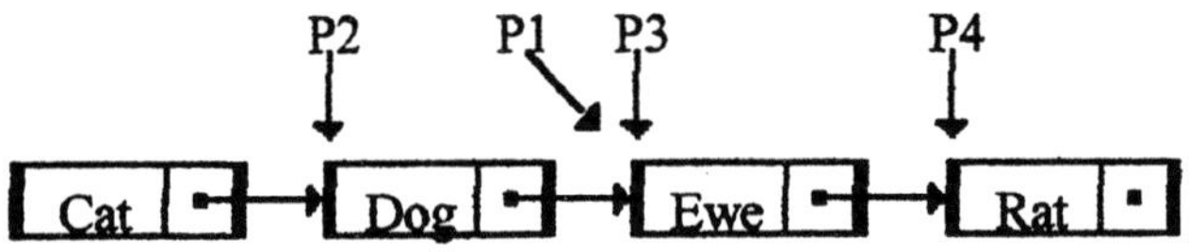

16.

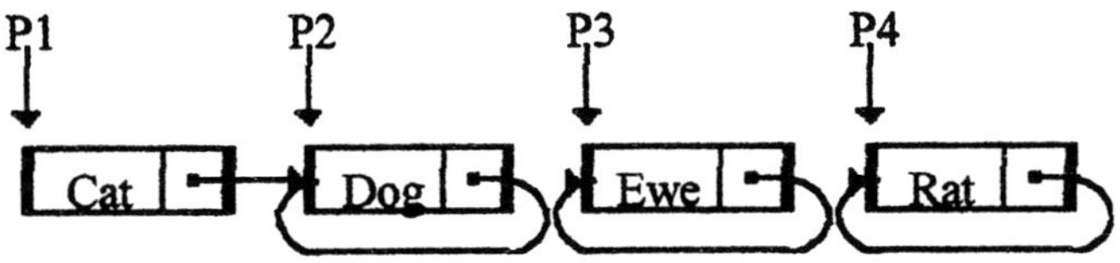

17.

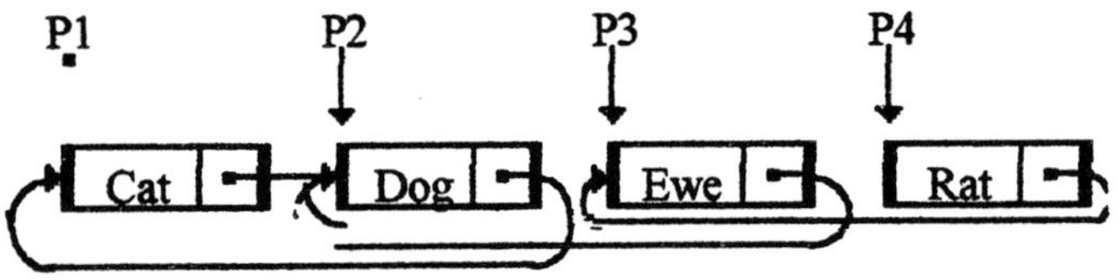

18. /* nonrecursive followed by a recursion version (#19) to count the # of nodes in a linked list */

```
int  NumNodes(Node* first)
{
      int count = 0;
      Node* ptr = first;

      while (ptr != 0)
      {
            count++;
            ptr = ptr->next;
      }
      return count;
}
```

19.
```
int  NumNodes(Node* first)
{
     if (first != 0)
          return 1 + NumNodes( first->next )
     else
          return 0;
}
```

20.
```
template<typename element>
class LinkedList          // ordered LL
{
  private:
     class Node
     {
       public:
          element   data;
          Node*          next;
     };
     Node*     first;
     int  mySize;
     Node* copyLL(Node*);          // private helper functions
     void  deleteLL();

  public:
     LinkedList();              //* one constructor
     LinkedList(const LinkedList<element>&); //* copy constructor
     ~LinkedList();                          //* destructor

     LinkedList<element>& operator=(const LinkedList<element>&);
                              //* assignment

     bool empty() const;
     void insert(element, unsigned);
     void delete(element);
     void traverse();
     Node* search();
};

template <typename element>
LinkedList<element>::LinkedList()
{
     mySize = 0;
     first = 0;           //   no   memory   allocated   until   element
inserted into LL
}
```

```
template <typename element>
Node* LinkedList<element>::copyLL(Node* source)
{
    if (source == 0)
      return 0;
    else
    {
      Node* newH = new Node;
      newH->data = source->data;
      Node* tempP = newH;
      source = source->next;

      while (source != 0)
      {
            tempP->next = new Node;
            tempP = tempP->next;
            tempP->data = source->data;
            source = source->next;
      }
      tempP->next = 0;
    }

    return newH;
}

template <typename element>
LinkedList<element>::LinkedList(const LinkedList<element>& source)
//copy constructor
{
      mySize = source.mySize;
      first = copyLL(source.first);
}

template <typename element>
void LinkedList<element>::deleteLL()
{
      Node*  tempP = first;

      while (tempP != 0)
      {
            Node* disposeP = tempP;
            tempP = tempP->next;
            delete disposeP;
      }
      return;
}
```

see p. 436 copy constructor

LinkedList :: LinkedList (const LinkedList & source)

```
template <typename element>
LinkedList<element>::~LinkedList()
{
     deleteLL();          // deallocate in destructor
}


template <typename element>
LinkedList<element>&
LinkedList<element>::operator=(const LinkedList<element>& s)
{
  if (this != &s)
  {
     deleteLL();
     mySize = s.mySize;

     first = copyLL(s.first);
  }
  return *this;
}

template <typename element>
bool LinkedList<element>::empty()
{
     return first == 0;        // could also compare mySize to 0
}


template <typename element>
void LinkedList<element>::insert(element item, unsigned pos);
{
   if (pos > mySize + 1)
   {
     cerr << "Illegal position to insert " << pos << endl;
     return;
   }
   // else
   mySize++;
   Node* newNode = new Node;
   newNode->data = item;

   Node* prev = 0;
   for (int i = 1; i < pos; i++)  // move prev to position
       prev = prev->next;           //  before insert position
   newNode->next = prev->next;
   prev->next = newNode;
}
```

```
template <typename element>
void LinkedList<element>::delete(element item)
{
     mySize--;

     Node*          tempP = first;
     Node*          prev = 0;

     while (tempP != 0 && tempP->data != item)
                              //find item in LL
     {
          prev = tempP;
          tempP = tempP->next;
     }

     if (tempP != 0 && tempP->data == item)
     {
          prev->next = tempP->next;
          delete tempP;
     }
     else
          cerr << "Item to delete not found"  << endl;
     return;
}


template <typename element>
void LinkedList<element>::traverse()
{
     Node*          tempP = first;

     while (tempP != 0)       //find item in ordered LL
     {
          Process( tempP->data);
          tempP = tempP->next;
     }
     return;
}

template <typename element>
void LinkedList<element>::search(element item)
{
     Node*          tempP = first;
     Node*          prev = 0;

     while (tempP != 0  && tempP->data != item)
                         //find item in LL
     {
     prev = tempP;
```

```
        tempP = tempP->next;
        }

        if (tempP != 0)
             return tempP;
        else
             return 0;
}
```

21.

```
template <typename element>
void LinkedList<element>::reverse()
{
        Node* prev = 0;
        Node* currentP = first;

        while (currentP)
        {
             Node* nextP = currentP->next;
             currentP->next = prev;
             prev = currentP;
             currentP = nextP;
        }
        first = prev;        // new head of (reversed) linked list
        return;
}
```

22.

```
template <typename element>
bool LinkedList<element>::ascend()
{
        Node*     tempP = first;
        Node*     prev = 0;
        while (tempP != 0 && prevP->data <= tempP->data)
        {
             prev = tempP;
             tempP = tempP->next;
        }

        if (first == 0 || first->next == 0)
                  //empty or one element list
             return true;
        else if (tempP != 0)
             return false;
        else
             return true;
}
```

23. **/* member functions are usually not recursive; without an incoming argument, one cannot devise a recursive version with a reachable terminating condition. One can employ a private, recursive, helper member function */**

```
template <typename element>
bool LinkedList<element>::ascend()
{
     return helperRec(first);
}

template <typename element>
bool LinkedList<element>::helperRec(Node* where)
{
     if (where == 0)
          return true;
     else if (where->next == 0)
          return true;
     else if (where->data > where->next->data)
          return false;
     else
          return ascend(where->next);
}
```

8.7 Exercises

1. /* This exercise and the next one are essentially the same as Problem #4 in chapter 2.

   Several of the previously discussed data structures (arrays, linked lists, vectors) can be used within the class to hold the digits of the large integers. The use of vectors would support dynamic sizing, as would linked lists, but require substantial overhead.

```
*/
// BigInt.h
/* This file contains the interface for the class BigInt,
 * written by Ed Ball for C++: An Introduction to Programming.
 ******************************************************/
#ifndef BIGINT_H
#define BIGINT_H

#include <iostream>                     // cin, cout, >>, <<
#include <iomanip>                      // setfill()
#include <list>                         // list<T>
#include <algorithm>                    // reverse()
using namespace std;
class BigInt
{
  public:
     BigInt();
     BigInt(int n);
     void ReadBig(istream & in);
     void PrintBig(ostream & out);
     BigInt operator=(const BigInt & int2);
     friend bool operator<(BigInt int1, BigInt int2);
     friend BigInt operator+(BigInt int1, BigInt int2);
     friend BigInt operator-(BigInt int1, BigInt int2);
  private:
     char mySign;
     list<short int> myList;
};


inline BigInt::BigInt()
{
     mySign = '+';
}

inline BigInt::BigInt(int n)
{
     myList.push_back(n);
     mySign = '+';
}
```

```
inline BigInt BigInt::operator=(const BigInt & int2)
{
     mySign = int2.mySign;
     myList = int2.myList;

     return *this;
}


inline istream & operator>>(istream & in, BigInt & x)
{
     x.ReadBig(in);

     return in;
}


inline ostream & operator<<(ostream & out, BigInt x)
{
     x.PrintBig(out);

     return out;
}

#endif

// BigInt.cpp
/* This file contains the implementation for class BigInt.
 *****************************************************/

#include "BigInt.h"
/* ReadBig reads a BigInt.
 *
 * Receive:   istream in
 * Pass back: istream with a BigInt value removed from
 *            it and x with this value assigned to it
 *******************************************************/
void BigInt::ReadBig(istream & in)
{
     short int block;
     for (;;)
     {
          in >> block;
          if (block < 0) return;
          myList.push_back(block);
     }
}
```

```
/* PrintBig displays a BigInt.
*
* Receive:   ostream out
* Pass back: ostream with a BigInt value inserted
* Output:    x
*****************************************************/
#include <iomanip>              // setfill, setw
using namespace std;
void BigInt::PrintBig(ostream & out)
{
     out << mySign << setfill('0');
     int count = 1;
     for (list<short int>::iterator it = myList.begin();
                                    it != myList.end(); it++)
     {
          out << setw(3) << *it << ' ';
          if (count % 20 == 0) out << endl;
          count ++;
     }
     out << endl;
}


/* operator< comparess two BigInts.
*
* Receive:   BigInts int1 and int2
* Pass back: truth or falsity of int1 < int2
*****************************************************/
bool operator<(BigInt int1, BigInt int2)
{
     if (int1.mySign != int2.mySign)
          return (int1.mySign == '-') && (int2.mySign == '+');
                                                  // neg. < pos
     // they have the same sign
     list<short int> :: iterator it1 = int1.myList.begin(),
                                 it2 = int2.myList.begin();
     while (it1!= int1.myList.end() && *it1 == *it2)
     {
          it1++;
          it2++;
     }
     if (it1 == int1.myList.end())     // they're equal
          return false;

     if (*it1 < *it2)
          return int1.mySign == '+';
     // else
          return int1.mySign == '-';
}
```

```
BigInt operator+(BigInt int1, BigInt int2);
/* operator+ adds two BigInts.
 *
 * Receive:    BigInts int1 and int2
 * Pass back : int1 + int2
 ***************************************************/
BigInt operator+(BigInt int1, BigInt int2)
{
   short int first,          // a block of int1
             second,         // a block of int2
             result,         // a block in their sum
             carry = 0;      // the carry in adding two blocks
   BigInt answer;            // the sum

   reverse(int1.myList.begin(), int1.myList.end());
   reverse(int2.myList.begin(), int2.myList.end());
   list<short int>::iterator it1 = int1.myList.begin();
   list<short int>::iterator it2 = int2.myList.begin();

   for(;;)
   {
      if (it1 == int1.myList.end() &&
                                it2 == int2.myList.end())
break;
      if (it1 != int1.myList.end())
      {
         first = *it1;
         it1++;
      }
      else
         first = 0;
      if (it2 != int2.myList.end())
      {
         second = *it2;
         it2++;
      }
      else
         second = 0;
      short int temp = first + second + carry;
      result = temp % 1000;
      carry = temp / 1000;
      answer.myList.push_back(result);
   }
   if (carry > 0)
      answer.myList.push_back(carry);
   reverse(answer.myList.begin(), answer.myList.end());

   return answer;
}
```

```
/* operator- subtracts two BigInts.
 *
 * Receive:    BigInts int1 and int2
 * Pass back : int1 - int2
 ******************************************/
BigInt operator-(BigInt int1, BigInt int2)
{
   short int first,          // a block of int1
             second,         // a block of int2
             result,         // a block in their difference
             borrow = 0;
                        // the carry in subtracting two blocks
   BigInt temp,              // used to swap int1 and int2
          answer;            // the difference
   if (int1 < int2)
   {
     temp = int1;
     int1 = int2;
     int2 = temp;
     answer.mySign = '-';
   }

   reverse(int1.myList.begin(), int1.myList.end());
   reverse(int2.myList.begin(), int2.myList.end());
   list<short int>::iterator it1 = int1.myList.begin(),
                             it2 = int2.myList.begin();
   for(;;)
   {
      if (it1 == int1.myList.end() &&
                                it2 == int2.myList.end())
break;
      if (it1 != int1.myList.end())
      {
         first = *it1;
         it1++;
      }
      else
         first = 0;
      if (it2 != int2.myList.end())
      {
         second = *it2;
         it2++;
       }
      else
         second = 0;
      result = first - second - borrow;
      if (result < 0)
      {
         result += 1000;
```

```
                borrow = 1;
            }
            else
                borrow = 0;
            answer.myList.push_back(result);
        }
        if (borrow > 0)
            answer.mySign = '-';
        reverse(answer.myList.begin(), answer.myList.end());
        return answer;
    }
```

2. a) a challenging exercise. The idea is to use partial products, i.e. repetitively: multiply the first number by a block in the second to get a partial product, pad it with enough zeroes (to the right), then use BigInt + to add this partial product to the running sum. When all blocks of the second number have been used the sum is the final product.

   b) a simple extension of #1 above.

   c) major endeavor and suitable for a significant programming project. Without extensive limitations, dividing two large integers, represented as lists is a huge undertaking.

Problem 6 in the first printing is misplaced; it should be in Chapter 12.

In later printings it will be replaced by:

> *6. Extend the class Polynomial from Exercise 3 by adding a member function Evaluate() that receives a double value x and returns the value of the polynomial at x.*

3-6:

```
    // Polynomial.h
   /* This file is the interface for class Polynomial,
    * written by Ed Ball for C++: An Introduction to Programming.

*************************************************************/
        #ifndef POLYNOMIAL
        #define POLYNOMIAL
        #include <iostream>
        #include <list>
        using namespace std;
        class Polynomial
        {
         public:
          // SetCoefficient -- set a coefficient of the polynomial
          void SetCoefficient(double coeff, int expo);
          // GetCoefficient -- get a coefficient of the polynomial
          double GetCoefficient(int expo);
```

```
  // Evaluate -- evaluate a polynomial
  double Evaluate(double value);
  // operator+ -- add two polynomials
  Polynomial operator+(Polynomial p);
  // operator* -- multiply two polynomials
  Polynomial operator*(Polynomial p);
  // Print -- output a polynomial to an ostream
  void Print(ostream & out);
  // Input -- input a polynomial from an istream
  void Input(istream & in);

private:
  struct PolyTerm
  {
    double myCoeff;
    int myExp;
    // constructor
    PolyTerm(double coef = 0.0, int expo = 0)
    { myCoeff = coef;  myExp = expo; }
  };

  // Define == to mean have the same exponent
  friend bool operator==(PolyTerm term1, PolyTerm term2)
  { return term1.myExp == term2.myExp;}
  friend bool operator!=(PolyTerm term1, PolyTerm term2)
  { return term1.myExp != term2.myExp;}
  // Define < to mean has a smaller exponent
  friend bool operator<(PolyTerm term1, PolyTerm term2)
  { return term1.myExp < term2.myExp;}
  list<PolyTerm> myList;
};


inline ostream & operator<<(ostream & out, Polynomial poly)
{
  poly.Print(out);
  return out;
}


inline istream & operator>>(istream & in, Polynomial & poly)
{
  poly.Input(in);
  return in;
}

#endif
```

```
//Polynomial.cpp:
/* This file is the implementation for class Polynomial.
   ***********************************************/
#include "Polynomial.h"
#include <cmath>
#include <algorithm>
using namespace std;
void Polynomial::SetCoefficient(double coeff, int expo)
{
  // search for a term with this exponent
  Polynomial::PolyTerm term(coeff, expo);
  list<PolyTerm>::iterator it =
              find(myList.begin(), myList.end(), term);
  if (it != myList.end())
  // term found
  {
    if (coeff == 0.0)             // term to be removed
      myList.erase(it);
    else                     // change coefficient in term
      (*it).myCoeff = coeff;
    return;
  }
  // no term with this exponent found -- have to insert one
  myList.push_back(term);
  myList.sort();                  // keep terms in order}
}

double Polynomial::GetCoefficient(int expo)
{
  // search for a term with this exponent
  Polynomial::PolyTerm term(0.0, expo);
  list<Polynomial::PolyTerm>::iterator it =
              find(myList.begin(), myList.end(), term);
  if (it != myList.end())  // term found, return coefficient
    return (*it).myCoeff;
  return 0.0;              // no term found, return 0
}

double Polynomial::Evaluate(double value)
{
  double answer = 0.0;
  for (list<Polynomial::PolyTerm>::iterator
          it = myList.begin(); it != myList.end(); it++)
    if ((*it) != 0)
      answer += (*it).myCoeff * pow(value, (*it).myExp);
    else
      answer += (*it).myCoeff;
  return answer;
}
```

```
Polynomial Polynomial::operator+(Polynomial p)
{
  Polynomial answer = p;
  for (list<Polynomial::PolyTerm>::iterator
          it = myList.begin(); it != myList.end(); it++)
  {
    double coeff =
          (*it).myCoeff + p.GetCoefficient((*it).myExp);
    answer.SetCoefficient(coeff, (*it).myExp);
  }
  return answer;
}

Polynomial Polynomial::operator*(Polynomial p)
{
  Polynomial answer;
  int expo;
  double coeff;

  for (list<Polynomial::PolyTerm>::iterator
          it1 = myList.begin(); it1 != myList.end(); it1++)
    for (list<Polynomial::PolyTerm>::iterator
               it2 = p.myList.begin();
               it2 != p.myList.end(); it2++)
    {
      expo = (*it1).myExp + (*it2).myExp;
      coeff = answer.GetCoefficient(expo) +
              (*it1).myCoeff * (*it2).myCoeff;
      answer.SetCoefficient(coeff, expo);
    }
  return answer;
}


void Polynomial::Print(ostream & out)
{
  list<Polynomial::PolyTerm>::iterator it = myList.begin();

  if(!myList.empty())
  {
    if ((*it).myExp == 0 ||
        ((*it).myCoeff != 1.0 && (*it).myCoeff != -1.0))
      out << (*it).myCoeff;
    if ((*it).myExp >= 1)
      out << 'x';
    if ((*it).myExp >= 2)
      out << '^' << (*it).myExp;
    it++;
  }
```

```
    else
    {
      out << '0';
      return;
    }
    while (it != myList.end() )
    {
      out << (((*it).myCoeff < 0.0) ? " - " : " + ");
      if ((*it).myExp == 0 ||
            ((*it).myCoeff != 1 && (*it).myCoeff != -1))
        out << (((*it).myCoeff < 0.0) ? -(*it).myCoeff :
                                              (*it).myCoeff);
      if ((*it).myExp >= 1)
        out << 'x';
      if ((*it).myExp >= 2)
        out << '^' << (*it).myExp;
      it++;
    }
  }


  void Polynomial::Input(istream & in)
  {
    int expo;
    double coeff;
    for (;;)
    {
      cout << "\n  Exponent (-1 to stop): ";
      cin >> expo;
      if (expo< 0) break;
      cout << "  Coefficient for x^" << expo<< ": ";
      cin >> coeff;
      (*this).SetCoefficient(coeff, expo);
    }
  }
```

Programming Problems (p 464)

1. This problem is essentially a driver for the Polynomial class with the addition of a menu-driven user interface. Aside from structuring the interface, one needs to instantiate at least two objects from the Polynomial class, and test the capabilities of addition, multiplication, display, etc.

See the driver developed for #17 and #18.

2. Most of the code is given in the text.

3. & 4. These two problems are straight-forward applications of lists.
One needs to instantiate a list object for ticket orders (including name, address, and number of tickets requested).

#3 requires construction of the list from user input and scan of the complete list for output.

#4 adds the additional requirement of limiting the number of ticket sold to each party and the duplication of requests. A conditional check before insertion into the list satisfies these additional restrictions.

```
/* Hoops basketball-ticket program.
 *
 * Input (keyboard): number of tickets available,
 * Input (file):     names, addresses of people ordering
                     tickets,
 *                     and number of tickets requested
 * Output:           mailing labels for ticket orders .
 * Condition:        no person receives more than MAX_TICKETS
                     tickets
 *                     and multiple requests are not allowed.
 *
 * Written by Ed Ball for C++: An Introduction to Computing

 *********************************************************/

#include <fstream>
#include <string>
#include <list>
#include <algorithm>
using namespace std;
const MAX_TICKETS = 4;
```

```
class TicketOrder
{
 public:
   void Read(ifstream & in);
   void PrintLabel(ostream & out) const;
   short int NumRequested() const;
   void SetRequest(short int num);
   bool DupOrder(TicketOrder order2) const;

 private:
   string myName,
          myStreetAddress,
          myCity_and_Street;
   unsigned myZip;
   short int myRequest;
 };


// Read a ticket order from a file
void TicketOrder::Read(ifstream & in)
{
   char ch;
   getline(in, myName);
   getline(in, myStreetAddress);
   getline(in, myCity_and_Street);
   in >> myZip >> myRequest;
   if (myRequest > MAX_TICKETS)
      myRequest = 4;
   ch = in.get();    // chew up end-of-line mark
 }


// Display a mailing label
void TicketOrder::PrintLabel(ostream & out) const
{
   cout << endl << myName << endl
        << myStreetAddress << endl
      << myCity_and_Street << myZip << endl
      << "------------------------ " << myRequest << "
tickets\n\n";
}


// Retrieve # of tickets ordered
inline short int TicketOrder::NumRequested() const
{
  return myRequest;
}
```

```
// Change the # of tickets ordered
inline void TicketOrder::SetRequest(short int num)
{
   myRequest = num;
}


// Function to check if two ticket orders are from same person
bool TicketOrder::DupOrder(TicketOrder order2) const
{
   return myName == order2.myName &&
          myStreetAddress == order2.myStreetAddress &&
          myCity_and_Street == order2.myCity_and_Street &&
          myZip == order2.myZip;
 }


// Operation ==
inline bool operator==(TicketOrder order1, TicketOrder order2)
{
  return order1.DupOrder(order2);
}


// Operation !=
inline bool operator!=(TicketOrder order1, TicketOrder order2)
{
   return !order1.DupOrder(order2);
}
// End of file for class TicketOrder


// Function to output a list of ticket orders to the screen
ostream & operator<<(ostream & out, list<TicketOrder> orders)
{
   for (list<TicketOrder>::iterator it = orders.begin();
                                    it != orders.end(); it++)
      (*it).PrintLabel(out);

   return out;
 }


 int main()
 {
    int ticketsAvailable;
    cout << "How many tickets are available? ";
    cin >> ticketsAvailable;
    string fileName;
```

```
   cout << "Enter name of file containing orders: ";
   cin >> fileName;
   ifstream inStream (fileName.data());
   if (!inStream.is_open())
   {
      cerr << "Error in opening file " << fileName << endl;
      exit(1);
   }
   list<TicketOrder> orders;
   TicketOrder anOrder;
   for (;;)
   {
      anOrder.Read(inStream);
      if (anOrder.NumRequested() < 0) break;   // end of data
      if (find(orders.begin(), orders.end(),
                  anOrder) != orders.end())
      {
         anOrder.PrintLabel(cerr);
         cerr << "The above order was processed earlier\n";
      }
      else
      {
         if (anOrder.NumRequested() > ticketsAvailable)
            anOrder.SetRequest(ticketsAvailable);
         orders.push_back(anOrder);
         ticketsAvailable -= anOrder.NumRequested();
      }

      if (ticketsAvailable <= 0)
      {
         cout << "\n\n\n*** NO MORE TICKETS ***\n";
         break;
      }
   }

   cout << "Mailing labels for the valid orders: \n"
        << orders;
   return 0;
}
```

5. - 14. All these problems involve writing drivers.

The first two (#5 & #6) involve writing drivers for the Queue class template.
See the driver developed for the programming problems in chapter 5.

The last two (#13 & #14) involve writing drivers for the BigInt class. These drivers are very similar to the numerical evaluation done using polynomials.

```
/* prog13-1.cpp is a driver program to test class BigInt.
        *
        * Input:  operation (+, -, Q) and two BigInts
```

```
 * Output: The sum or difference of the BigInts
 *
 * Written by Ed Ball for C++: An Introduction to Computing
 ***********************************************/
#include <iostream>
using namespace std;
#include "BigInt.h"
int main()
{
   cout << "Enter BigInts in blocks of 3 digits
            (-1 to stop).\n";
   char option;
   for (;;)
   {
      cout << "\nEnter +, -, *, /, or Q (to quit): ";
      cin >> option;
      if (option == 'Q' || option == 'q') break;
      BigInt int1, int2, answer;
      cout << "Enter first BigInt:  ";
      cin >> int1;
      cout << "Enter second BigInt: ";
      cin >> int2;
      switch (option)
      {
         case '+' : cout << int1 + int2 << endl;
                    break;
         case '-' : cout << int1 - int2 << endl;
                    break;
         case '*' : cout << int1 * int2 << endl;
                    break;
         case '/' : cout << int1 / int2 << endl;
                    break;
         default  : cerr << "Illegal operation\n";
      }
   }
}
```

#7 - #12 involve writing drivers for the LinkedList class template and associated utility functions.
A driver program follows.

```
#include "LinkedListT.h"
#include <iostream>
using namespace std;
int main()
{
  LinkedList<int>          IntLL;
  LinkedList<double>       DoubleLL;
  LinkedList<char>         CharLL;
```

```
    for (int index = 0; index < 25; index++)
    {
        IntLL.insert(index * 3);
        DoubleLL.insert(index * 2.75);
        CharLL.insert(index + 41);
    }


    for (int index = 0; index < 25; index++)
    {
        IntLL.insert(index * 2);
        DoubleLL.insert(index * 1.75);
        CharLL.insert(index + 61);
    }

    IntLL.traverse();
    CharLL.traverse();
    DoubleLL.traverse();

    LinkedList<int>     Int2LL;
    Int2LL = IntLL;

    for (int index = 0; index < 15; index++)
    {
        IntLL.delete(index);
        DoubleLL.delete(index * 2.25);
        CharLL.insert(index + 51);
    }


    IntLL.traverse();
    Int2LL.traverse();
    CharLL.traverse();
    DoubleLL.traverse();

    return 0;
}
```

15. This problem is a duplicate of #3 and #4 and will be removed in later printings and/or editions.

16. See Evaluate() function above

Problem 19 in the first printing is misplaced; it should be in Chapter 12.

In later printings, the following changes are made:

> *18. Extend your program from Prob. 17 to subtract two polynomials using the modified class Polynomial in Exercise 5.*
>
> *19. Extend your program from Prob. 18 to multiply two polynomials using" the modified class Polynomial in Exercise 5.*

17. - 18. Similar to problems 13 and 14.

19. Omit

20. This problem is an application of priority queues.

A *priority queue* is a queue in which the insertion (addQ) routine has been modified so that an element is not just simply added onto the back of the queue. Instead, each element has a priority, and the queue is ordered in non-increasing order of priority, i.e. the first element in the queue has the highest priority; the last element has the lowest. Hence the addQ routine now must linearly scan the queue from front to (in the worst case) back to find the point at which to insert the new element. This modification results in an O(n) insertion rather than O(1) for regular queues.

In addition to increased complexity, priority queues also permit elements to wait indefinitely in the queue, should they constantly be pre-empted by the addition of higher priority items.

It should be clear that linked lists (rather than arrays) are the preferred implementation of priority queues.

Once priority queues are implemented, the student just needs to construct a user-interface that translates the requested action into the appropriate priority queue method.

```
// PQueue.h
          /* This is the file for class template PQueue.
           *
           * Written by Ed Ball for C++: An Introduction to Computing
           ******************************************/
          #ifndef PQUEUE
          #define PQUEUE
          #include <iostream>
          #include <list>
          using namespace std;
```

```
template <typename T>
class PQueue
{
public:
  // Add -- add an element to the queue
  void Add(T item, int priority);
  // Remove -- remove the next element from the queue
  bool Remove(T & data);
  // Print -- output elements to stream
  void Print(ostream & out);
private:
  struct PQElement
  {
    T myData;
    int myPriority;
    PQElement()
    {}
    PQElement(T data, int priority)
    { myData = data; myPriority = priority; }
  };
  list<PQElement> myList;
};


template <typename T>
void PQueue<T>::Add(T item, int priority)
{
  PQueue<T>::PQElement value(item, priority);
  if (myList.empty())
  {
    myList.push_back(value);
    return;
  }
  if (priority > myList.front().myPriority)
  {
    myList.push_front(value);
    return;
  }

  // Search list for place to insert item
    list<PQueue<T>::PQElement>::iterator it =
                            myList.begin();
    for (;;)
    {
       if (it == myList.end())              // end of list
       {
         myList.push_back(value);
         return;
       }
```

```
        if (priority > (*it).myPriority)
        {
          myList.insert(it, value);
          return;
        }
        it++;
      }
}


template <typename T>
bool PQueue<T>::Remove(T & data)
{
  if (myList.empty())
    return false;
  PQElement item  = myList.front();
  data = item.myData;
  myList.pop_front();
  return true;
}


template <typename T>
void PQueue<T>::Print(ostream& out)
{
  for (list<PQueue<T>::PQElement>::iterator it =
            myList.begin(); it != myList.end(); it++)
     out << (*it).myData << endl;
}


#endif


/* Program that uses the class PQueue.
 *
 * Input:  codes for operations to perform and
 *            items to add to priority queue
 * Output: results of operation.
 *
 * Written by Ed Ball for C++: An Introduction to Computing
 *******************************************/
#include <iostream>
using namespace std;
#include "PQueue.h"
const char HELP_TEXT[] =
  "\nValid Commands:\n"
  "A <entry> <priority> - add an entry\n"
  "R - remove the next item in the queue\n"
```

```
  "P - display the items in the queue\n"
  "H - this help text\n"
  "Q - quit the program\n";

int main()
{
  cout << "This program demonstrates a priority queue.\n";
  PQueue<unsigned> pq;
  unsigned job;
  int priority;
  for (;;)
  {
    char command;
    cout << "\nCommand (H = help): ";
    cin >> command;
    if (command == 'q' || command == 'Q') break;
    switch (command)
    {
      case 'a': case 'A':
                          cin >> job >> priority;
                          pq.Add(job, priority);
                          cout << "Job " << job
                              << " added.\n";
                          break;
      case 'r': case 'R':
                          if (pq.Remove(job))
                            cout << "Job " << job
                              << " removed.\n";
                          else
                            cout << "Priority queue
                                   is empty!\n";
                          break;
      case 'p': case 'P':
                          cout << "List of jobs in
                                   priority queue:\n";
                          pq.Print(cout);
                          break;
      case 'h': case 'H':
                          cout << HELP_TEXT;
                          break;
      default:
                          cout << "Illegal command -
                                   select one of"

                              << HELP_TEXT;
    }
  }
}
```

21 - 22. These two programs are straight-forward application of lists. The student must instantiate list objects, open files for input and then read the data into the appropriate list. Once initialized, each list is used when user responses are processed from the keyboard. For #21, user input results in the list being scanned and possibly an insertion (if the given answer does not match any stored answers). For #22, user input results in display(s).

```
/* Program reads student records, stores them in a vector of sorted
 * lists, one for each class, then displays each list.
 *
 * input(keyboard): name of student file
 * input(file):     the student records
 * output(screen):  lists of student records
 *
 * Written by Ed Ball for C++: An Introduction to Computing
 *****************************************************/

#include <iostream>
#include <fstream>
#include <string>
#include <list>
#include <vector>
using namespace std;
struct StudentRecord
{
   int myNumber;
   string myFirstName, myLastName;
   char myMiddleInit;
   string myCity, myState;
   string myPhoneNumber;
   char myGender;
   int myYear;
   string myMajor;
   int myCredits;
   double myGPA;
   void Print(ostream & out);
   void Read(istream & in);
};

void StudentRecord::Print(ostream & out)
{
   out << "\n#" << myNumber << ' ' << myLastName << ' '
       << myFirstName << ' ' << myMiddleInit << ".\n"
       << myCity << ' ' << myState
       << "\nPhone: " << myPhoneNumber
       << (myGender == 'F' ? "   Female" : "   Male")
       << "   Year: " << myYear
       << "\nMajor: " << myMajor << "   Credits:" << myCredits
       << "   GPA: " << myGPA << endl;
}
```

```
void StudentRecord::Read(istream & in)
{
   in >> myNumber >> myLastName >> myFirstName >> myMiddleInit
      >> myCity >> myState
      >> myPhoneNumber >> myGender >> myYear >> myCredits
        >> myGPA >> myMajor;
}

bool operator<(StudentRecord one, StudentRecord two)
{
  return one.myNumber < two.myNumber;
}

int main()
{
   string fileName;
   cout << "Enter name of file containing student records: ";
   cin >> fileName;
   ifstream inStream (fileName.data());
   if (!inStream.is_open())
   {
      cerr << "Error in opening student file " << fileName
             << endl;
      exit(1);
   }

   vector< list<StudentRecord> > stuList(5);
   StudentRecord stuRec;

   for (;;)
   {
      stuRec.Read(inStream);
      if (inStream.eof()) break;
      if (stuRec.myYear < 1 || stuRec.myYear > 5)
         cerr << "*** Bad Student Record for "
              << stuRec.myNumber << " ***\n";
      else
         stuList[stuRec.myYear - 1].push_back(stuRec);
   }

   for (int i = 0; i < 5; i++)
   {
      stuList[i].sort();
      cout << "\nList of students for year " << i + 1 << endl;
      for (list<StudentRecord>::iterator
             it = stuList[i].begin(); it != stuList[i].end();
                                                      it++)
        (*it).Print(cout);
```

```
            cout << endl << endl;
        }
    }
```

23 - 25. These programs are nice exercise to reinforce the manipulation of lists.

```
/* This program lists the words and their frequencies of a file.
 *
 * input(keyboard): name of file
 * input(file):     text from the file
 * output(screen):  lists of words and their frequencies
 *
 * Written by Ed Ball for C++: An Introduction to Computing
 ******************************************************/

#include <iostream>
#include <fstream>
#include <cctype>
#include <string>
#include <list>
#include <algorithm>
using namespace std;

struct WordInfo
{
  string myWord;
  int myTimes;
  WordInfo(string w = "", int t = 0)
  { myWord = w; myTimes = t; }

};


bool operator<(WordInfo one, WordInfo two)
{
   return one.myWord < two.myWord;
}


bool operator==(WordInfo one, WordInfo two)
{
   return one.myWord == two.myWord;
}

bool operator!=(WordInfo one, WordInfo two)
{
   return !(one.myWord == two.myWord);
}
```

```
ostream & operator<<(ostream & out, list<WordInfo> l)
{
  for (list<WordInfo>::iterator it = l.begin();
                                     it != l.end(); it++)
    out << (*it).myWord << " (" << (*it).myTimes << ")\n";
}


class Concordance
{
public:
  Concordance(int n);
  void Insert(string word);
  friend ostream & operator<<(ostream & out,
                                      const Concordance & c);

private:
  list<WordInfo> myWords[27];
};


// Implementations of Concordance operations
Concordance::Concordance(int n)
{ }

void Concordance::Insert(string word)
{
  char firstChar = word[0];
  int index;
  if (isalpha(word[0]))
    index = int(firstChar - 'A' + 1);
  else
    index = 0;
  list<WordInfo>::iterator it =
                 find(myWords[index].begin(),
                      myWords[index].end(),
                      WordInfo(word, 0));

  if (it != myWords[index].end())
                          // word already in concordance
    (*it).myTimes++;
  else
  {
    myWords[index].push_back(WordInfo(word, 1));

    if (myWords[index].size() > 1)
      myWords[index].sort();
  }
}
```

```
ostream & operator<<(ostream & out, const Concordance & c)
{
  for (int i = 0; i < 27; i++)
    if (!c.myWords[i].empty())
    {
      if (i == 0)
        out << endl << "Words not beginning with a letter:\n";
      else
        out << endl << char('A' + i - 1) << "-words:\n";

      out << c.myWords[i];
    }

  return out;
}


int main()
{
   string fileName;
   cout << "Enter name of file containing text: ";
   cin >> fileName;
   ifstream inStream (fileName.data());
   if (!inStream.is_open())
   {
      cerr << "Error in opening file " << fileName << endl;
      exit(1);
   }
  Concordance words(27);
  string aWord;

  while (!inStream.eof())
  {
    inStream >> aWord;
    // remove trailing punctuation
    int i = aWord.length() - 1;
    while (!isalpha(aWord[i]))
    {
      aWord = aWord.substr(0, i);
      i--;
    }

    words.Insert(aWord);
  }
  cout << "\nConcordance:\n" << words << endl;
}
```

26. This problem is a programming project. It is similar, but requires more detail, than #25.

Chapter Nine: Other Linked Structures

9.1 Exercises

1. Top of stack : Q, X

2. /* Stack class template */

```
template <typename element>
class Stack
{
 private:
     class Node
     {
       public:
          element   data;
          Node*     next;
     };

     Node*      myTop;

     void copyLL();        // auxiliary functions
     void deleteLL();

  public:
     Stack();               // constructor
     Stack(const Stack<element>&);      // copy constructor
     ~Stack();                        // destructor

     Stack<element>& operator=( const Stack<element>&);
     //assignment

     bool empty() const;
     void push(element);
     void pop();
     element top();
     void output(ostream&);
};


template <typename element>
Stack<element>::Stack()
{
     myTop = 0;            // stack initially empty
}
```

```
template <typename element>
Stack<element>::Stack(const Stack<element>& S)
{
     if (S.empty())
          myTop = copyLL(S);        // deep copy of stack S
}


template <typename element>
Stack<element>::~Stack()
{
     deleteLL();            // deallocate in destructor
}



template <typename element>
Node* Stack<element>::copyLL(Node* source)
{
   if (source == 0)
     return 0;
   else
   {
     Node* newH = new Node();
     newH->data = source->data;

     Node* tempP = newH;
     source = source->next;

     while (source != 0)
     {
          tempP->next = new Node;
          tempP = tempP->next;
          tempP->data = source->data;

          source = source->next;
   }
   tempP->next = 0;
   }

   return newH;
}


template <typename element>
```

```
void Stack<element>::deleteLL()
{
     Node*  tempP = myTop;

     while (tempP != 0)
     {
          Node* disposeP = tempP;
          tempP = tempP->next;
          delete disposeP;
     }
     return;
}


template <typename element>
Stack<element>&
Stack<element>::operator=(const Stack<element>& source)
{
  if (this != &source)
  {
     deleteLL();

     myTop = copyLL(source);
  }
  return *this;
}


template <typename element>
bool Stack<element>::empty()
{
     return myTop == 0;
}


template <typename element>
void Stack<element>::push(element item)
{
     Node* newNode = new Node;
     newNode->data = item;

     newNode->next = myTop;
     myTop = newNode;
     return;

}
```

```
template <typename element>
void Stack<element>::pop()
{
     if (empty())
     {
          cerr << "Stack empty: cannot pop" << endl;
          return;
     }
     // else
     Node* tempP = myTop;
     myTop = myTop->next;

     delete tempP;

     return;
}


template <typename element>
element Stack<element>::top()
{
     if (empty())
     {
          cerr << "Cannot retrieve from empty stack" << endl;
          return element();
     }
     else return myTop->data;
}




template <typename element>
void Stack<element>::output(ostream& out)
{
     Node*     tempP = first;
     while (tempP != 0)        //print each item
     {
          out <<  tempP->data; // assumes can be output
          tempP = tempP->next;
     }
     return;
}
```

3. Front of queue: A, Q

4. /* Queue template */

```
template<typename element>
class Queue
{
  private:
     class Node
     {
       public:
          element   data;
          Node*           next;
     };

     Node* first;
     Node* last;

     Node* copyLL(Node*);      // private helper functions
     void  deleteLL();
     Node* findLast();

  public:
     Queue();               //* one constructor
     Queue(const Queue<element>&); //* copy constructor
     ~Queue();                     //* destructor

     Queue<element>& operator=(const Queue<element>&);
                            //* assignment

     bool empty() const;
     void addQ(element);
     void removeQ();
     element front();
     void output(ostream&);
};


template <typename element>
Queue<element>::Queue()
{
      last = 0;
      first = 0;            // no memory allocated until
                            // element inserted into Queue
}
```

```
template <typename element>
Queue<element>::Queue(const Queue<element>& source)
//copy constructor
{
     first = copyLL(source);
     last = findLast();
}


template <typename element>
Node* Queue<element>::findLast(Node* source)
{
     Node* prev = 0;
     Node* current = first;

     while(current != 0)
     {
          prev = current;
          current = current->next;
     }
     return prev;
}


template <typename element>
Node* Queue<element>::copyLL(Node* source)
{
   if (source == 0)
     return 0;
   else
   {
     Node* newH = new Node;
     newH->data = source->data;
     Node* tempP = newH;
     source = source->next;
     while (source != 0)
     {
          tempP->next = new Node;
          tempP = tempP->next;
          tempP->data = source->data;
          source = source->next;
     }
     tempP->next = 0;
   }
   return newH;
}
```

```
template <typename element>
void Queue<element>::deleteLL()
{
     Node*  tempP = first;
     while (tempP != 0)
     {
          Node* disposeP = tempP;
          tempP = tempP->next;
          delete disposeP;
     }
     return;
}


template <typename element>
Queue<element>::~Queue()
{
     deleteLL();          // deallocate in destructor
}


template <typename element>
Queue<element>&
Queue<element>::operator=(const Queue<element>& sourc)
{
  if (this != &sourc)
  {
     deleteLL();
     first = copyLL(sourc.first);
     last = findLast();
  }

  return *this;
}
template <typename element>
bool Queue<element>::empty()
{
     return first == 0;
}


template <typename element>
void Queue<element>::addQ(element item)
{
     Node* newNode = new Node;
     newNode->data = item;
     newNode->next = 0;
```

```
          if (last != 0)
          {
               last->next = newNode;
               last = newNode;
          }
          else                         // first element in Queue
          {
               first = newNode;
               last = newNode;
          }
          return;
     }


     template <typename element>
     void Queue<element>::removeQ()
     {
          if (empty())
          {
               cerr << "Can't remove from an empty queue\n";
               return;
          }
          else
          {
               Node * tempP = myTop;
               first = first->next;
               delete tempP;

               if (first== 0)  // Was a one-element queue
                    last = 0;
          }
      }

     template <typename element>
     element Queue<element>::front()
     {
          if (empty())
          {
               cerr << "Can't retrieve front of an empty queue\n";
               return element();  // default element value
          }
          // else
               return first->data;
     }


     template <typename element>
```

```
void Queue<element>::output(ostream& out)
{
     Node*          tempP = first;

     while (tempP != 0)        //output Queue
     {
          out << tempP->data; // assumes can be output
          tempP = tempP->next;
     }
     return;
}
```

5.

```
/* A priority queue is a queue with a specialized addQ()
routine since addition is not perform unconditionally at the
back of the Queue.

The Queue is maintained in an ordered fashion, with the
highest priority item at the front.

Hence, the class template for Queue as developed above can be
used with the replacement addq() given below.

Note that each item held in the queue is associated with a
priority.  Here, we assume that the data value itself can be
ordered.  If not, an additional field in the Node class must
be added to contain priority keys.
*/
```

```
template <typename element>
void PriorityQueue<element>::addQ(element item)
{
     Node* newNode = new Node;
     newNode->data = item;
     newNode->next = 0;

     if (first == 0)                  // only element in Queue
     {
          first = newNode;
          last = newNode;
     }
     else                   // must search for insertion point
     {
```

```
            Node* prev = 0;
            Node* current = first;

            while (current != 0 && current->data > item)
            {
                 prev = current;
                 current = current->next;
            }

            if (prev != 0)
            {
                 newNode->next = prev->next;
                 prev->next = newNode;
                 if (current == 0)    // new last element in Q
                      last = newNode;
            }
            else                     // new first element in Queue
            {
                 newNode->next = first;
                 first = newNode;
            }
       }
       return;
}
```

6. see page 470.

7.
```
/* delete node.
     Assume address of predecessor of node to delete is given
     If not, just add scan (see 8 & 9) to find it
   */

     //predptr-> is non-null address of item
     // BEFORE point of deletion


     Node*  tempP = predptr->next;

     predptr->next = predptr->next->next;
     delete tempP;
```

8. /* search process for circularly linked lists */

```
if (first == 0)
     return 0;
else if (first->data == item)
     return first;
else      // 2 or more nodes
{
     ptr = first->next;
     for (;;)
          if (ptr == first)       /**/
               return 0;
          else if (ptr->data == item)
               return ptr;
          else
               ptr = ptr->next;
}
```

9. Change statement marked with /**/ in Problem 8 to:

```
     if (ptr == first || ptr->data > item)
```

10. /* nth successor */

```
if (first != 0 )     // list non-empty
{
     Node*  ptr = first;
     Node* where = 0;

     do
     {
          item = ptr->data;
          where = ptr;
          ptr = ptr->next;
     }
     while (ptr !=first && item != given_item);

     if (item == given_item)        //item found
     {
          for (int count = 0; count < n; count++)
               where = where->next;            // wrapsaround

          return where->data;
```

```
        }
        else
             return 0;
}
else
        return 0;
```

11. The changes to #4 are relatively minor.

The trick is realizing that in a circularly linked list, last->next is equivalent to first.

Hence, if the Queue template uses only one data member (last), the front of the queue is reachable from last->next. (One can track cycles by maintaining a count of the number of elements in the queue.) Whereever first is manipulated in the original implementation, use last->next.

12. – 13. Recall that a deque is a double-ended queue allowing additions and deletions to both the front and the back of the queue. Hence the Queue class template must be modified to allow additions to the front and deletions from the rear, i.e. add the capabilites of push_front and remove_back.

#12 is easily acquired from #4 with these modifications.
Likewise, #13 can be derived from #11. See #11 comments.

14. Algorithm to perform a shuffle merge of two circularly linked lists with head nodes:

```
1) GetNode (MergedList).

2)
Last = MergedList,
Ptr1 = CList1->Next,
Ptr2 = CList2->Next

3) while (Ptr1 != CList1 && Ptr2 !=  CList2)

     a.  GetNode (Temp).

     b. Temp->Data = Ptr1->Data
        Last->Next = Temp.

     c. Last = Temp,
        Ptr1 = Ptr1->Next

     d. GetNode (Temp)
```

```
    e. Temp->Data = Ptr2->Data
       Last->Next = Temp.

    f. Last = Temp,
       Ptr2 = Ptr2->Next


4) while (Ptr1 != CList1)
    a.  GetNode (Temp).

    b. Temp->Data = Ptr1->Data
       Last->Next = Temp.

    c. Last = Temp,
       Ptr1 = Ptr1->Next

5) while (Ptr2 != CList2)

    a.  GetNode (Temp).

    b. Temp->Data = Ptr2->Data
       Last->Next = Temp.

    c. Last = Temp,
       Ptr2 = Ptr2->Next

    d. Last->Next = MergedList.
```

15.

Algorithm to perform a shuffle-merge of two circularly linked lists with head nodes, without copying data items into new nodes.

```
If (CList1->Next == CList1)
     MergedList = CList2
Else
     1.   MergedList = CList1.
     2.   Ptr1 = CList1->Next
          Ptr2 = CList2->Next
     3.   while (Ptr1 != CList1 && Ptr2 != CList2)
               a.  Temp = Ptr1.
               b.  Ptr1 = Temp->Next
               c.  Temp->Next = Ptr2.
               d.  Temp = Ptr2.
               e.  Ptr2 = Temp->Next
               f.  If (Ptr1 !=CList1)
                          Temp->Next = Ptr1.
```

```
4.   If (Ptr1 == CList1) //find last node in CList2
          a. while (Ptr2 != CList2)
               i. Temp = Ptr2.
               ii. Ptr2 = Ptr2->Next
          b. Temp-> = MergedList.
```

16. Algorithm to return circular linked list to storage pool.

```
1.   tempPtr = first
2.   first = free
3.   free = tempPtr
```

17.

```
/* This problem is essentially one of repetitively
removing nodes from a circularly linked list until only
one remains.

Each element of the linked list contains an integer
indicating the id of the soldier.

This problem could be easily solved using vectors but
for practice, we use linked lists here
*/

#include <iostream>
#include <cstdlib>
using namespace std;

Node* CreateLL(int& numS)
{
     numS = 0;
     while (numS < 1)
     {
          cout << "Please enter number of soldiers
               present" << endl;
          cin >> numS;
     }

     Node* temp = new Node(1,0);
     Node* head = temp;
     Node* prev = temp;

     for (int num = 0; num < numS; num++)
     {
          temp = new Node(num, 0);
          prev->next = temp;
```

```
        prev = temp;
    }
    prev->next = head;          //make list circular
    return head;
}


void PickMessenger(Node* head, int NumS)
{
    Node* StartP = head;
    int n = rand() % numS;

    for (int advance = 0; advance < n; advance++)
        StartP = StartP->next;

    Node* prev = StartP;
    StartP = StartP->next;

    n = rand() % numS;

    while (StartP->next != StartP)      // > 1 left
    {
        for (int advance = 0; advance < n; advance++)
        {
            prev = StartP;
            StartP = StartP->next;
        }
        prev->next = StartP->next;     // remove node

        cout << "Soldier #" << StartP->data <<
                " is not chosen" << endl;

        delete(StartP);
        numS--;
        StartP = prev->next;
    }

    cout << "Messenger is soldier #" << StartP->data
        << endl;
}
```

```
int main()
{
     int num;
     Node* first = CreateLL(num);

     srand(17);
     PickMessenger(first, num);

     return 0;
}
```

9.2 Exercises

```
1. - 5.  /* Add the following functionality to the Polynomial
   class template.  */


template<typename CoeffType>
void Polynomial< CoeffType >::Input(istream& in)
{
     cout << "Enter polynomial coefficients with exponents in
               increasing order (0 to terminate):" << endl;

     CoeffType coeff;

     int expo;

     PolyNode* prev = 0, temp = 0;

     in >> coeff;
     in >> expo;

     myFirst = 0;

     while (coeff !=0)
     {
          prev = temp;
          temp = new PolyNode(coeff, expo, 0);

          if (!myFirst)
               myFirst = temp;
          else
               prev->next = temp;

          cout << "Next coefficient and exponent: " << endl;
          in >> coeff;
          in >> expo;
     }
     return;
}
```

```
template<typename CoeffType>
void Polynomial< CoeffType >::Output(ostream& out)
{
     PolyNode*  scan = myFirst;

     while (scan != 0)
     {
          out << scan->coef << "*x^" << scan->expo;

          if (scan->next != 0)
               out << " + ";

          scan = scan->next;
     }
     out << endl;

     return;
}


template<typename CoeffType>
CoeffType Polynomial< CoeffType >::Value(CoeffType a)
{
     CoeffType sum = 0.0;

     double power = 1.0;
     double prevE = 0.0;

     PolyNode* scan = myFirst;

     while (scan != 0)
     {
          for (int rep = prevE; rep < scan->expo ; rep++)
               power *=a;

          sum += scan->coef*power;

          prevE = scan->expo;
          scan = scan->next;
     }
     return sum;
}
```

```
template<typename CoeffType>
Polynomial<CoeffType> Polynomial< CoeffType >::derivative()
{
     PolyNode*  temp = 0, Dprev;
     PolyNode*  FirstDer = temp;
     PolyNode*  scan = myFirst;

     while (scan != 0)
     {
          if (scan->expo != 0)
          {
               Dprev = temp;
               temp = new PolyNode( scan->coef * scan->expo,
                                         scan->expo - 1, 0);

               if (!FirstDer)
                    FirstDer = temp;
               else
                    Dprev->next = temp;
          }
          scan = scan->next;
     }
     return FirstDer;
}
```

9.3 Exercises

1.

0	44
1	12
2	80
3	36
4	26
5	5
6	92
7	59
8	40
9	42
10	55

2.

0	44		
1	12		
2			
3	80	36	36
4	59	92	26
5	60	5	
6			92
7	40		
8			
9	42		
10			

3.

0	RATE
1	BETA
2	MEAN
3	WAGE
4	FREQ
5	SUM
6	KAPPA
7	ALPHA
8	NUM
9	PAY
10	BAR

4.

0	FREQ	RATE
1	ALPHA	BETA
2	NUM	MEAN
3	WAGE	
4		
5	SUM	
6	KAPPA	
7		
8		
9	PAY	
10	BAR	

5.

0	44
1	92
2	12
3	36
4	26
5	5
6	59
7	40
8	80
9	42
10	60

6.
```
template<typename ElementType>
class Hash
{
   public:
     Hash(int);
     Hash(const Hash&);
     ~Hash();
     void Insert(ElementType);
     void Search(ElementType);

   private:
     vector<list<ElementType> > data;
     static int hash(ElementType);
};
```

```
template<typename ElementType>
Hash<ElementType>::Hash()
{
     data.reserve(n);     // sets up table of n empty lists
}


template<typename ElementType>
Hash<ElementType>::~Hash()
{}        // vector and list destructors adequate here


template<typename ElementType>
int Hash<ElementType>::Search(ElementType item)
{
     int loc = hash(item);
          // use search from <algorithm> to search v[loc]

     if (search(v[loc], item) != v[loc].end())
          return loc;
     else
     {
          cerr << "Item not found -- returning -1\n";
          return -1;
     }
}


template<typename ElementType>
void Hash<ElementType>::Insert(ElementType item)
{
     int loc = hash(item);
     int where = Search(item);
     if (where < 0)
          data[loc].push_front(item);
     else
          cerr << "Item already in table.\n";
     return;
}
```

9.4 Exercises

1. I

2. R

3. 0

4. p2

5. pl

6. I

7. 0

8. R

9.
```
ptr = p1-> prev;
while (ptr != 0)
{
      cout << ptr->data << "   ";
      ptr = ptr->next;
}
```

10.
```
ptr = p1;
ptr->prev->data = "M";
ptr->next->data = "S";
```

11.
```
ptr = p1->next->next;
ptr->prev->next = ptr->next;
ptr->next->prev = ptr->prev;
delete ptr;
```

12.
```
ptr = p2->prev->prev->prev;
while (ptr != 0)
{
      cout << ptr->data << "   ";
      ptr = ptr->next;
}
```

13.
```
ptr = p2->prev->prev;
ptr->prev->data = "M";
ptr->next_>data = "S";
```

14.
```
ptr = p2;
ptr->prev->next = ptr->next;
ptr->next->prev = ptr->prev;
delete ptr;
```

15. B

16. E

17. p2

18. p2

19. p1

20. B

21. p2

22. E

23.
```
ptr = p1;
do
{
      cout << ptr->data << "    ";
      ptr = ptr->next;
}
while (ptr != p1);
```

24.
```
ptr = p1;
temp = new Node;
temp->data = "L";
temp->prev = ptr;
temp->next = ptr->next;
ptr->next = temp;
temp->next->prev = temp;
ptr->next->next->data = " A";
```

25.
```
ptr = p1->prev;
ptr->prev->next = ptr->next;
ptr->next->prev = ptr->prev;
delete ptr;
```

26.
```
ptr = p2->next->next;
do
{
     cout << ptr->data << "    ";
     ptr = ptr->next;
}
while (ptr != p1);
```

27.
```
ptr = p2->next->next;
temp = new Node;
temp->data = "L";
temp->prev = ptr;
temp->next = ptr->next;
ptr->next = temp;
temp->next->prev = temp;
ptr->next->next->data = " A";
```

28.
```
ptr = p2->next;
ptr->prev->next = ptr->next;
ptr->next->prev = ptr->prev;
delete ptr;
```

29. - 35.
```
/* BigInt enhancements

     For 29, 30, 31, 33, and 35, see the solution to
     Exercises 1 & 2 in Sec. 8.7.

     32 & 34 are straightforward.
     32 follows.  34 is similar.
*/


#include "BigInt.h";
#include <iostream>
using namespace std;
```

```
int main()
{
     BigInt Fib1(1);
     BigInt Fib2(1);

     cout << "Enter what Fibonacci number you would like
               to see" << endl;
     int n;
     cin >> n;

     BigInt FibN = Fib1;

     for (int iter = 0; iter < n; iter++)
     {
          FibN = Fib1 + Fib2;
          Fib1 = Fib2;
          Fib2 = FibN;
     }
     return 0;
}
```

9.5 Exercises

1.

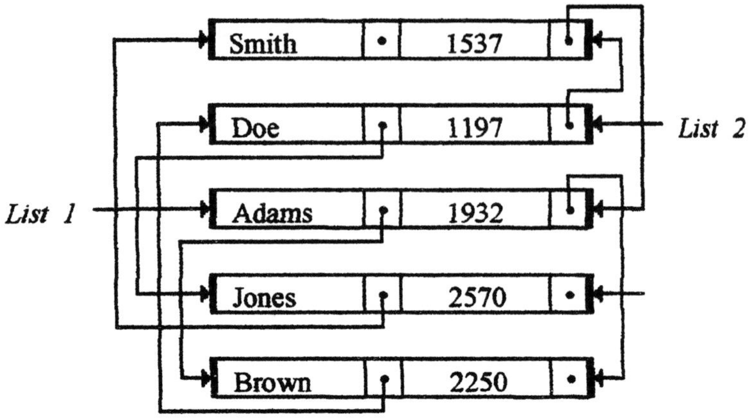

2.

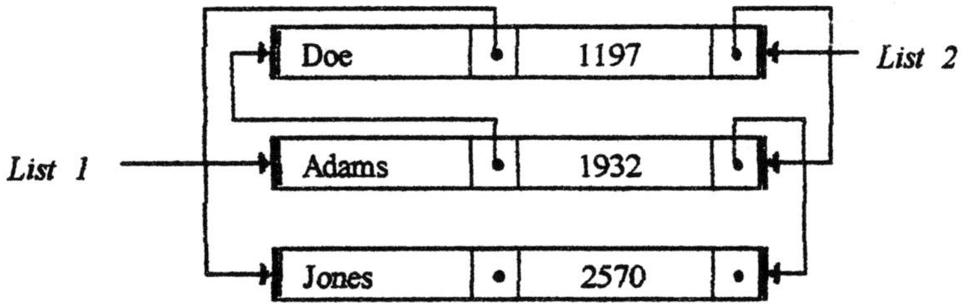

3.

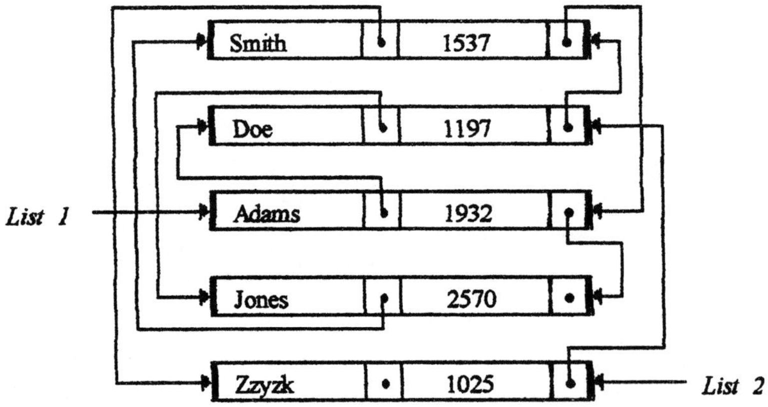

4.

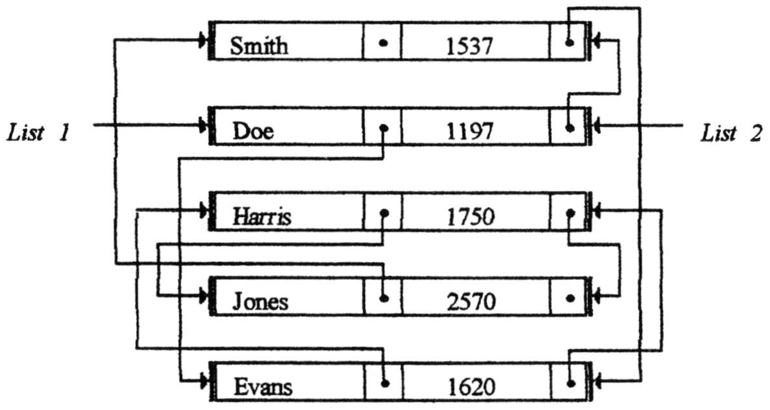

5.

```
struct Node
{
  string data1;
  Node * next1;
  int data2;
  Node * next2;
};

typedef Node * Nodeptr;
Nodeptr first1, first2;
```

or

```
struct Node
{
  string data1;
  int data2;
  Node * next[2];
};
```

6.

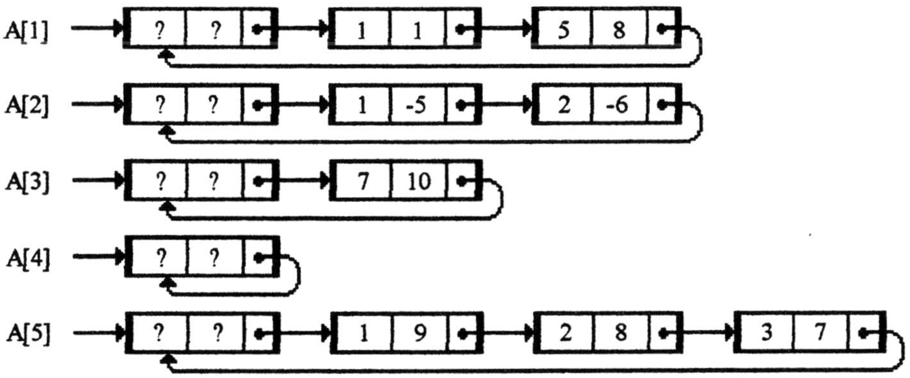

7.

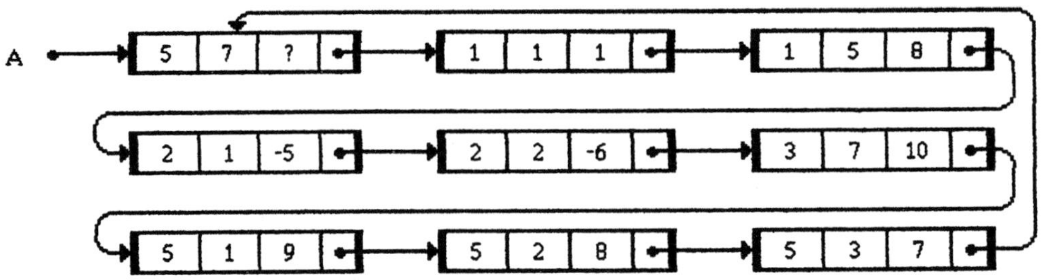
A
5
7
?
1
1
1
1
5
8
2
1
-5
2
2
-6
3
7
10
5
1
9
5
2
8
5
3
7

8.

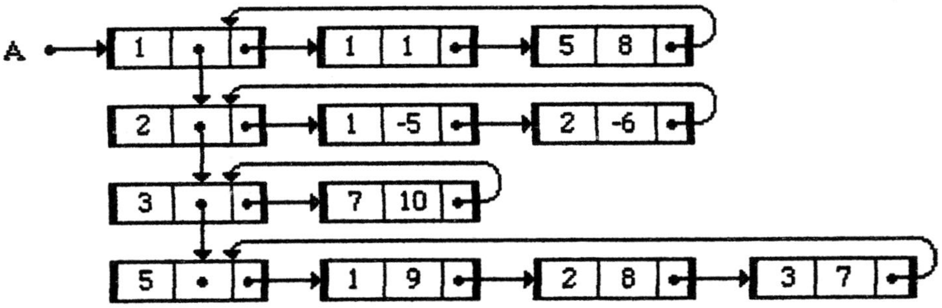
A
1
1
1
5
8
2
1
-5
2
-6
3
7
10
5
1
9
2
8
3
7

9.

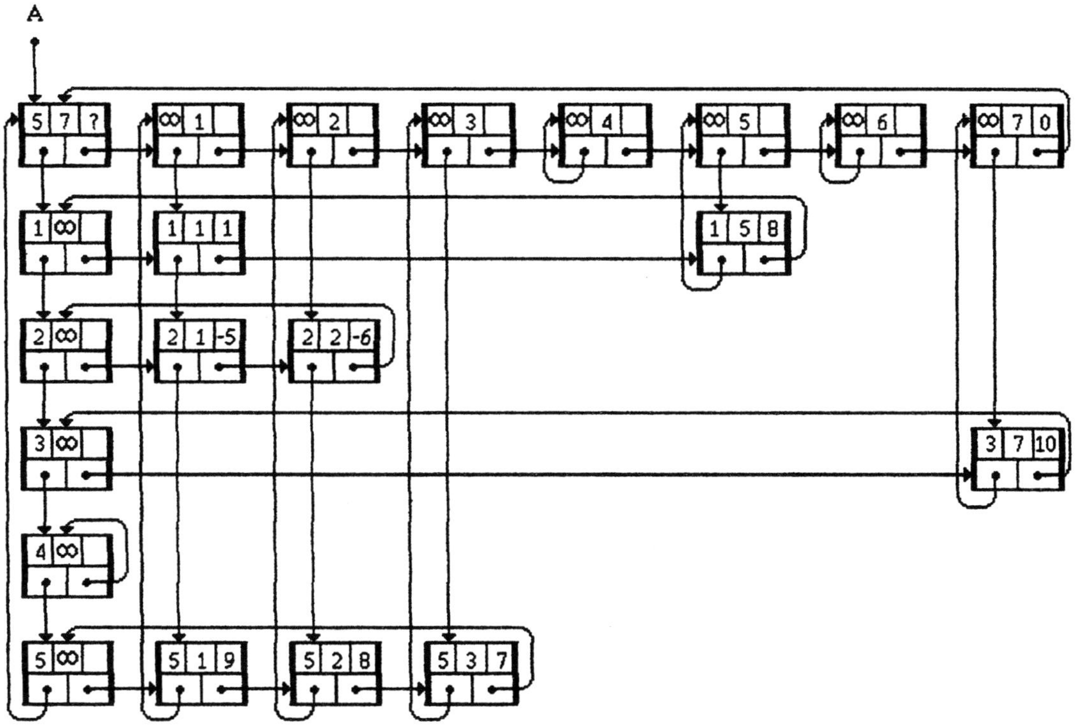

10.
```
struct Node
{
     int  data;
     int  col;
     Node* next;
}
typedef Node* Nodeptr;
const int MAXROWS = some_value;

Nodeptr   A[MAXROWS];
```

11.
```
struct Node
{
     int  data;
     int  row, col;
     Node* next;
}
```

```
typedef Node* Nodeptr;
Nodeptr   A;
```

12.

```
struct Node
{
     int  data;
     int  col;
     Node* next;
}

struct Head
{
     int  row;
     Head* next;
     Node* rowptr;
}

typedef Head* Headptr;

Headptr   A;
```

13.

```
struct Node
{
     int  data;
     int  row, col;
     Node* nextrow, nextcol;
}
typedef Node* Nodeptr;

Nodeptr   A;
```

14.

```
// use Nodeptr from #10

void AddMatrices(Nodeptr A[], Nodeptr B[], Nodeptr C[],
                                                int numrows)
{
     Nodeptr Aptr, Bptr, Cptr = 0, temp;

     for (int index = 0; index < numrows; index++)
     {
          C[index] = new Node;
```

```
        C[index]->next = Cptr;

        Cptr = C[index];
        Aptr = A[index]->next;
        Bptr = B[index]->next;

        while (Aptr != A[index] && Bptr != B[index])
        {
            temp = new Node;
            if (Aptr->col == Bptr->col)
            {
                temp->data = Aptr->data + Bptr->data;
                temp->col = Aptr->col;
                Aptr = Aptr->next;
                Bptr = Bptr->next;
            }
            else if (Aptr->col < Bptr->col)
            {
                temp->data = Aptr->data;
                temp->col = Aptr->col;
                Aptr = Aptr->next;
            }
            else
            {
                temp->data = Bptr->data;
                temp->col = Bptr->col;
                Bptr = Bptr->next;
            }
            temp->next = C[index];
            Cptr->next = temp;
            Cptr = temp;
        }
    }
    return;
}
```

```
15.  /* Use typedef from #11 */

void AddMatrices(Nodeptr A, Nodeptr B, Nodeptr C)
{
    Nodeptr Aptr, Bptr, Cptr = 0, temp;

    C = new Node;
    C->next = Cptr;
    C->row = A->row;
    C->col = A->col;
```

```
Cptr = C;
Aptr = Aptr->next;
Bptr = Bptr->next;

while (Aptr != A&& Bptr != B)
{
     temp = new Node;

     if (Aptr->row == Bptr->row)

          if (Aptr->col == Bptr->col)
          {
               temp->data = Aptr->data + Bptr->data;
               temp->col = Aptr->col;
               temp->row = Aptr->row;
               Aptr = Aptr->next;
               Bptr = Bptr->next;
          }
          else if (Aptr->col < Bptr->col)
          {
               temp->data = Aptr->data;
               temp->col = Aptr->col;
               temp->row = Aptr->row;
               Aptr = Aptr->next;
          }
          else
          {
               temp->data = Bptr->data;
               temp->col = Bptr->col;
               temp->row = Aptr->row;
               Bptr = Bptr->next;
          }
     else if (Aptr->row == Bptr->row)
     {
          temp->data = Aptr->data;
          temp->col = Aptr->col;
          temp->row = Aptr->row;
          Aptr = Aptr->next;
     }
     else
     {
          temp->data = Bptr->data;
          temp->col = Bptr->col;
          temp->row = Bptr->row;
          Bptr = Bptr->next;
     }
```

```
            temp->next = C;
            Cptr->next = temp;
            Cptr = temp;
        }
        return;
}
```

16. Very similar to #15

17. - 19.

```
/* input, output and addition for sparse matrices:
          use implementation from #13, wrapped in class

   Execises 17-19 make a nice project using multiply linked
   lists.  Implementing the operations is not difficult but
   does require some time and effort to get them right.

   Class declaration follows
*/

class SparseMatrix
{
   public:
     SparseMatrix();
     SparseMatrix(const SparseMatrix&);
     ~SparseMatrix();

     void Input(istream&);
     void Output(ostream&);
     friend SparseMatrix operator+(const SparseMatrix& A,
                                   const SparseMatrix& B);
   private:
     struct Node
     {
          int  data;
          int  row, col;
          Node* nextrow, nextcol;
     }
     Node* first;
};
```

20. 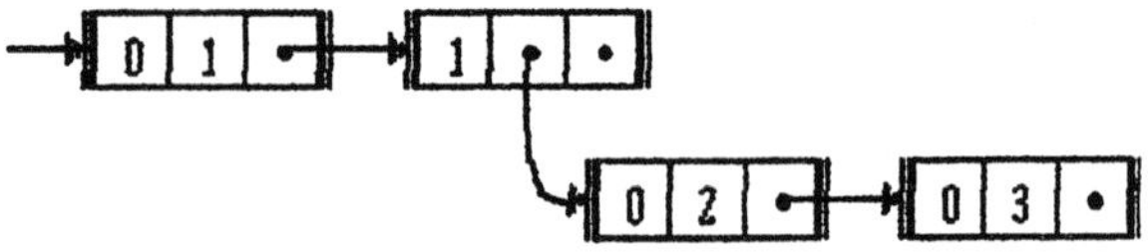

21. 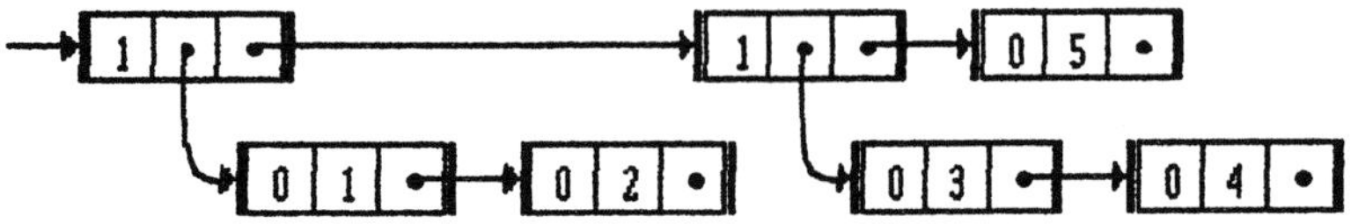

22. 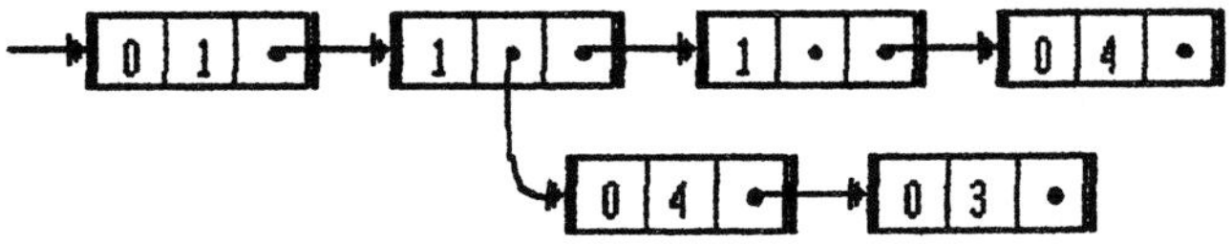

23. 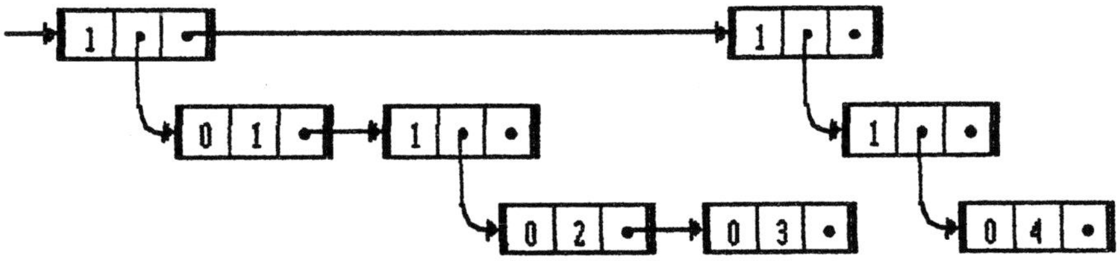

24. $7 + (3x + 5x^3)y - 17y^2$

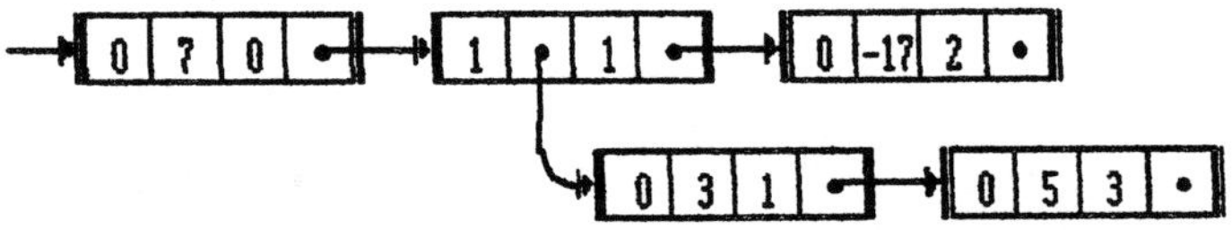

25. $(6 - 5x + 4x^{2}) + (-2x^{3} + 6x^{5} - x^{9})y^{4} + y^{8}$

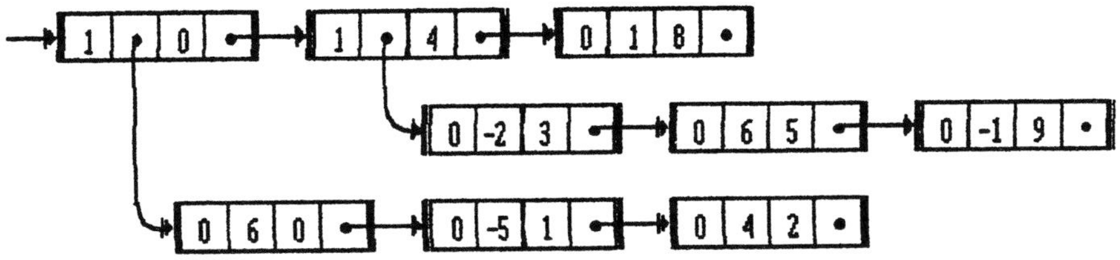

26. $((6 - 5x + 4x^{2}) - 2x^{3}y^{4}) + ((6x^{5} - x^{9})y^{4} + y^{8})z^{3} + z^{7}$

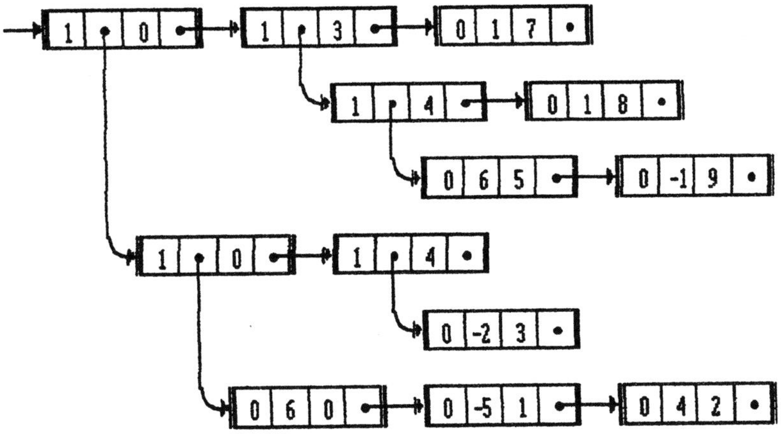

Programming Problems

1. - 13.
These problems require writing driver programs or they use programs given in the text and are very straightforward.

#1 & #2 deal with stack implementations. Any of the drivers for stacks from chapter 4 will suffice.

#3 – 7 deal with queue implementations. Any of the drivers for queues from chapter 5 will suffice.

#8 & #9 deal with deque implementations. Any of the drivers for deques from chapter 6 will suffice.

#10 involves adding trace output to Exercise #17 in Section 9.1 See the solution to Exercise 17 in Section 9.1.

#11 – 13 deal with the Polynomial class implementation. One needs to instantiate several Polynomial objects and then manipulate them to test the functionality of the class template.

Instantiation with different types of coefficients is needed.

14. – 15. Both these problems use the Polynomial class in standard numerical algorithms for finding the root of a Polynomial (bisection and Newton's methods).

The code for 14 follows, with modifications noted for 15.

```
/* Find approximate root of polynomial in the interval
 * (left, right) using the bisection algorithm.
 *******************************************/

template <typename CoefType>
CoefType Polynomial::Root(CoefType left, CoefType right)
{

  const double ACCURACY = 1E-7;
                    // accuracy of approximate root

  CoefType      width = right - left, // interval width
                midPt,          // midpoint of interval
                value_mid;
                    // value of polynomial at midpt
```

```
        while (width / 2.0 > ACCURACY)
        {
                  midPt = (left + right) / 2.0;
                  value_mid = Value(midPoint);
                  if (Value(left) * value_mid < 0)
                                // root is in left half
                    right = midPt;
                  else          // root is in right half
                    left = midPt;
                  width /= 2.0;
        }
        return midPt;
}
```

15. For Newton's method, replace the body of `Root()` in Problem 14 with:

```
const double ACCURACY = 1E-7;
const int ITERATION_LIMIT = 100;

CoefType xOld = (left + right) / 2.0,   // old approx
         xNew;                          // new approx

for (int i = 1; i <= ITERATION_LIMIT; i++)
{
     xNew = xOld + Value(xOld) / derivative.Value(xOld);
     if Value(xNew) < ACCURACY)
          return xNew;
     xOld = xNew;
}
cerr << "No convergence to root in " << ITERATION_LIMIT
   << " iterations -- returning last approximation.\n";

return xNew;
```

16. This problem is a simple driver of the Hash class.

17. This problem is a straight-forward application of hash tables. The program:
    1) reads in a collection of ids and passwords
    2) stores them in a hash table
    3) reads in individual ids and passwords
    4) verifies that they are in the table

Presumably, the class Hash has a good (random) hash function. So, for step 2, we can convert the strings input to numeric form for the hash function by:

```
int sumOfChars = 0;
for (int i = 0; i < userId.length(); i++)
     sumOfChars += userId[i];
```

and pass `sumOfChars` to the hash function.

18. This program is a little simpler than the previous one since one needs only to:
    generate random numbers,
    store them according to the provided hash function, and
    keep track of statistics on collisions.

19. /* First Fit */

```
void FirstFit(Node* free, int want, bool& avail, int& where)
{
     avail = false;
     Node* ptr = free->next;
     Node* prev = free;

     while (ptr != free && !avail)
     {
          if (ptr->size >= want)
          {
               avail = true;
               where = ptr->address + ptr->size - want;
               ptr->size -= want;
               if (ptr->size == 0)
               {
                    prev->next = ptr->next;
                    delete ptr;
                    ptr = prev->next;
               }
               else
               {
                    prev = ptr;
                    ptr = ptr->next;
               }
          }
          else
          {
               prev = ptr;
               ptr = ptr->next;
          }
          return;
 }
```

```
20.  /* Best Fit */
#include <climits>
using namespace std;
void BestFit(Node*  free, int want, bool& avail, int& where)
{
     avail = false;
     Node* ptr = free->next;
     Node* prev = free;

     int smallestfit = INT_MAX;
     Node* sfptr = free;

     while (ptr != free)
               // find smallest block that big enough
     {
          if (ptr->size >= want && ptr->size < smallestfit)
          {
               sfptr = ptr;
               smallestfit = ptr->size;
               avail = true;
          }
          prev = ptr;
          ptr = ptr->next;
     }

     if (avail)
     {
          where = sfptr->address + sfptr->size - want;
          sfptr->size -= want;

          if (sfptr->size != 0)
          {
               prev->next = sfptr->next;
               delete sfptr;
               sfptr = prev->next;
          }

     }
}
```

21 & 22. Both these problems deal with multiply linked lists and hence involve a lot of bookkeeping details. Tracking multiple links can be difficult. Essentially, one must first order the list by id and then order it by name. (It is far easier to order a list upon construction then to reorder an existing list. However, to order the second set of links, one must work with the existing list.)

Note that two external pointers must be kept:
One to the first id in the list.
Another to the first name in the list.

Sketch of approach:

1) read in id & associated name
2) insert it in list ordered by id
3) repeat 1 & 2 until EOF
4) initialize nameptr & prevnameptr to null
5) find smallest unmarked name in list
6) mark it
7) if it's the first name,
   initialize nameptr & firstname
   else
   link this newlyfoundname to previous one
   prevnameptr = nameptr
   nameptr = newlyfoundname
8) repeat 5 – 7 until all names marked

#22 insertion or deletion may be accomplished through scan of the appropriate link (either name link or id link)

23 & 24 are driver programs.

Chapter 10: Binary Trees

10.1 Exercises

1. 4, 6

2. 4, 1, 2, 3

3. 4, 6, 5

4. 4, 1, 0

5. 4, 6, 7, 8

6.
```
v.push_back(item);

bool found = false;
int loc = 0;

for (;;)
{
     if (item == v[loc])
          break;
     else
          loc++;
}
found = (loc != v.size());
```

7.
```
/* linear search for items in an ordered lists can terminate
      when an element v[loc] is found with item > v[loc]..
   Hence, use a while loop.  Refer to #6
*/
```

8. /* Recursive linear search
*/

```
void RecLinSearch(const vector<ElementType> & v,
            ElementType item, int & loc, bool & found)
{
      if (loc >= v.size())
            found = false;
      else if (item == v[loc])
            found = true;
      else
            RecLinSearch v, item, loc + 1, found);
}
```

9. /* LinkedLinearSearch */

```
void LinkedLinS(Node* Head, ElementType item,
                    Node* where, bool& found)
{
      if (Head == 0)
            found = false;
      else if (item == Head->data)
      {
            found = true;
            where = Head;
      }
      else
            LinkedLinS(Head->Next, item, where, found);

      return;
}
```

10. /* LinkedListBinarySearch essentially forces a sequential traversal of the linked list. Hence, the time complexity is O(n)
*/

```
void BinLinS(Node* Head, ElementType item, Node* where)
{
      bool        found = false;
      int         n = 0;
      int         first = 1;
      int         mid, last;

      Node*       binptr;
      Node*       ptr = Head;
```

```
     while (ptr != 0)
     {    // already O(n)  & haven't found anything yet
          ptr = ptr->next;
          n++;
     }

     last = n;
     ptr = Head;

     while (!found && first <= last)
     {
          mid = (first +last) / 2;
          binptr = ptr;
          for (int inc = 1; inc < mid; inc++)
               binptr = binptr->next;

          if (item < binptr->data)
               last = mid - 1;
          else if (item > binptr->data)
          {
               first = mid + 1;
               ptr = binptr->next;
          }
          else
          {
               found = true;
               where = binptr;
          }
     }

     if (!found)
          where = 0;
     return;
}
```

11. /* Move to the front is expensive with arrays: O(n) */

```
void MoveLinS(ElementType x[], int n, ElementType item,
                              int& loc, bool& found)
{
     loc = 0;
     found = false;

     while (!found && loc < n)
```

```
        if (item == x[loc])
          found = true;
        else
          loc++;

     if (found)
     {
          for (int index = loc - 1; index > 0; index++)
               x[index + 1] = x[index];

          x[0] = item;
     }
     return;
}
```

12. /* Move to the front is O(1) with linked lists */

```
void MoveLinkedLinS(Node* Head, ElementType item,
                                        Node* where)
{
     bool       found = false;
     Node*      prev = 0;

     where = Head;

     while (!found && where)
        if (item == where->data)
          found = true;
        else
        {
          prev = where;
          where = where->next;
        }


     if (found && where !=head)
     {
          prev->next = where->next;
          where->next = Head;
          Head = where;
     }
     else if (!found)
          where = 0;

     return;
}
```

13. See #11. Instead of moving all items up to the location where the item is found, just interchange the found item with its predecessor, i.e. replace the for-loop with a swap. Hence, move up strategy is cheaper, O(1).

14. See #12. Instead of moving the found item to the front, just change the links with its predecessor. Complexity is still O(1).

15.

```
void InterpS(ElementType x[], int n, ElementType item,
                                int& loc, bool& found)
{
     int  first = 0, last = n-1;

     if (item < x[first] || x > x[last])
          found = false;
     else if (first == last && item == x[first])
     {
          found = true;
          loc = first;
     }
     else
     {
          found = false;
          while (!found && first < last)
          {
               loc = first + (int) (
          ( (item - x[first]) / (x[last] - x[first]) )
                                   * (last - first) );


               if (item < x[loc])
                    last = loc -1;
               else if (item > x[loc])
                    first = mid+1;
               else
                    found = true;
          }
     }
     return;

}
```

10.3 Exercises

1.

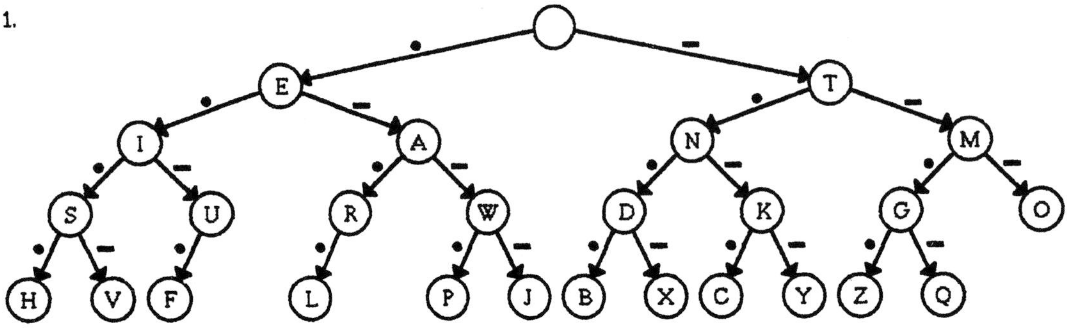

2.

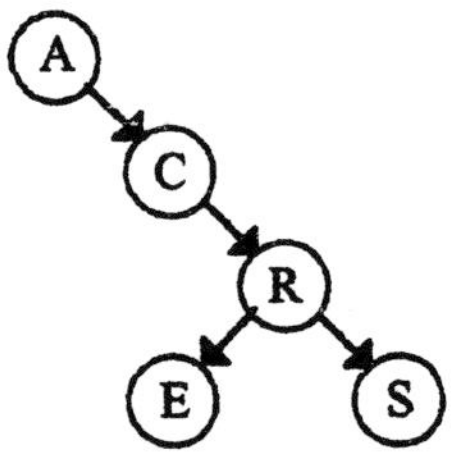

3.

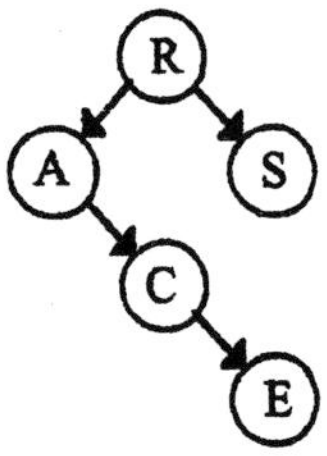

4.

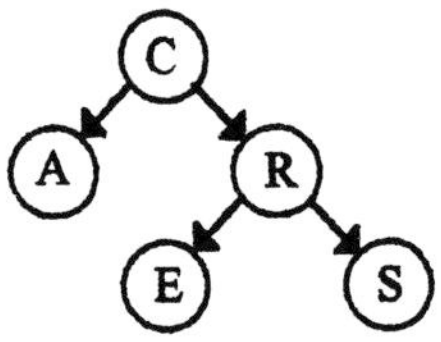

5.

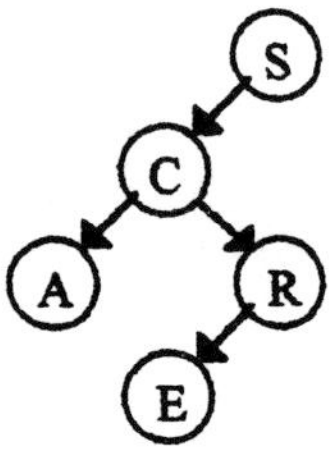

6.

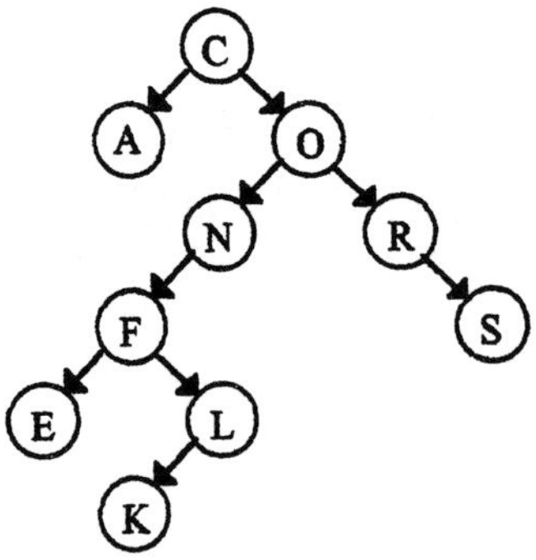

7.

i	0	1	2	3	4	5	6	...	13	14	
T[i]	A		C				R		E	S	

8.

i	0	1	2	3	4	5	6	7	8	9	10	
T[i]	R	A	S		C						E	

9

i	0	1	2	3	4	5	6
T[i]	C	A	R			E	S

10.

i	0	1	2	3	4	5	6	7	8	9	
T[i]	S	C		A	R					E	

11.

i	0	1	2	3	4	5	6	...	12	...	15	...	24	25	...	50
T[i]	C	A	0			N	R		F		S		E	L		K

12. **/* recursive Binary Search */**

```
void BSTrec(Node* root, ElementType item, bool& found,
                              Node* where)
{
        if (root == 0)
            found = false;
        else
        {
            if (root->data < item)    // go left
               BSTrec(root->left, item, found, where);
            else if (root->data > item)
               BSTrec(root->right, item, found, where);
            else
            {
               where = root;
               found = true;
            }
        }
        return;
}
```

13. **/* level of item, if found, in BST tree */**

```
int BSTlevel(Node* root, ElementType item)
{
        bool found = false;
        int count = 0;
        Node* ptr = root;

        while (!found && ptr != 0)
            if (item < ptr->data)
            {
               count++;
               ptr = ptr->left;
            }
            else if (item > ptr->data)
            {
               count++;
               ptr = ptr->right;
            }
            else
               found = true;

        if (found)
            return count;
        else
            return -1;
}
```

14. /* recursive version of #13 */

```
int BSTlevel(Node* root, ElementType item, bool& found)
{
      if (root == 0)
      {
         found = false;
         return -1;
      }
      else
         if (item < root->data)
            return 1+ BSTlevel(root->left, item, found);
         else if (item > ptr->data)
            return 1 + BSTlevel(root->right, item, found);
         else
         {
            found = true;
            return 0;
         }
      }
}
```

15. /* height of BST */

```
int BSTheight(Node* root)
{
      if (root == 0)
         return 0;
      else
      {
         int leftht  = BSTheight(root->left);
         int rightht = BSTheight(root->right);

         if (leftht < rightht)
            return 1 + rightht;
         else
            return 1 + leftht;

      }
}
```

10.4 Exercises

1.

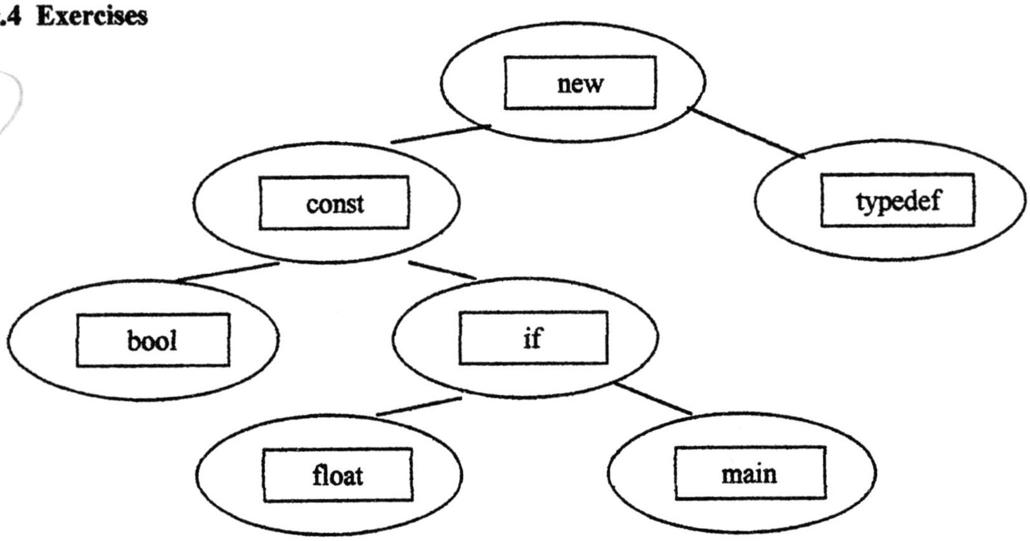

2.

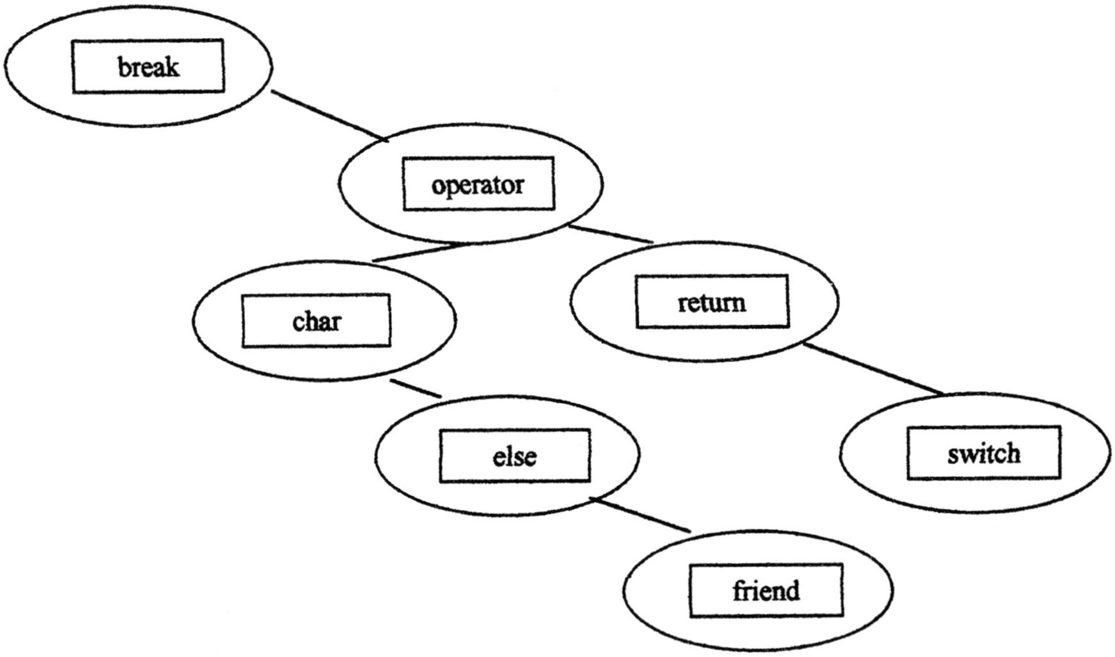

3.

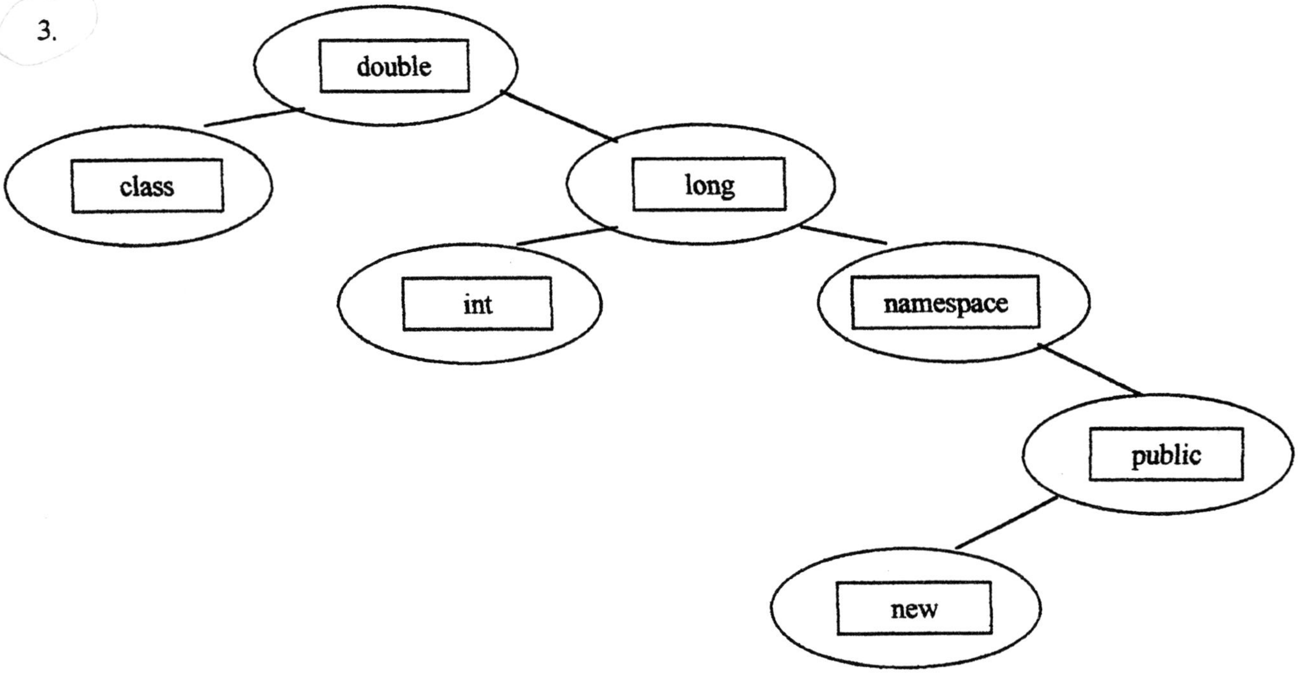
double
class
long
int
namespace
public
new

4.

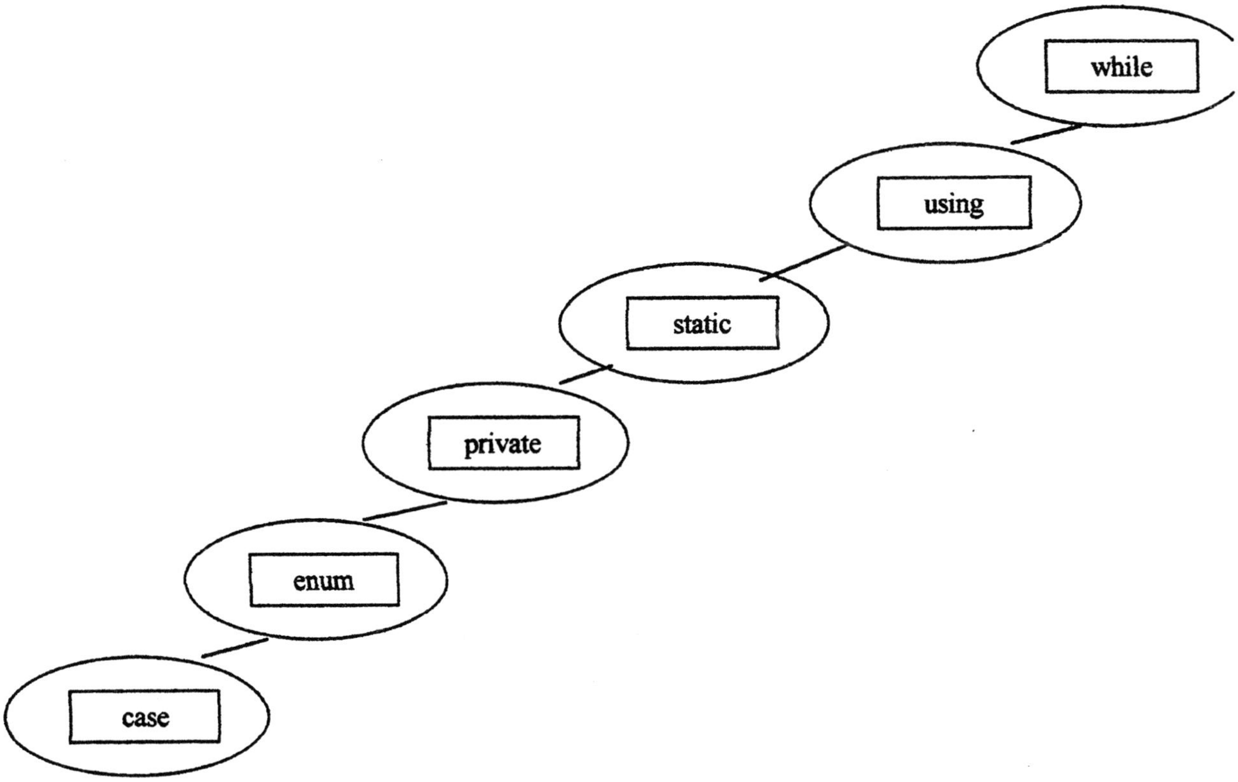
while
using
static
private
enum
case

5.

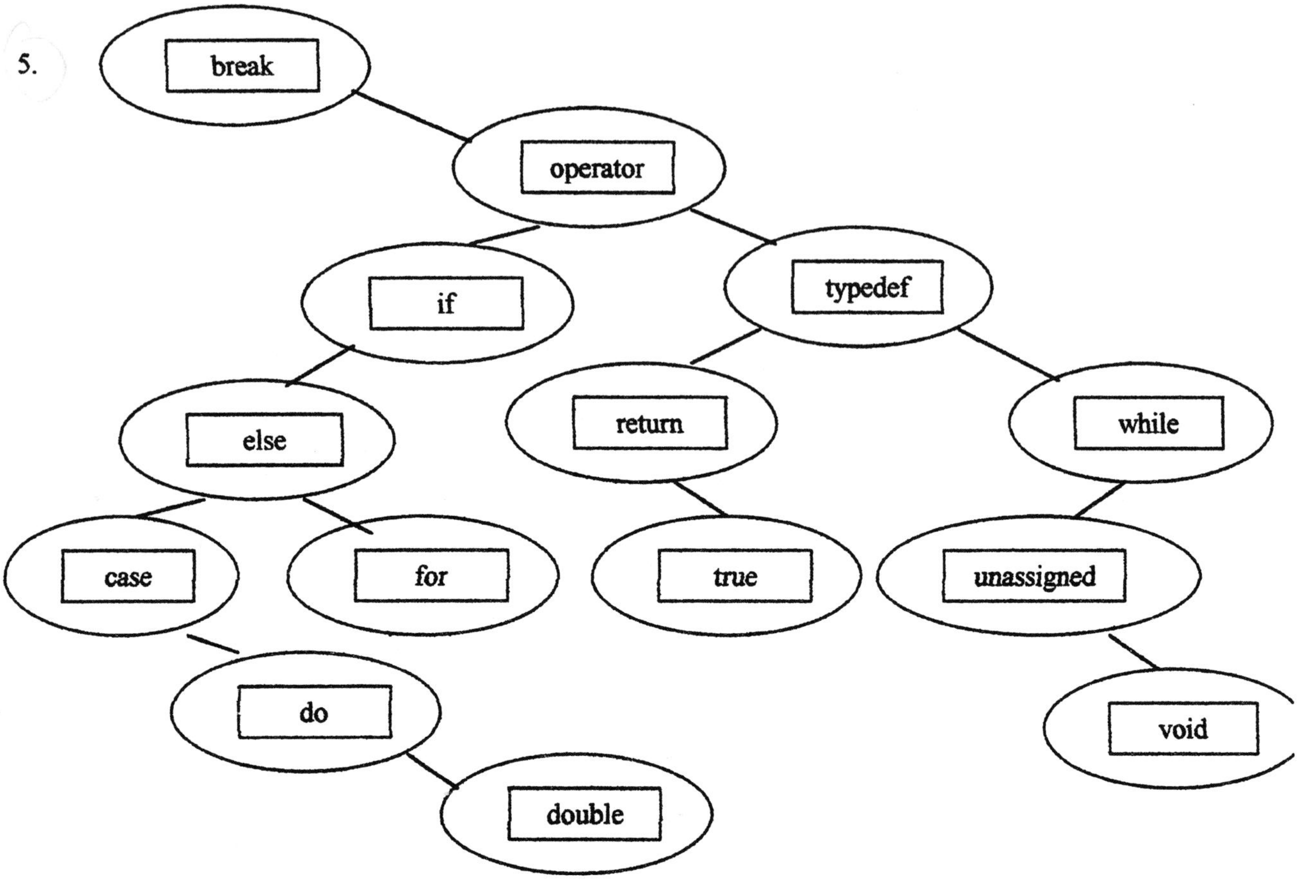
break
operator
if
typedef
else
return
while
case
for
true
unassigned
do
void
double

6.

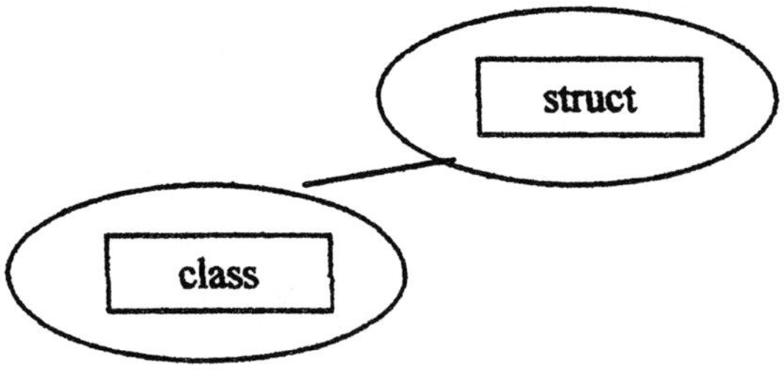
struct
class

7. preorder: new, const, bool, if, float, main, typedef
inorder: bool, const, float, if, main, new, typedef
postorder: bool, float, main, if, const, typedef, new

8. preorder: break, operator, char, else, friend, return, switch
inorder: break, char, else, friend, operator, return, switch
postorder: friend, else, char, swithc, return, operator, break

9. preorder: double, class, long, int, namespace, public, new
inorder: class, double, int, long, namespace, new, public
postorder: class, int, new, public, namespace, long, double

10. preorder: while, using, static, private, enum, case
inorder: case, enum, private, static, using, while
postorder: same as inorder

11. preorder: break, operator, ief, else, case, do, double, for, typedef, return, true, while,unsigned, void
inorder: break, case, double, do, for, else, if, operator, true, return typedef, void, unsigned, while
postorder: double, do, case, for, else, if, true, return, void, unsigned while, typedef, operator, break

12. preorder: struct, class
inorder: class, struct
postorder: class, struct

13.

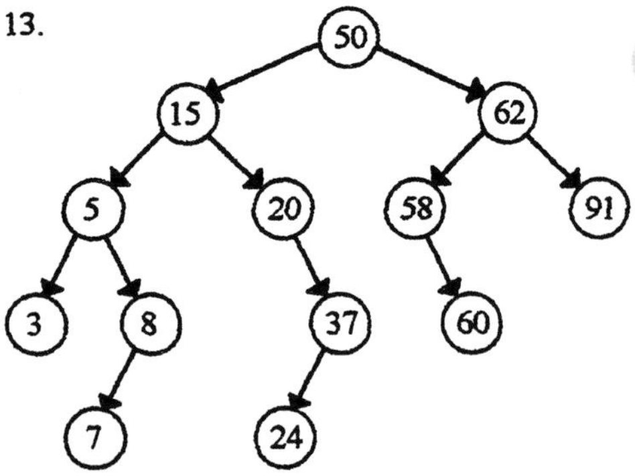
50
15
62
5
20
58
91
3
8
37
60
7
24

14.

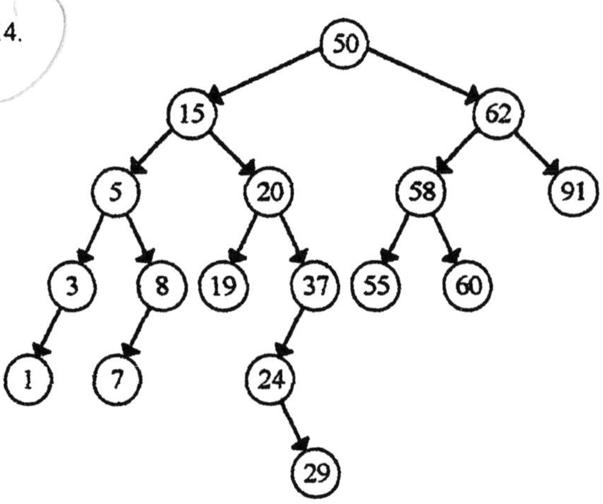
50
15
62
5
20
58
91
3
8
19
37
55
60
1
7
24
29

15.

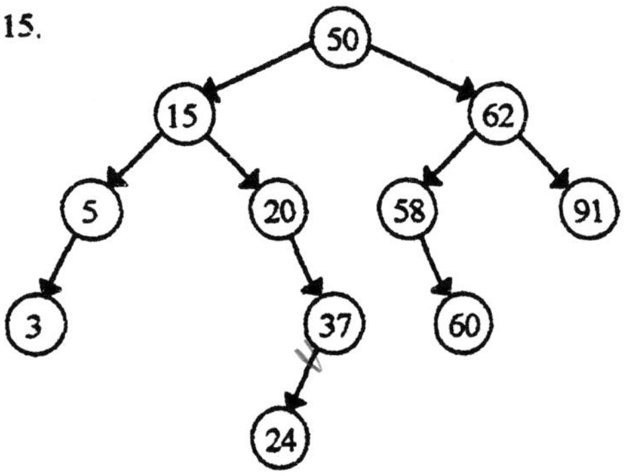
50
15
62
5
20
58
91
3
37
60
24

16.

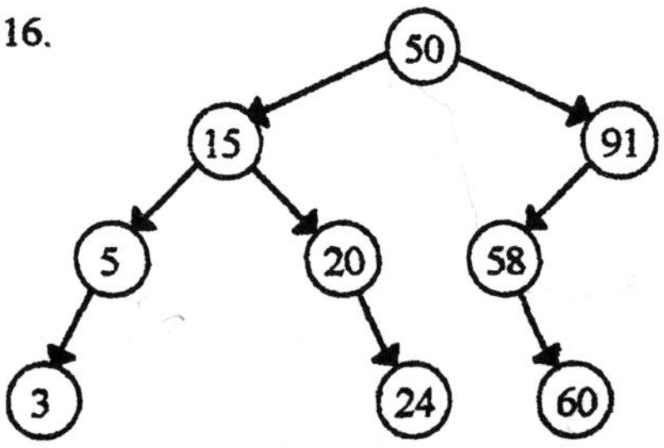
50
15
91
5
20
58
3
24
60

17.

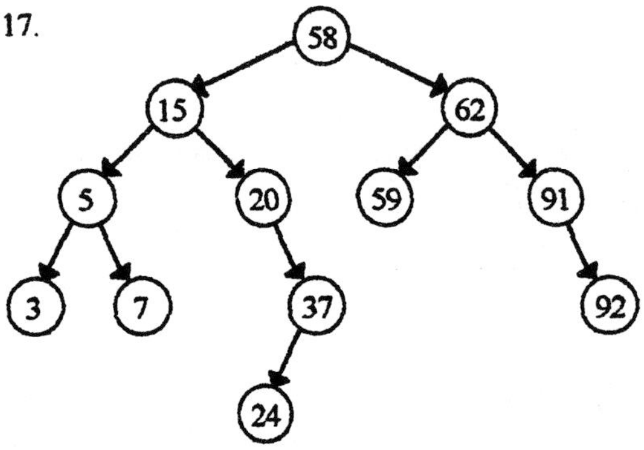
58
15
62
5
20
59
91
3
7
37
92
24

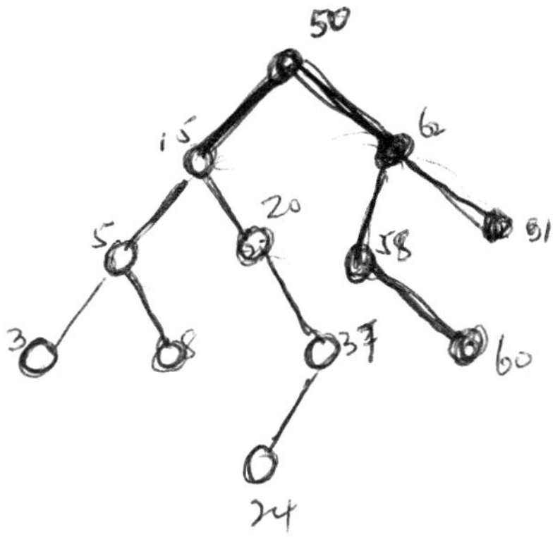

18. 3, 5, 8, 15, 20, 24, 37, 50, 58, 60, 62, 91

19. 50, 15, 5, 3, 8, 20, 37, 24, 62, 58, 60, 91

20. 3, 8, 5, 24, 37, 20, 15, 60, 58, 91, 62, 50

21.
LLLLU/3
RUU/5
RLU/8
RUUU/15
RLU/20
RLLU/24
RUU/37
RUUUU/50
RLLU/58
RLU/60
RUUU/62
RLU/91
RUUUU

22. /* iomanip or C-style tabs should be used for formatting. Algorithm given below*/

```
void displayPre(Node* root)
{
   if (root != 0)
   {
         cout << root->data;
         if (root->left != 0)
               cout << root->left->data;
         else
               cout << "   ";
         if (root->right != 0)
               cout << root->right->data;
         else
               cout << "   ";
         cout << endl;

         displayPre(root->left);
         displayPre(root->right);
   }

   return;
}
```

23.

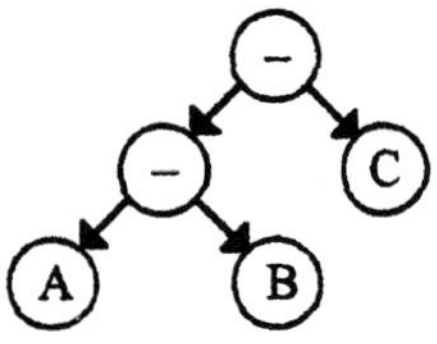

Preorder: - - A B C
Postorder: A B - C -

24.

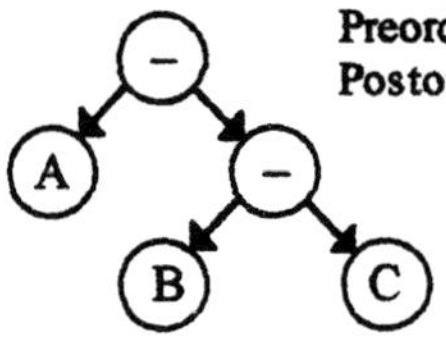

Preorder: - A - B C
Postorder: A B C - -

25.

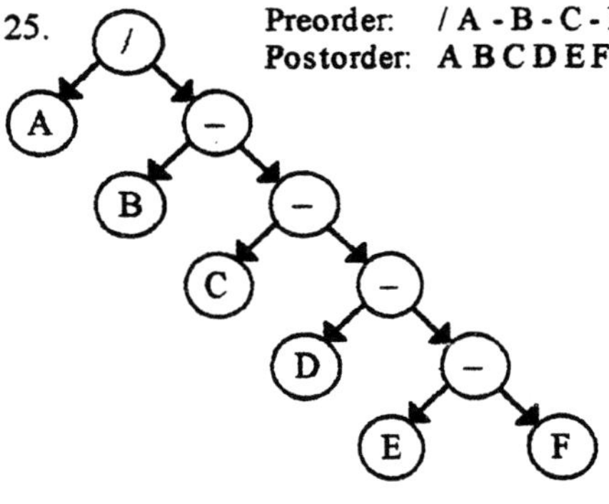

Preorder: / A - B - C - D - E F
Postorder: A B C D E F - - - - /

26.

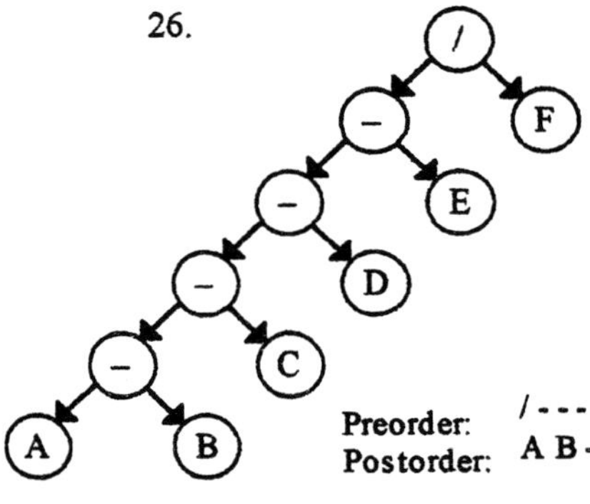

Preorder: / - - - - A B C D E F
Postorder: A B - C - D - E - F /

27.

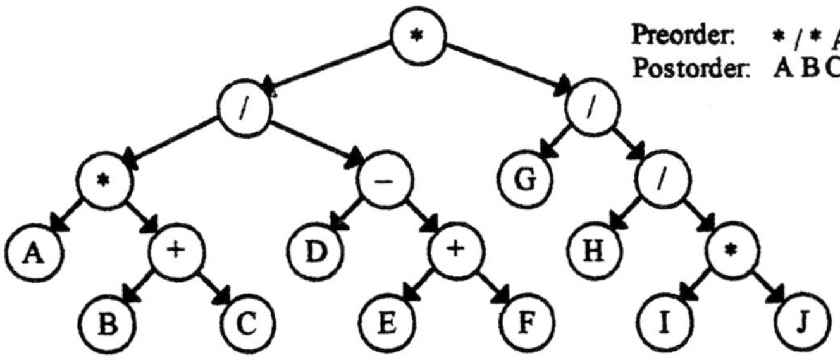

Preorder: * / * A + B C - D + E F / G / H * I J
Postorder: A B C + * D E F + - / G H I J * / / *

28.

index	0	1	2	3	4	5	6	7	8	9	10	11	12...	21
content	50	15	62	5	20	58	91	3	8		37		60	24

29.

index	0	1	2	3	4	5	6	7	8	9	10
content	new	const	typedef	bool	if					float	min

30.

index	0	1	2	3	4	5	6...	12	13	14...	26
content	break		operator			char	return	else		switch	friend

31.

index	0	1	2	3	4	5	6...	14...	29
content	double	class	operator			int	namespace	public	new

32.

index	0	1	2	3...	7...	15...	31
content	while	using		static	private	enum	case

33.

index	0	1	2	3	4	5	6...	11	12	13	14...
content	break		operator			if	typedef	else		return	while

index	23	24...	28	29...	48...	60...	98
content	case	for	true	unsigned	do	void	double

34.

index	0	1
content	struct	class

35.

index	0	1	2	3	4
content	-	-	C	A	B

36.

index	0	1	2	3	4	5	6
content	-	A	-			B	C

37.

index	0	1	2	3	4	5	6...	13	14..	29	30..	61	62
content	/	A	-			B	-	C	-		D	E	F

38.

index	0	1	2	3	4...	7	8...	15	16...	31	32
content	/	-	F	-	E	-	D	-	C	A	B

39.

index	0	1	3	3	4	5	6	7	8	9	10...
content	*	/	/	*	-	G	/	A	+	D	+

index	13	14...	17	18...	21	22...	29	32
content	H	*	B	C	E	F	I	J

40.

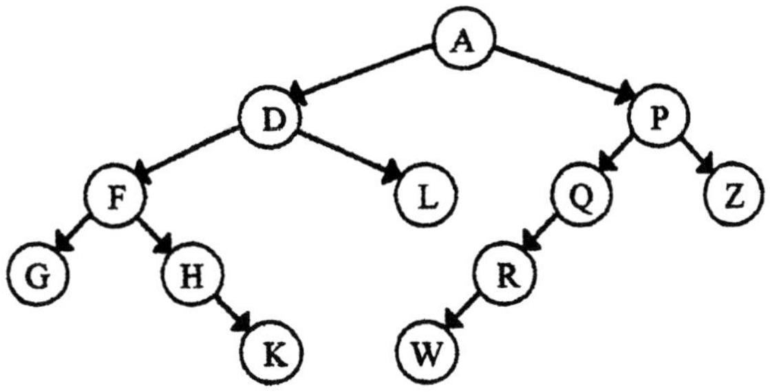

41.

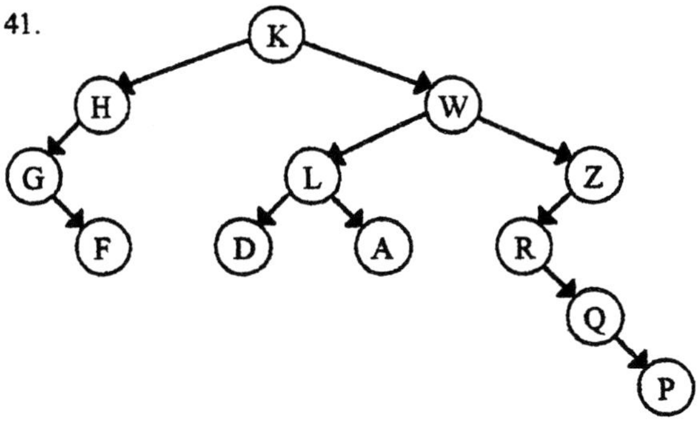

41.

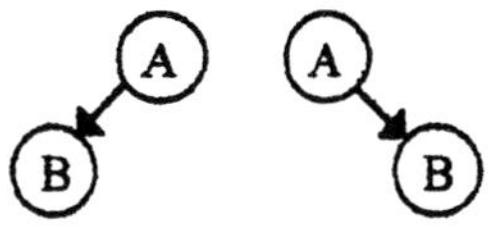

42. /* recursive LeafCount */

```
int LeafCount(Node* root)
{
   if (root == 0)
        return 0;
   else if (root->left == 0 && root->right == 0)
        return 1;
   else
        return LeafCount(root->left) + LeafCount(root->right);
}
```

43. /*nonrecursive InOrder: use stack to retain address of nodes.
Output statement may be replaced with appropriate action upon visiting a node
*/

```
#include "StackP.h"     //stack of pointers
        // alternatively use STL stack & instantiate with pointer

#include <iostream>
using namespace std;

void InOrder(Stack& S, Node* root)
{
   S.push(root);

   while (!S.empty())
   {
        root = S.top();
        S.pop();

        if (root != 0)
        {
             S.push(root->right);
             S.push(root);
             S.push(root->left);
        }
        else if (!S.empty())
        {
             root = S.top();
             S.pop();
             cout << "visiting node " << root->data;
        }
   }
   return;
}
```

44. /* nonrecursive level traversal: use queue to retain address of nodes
Output statement may be replaced with appropriate action upon visiting a node
*/

```
#include "QueueT.h"     // queue to store pointers

#include <iostream>
using namespace std;

void LevelTraverse(Queue Q, Node* root)
{
   Q.addQ(root);

   while (!Q.empty())
   {
        root = Q.front();
        Q.removeq();

        cout << "visiting node " << root->data;

        if (root->left)
             Q.addQ(root->left);
        if (root->right)
             Q.addQ(root->right);
   }
   return;
}
```

45. - 49. To effectively trace any program, one must determine the critical control points. In the recursive `DeleteAux()` given in the text there are 6 important junctions:

a) descend left (recursive call)

b) descend right (recursive call)

c) item found: no left child

d) item found: no right child

e) item found: two children

f) recursive call

These points are labelled below. Then execution is traced via reference to these control points in each of the problems 45 - 49. From these traces, trees may be drawn.

```
if (item < root->data)                // a
     DeleteAux(ite, root->left);

else if (item > root->data)           // b
     DeleteAux (ite, root->right);

else
{
     BinNodePointer ptr;
     if (root->left == 0)             // c
     ...
     else if (root->right == 0)       // d
     ...
     else                             // e
     ...
     DeleteAux(ptr->data, root->right); // f
}
```

45. First call is `DeleteAux` (root, 24) where root is pointer to node with data field 50.

Then the function call at (* a *) is executed:
`DeleteAux` (root->left, 24) where root->left is pointer to node with data field 15.

Then the function call at (* b *) is executed:
`DeleteAux` (root->right, 24) where root->right is pointer to node with data field 20.

Then the function call at (* b *) is executed:
`DeleteAux` (root->right, 24) where root->right is pointer to node with data field 37.

Then the function call at (*a *) is executed:
`DeleteAux` (root->left, 24) where root->left is pointer to node with data field 24.

Then statements at (* c *) are executed where root is pointer to node with data field 24.

ptr is set to null.
delete node with data field containing 24.
root (which is left in node with 37 in data field) is set to null.

46. First call is `DeleteAux` (root, 58) where root is pointer to node with data field 50.

Then the function call at (* b *) is executed:
`DeleteAux` (root->right, 58) where root->right is pointer to node with data field 62.

Then the function call at (* a *) is executed:
`DeleteAux` (root->left, 58) where root->left is pointer to node with data field 58.

Then statements at (* c *) are executed where root is pointer to node with data field 58.

ptr is set to a pointer to node with data field 60.
Delete node with data field containing 58.
root (which is left in node with 62 in data field) is set to a pointer to node with data field 60.

47. First call is `DeleteAux` (root, 37) where root is pointer to node with data field 50.

Then the function call at (* a *) is executed:
`DeleteAux` (root->left, 37) where root->left is pointer to node with data field 15.

Then the function call at (* b *) is executed:
`DeleteAux` (root->right, 37) where root->right is pointer to node with data field 20.

Then the function call at (* b*) is executed:
`DeleteAux` (root->right, 37) where root->right is pointer to node with data field 37.

Then statements at (* d *) are executed where Root is pointer to node with data field 37.

ptr is set to a pointer to node with data field 24.
Delete node with data field containing 37.
root (which is right in node with 20 in data field) is set to a pointer to node with data field 24.

48. First call is `DeleteAux` (Root, 15) where Root is pointer to node with data field 50.

Then the function call at (* a *) is executed:
`DeleteAux` (root->left, 15) where root->left is pointer to node with data field 15.

Then the statements at (*e*) are executed where root is pointer to node with data field 50

Then the function call at (* f *) is:

`DeleteAux` (root->right, 37) where root->right is pointer to node with data field 20.

Then statements at (* c *) are executed where root is pointer to node with data field 20.

ptr is set to a pointer to node with data field 37.
Delete node with data field containing 20.
root is set to a pointer to node with data field 37.

49. First call is `DeleteAux` (Root, 5) where Root is pointer to node with data field 50.

Then the function call at (* a *) is executed:
`DeleteAux` (root->left, 5) where root->left is pointer to node with data field 15.

Then the function call at (* a *) is executed:
`DeleteAux` (root->left, 5) where root->left is pointer to node with data field 5.

Then the statements at (*e *) are executed where root is pointer to node with data field 5:
ptr is set to a pointer to node with data field 8.
Root->data is set to 8 (was 5)

and the function call at (* f *) is executed:

`DeleteAux` (root->right, 8) where root->right is pointer to node with data field 8.

Then statements at (*c *) are executed where Root is pointer to old node with data field 8.

ptr is set to NIL.
Delete old node with data field containing 8.
root is set to NIL (it is right of new node with data field 8).

10.5 Exercises

1. Morse code is not unambiguously (immediately) decodable because its codes do not have unique prefixes. The given string can be decoded as NSGE or DIMI.

2. BAD

3. DEAD

4. CAD

5. BEADED

6. Note for #6 and #7, several codes are possible, depending on whether the nodes are placed in the left or right subtrees.

int	10
main	11
while	000
if	01
for	001

7.

a	111
b	100
c	1100
d	1101
e	0
f	1010
g	10110
h	101115

8.

1010	0	0	1101	111	1101	0	111	1010
F	E	E	D	A	D	E	A	F

111	10110	0	1101	10111	111	10110
A	G	E	D	H	A	G

9. As in #6 and #7, the code formed depends on the placement of nodes in the left or right subtree.

case	001011
class	100
do	00111
else	1010
false	00110
for	010
goto	001010
if	011
int	110
main	111
static	101101
struct	00100
switch	101101
true	10111
while	000

Programming Problems

1. - 10. These problems are all drivers for searching routines. #5 and #10 require the search space to be sorted. The remainder do not.

One needs to construct a search space (ordered if necessary) and then search for selected items.

In testing any search, one should look for an item lying on each extreme, an item in the middle and an item not in the list at all.

A driver for #1 follows. It is easily altered for the remaining problems by simply replacing the searching algorithm invoked.

```
#include "SearchFns.h"
#include <iostream>
#include <cstdlib>
using namespace std;

int main()
{
  const int MAXLGTH = some_value;

  vector<int>     order(MAXLGTH);
  vector<int>     reverse(MAXLGTH);
  vector<int>     random(MAXLGTH);

  int seed;

  cout << "Please enter the seed for the
              random number generator" << endl;
  cin >> seed;

  srand(seed);

  for (int index = 0; index < MAXLGTH; index++)
  {
       order[index] = index;
       reverse[index] = MAXLGTH - index;
       random[index] = rand();
  }
```

```
bool found = false;
int where = -1;
LinearSearch(ordered, MAXLGTH-3, found, where);

if (found && where = MAXLGTH-3)
     cout << "LinearSearch on ordered list OK "
          << endl;
else
     cout << "LinearSearch on ordered list OK "
          << endl;


found = false;
where = -1;
LinearSearch(reversed, MAXLGTH-3, found, where);

if (found && where = 3)
     cout << "LinearSearch on reversed list OK "
          << endl;
else
     cout << "LinearSearch on reversed list OK "
          << endl;

found = false;
where = -1;
LinearSearch(reversed, MAXLGTH, found, where);

//same as searching ordered for 0
// test the lower boundary

if (found && where = MAXLGTH)
     cout << "LinearSearch on reversed list OK "
          << endl;
else
     cout << "LinearSearch on reversed list OK "
          << endl;

found = false;
where = -1;
LinearSearch(reversed, 0, found, where);
//test upper boundary

if (found && where = 0)
     cout << "LinearSearch on reversed list OK "
          << endl;
else
     cout << "LinearSearch on reversed list OK "
          << endl;
```

```
  found = false;
  where = -1;
  LinearSearch(random, MAXLGTH-3, found, where);

  if (found )
       cout << "LinearSearch on random list found  "
            << MAXLGTH-3
            << " at index "  << where << endl;
  return 0;
}
```

11. This problem is very similar to the concordance problem presented in chapter 8. The addition of the user interface, the initialization of the lists and searching for specific values are all straight-forward.

12. & 13. One can use a system call like clock() to collect timing statistics before a search call and immediately after a return from a search call. In this manner, comparative statistics can be gathered.

14.

```
#include "BST"
#include <iostream>
#include <cstdlib>
using namespace std;

BST<char> GenerateBST(int n)
{
  BST<char> B;
  srand(11);

  int index = -1;
  char      ALPHA[26] = "ABCDEFGHIJKLMNOPQRSTUVWXYZ";
  for (int count = 0; count < n; count++)
  {
       index = rand() % 26;
       cout << "The " <<count << " random character is "
            << ALPHA[index] << endl;
       B.insert(ALPHA[index]);
  }
  return B;
}
```

15. - 17.

```
#include "BST"
#include <iostream>
#include <cstdlib>
using namespace std;

BST<char> GenerateBST(int n)

int main
{
  BST<char> One, Two;
  int size = -1;
  while (size < 1)
  {
       cout << "Please enter the size of the BST
            you wish to construct" << endl;
       cin >> size;
  }

  One = GenerateBST(size);

  size = -1;
  while (size < 1)
  {
       cout << "Please enter the size of the BST
            you wish to construct" << endl;
       cin >> size;
  }

  Two = GenerateBST(size);

  char      ALPHA[26] = "ABCDEFGHIJKLMNOPQRSTUVWXYZ";
  for (int count = 0; count < 26; count++)
  {
       cout << ALPHA[count] << " is on level  "
            << One.level(ALPHA[index])
            << "of BST One " << endl;
       cout << ALPHA[count] << " is on level  "
            << Two.level(ALPHA[index])
            << "of BST Two " << endl;
  }
  cout << "Height of BST One is "  << One.Height()
            << endl;
  cout << "Height of BST Two is "  << Two.Height()
            << endl;
  return 0;
}
```

18 - 20. /* Since we are working with a fixed-size data structure now, for initialization, we can exploit the indexing of arrays according to heap properties. That is, the root is at index 0, and for any interior node at index x, its left child is at index 2*x and its right child is at index 2*x+1. Deletion and insertion operate in the manner discussed in section 8.3 of the text
*/

```
template<typename ElementType>
class BST
{
 public:
  BST();
  void Insert(const ElementType&);
  void Search(ElementType&, bool&, int&);

 private:
  struct NodeType
  {
       ElementType    data;
       int        left;
       int        right;
  };

  const int NumNodes = some_value;

  NodeType  node[NumNodes];
  int       root;
  int       num
};


template<typename ElementType>
BST::BST()
{
  root = 0;
  num = 0;

  for (int index = 0; index < NumNodes/2 -1; index++)
  {
       node[index].left = 2*index;
       node[index].right = 2*index + 1;
       node[index].data = invalid_value;
  }
```

```
    for (int index = NumNodex/2 - 1; index++)
    {
         node[index].left = -1;
         node[index].right = -1;
         node[index].data = invalid_value;
    }
}


template<typename ElementType>
void BST::Search(const ElementType& what, bool& found,
                                    int& where,)
{
    found = false;
    where = -1;

    int first = root;

    while (first != -1 && !found)
    {
         if (node[first].data == what)
         {
              found = true;
              where = first;
         }
         else if (node[first].data < what)
              first = node[first].left;
         else
              first = node[first].right;
    }
    return;
}
```

```
template<typename ElementType>
void BST::Insert(const ElementType& what)
{
   if (num == 0)
   {
        node[root].data = what;
        num++;
   }
   else
   {
        int probe = root;

        while (probe != -1  && !done)
        {
             if (node[probe].data == what)
                  done = true;    // discard duplicates
             else if (node[probe].data == invalid_value)
             {
                  node[probe].data = what;
                  num++;
             }
             else if (node[probe].data < what)
                  probe = node[probe].left;
             else
                  probe = node[probe].right;
        }
   }
   return;
}
```

21 - 24.

```
#include "BST"
#include <iostream>
#include <cstdlib>
using namespace std;

BST<char> GenerateBST(int n)

int main
{
   BST<char> One, Two;
   int size = -1;
   while (size < 1)
   {
        cout << "Please enter the size of the BST
                  you wish to construct" << endl;
```

```
        cin >> size;
    }

    One = GenerateBST(size);
    One.DisplayPreOrder();
    One.DisplayInOrder();
    One.LevelByLevel();

    size = -1;
    while (size < 1)
    {
        cout << "Please enter the size of the BST
                    you wish to construct" << endl;
        cin >> size;
    }


    Two = GenerateBST(size);
    Two.DisplayPreOrder();
    Two.DisplayInOrder();
    Two.LevelByLevel();

    cout << "Number of leaves in BST One is "
        << One. LeafCount()  << endl;
    cout << "Number of leaves in BST Two is "
        << Two. LeafCount() << endl;

    return 0;
}
```

25. This program is not much more than a user interface added to the BSTgenerator and drivers written above in exercises 14 - 17 and 21 - 24.

26. This program involves constructing a BST of strings from a file, reading in a string from the user, searching for the string in the BST and responding whether the word was found (spelled correctly) or not (misspelled).

27. - 28. As in the previous problems, this programming assignment deals with constructing a BST of strings from a file, reading in a string from the user, searching for the string in the BST and responding whether the word was found or not (not in file). Variety is provided by using an array of BSTs (one for each letter of the alphabet) rather than one BST. Note that for #27 only one copy of each word is stored, so finding a word is equivalent to displaying the place of its first occurrence. #28 stores all copies (& reference points) of each word, so finding a word is equivalent to displaying the places of all of its occurrences.

29. /* A classic illustration of the greedy paradigm. One implementation is given in the text (Figure 10.7). An alternate one follows (main difference is that text builds the tree as each character is read in. Here, all characters are read in and then the tree is built. The approach given here is appropriate for #30)

Structure the BST used so that each node contains both the character and its associated weight.

An array implementation of the BST is the common approach (the number of nodes is fixed).

A sketch of the program follows:

a) read in the characters, one by one, and their associated weights
b) place in the Huffman tree (under construction), initializing the left and right links to zero
c) scan the tree to find the smallest (unused) weight, mark as used
d) scan the tree to find the second smallest (unused) weight, mark as used
e) create a new node,
    1) give it the combined weight of the two (childre) nodes,
    2) add it to the tree
    3) link it to its children
f) repeat steps c) - e) until all weights (but one, the root) marked as used
*/

30. A sketch of an approach to this project:

a. Initialize an array to correspond to the applicable portion of the ASCII table to covered in the file. This array, charCount, will be used to count the occurrences of characters. Hence, it is an array of integers, indexed by characters. Initialize each element to zero.

b. Read in the file, character by character, incrementing the total character count and updating the charCount array.

c. Close the file, calculate the frequency of occurrence for each character.

c. Construct the Huffman code using the character frequencies as weights. See #29 above

e. Open the input (uncompressed) file again.

f. Create an output (compressed) file.

g. While (input_file_not_empty)
read character
encode character
write encoded character to output file

h. Close both files

Chapter Eleven: Sorting

11.1 Exercises

1. After first pass, elements of x are: 10 50 70 30 40 60.

   After second pass: 10 30 70 50 40 60.

2. (a) 60 70 50 40 20 10

   70 60 50 40 20 10

   (b) 3, since no interchanges occur on the third pass.

   (c) Worst case is when elements are in reverse order.

3. (a) After x [4] is positioned: 20 30 40 60 10 50

   After x [5] is positioned: 10 20 30 40 60 50

   (b) If list is in increasing order, no interchanges.

4. (a) After one pass: 10 50 60 30 40 70
   After two passes: 10 30 40 50 60 70

   (b) Algorithm for double-ended selection sort:

Do the following for i = 1 to n / 2:

- a. minindex = i.
- b. min = x [i].
- c. maxindex = i.
- d. max = x [i].
- e. Do the following for j = i + 1 to n - i + 1:
  1. If x [j] < min then
     - i. minindex = j.
     - ii. min = x [minindex].
  2. If x [j] > max then
     - i. maxindex = j.
     - ii. max = x [maxindex].
- f. x [minindex] = x [i].
- g. x [i] = min.
- h. x [maxindex] = x [n - i + 1].
- i. x [n - i + 1] = max.

5. (a) After step 1 executes, x[i]'s are: 30 50 90 10 60 70 20 100 80 40

There are 5 passes for step 2. x[i]'s are:

After first pass:	10	50	40	20	60	70	30	90	80	100
After second pass:	10	20	40	30	60	70	50	80	90	100
After third pass:	10	20	30	40	60	70	50	80	90	100
After fourth pass:	10	20	30	40	50	60	70	80	90	100
After fifth pass:	10	20	30	40	50	60	70	80	90	100

(b) The program below implements Smallest-Max Sort.

```
void swap(int  x[], int a, int  b);
{
   int temp = x[a];
   x[a]  = x[b];
   x[b]  = temp;
}

void MinMax(int x[], int size)
{
   for (int index = 0; index < size/2; index++)
      if (x[index] > x[size - index])
         swap(x, index, size - index);

   for (int index = 0; index < size/2; index++)
   {
      int minindex = index;
      int min = x[index];

      for (int index2 = index + 1; index < size/2; index++)
         if (x[index2} < min)
         {
            minindex = index2;
            min = x[index2];
         }
      x[minindex]  = x[index];
      x[index]  = min;

      int maxindex = size - index;
      int max = x[maxindex];

      for (int index2 = index + 1; index < size/2; index++)
         if (x[index2} > max)
         {
            maxindex = index2;
            max = x[index2];
         }
```

```
        x[maxindex] = x[size - index];
        x[size - index] = max;

        if (x[minindex] > x[size - minindex])
           swap(x, minindex, size - minindex);
        if (x[maxindex] < x[size - maxindex])
           swap(x, maxindex, size - maxindex);
    }
    return;
}
```

```
6. /* recursive SelectionSort, called with index = 1 */
void recSelectSort(int  x[], int size, int index)
{
    if (index < size)
    {
        int minindex = index;
        int min = x[minindex];


        for (int index2 = index + 1; index < size/2; index++)
            if (x[index2} < min)
            {
                minindex = index2;
                min = x[index2];
            }

        x[minindex] = x[index];
        x[index] = min;

        recSelectSort(x, size, index+1);
    }
    return;
}
```

```
7. /* recursive Bubblesort, called with numpairs = size-1 */
void recBubble(int  x[], int numpairs)
{
    int last = 0;
    if (numpairs)
    {
        for (int index = 0; index < numpairs; index++)
            if (x[index] > x[index + 1])
            {
                int temp = x[index];
                x[index] = x[index + 1];
                x[index + 1] = temp;
```

```
                last = index;
            }

        recBubble(x, last - 1);
    }
    return;
}
```

8. Bubblesort algorithm for a linked list:

```
a) initialize ptr = null, lastswap = first
b) while (lastswap->next)    // assumes non-empty LL
        lastswap = lastswap->next
c) while (lastswap != first->next)
        ptr2= first->next
        while (ptr2 != lastswap)
            if (ptr2->data > ptr2->next->data)
                swap(ptr2->data, ptr2->next->data)
                ptr = ptr2
            ptr2 = ptr2->next
        lastswap = ptr
```

9. (a) Elements of x after each pass:

left to right:	30 80 20 60 70 10 90 50 40 100
ight to left:	10 30 80 20 60 70 40 90 50 100
left to right:	10 30 20 60 70 40 80 50 90 100
right to left:	10 20 30 40 60 70 50 80 90 100
left to right:	10 20 30 40 60 50 70 80 90 100
right to left:	10 20 30 40 50 60 70 80 90 100
left to right:	10 20 30 40 50 60 70 80 90 100
right to left:	10 20 30 40 50 60 70 80 90 100

(b) Algorithm for two way bubble sort: $O(n^2)$.

1. *Do*
   a. Set NoInterchanges to true.

   b. For i = 1 to n-1 do the following:
   □
      If x[i] > x[i+1] then

      i. Interchange x[i] and x[i+1]
      ii. Set NoInterchanges to false.

```
        c.  If NoInterchanges is false then
                For i = n-1 downto 1 do the following:
                    If x[i+1] < x[i] then
                        i.  Interchange x[i] and x[i+1]
                        ii. Set NoInterchanges to false
        while NoInterchanges is false.
```

10. Algorithm to insertion sort a linked list with head node pointed to by L.

```
1.  Ptr = L,                        // Ptr points to the predecessor of the place to insert the new node
    PredPtr = Ptr->Next,            // PredPtr points to the predecessor of the next node to be inserted
    NextElPtr = PredPtr->Next.      // NextElPtr points to the node of the next element to be inserted

2.  While (NextElPtr != null_value)
    a.  While (Ptr->Next != NextElPtr && Ptr->Next_>Data < NextElPtr->Data)
            Ptr = Ptr->Next

    b.  If ( Next(Ptr) != NextElPtr )
            1. PredPtr->Next = NextElPtr->Next.
            2. NextElPtr->Next = Ptr->Next
            3. Ptr->Next = NextElPtr.
            4. NextElPtr = PredPtr->Next
        Else
            1. PredPtr = NextElPtr.
            2. NextElPtr = NextElPtr->Next.

    c.  Ptr = L.
```

11. (a) Algorithm for binary insertion sort.

```
for index = 0 to end of array, do
        if x[index] > x[index +1]       // adjustment needed
            first = 0, last = index, found = false
            while (!found && last - first > 1)      //binary search
                loc = (first + last) /2;
                if x[index] = x[loc]
                    found = true
                else if x[index] < x[loc]
                    last = loc;
                else
                    first = loc;
            if found
                shift elements up to index
                place element in hole
            else
                shift elements up & reposition element
```

(b)

Insert 90:	90	100	60	70	40	20	50	30	80	10
Insert 60:	60	90	100	70	40	20	50	30	80	10
Insert 70:	60	70	90	100	40	20	50	30	80	10
Insert 40:	40	60	70	90	100	20	50	30	80	10
Insert 20:	20	40	60	70	90	100	50	30	80	10
Insert 50:	20	40	50	60	70	90	100	30	80	10
Insert 30:	20	30	40	50	60	70	90	100	80	10
Insert 80:	20	30	40	50	60	70	80	90	100	10
Insert 10:	10	20	30	40	50	60	70	80	90	100

Count for number of shifts is 35.

(c) The solution is the same as that of (b).

12. /* shellsort */

(a)

```
40  10  50  30  80  20  60  70  100  90
10  20  30  40  50  60  70  80  90  100
```

(b)

```
/*---Incremented Insertion Sort---*/
      void IncrInsertSort(ElementType x[], int numElements,
                          int start, int gap)
      {
        ElementType nextElement;
        int j;

        for (int i = start + gap; i <= numElements; i += gap)
        {
          // Insert x[i] into its proper position among
          // x[start], x[start + gap], . . .

          nextElement = x[i];
          j = i;

          while (j - gap >= start && nextElement < x[j - gap])
          {
              // Shift element gap positions to right to open a spot
             x[j] = x[j - gap];
             j -= gap;
          }
          // Now drop next Element into the open spot
          x[j] = nextElement;
        }
      }
```

```
/*--- ShellSort x[1], x[2], ...., x[numElements] ---*/
void ShellSort(ElementType x[], int numElements)
{
   int gap = 1;
        // Find largest value in incr. seq. <= numElements

   while (gap < numElements)
      gap = 3 * gap + 1;

   gap /= 3;
   while (gap >= 1)
   {
     for (int i = 1; i <= gap ; i++)
         IncrInsertSort(x, numElements, i, gap);
     gap /= 3;
   }
   return;
}
```

13. - 14.

```
/* array Treesort & supporting routines
       Array and linked list implementations are similar
  The primary difference is one of traversal:
          A index (for loop) is used for an array
          A temporary pointer, continually updated to the
   contents of the next field (while loop), is used for a linked list
  */
void inOrder(Node* root, int x[], int index)
{
     if (root)
     {
          inOrder(root->left, x, index);
          index++;
          x[index] = root->data;
          inOrder(root->right, x, index);
     }
     return;
}


void treeSort(int  x[], int size)
{
     Node* BST;
     for (int index = 0; index < size; index++)
          RecBSTInsert(BST, x[index]);

     InOrder(BST, x, 0)
     return;
}
```

11.2 Exercises

1. The tree is not complete because there are nodes with fewer than 2 children.

2.

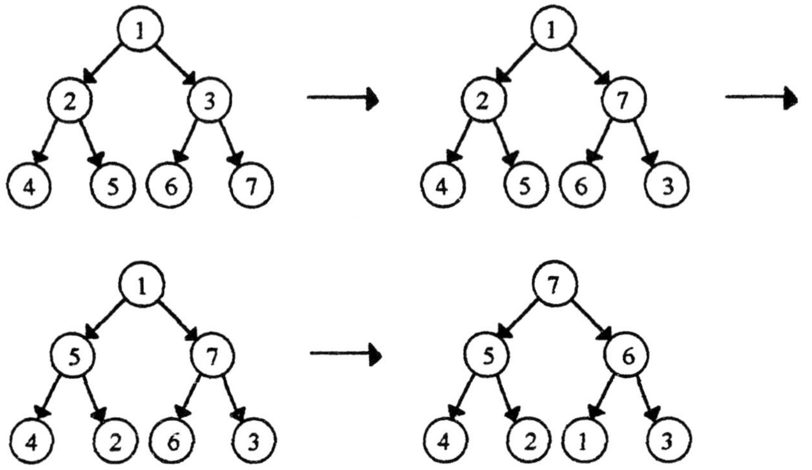

3.

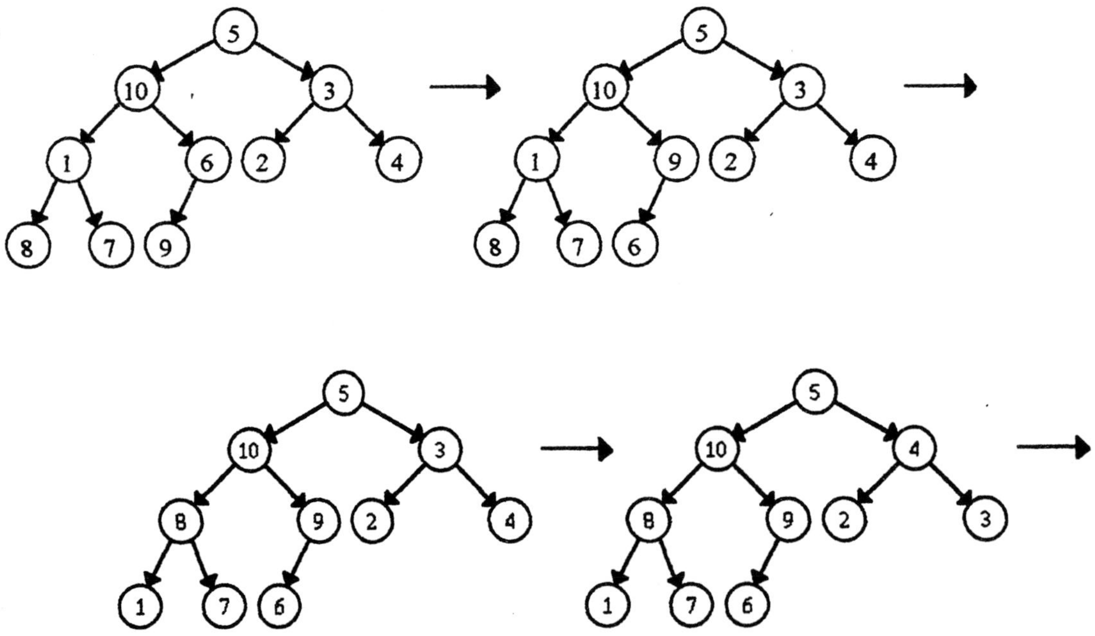

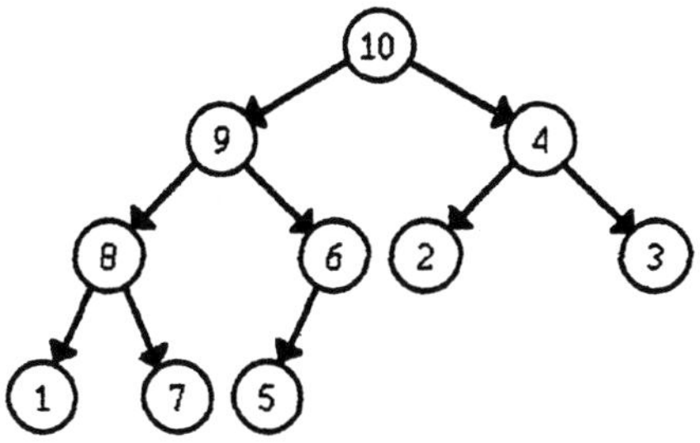

4.

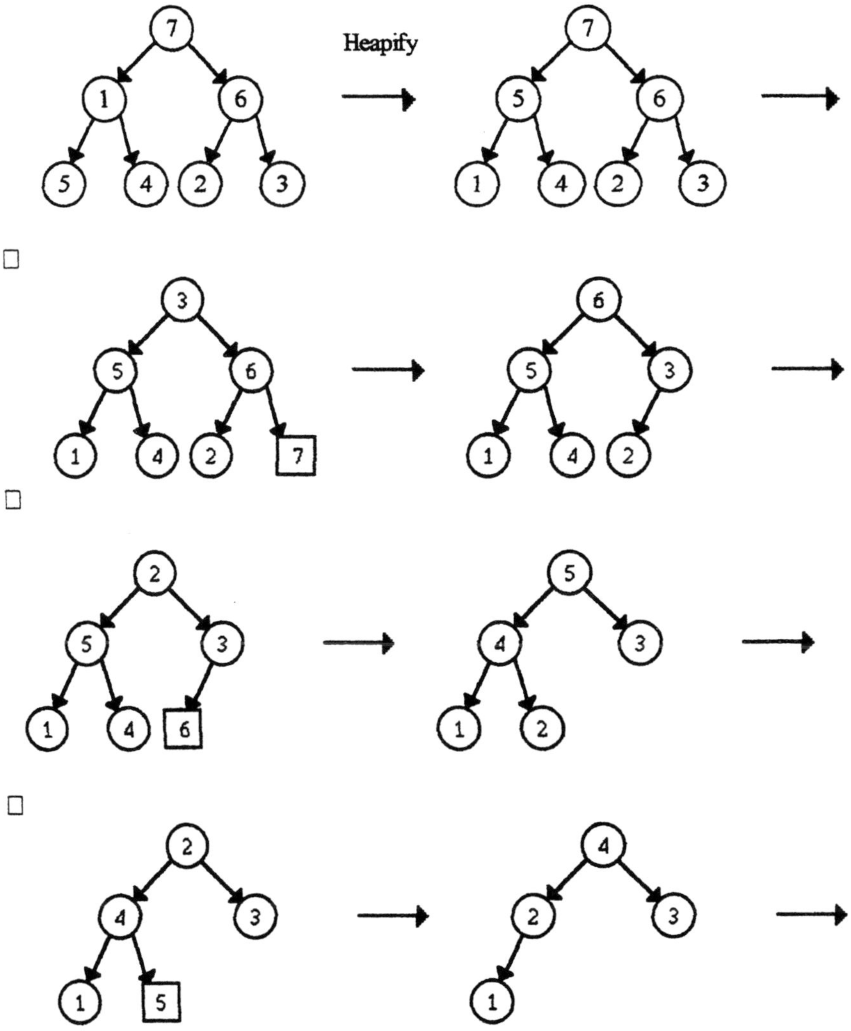

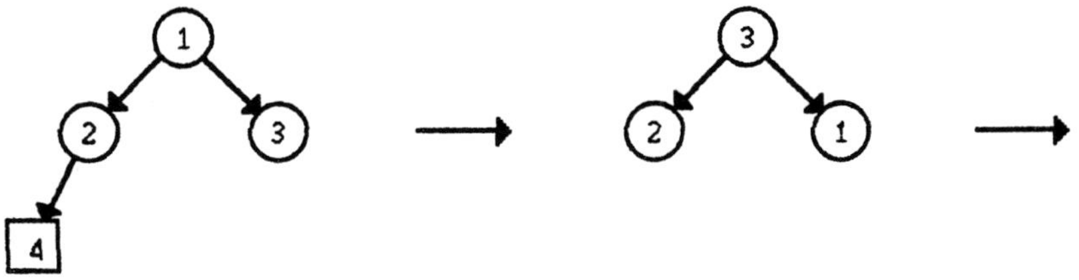

□

□

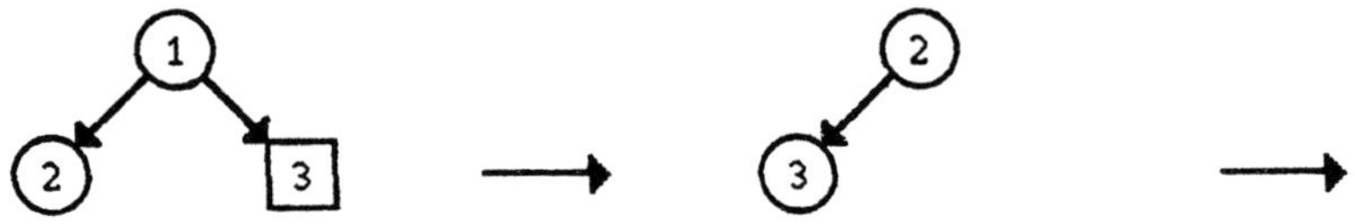

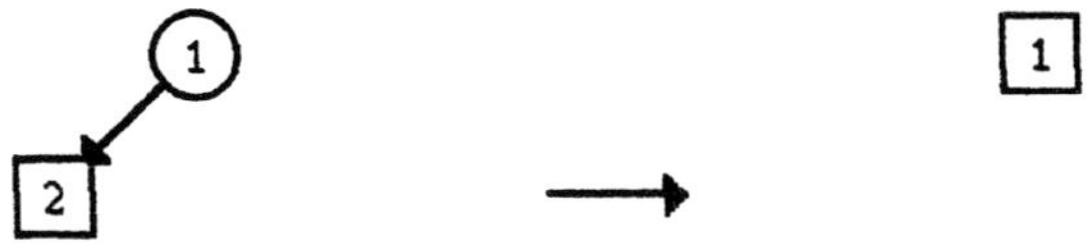

□

□

5.

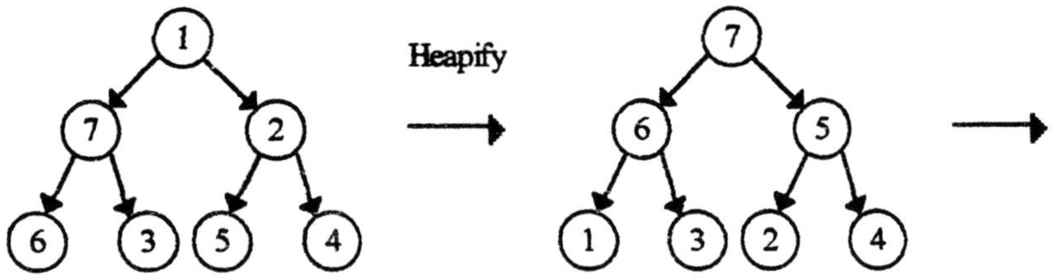

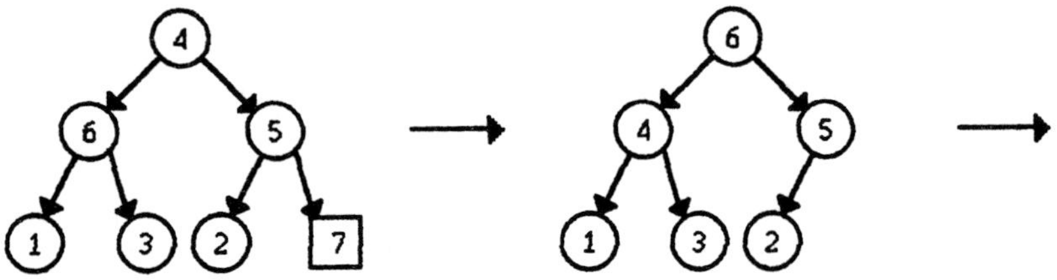

□

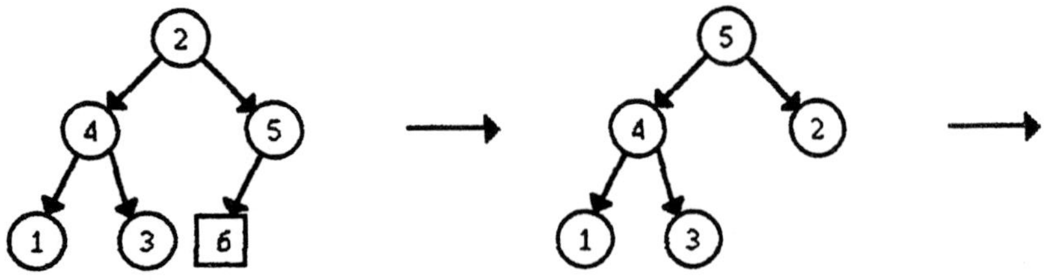

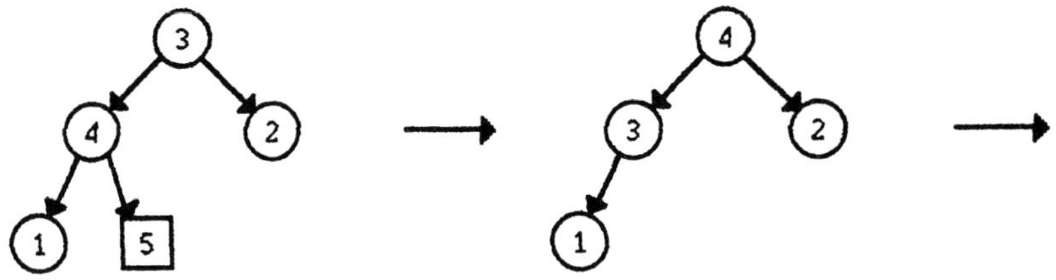

□

□

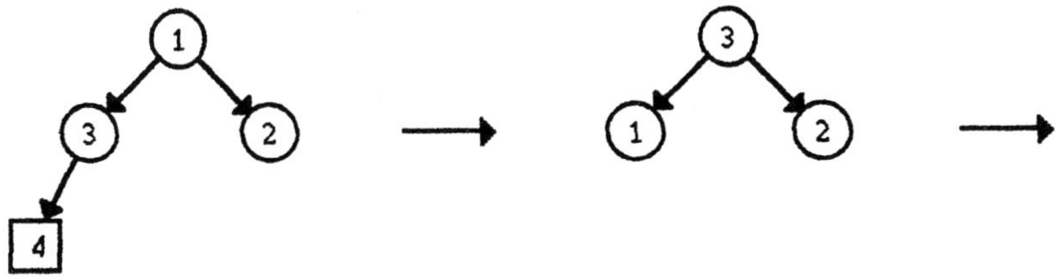

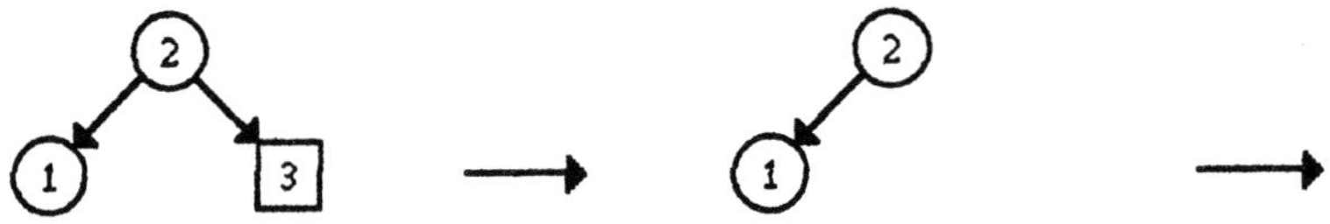

□

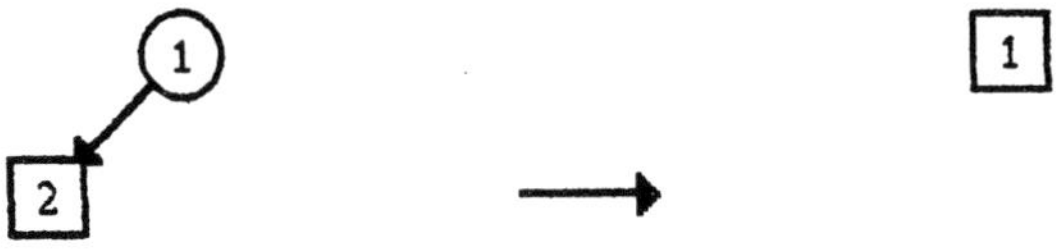

6.

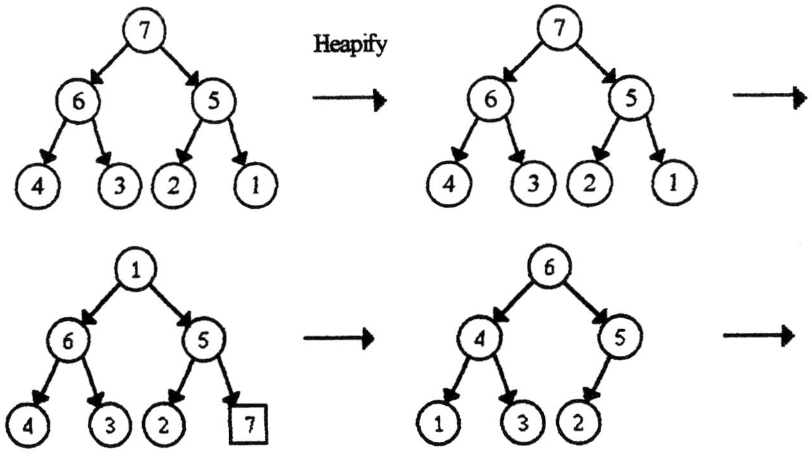

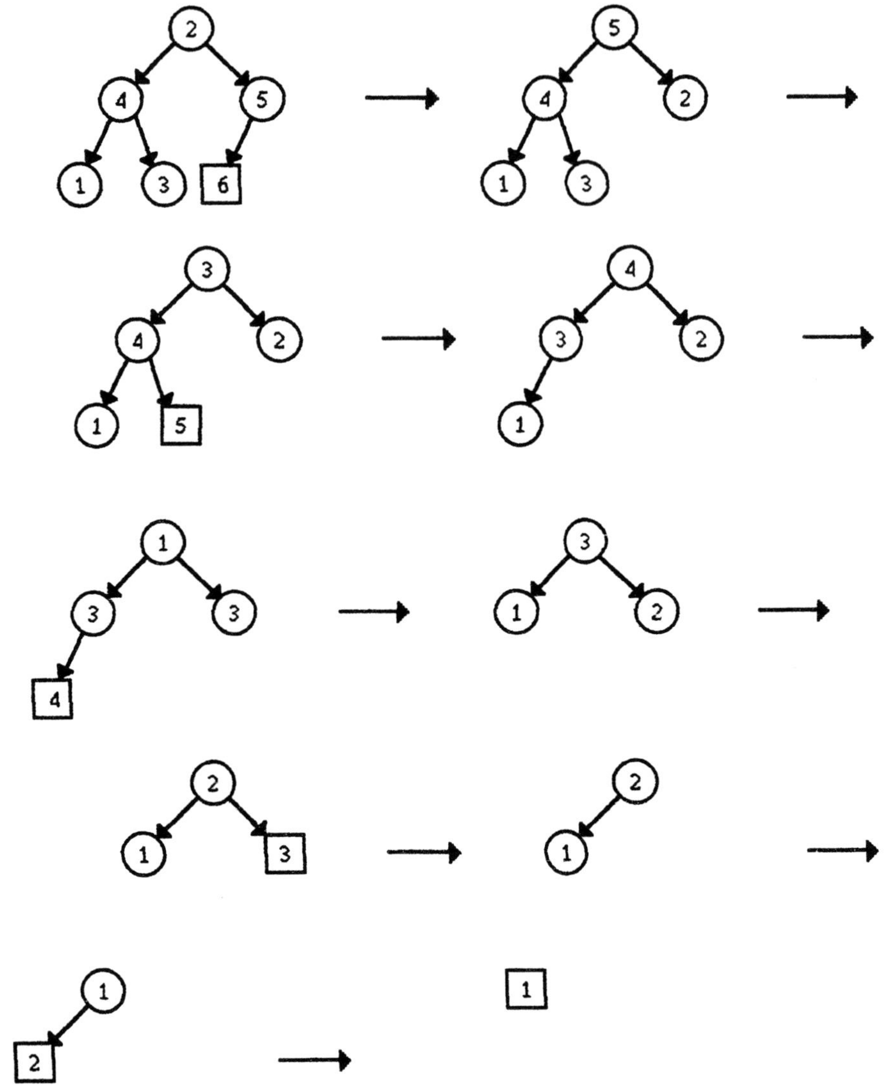

7.

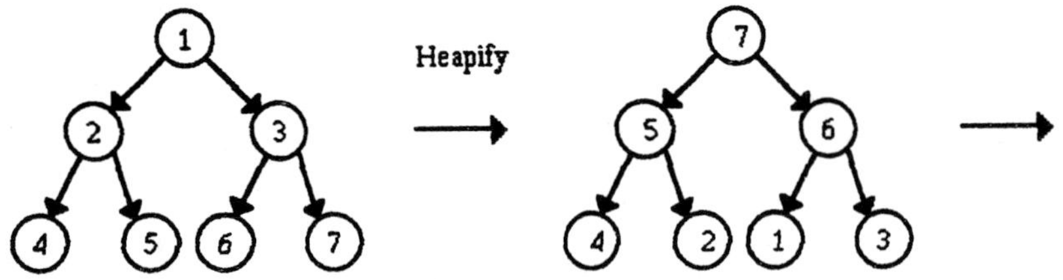

12. /* PercolateDown() */

```
template <typename ElementType>
void PercolateDown(ElementType x[], int n, int r)
{
  int c = 2*r;
  bool done = false;

  while (c < n && !done)
  {
        if (c < n && x[c] < x[c+1] )
              c++;

        if (x[r] < x[c])
        {
              ElementType temp = x[r];
              x[r] = x[c];
              x[c] = temp;
              r = c;
              c = 2*c;
        }
        else
              done = true;
  }
  return;
}
```

13. /* Heapify() */

```
template <typename ElementType>
void Heapify(ElementType x[], int n)
{
  for (int r = n/2; r > 0; r--)
        PercolateDown(x, n, r);

  return;
}
```

14. /* HeapSort() */

```
template <typename ElementType>
void HeapSort(ElementType x[], int n)
{
   Heapify(x,n);

   for (int index = n; index > 0; index--)
   {
         ElementType temp = x[1];
         x[1] = x[index];
         x[index] = temp;

         PercolateDown(x,n, index-1);
   }
   return;
}
```

15. /* Insert: Complexity O(nlogn) */

```
template <typename ElementType>
void Insert(ElementType x[], int& n, ElementType item)
{
   n++;
x[n] = item;
   Heapify(x, n);
   return;
}
```

16. /* Delete: Complexity O(nlogn) */

```
template <typename ElementType>
void Delete(ElementType x[], int& n, int remove)
{
x[remove] = x[n];
n--;
   Heapify(x, n);
   return;
}
```

17. /*HeapSearch() */
```
template <typename ElementType>
bool HeapSearch(ElementType x[], int n, int root, ElementType item)
{
   if (item == x[root])
        return true;
   else if (item > x[root])
        return false;
   else
   {
        bool found = HeapSearch(x, n, 2*root, item);
        if (!found)
             return HeapSearch(x, n, 2*root + 1, item);
        else
             return true;
   }
}
```

18. A queue is a specialized case of a priority queue because it adds items to the back of the queue unconditionally. Hence, it is as if one was always adding an item of lowest priority. All other functionality remains the same.

A stack is a specialized case of a priority queue because items are always unconditionally added to the front of the queue. Hence, it is as if one was always adding an item of highest priority. All other functionality remains the same.

19. /* Any of the queue implementations (array with empty slot, array with counter, linked list) can be modified for a priority queue. Here, as directed, we modify the first approach.
*/

```
#include <iostream>
using namespace std;

<template ElementType>
class PriorityQ
{
   public:
        PriorityQ();
        PriorityQ(int);

        void addQ(ElementType);
        ElementType front();
        void removeQ();
        bool empty();
        bool full();
        ElementType back();
        int size();
```

```
   private:
        const int       PRIORITYQ_CAPACITY = some_value;
        ElementType     myArray[PRIORITYQ_CAPACITY];
        int myFront;
        int myBack;
};


<template ElementType>
PriorityQ<ElementType>::PriorityQ()
{
   myFront = 0;
   myBack = 0;
}

<template ElementType>
bool PriorityQ<ElementType>::empty()
{
   return myFront == myBack;
}


<template ElementType>
void PriorityQ<ElementType>::addQ(ElementType item)
{
   if ((myBack +1)% PRIORITYQ_CAPACITY == myFront)
        cerr << "PriorityQ is full: cannot add to PriorityQ.
             Error!! " << endl;
   else
   {
        int size = myBack > myFront ? myBack - myFront:
                                      myFront - myBack;
        // must shift elements, yuck!, to insert
        int index = 0;
        int where, whereTo;
        bool lessthan = myArray[back].Priority() < item.Prority();
        while (index < size && lessthan)
        {
             whereTo = (myBack+index)%PRIORITYQ_CAPACITY;
             where = (myBack+index-1)%PRIORITYQ_CAPACITY;
             myArray[whereTo] = myArray[where];
             index++;
             lessthan = myArray[where].Priority() < item.Prority();
        }
        myArray[where] = item;
        myBack = (myBack+ 1) % PRIORITYQ_CAPACITY;
   }
   return;
}
```

```
<template ElementType>
ElementType PriorityQ<ElementType>::front()
{
   if (myFront == myBack)
   {
        cerr <<"PriorityQ is empty: cannot remove from PriorityQ.
                  Error!!" << endl;
        return string::npos;          // should be invalid data item;
   }
   else
        return myArray[myFront];
}

<template ElementType>
void PriorityQ<ElementType>::removeQ()
{
   if (myFront == myBack)
        cerr <<"PriorityQ is empty: cannot remove from PriorityQ.
                  Error!!" << endl;
   else
        myFront = (myFront+ 1) % PRIORITYQ_CAPACITY;
}

<template ElementType>
bool PriorityQ<ElementType>::full()
{
   return myFront == (myBack + 1)% PRIORITYQ_CAPACITY;
}

<template ElementType>
int PriorityQ<ElementType>::size()
{
   if (myFront == myBack)
        return 0;
   if (myFront > myBack)
        return myBack - myFront + PRIORITYQ_CAPACITY;
   return myBack - myFront;
}

<template ElementType>
ElementType PriorityQ<ElementType>::back()      //non-destructive
{
   int index_last;
   if (myBack == 0)
        index_last = PRIORITYQ_CAPACITY;
   else
        index_last = myBack-1;
   return myArray[index_last];
}
```

20.
```
/* Priority queue implementation with one queue (fixed-sized array)
   for each priority.  Note that a two-dimensional array can be used
   to store the data.  Now, insertion and deletion from the queue must
   look at the priority of the item in order to locate the correct row
   of the matrix. Also, empty(), full(), etc., are associated with a
   particular priority queue. We assume that p, the number of
   priorities is fixed, and that these priorities are numbered from 0.
   */

#include <iostream>
using namespace std;

<template ElementType>
class PriorityQ
{
   public:
        PriorityQ();
        PriorityQ(int);

        void addq(ElementType);
        ElementType front();
        void removeq();

        bool empty(int);
        bool full(int);

        ElementType back(int);
        int size(int);

   private:
        const int      PRIORITYQ_CAPACITY = some_value;
        const int      p = some_value2;

        ElementType    myArray[p][PRIORITYQ_CAPACITY];

        int myFront[p];
        int myBack[p];
};


<template ElementType>
PriorityQ<ElementType>::PriorityQ()
{
   for (int index = 0; index < p; index++)
   {
        myFront[index] = 0;
        myBack[index] = 0;
   }
}
```

```
<template ElementType>
bool PriorityQ<ElementType>::empty(int q)
{
  return myFront[q] == myBack[q];
}


<template ElementType>
void PriorityQ<ElementType>::addQ(int item)
{
  int q = item.Priority();

  if ((myBack[q] +1)% PRIORITYQ_CAPACITY == myFront[q])
       cerr << "PriorityQ is full: cannot add to PriorityQ.
            Error!! " << endl;
  else
  {
       myArray[q][myBack[q]] = item;
       myBack[q] = (myBack[q] + 1) % PRIORITYQ_CAPACITY;
  }
  return;
}


<template ElementType>
ElementType PriorityQ<ElementType>::front()
{
  int q = item.Priority();
  if (myFront[q] == myBack[q])
       cerr <<"PriorityQ is empty: no item in front.
                 Error!!" << endl;
       return string::npos;          // should be invalid data item
  }
  else
       return myArray[q][myFront[q]];
}


<template ElementType>
ElementType PriorityQ<ElementType>::remove()
{
  int q = item.Priority();
  if (myFront[q] == myBack[q])
       cerr <<"PriorityQ is empty: cannot remove from PriorityQ.
                 Error!!" << endl;
  else
       myFront[q] = (myFront[q] + 1) % PRIORITYQ_CAPACITY;
  return;
}
```

```
<template ElementType>
bool PriorityQ<ElementType>::full(int q)
{
   return myFront[q] == (myBack[q] + 1)% PRIORITYQ_CAPACITY;
}


<template ElementType>
int PriorityQ<ElementType>::size(int q)
{
   if (myFront[q] == myBack[q])
        return 0;
   else if (myFront[q] > myBack[q])
        return myBack[q] - myFront[q] + PRIORITYQ_CAPACITY;
   else
        return myBack[q] - myFront[q];
}


<template ElementType>
ElementType PriorityQ<ElementType>::back(int q)      //non-destructive
{
   int index_last;
   if (myBack[q] == 0)
        index_last = PRIORITYQ_CAPACITY;
   else
        index_last = myBack[q]-1;

   return myArray[q][index_last];
}
```

21. /* Priority queue implementation with p+1 pointers (indices into the data array) tracking the boundaries between the prioritized items.

    This implementation is very similar to the previous one. The key difference is one of visualization and boundaries. With p "prioritized" queues of equal length, one can think of the queue overall as a two-dimensional array, where the priority picks out the appropriate row of the matrix that corresponds to the queue for that priority. One still needs p front pointers and p back pointers to track where one is in an individual queue.

    With p queues of different length, one can think of the whole queue linearly. p+1 additional pointers are used to track the boundaries between the queues since one can no longer take advantage of a

```
     fixed-sized matrix (elements automatically delineated by rows in
     such structures) to do so.

     A design decision determines when the boundaries of the variable
     size queues will be determined.
     */

#include <iostream>
using namespace std;

<template ElementType>
class PriorityQ
{
   public:
        PriorityQ();
        PriorityQ(int);

        void addq(ElementType);
        ElementType removeq();

        bool empty(int);
        bool full(int);

        ElementType back(int);
        int size(int);

   private:
        const int      PRIORITYQ_CAPACITY = some_value;
        const int      p = some_value2;

        ElementType    myArray[PRIORITYQ_CAPACITY];

        int myFront[p];
        int myBack[p];

        int Qstart[p+1];
};


<template ElementType>
PriorityQ<ElementType>::PriorityQ()
{
   for (int index = 0; index < p; index++)
   {
        myFront[index] = 0;
        myBack[index] = 0;
        Qback[index] = 0;
   }
   Qback[p] = 0;
}
```

11.3 Exercises

1. The array elements are 10 20 40 30 45 80 60 70 50 90

The following diagram shows the sequence for trees for 2. Only the final trees of 3, 4 and 5 are given.

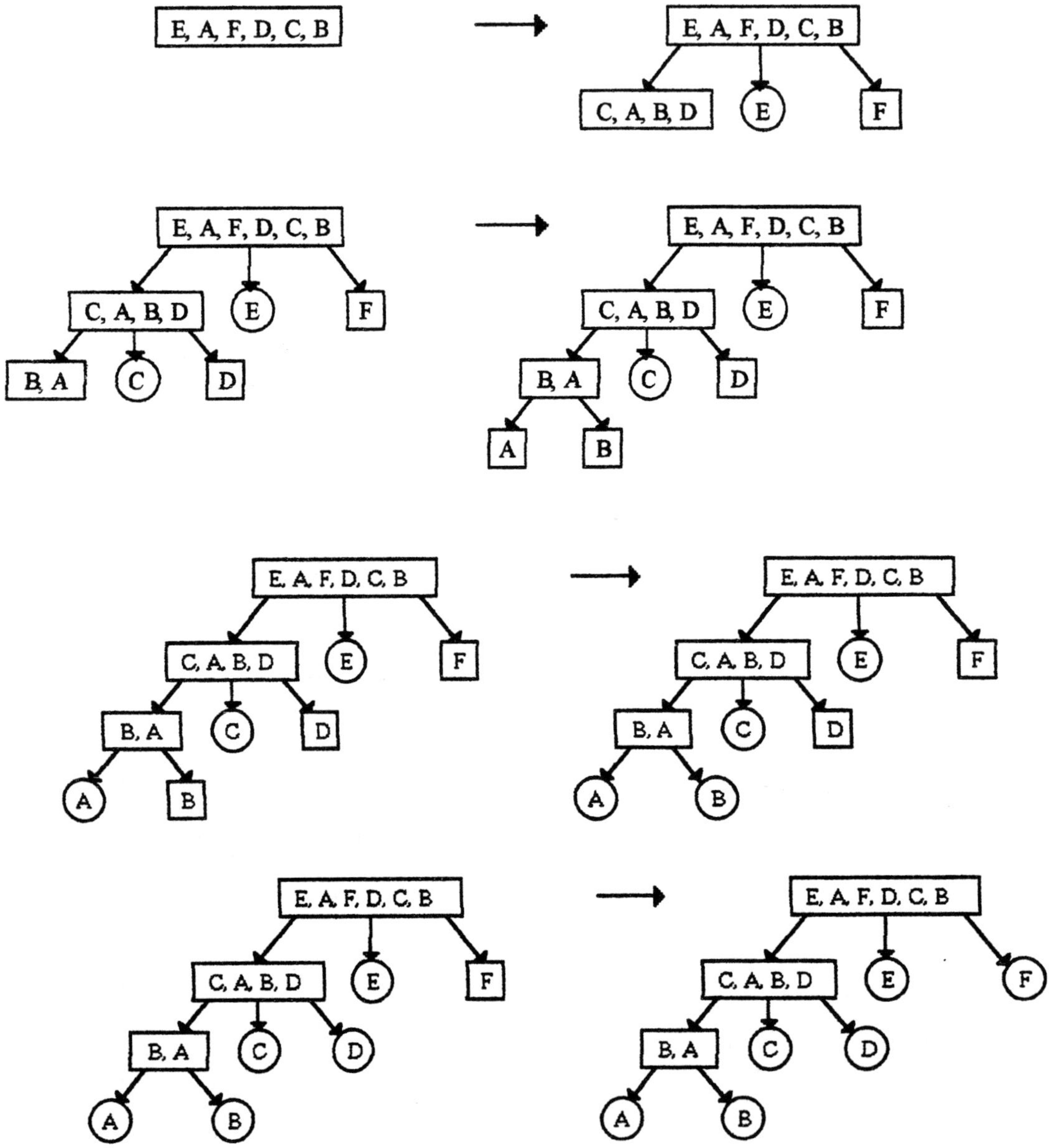

3.

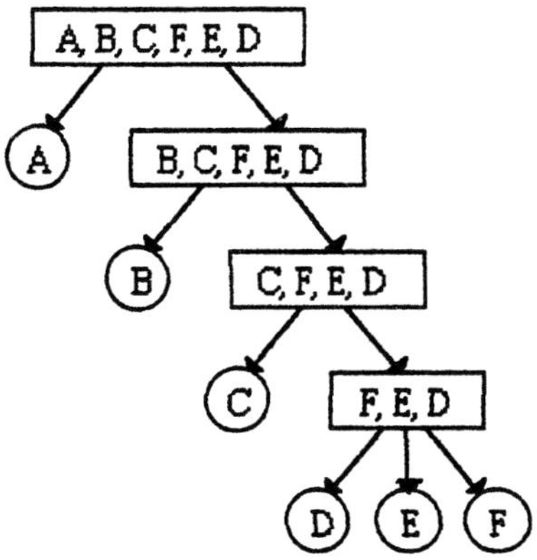
A, B, C, F, E, D
A
B, C, F, E, D
B
C, F, E, D
C
F, E, D
D
E
F

4.

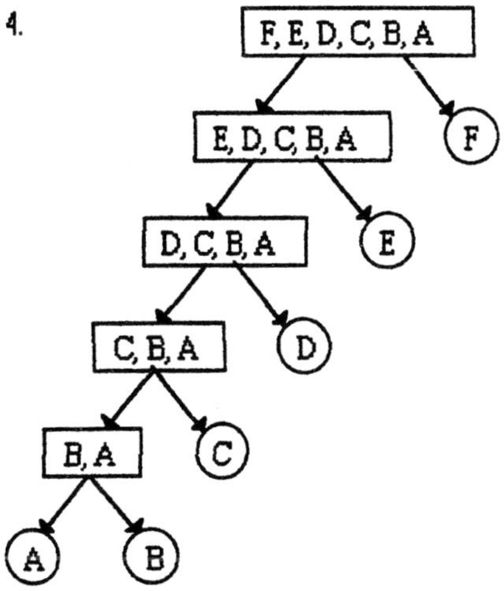
F, E, D, C, B, A
E, D, C, B, A
F
D, C, B, A
E
C, B, A
D
B, A
C
A
B

5.

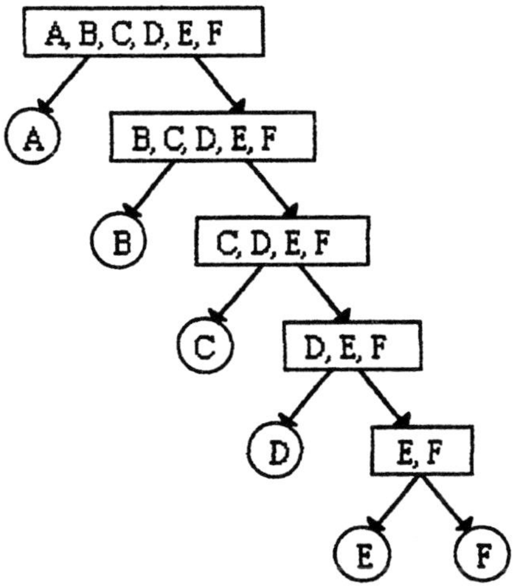
A, B, C, D, E, F
A
B, C, D, E, F
B
C, D, E, F
C
D, E, F
D
E, F
E
F

6. In #4, the compound boolean expression prevents the left pointer from going off the right end of the list.

7. /* modified Quicksort() */

```
template <typename ElementType>
void Quicksort(ElementType x[], int first, int last )
{
      int mid;
      if (first < last)
      {
            Split(x, first, last, mid);
            if ( (last - mid) < (mid - first) )
            {
                  Quicksort(x, mid+1, last);
                  Quicksort(x, first, mid-1);
            }
            else
            {
                  Quicksort(x, first, mid-1);
                  Quicksort(x, mid+1, last);
            }
      }
      return;
}
```

8. /* modified Quicksort() */

```
template <typename ElementType>
void Quicksort(ElementType x[], int first, int last )
{
      int mid;
      if (first < last)
      {
            Split(x, first, last, mid);
            if ( (mid - first) < LOWER_BOUND )
                  InsertionSort(x, first, mid-1);
            else
                  Quicksort(x, first, mid-1);

            if ( (last - mid) < LOWER_BOUND )
                  InsertionSort(x, mid+1, last);
            else
                  Quicksort(x, mid+1, last);
      }
      return;
   }
```

9. /* modified Quicksort() */

```
template <typename ElementType>
void Quicksort(ElementType x[], int first, int last)
{
     int mid;
     if (LOWER_BOUND < (last - first) )
     {
          Split(x, first, last, mid);
          Quicksort(x, first, mid-1);
          Quicksort(x, mid+1, last);
     }
     return;
  }
```

10. /* median of three to select pivot in Split() */

```
template <typename ElementType>
void Split(ElementType x[], int first, int last, int& mid)
{
        mid = (first + last) / 2;
        ElementType  item1 = x[first];
        ElementType  item2 = x[mid];
        ElementType  item3 = x[last];
        ElementType  pivot;

        if ( (( item2 < item1) && (item1 < item3))
                        || ((item3 < item1) && (item1 < item3)))
        {
                pivot = item1;
                mid = first;
        }
        else if  ( (( item1 < item2) && ( item2 < item3))
                        || ((item3 < item2) && (item2 < item1))
                pivot = item2;
        else
        {
                pivot = item3;
                mid = high;
        }

        int left = first;
        int right = last;

        while (first < last)
```

```
    {
            while (x[right] > pivot)
                    right--;
            while (left < right && x[left] <= pivot)
                    left++;
            if (left < right)
                    Swap(x[left], x[right]);
    }
    mid = right;
    x[first] = x[mid];
    x[mid] = pivot;

    return;
}
```

11. /* non-recursive Quicksort() Use a stack to store "recursive" calls*/

```
#include "StackT.h"             // stack template or could use STL
template <typename ElementType>
void Quicksort(ElementType x[], int first, int last)
{
        int mid;
        Stack<int>  S;

        S.push(first);
        S.push(last);

        while(!S.empty() )
        {
                last = S.top();
                S.pop();
                first = S.top();
                S.pop();
                if ( first < last)
                {
                        Split(x, first, last, mid);
                        S.push(last);
                        S.push(mid+1);
                        S.push(mid-1);
                        S.push(first);
                }
        }
        return;
}
```

12. /* Median */

```
template <typename ElementType>
int Median(ElementType x[], int first, int last)
{
        int mid = (first + last + 1) / 2;
        int pos;
        Split(x, first, last, pos);
        if (pos > mid)
                return Median(x, first, pos - 1);
        else if (pos < mid)
                return Median(x, pos+1, last);
        else
                return pos;
}
```

13. A simple modification of #12.
    Replace "int mid = (first + last + 1) / 2" with "int mid = k".

11.4 Exercises

1.

F [13 57 39 85 70 22 64 48]

F1 [13] [39] [70] [64]
F2 [57] [85] [22] [48]

F [13 57 39 85 22 70 48 64]

F1 [13 57] [22 70]
F2 [39 85] [48 64]

F [13 39 57 85 22 48 64 70]

F1 [13 39 57 85]
F2 [22 48 64 70]

F [13 22 39 48 57 64 70 85]

2.

F [13 57 39 85 99 70 22 48 64]

F1 [13] [39] [99] [22] [64]
F2 [57] [85] [70] [48]

F [13 57 39 85 70 99 22 48 64]

F1 [13 57] [70 99] [64]
F2 [39 85] [22 48]

F [13 39 57 85 22 48 70 99 64]

F1 [13 39 57 85] [64]
F2 [22 48 70 99]

F [13 22 39 48 57 70 85 99 64]

F1 [13 22 39 48 57 70 85 99]
F2 [64]

F [13 22 39 48 57 64 70 85 99]

3.

F [13 22 57 99 39 64 57 48 70]

F1 [13] [57] [39] [57] [70]
F2 [22] [99] [64] [48]

F [13 22 57 99 39 64 48 57 70]

F1 [13 22] [39 64] [70]
F2 [57 99] [48 57]

F [13 22 57 99 39 48 57 64 70]

F1 [13 22 57 99] [70]
F2 [39 48 57 64]

F [13 22 39 48 57 57 64 99 70]

F1 [13 22 39 48 57 57 64 99]
F2 [70]

F [13 22 39 48 57 57 64 70 99]

4.

F [13 22 39 48 57 64 70 85]

F1 [13] [39] [57] [70]
F2 [22] [48] [64] [85]

F [13 22 39 48 57 64 70 85]

F1 [13 22] [57 64]
F2 [39 48] [70 85]

F [13 22 39 48 57 64 70 85]

F1 [13 22 39 48]
F2 [57 64 70 85]

F [13 22 39 48 57 64 70 85]

5.

F [85 70 64 57 48 39 22 13]

F1 [85] [64] [48] [22]

F2 [70] [57] [39] [13]

F [70 85 57 64 39 48 13 22]

F1 [70 85] [39 48]

F2 [57 64] [13 22]

F [57 64 70 85 13 22 39 48]

F1 [57 64 70 85]

F2 [13 22 39 48]

F [13 22 39 48 57 64 70 85]

6.

F [13 57 39 85 70 22 64 48]

F1 [13 57] [70] [48]

F2 [39 85] [22 64]

F1 [13 57 70] [48]

F2 [39 85] [22 64]

F [13 39 57 70 85 22 48 64]

F1 [13 39 57 70 85]

F2 [22 48 64]

F [13 22 39 48 57 64 70 85]

7.

F [13 57 39 85 99 70 22 48 64]

F1 [13 57] [70]

F2 [39 85 99] [22 48 64]

F1 [13 57 70]

F2 [39 85 99] [22 48 64]

F [13 39 57 70 85 99 22 48 64]

F1 [13 39 57 70 85 99]

F2 [22 48 64]

F [13 22 39 48 57 64 70 85 99]

8.

F [13 22 57 99 39 64 57 48 70]

F1 [13 22 57 99] [57]

F2 [39 64] [48 70]

F [13 22 39 57 64 99 48 57 70]

F1 [13 22 39 57 64 99]

F2 [48 57 70]

F [13 22 39 48 57 57 64 70 99]

9.

F [13 22 39 48 57 64 70 85]

F1 [13 22 39 48 57 64 70 85]

F2

F [13 22 39 48 57 64 70 85]

10. This is the same as 5.

11. Selection sort is not stable. For example, given elements 5a, 5b, 3a, selection sort on the integer value will yield 3a, 5b, 5a, i.e. the relative order of the two5's has changed.

12. Bubblesort is stable.

13. Insertion sort is stable.

14. Heapsort is not stable. See the example from #11.

15. Quicksort is not stable. See the example from #11.

16. Binary Mergesort is not stable. Consider 5a, 5b, 1a, 6a, sorting on the integer values yields 1a, 5b, 5a, 4a, i.e. the relative order of the two 5's has changed.

17. Natural Mergesort is not stable. See example from #16.

18. /* Split(), Merge() & Mergesort() for files
Note the "end" of a subfile is when the next element is smaller than the current one in a file*/

```
#include <fstream>
using namespace std;


int Merge(fstream& outfile, fstream& infile1,
                                        fstream& infile2)
{
     int in1;
     int in2;

     int  numSubfiles = 0;
     bool inSub1 = true;
     bool inSub2 = true;
     int  oldone1, oldone2;

     while (infile1 >> in1  && infile2 >> in2)
     {
       while (inSub1 && inSub2)
```

```
    {
        if (in1 < in2)
        {
                outfile << in1;
                oldone1 = in1;
                infile1 >> in1;
                inSub1 = oldone1 < in1;
        }
        else
        {
                outfile << in2;
                oldone2 = in2;
                infile2 >> in2;
                inSub2 = oldone2 < in2;
        }
    }

    if (inSub2)
        while (inSub2)
        {
                outfile << in2;
                oldone2 = in2;
                infile2 >> in2;
                inSub2 = oldone2 < in2;
        }
    else
        while (inSub1)
        {
                outfile << in1;
                oldone1 = in1;
                infile1 >> in1;
                inSub1 = oldone1 < in1;
        }

    numSubfiles++;
}

if (in1)
        while (in1)
        {
                outfile << in1;
                oldone1 = in1;
                infile1 >> in1;
                if ( oldone1 < in1)
                        numSubfiles++;

        }
else
        while (in2)
```

```
            {
                  outfile << in2;
                  oldone2 = in2;
                  infile2 >> in2;
                  if ( oldone1 < in1)
                        numSubfiles++;
            }
      return numSubfiles++;
}


void Split(fstream& infile, fstream& outfile1,
                                    fstream& outfile2)
{
      bool inSub = true;
      int oldone;
      int value;

      while (infile >> value)
      {
            while (inSub)
            {
                  outfile1 << value;
                  oldone = value;
                  infile >> value;
                  inSub = oldone < value;
            }

            if (value)
            {
                  inSub = true;
                  while (inSub)
                  {
                        outfile2 << value;
                        oldone = value;
                        infile >> value;
                        inSub = oldone < value;
                  }
            }
      }
      return;
}


void Mergesort()
{
      string filename;
      cout << "Please enter the name of the input file F"
            << endl;
```

```
    cin >> filename;

    fstream infile(filename.c_str(), ios::in);
    while (!infile)
    {
         cout << "Error: unable to open file "
              << filename << endl;
         cout << "Please re-enter name"  << endl;
         cin >> filename;

         infile.open(filename.c_str(), ios::in);
    }
    infile.close();      // for consistency in while loop

    Tfilename1 = "hold1";
    fstream outfile1;


    Tfilename2 = "hold2";
    fstream outfile2;

    int subfiles = 2;
    while (subfiles > 1)
    {

         infile.open(filename.c_str(), ios::in);
         outfile1.open(Tfilename1.c_str(), ios::out);
         outfile2.open(Tfilename2.c_str(), ios::out);

         Split(infile, outfile1, outfile2);

         infile.close();
         outfile1.close();
         outfile2.close();

         infile.open(filename.c_str(), ios::out);
         outfile1.open(Tfilename1.c_str(), ios::in);
         outfile2.open(Tfilename2.c_str(), ios::in);

         subfiles = Merge(infile, outfile1, outfile2);

         infile.close();
         outfile1.close();
         outfile2.close();

    }
    return;
}
```

19. See #18, the process is essentially the same: the source of data has changed the external sort to an internal sort. Now, the *array limits* control the iteration rather than the EOF.

20. See #18, the process is essentially the same: the source of data has changed the external sort to an internal sort. Now the *end of the linked list* controls the iteration rather than the EOF.

21. We need to modify only Split()

```
void Split(fstream& infile, fstream& outfile1,
                                    fstream& outfile2)
{
    const int SIZE = some_value;

    bool inSub = true;
    int  oldone;
    int  value;
    int  InternalStore[SIZE];

    int filenum = 1;
    while (!infile.eof())
    {
        int count = 1;
        while (count <=size && infile >> value)
        {
            InternalStore[count] = value;
            count++;
        }

        Quicksort(InternalStore, 1, count-1);

        if (filenum ==1)
            for (int index = 1; index < count; index++)
                outfile1 << InternalStore[index];
        else
            for (int index = 1; index < count; index++)
                outfile1 << InternalStore[index];
        filenum = 3 - filenum;
    }
    return;
}
```

22. A three-way merge is similar to a two-way merge, except now the comparison is between three files and the smallest element of the three starts the copying of that subfile to the output file.

Programming Problems

1. - 6. These problems are all drivers for sorting routines. Hence one needs to construct unordered lists and then sort them.

   To compare effectiveness, at least three lists are needed:
   an ordered list (to insure it is not altered by a sort),
   a list in reverse order and
   a randomly unordered list.
   Sort each of the three and then verify that the sort worked correctly.

A driver for #1 follows. It is easily altered for the remaining problems by simply replacing the sorting algorithm invoked.

```
#include "SortFns.h"
#include <iostream>
#include <cstdlib>
using namespace std;

int main()
{
     const int MAXLGTH = some_value;

     int  order[MAXLGTH];
     int  reverse[MAXLGTH];
     int  random[MAXLGTH];

     int seed;

     cout << "Please enter the seed for the
          random number generator" << endl;
     cin >> seed;

     srand(seed);

     for (int index = 0; index < MAXLGTH; index++)
     {
          order[index] = index;
          reverse[index] = MAXLGTH - index;
          random[index] = rand();
     }

     selectionSort(ordered, MAXLGTH);
     bool sorted = true;
     for (int index = 0; index < MAXLGTH-1, index++)
          if (ordered[index] > ordered[index+1])
               sorted = false;
```

```
if (sorted)
     cout << "SelectionSort on ordered list OK "
          << endl;
else
     cout << "SelectionSort on ordered list NOT OK "
          << endl;


selectionSort(reverse, MAXLGTH);
sorted = true;
for (int index = 0; index < MAXLGTH-1, index++)
     if (reverse[index] > reverse[index+1])
          sorted = false;

if (sorted)
     cout << "SelectionSort on reversed list OK "
          << endl;
else
     cout << "SelectionSort on reversed list NOT OK "
           << endl;


selectionSort(random, MAXLGTH);
sorted = true;
for (int index = 0; index < MAXLGTH-1, index++)
     if (random[index] > random[index+1])
          sorted = false;
if (sorted)
     cout << "SelectionSort on random list OK "
          << endl;
else
     cout << "SelectionSort on random list NOT OK "
          << endl;

return 0;

}
```

7 & 8 Both of these programs involve essentially developing a user interface to read in data, storing the data in an array of structs or classes, overloading < and == for these structs/classes,and then sorting the array. It may be tedious but it is not difficult given that the sorting routines have already been written.

9. As in earlier chapters, one can use a system call like clock() to collect timing statistics before a sort call and immediately after a return from a sort call.

10 - 15. These problems are all drivers for heaps. 10 - 12 can be exercised in the construction of a heap. 13 - 15 can be exercised by making two identical heap objects, modifying one by insertion, then undoing the change by deletion and comparing the result to the unmodified original.

16 - 18. These drivers all test various implementations of a priority queue class template. To test a priority queue, one needs to add items of varying priorities to the queue and then insure that upon retrieval they are in order of highest to lowest priority.

The driver that follows can be used for each of the three.

```
#include "PriorityQT.h"
#include <iostream>
using namespace std;

int main()
{
     PriorityQ<int>      Q;

     for (int index = 0; index < Q.size(); index++)
          Q.addQ(index);

     //Q should be full here
     if (Q.full())
          cout << "OK, queue full"  << endl;

     bool reverse = true;
     int lastElem = Q.size() + 1;
     for (int index = 0; index < Q.size(); index++)
     {
          int item = Q.front();
          Q.remove();

          reverse = item < lastElem;
          lastElem = item;
     }
     if (reverse)
          cout << "OK, items ordered by priority" << endl;

     //Q should be empty here
     if (Q.empty())
          cout << "OK, queue empty"  << endl;
     return 0;
}
```

19. Like #7 & #8, this problem involves putting a user interface on top of data structure construction and modification.

Specifically, read in data, construct a heap, then process arbitrary insertions and deletions as received from the user.

Finally, apply heapsort to display the collected data in sorted fashion.

20. This problem is an extensive project involving priority queue construction and maintenance as well as the tracking of several statistical measures.

21. - 25. Like 1 - 6, these problems are all drivers for sorting routines; here, various versions of `Quicksort()` are functions targeted for exercise. Again, one needs to construct unordered lists and then sort them. To compare effectiveness, at least three lists are needed: an ordered lists (to insure it is not altered by a sort), a list in reverse order and a randomly unordered list. Sort each of the three and then verify that the sort worked correctly.

See the driver developed for #1

26 & 27. These drivers test functions written to find specific elements in unordered collections. A program covering the exercising of both functions follows.

```
#include "SelectFns.h"
#include <iostream>
#include <cstdlib>
using namespace std;

int main()
{
     const int MAXLGTH = some_value;

     int  order[MAXLGTH];
     int  reverse[MAXLGTH];
     int  random[MAXLGTH];
     int seed;

     cout << "Please enter the seed for the
                random number generator" << endl;
     cin >> seed;
```

```
    srand(seed);

    for (int index = 0; index < MAXLGTH; index++)
    {
         order[index] = index;
         reverse[index] = MAXLGTH - index;
         random[index] = rand();
    }
              // medians of first two should be the same
    cout << "The median of the ordered list is "
         << median(ordered, MAXLGTH) << endl;

    cout << "The median of the reversed list is "
         << median(reversed, MAXLGTH) << endl;

    cout << "The median of the random list is "
         << median(random, MAXLGTH) << endl;

    int k = 0;
    while (k < 1 || k > MAXLGTH)
    {
         cout << "Please enter the element you wish to find
               (1 for smallest, " << MAXLGTH
              << " for largest): " << endl;
         cin >> k;
    }
              // kth element of first two should be same
    cout << "The kth element of the ordered list is "
         << kth(ordered, MAXLGTH) << endl;

    cout << "The kth element of the reversed list is "
         << kth(reversed, MAXLGTH) << endl;

    cout << "The kth element of the random list is "
         << kth(random, MAXLGTH) << endl;
    return 0;
}
```

28 - 30. & 32. Like 1 - 6, these problems are all drivers for sorting routines; here, various versions of Mergesort() (and its auxiliary functions Split() and Merge()) are targeted for exercise. Again, one needs to construct unordered lists and then sort them. To compare effectiveness, at least three lists are needed: an ordered lists (to insure it is not altered by a sort), a list in reverse order and a randomly unordered list. Sort each of the three and then verify that the sort worked correctly.

See the driver developed for #1

31. Similar to #7 & #8 & #19, this problem involves putting a user interface on top of data structure construction and sorting. Specifically, read in and store data and then sort and display (for verification of the sort) the sorted results.

33 - 35. Note that a three-way merge is similar to the two-way merge, but the smallest element in the files is found and written to the final file, and then the next element in that file is read.

Like 1 - 6, these problems are all drivers for sorting routines; here, various versions of `TernaryMergesort()` are targeted for exercise. Again, one needs to construct unordered lists and then sort them. To compare effectiveness, at least three lists are needed: an ordered lists (to insure it is not altered by a sort), a list in reverse order and a randomly unordered list. Sort each of the three and then verify that the sort worked correctly.

See the driver developed for #1

36. As in #9, one can use a system call like clock() to collect timing statistics before a sort call and immediately after a return from a sort call.

37. See #31.

38. This programming project is a straight-forward application of mergesort. One needs to establish a method for determining a keyword.

Chapter Twelve: OOP and ADT

12.2 Exercises

1. One can view instances of a derived class as consisting of two components: the portion inherited (data members and functionality defined by the base class) and the portion explicitly declared in the derived class definition. Access to each component is governed by the declared accessibility in the class definitions as well as the method of inheritance.

Public inheritance allows instances of the derived class to access the public and protected members of its base class component. For example, object.publicBasefn() is a legal call. Moreover, these members retain their visibility for any descendants of the derived class. This form of inheritance provides the most accessibility to the base class component: only private members of the base class are not directly accessible in the derived class.

Protected inheritance allows instances of the derived class to access the public and protected members of its base class component only in a protected manner. So, object.publicBasefn() is NOT a legal call but within the derived class' method implementation, publicBasefn() would be a legal call. Also, any descendants of the derived class would also be able to use the inherited members internally. This form of inheritance allows the derived class to use the public and protected members of the base in an internal manner but not to open them up to the "world".

Private inheritance essentially prevents the derived class from accessing any members of the base class externally or from passing on access to these members to any descendants. It is not commonly used. An example use is when one wants to completely redefined the interface of the base class but wants to use that interface internally.

2.

Is-a relationships refer to relationships between two object when one is defined (even if only partially) by the other, i.e. inheritance. For example, a priority queue is-a queue. The relationship must be defined by innate characteristics or functionality NOT by implementation. For example, a stack may be implemented by an array but a stack is-a array is an invalid statement.

Has-a relationships refer to containment, when one object contains another. For example, an employee has-a address.

Uses-a relationships refer to interaction between objects not related by inheritance or composition. That is, when one object employs the functionality of another.

3. Rectangle has-a line

4. At first pass, one is tempted to say a Square is-a rectangle but this specific example is a hotly contested issue in OO circles. Why? Because the property of being a square rests on all sides being equal. If the rectangle class provides the capability of increasing the x or y dimensions of a rectangle then the derived class (inheriting this functionality) could alter one dimesion thus violating the all-sides-equal property. One prevents such a violation only by overriding the behavior. See Rumbaugh, Journal of OOP, 9/96.

5. No direct relationship (both could be descendants of Shape)

6. Student has-a GPA

7. Student uses-a library

8. Professor is-a employee

9. Employee is-a person

10. No direct relationship

11. Stack is-a deque (restricted (contracted) version)

12. Queue is-a deque (restricted (contracted) version)

13. Binary Search tree is a binary tree

14. vector is-a container

15. Computer is-a electronic equipment

16. Computer uses-a Operating Systems

17. No direct relationship

18. Computer has-a CPU

12.3 Exercises

1. class Administrator: public Employee

```
{
  public:
     void setSalary(double);
     void setBonus(double);
     double getSalary();
     double getBonus();
  private:
     double salary;
     double bonus;
};
```

2. class FactoryEmployee: public Employee

```
{
  public:
     void setSalary(double);
     void setUnits(int);
     double getSalary();
  private:
     double salary;
     int numUnits;
};
```

3. class SalesPerson: public Employee

```
{
  public:
     void setSalary(double);
     void setCommission(double);
     double getSalary();
     double getCommission();
  private:
     double salary;
     double Commission;
};
```

4.
```
template <typename ElementType>
class Scroll: public Stack<ElementType>
{
 public:
     void push_bottom(const ElementType&);
};
```

5.
```
template <typename ElementType>
class Deque: public Stack<ElementType>
{
 public:
     void push_bottom(const ElementType&);
     ElementType pop_bottom();
     ElementType bottom();
};
```

6.
```
template <typename ElementType>
class LookAheadStack: public Stack<ElementType>
{
 public:
     void push(const ElementType&);
};

template<typename ElementType>
void LookAheadStack<ElementType>::push(const ElementType& value)
{
     if ( value != top() )
            Stack<ElementType>::push(value);
}
```

Programming Problems

All programming problems here are essentially drivers. The characteristics of drivers programs remain the same: exercise the functionality (exhaustively) of the targeted function and/or data structures. When working with derived objects, it is critical to remember to test the two components of the derived object -- that inherited from the base class and that defined directly. In this manner, overriding, polymorphism, and consistency can all be tested.

The following driver can be used for #6 & #7. The remaining drivers are similar.

```
#include <iostream>
using namespace std;

int main
{
     Deque<int>     pal;

     cout << "please input your candidate palindrome
           string (numeric or alphabetic)" << endl;

     char symbol;
     while (cin >> symbol && !pal.full())
          pal.push_back(symbol);

     if (pal.full())
     {
          cout << "Your string was too long "  << endl;
          return 1;
     }

     bool yesPal = true;

     while (!pal.empty() && pal.size() > 1 && yesPal)
     {
          char compare = pal.pop_front();
          symbol = pal.pop_back();

          yesPal = compare == symbol;
     }
     if (yesPal && pal.size() <= 1)
          cout << "Your string is a palindrome!"
               << endl;
     else
          cout << "Sorry, your string is not a
               " palindrome"  << endl;
     return 0;
}
```

Chapter Thirteen: Trees

13.1 Exercises

1.

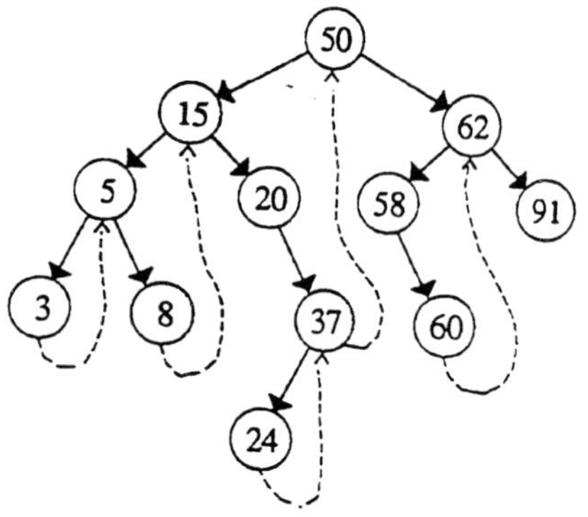

2.

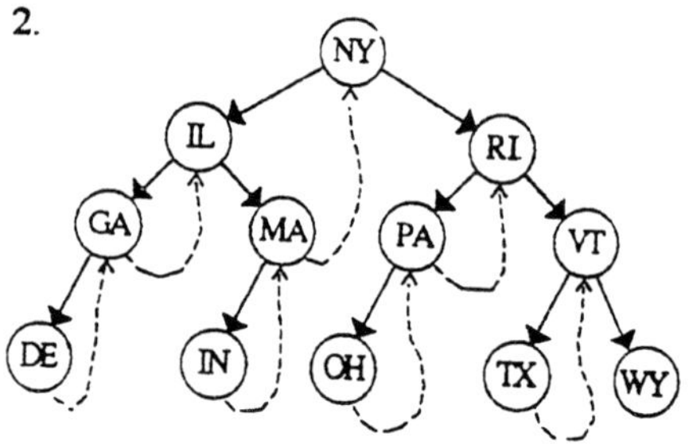

3.

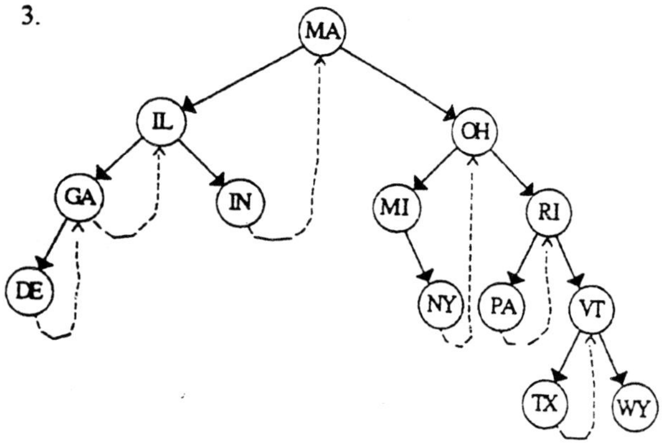

4.

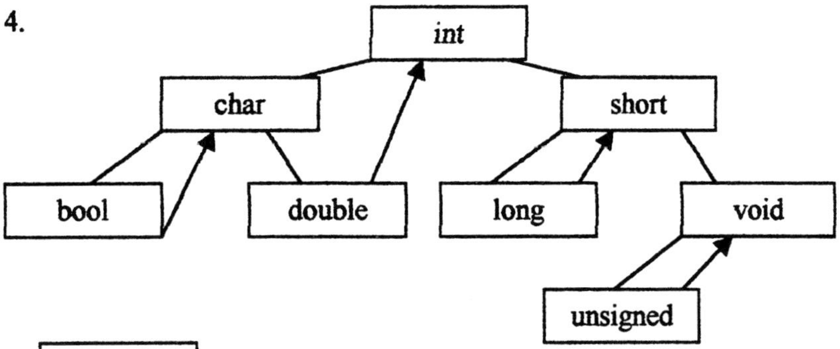
int
char
short
bool
double
long
void
unsigned

5.

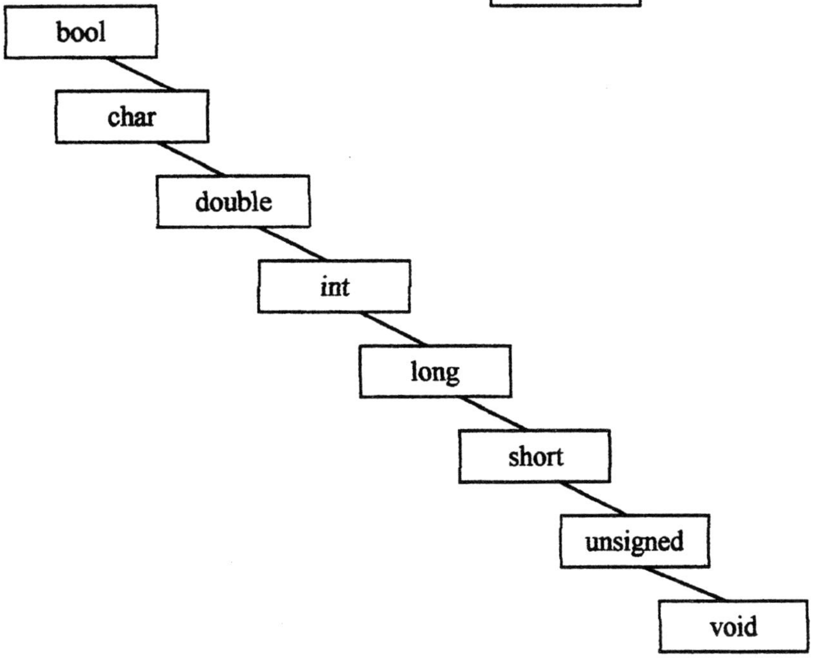
bool
char
double
int
long
short
unsigned
void

6.

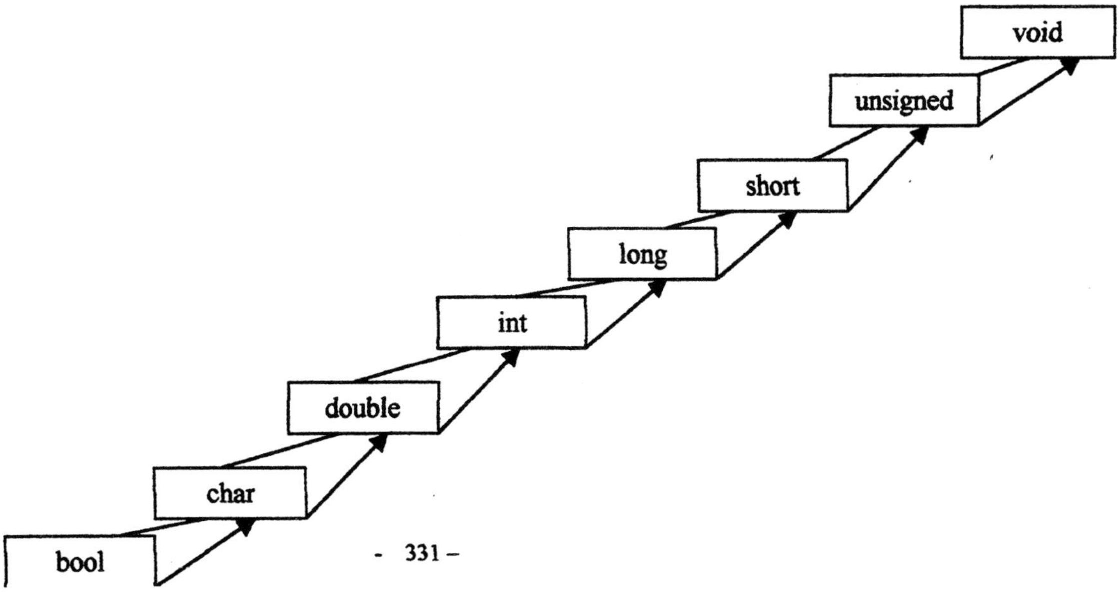
void
unsigned
short
long
int
double
char
bool

7.

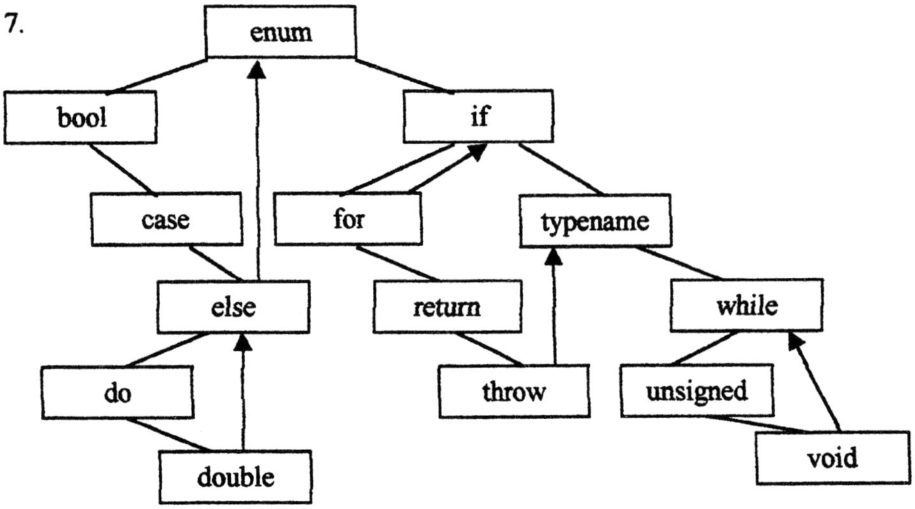

8. /* inorder for right-threaded BST
Note: recursion no longer needed
Output statement may be replaced by appropriate processing at node
*/

```
#include <iostream>
using namespace std;

void inOrder(Node* root)
{
   Node* ptr = root;

   while(ptr != 0)
   {
         while (ptr->left != 0)
               ptr = ptr->left;
         cout << "At node " << ptr->data << endl;

         // use bool field to distinguish between threads and links
         // see text
         while (ptr->right != 0 && ptr->rightThread)
         {
               ptr = ptr->right;
               cout << "At node " << ptr->data << endl;
         }

         ptr = ptr->right
   }
   return;
}
```

```
9. /* rightThreading a BST */

void Thread(Node* BST, Node* inOrderp)
{
   if (BST != 0)
   {
        Thread(BST->left, inOrderp);

        if (inOrderp != 0)
        {
             if (!inOrderp->right != 0)
             {
                  inOrderp->right = BST;
                  inOrderp->rightThread = true;
             }

             inOrderp = BST;
             Thread(BST->right);
        }
   }
   return;
}


void rightThread(Node* root)
{
   Node* pred = null;
   Thread(root, pred);
}
```

10. Algorithm for preorder traversal involves replacing the null right links of leaves with their preorder successors. The trick is realizing that the preorder successor of node A is the right child of the nearest ancestor (all ancestors are visited before a leaf) of A such that this ancestor's right child is not an ancestor of A. Thus, the algorithm reduces to:

   a) perform a preorder traversal.

   b) Whenever a leaf A is encountered (null left & right links)
      Replace the leaf's null right link with a link to its preorder successor.

11.

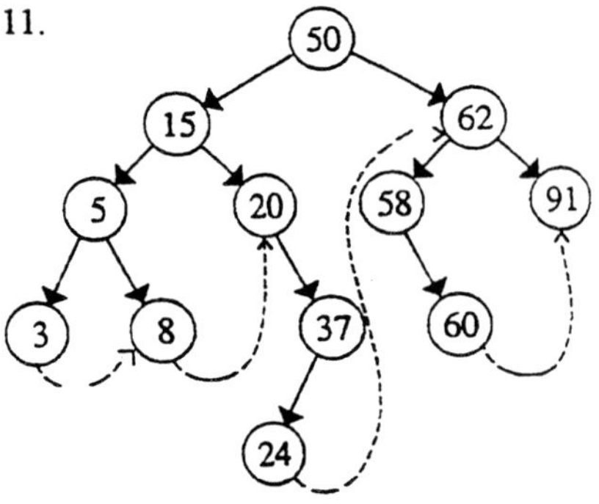
50
15
62
5
20
58
91
3
8
37
60
24

12.

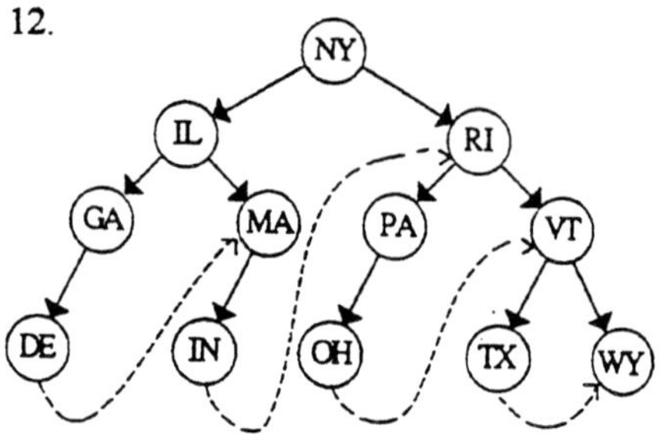
NY
IL
RI
GA
MA
PA
VT
DE
IN
OH
TX
WY

13.

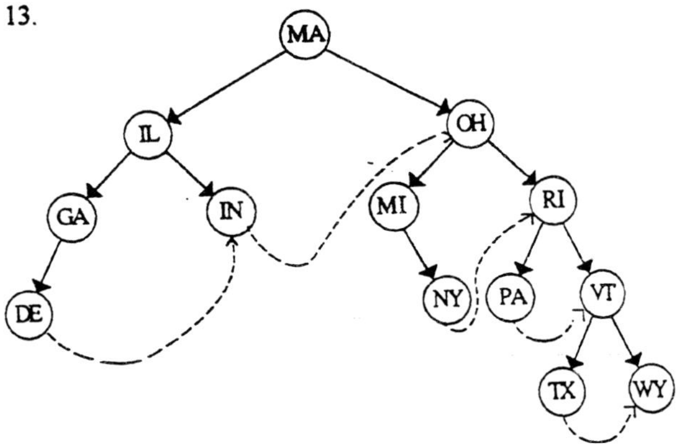
MA
IL
OH
GA
IN
MI
RI
DE
NY
PA
VT
TX
WY

14.

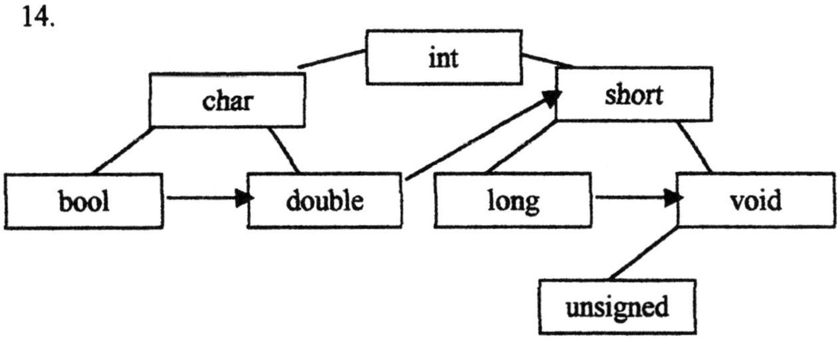

15. no rightThreads for preorder traversal. Tree is simply the underlying BST shown in #5 without any thread replacements.

16. Again, no rightThreads for preorder traversal. Tree is simply the underlying BST shown in #6 without any thread replacements.

17.

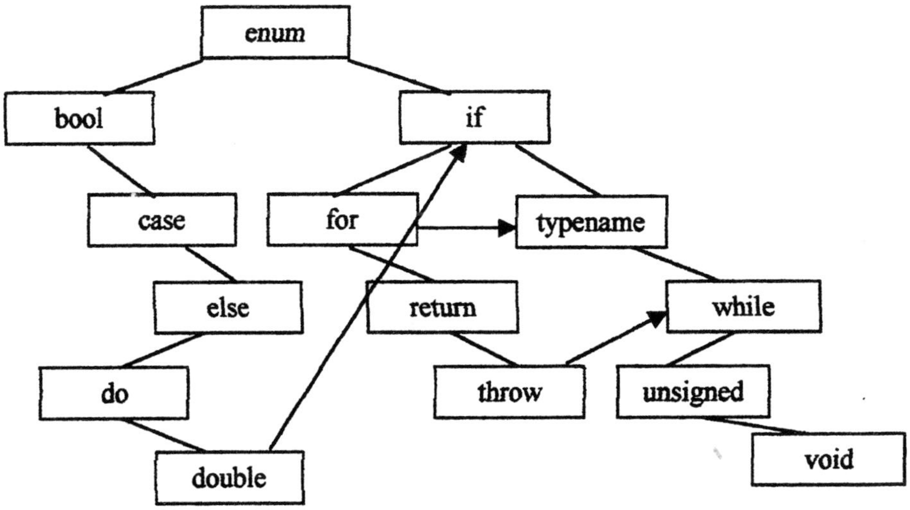

18. Algorithm to carry out a preorder traversal of a BST threaded as described in Exercise 10:

    1. Node* p = Root.

    2. bool done = (p == 0)

    3. While (!done)
        a. Visit the node pointed to by p.
        b. While (p->left != 0)
            i. p = p->left
            ii. Visit the node pointed to by p.
        c. If (p->right != 0)
            i. p = p->right
            ii. Visit the node pointed to by p.
           Else
              done = TRUE.

19. Algorithm to find preorder successor of node pointed to by p in an inorder-threaded BST. Assume p is non-null, i.e. points to a valid node.

```
If (p->left != 0 )
     PreOrdSucc = p->left
Else
     a. Node* q = p.
     b. While (q->right != 0 && q->rightThread)
              q = q->right
     c. PreOrdSucc = q->right
```

20. Algorithm to carry out a preorder traversal of an inorder-threaded BST.

    1. p = Root.

    2. While (p != 0)
        a. Visit the node pointed to by p.
        b. p = PreOrdSucc(p).

21. Algorithm to insert a node into a right-threaded BST:

```
1.  temp = new Node.
2.  temp->data = item
3.  temp->left = null
4.  temp->right = null, temp->rightThread = false

5.  If (BST == 0)       //tree empty
        BST = temp

6.  bool done = false;  root = BST.
7.  While (!done)
      If temp->data < root->data
        If (root->left == 0)
             (i)   root->left = temp;
             (ii)  temp->right = root;
             (iii) temp->rightThread = true;
             (iv)  done = true
        Else
             root = root->left
      Else if ( temp->data > root->data )
        If (root->right == 0)
             (i)   root->right = temp
             (ii)  temp->right = null
             (ii)  done = true.

        Else if ( root->rightThread)
             (i)   temp->right = root->right
             (ii)  temp->rightThread = true;
             (iii) root->right = temp
             (iv)  root->rightThread = false
             (v)   done = true
        Else
             Root = root->right
      Else display a message that item is already in the list.
```

22.

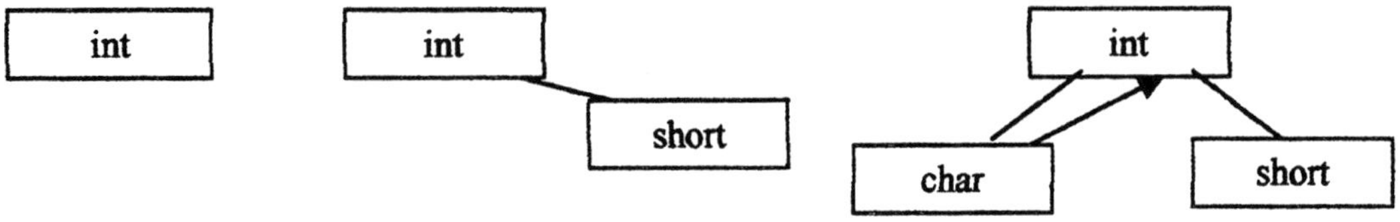
int
int
short
int
char
short

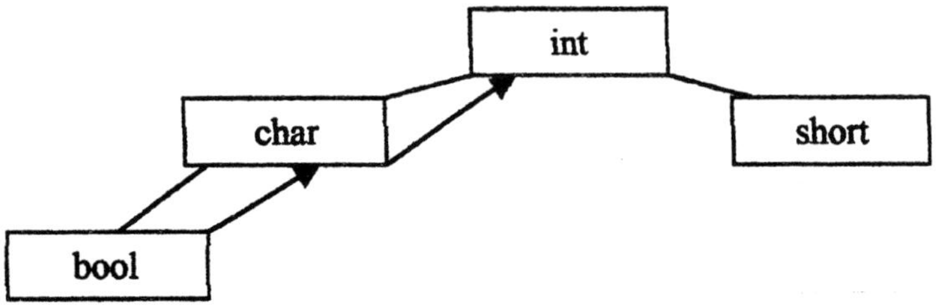
int
char
short
bool

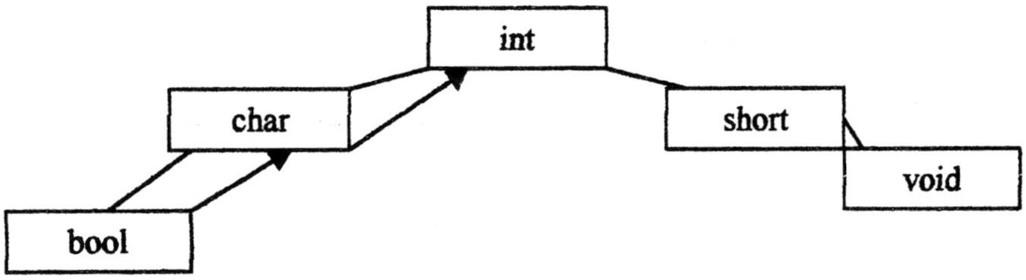
int
char
short
void
bool

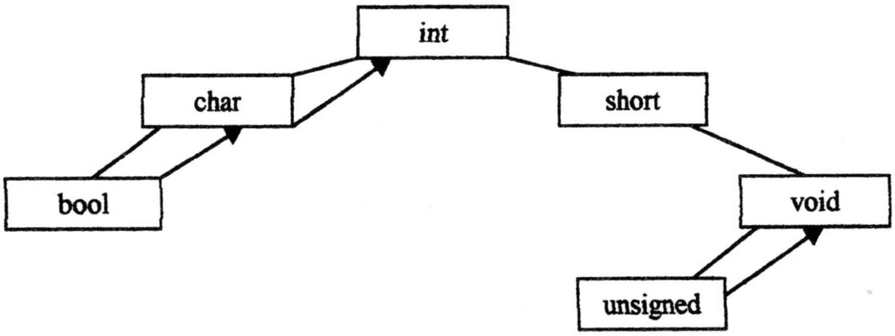
int
char
short
bool
void
unsigned

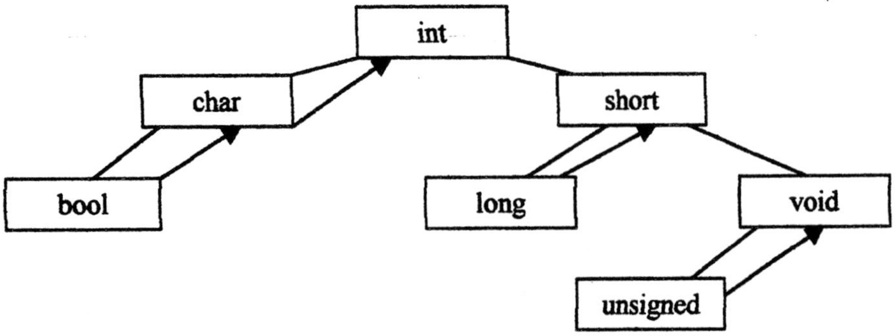
int
char
short
bool
long
void
unsigned

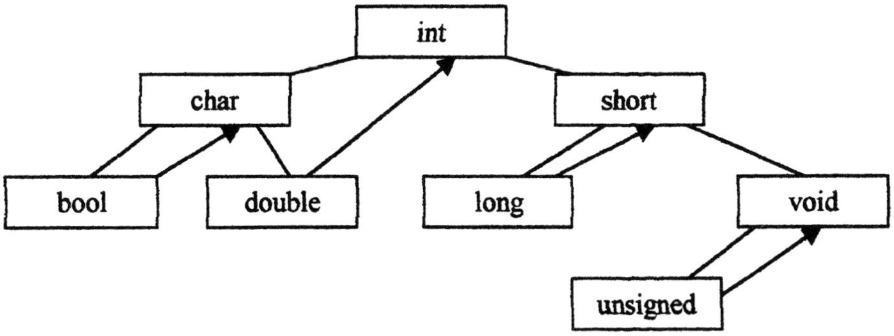

23. No rightThreads for in this traversal. Tree is simply the underlying BST shown in #6 without any thread replacements.

24. Two auxiliary algorithms are given first.

Algorithm to find inorder successor of a node p:

1. pSucc = p->right
2. If (!p->rightThread)
   While (pSucc->left != 0)
   pSucc = pSucc->left

Algorithm to find inorder predecessor of a node p

1. pPred = root.
2. pSucc = InorderSucc(pPred).
3. While pSucc != p
   a. pPred = pSucc
   b. pSucc = InorderSucc(pPred).

Algorithm to delete a node from a right-threaded BST, preserving right-threadness

1. BSTSearch(root, item, found, p, parent).

2. If (!found)
   Print an error message and stop execution.

3. Node* pSucc = InorderSucc(p).

4. If (p->right != 0 && p->left != 0 && !p->rightThread) // p has two children
   a. If (p->right == pSucc)
          parent = p
      Else
          i. parent = p->right
          ii. While (parent->left!= pSucc)
              Set parent = parent->left
   b. p->data = psucc->data
   c. temp = p
   d. p = pSucc
   e. pSucc = temp

5. Node* pPred = InorderPred(p).

6. If (pPred->right == p)
   pPred->right = pSucc.

7. Node* Subtree = p->left

8. If (Subtree == 0)
   Subtree = p->left

9. If (parent == 0)
       root = Subtree
   Else if (parent->left == p)
       parent->left = Subtree
   Else
       parent->right = Subtree
       parent->rightThread = p->rightThread

10. Delete node p.

25.

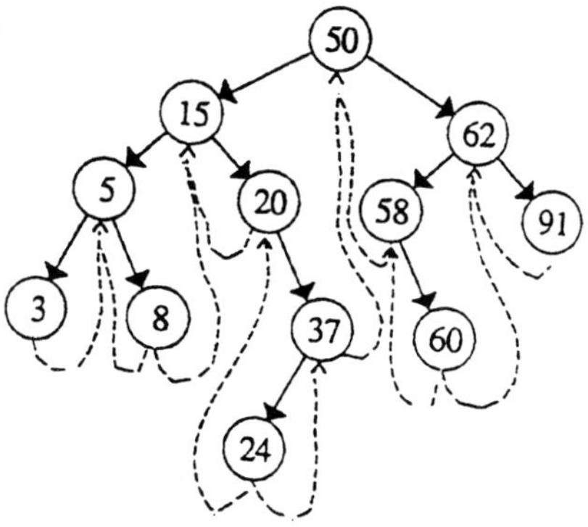
50
15
62
5
20
58
91
3
8
37
60
24

26.

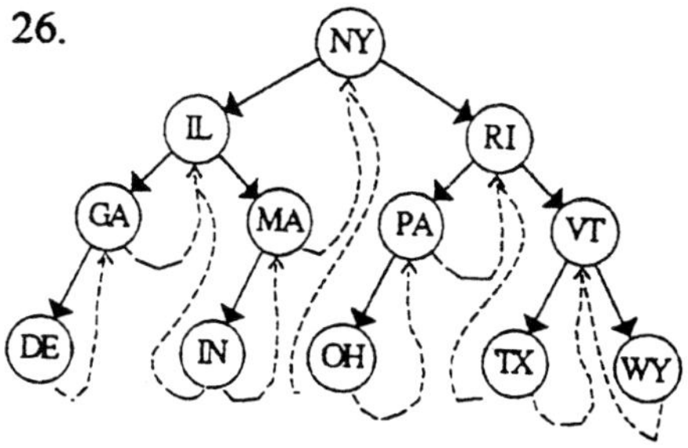
NY
IL
RI
GA
MA
PA
VT
DE
IN
OH
TX
WY

27.

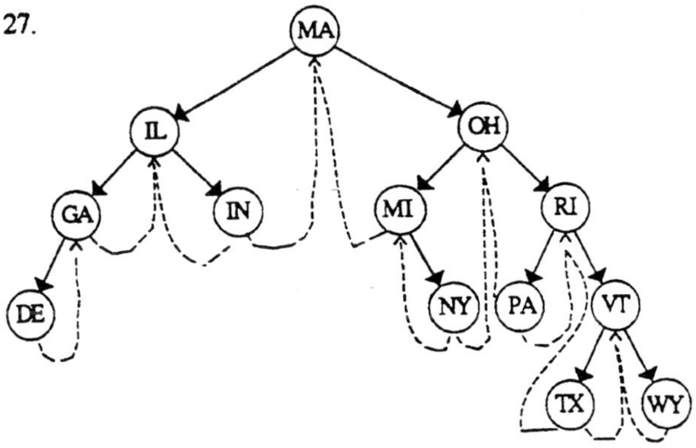
MA
IL
OH
GA
IN
MI
RI
DE
NY
PA
VT
TX
WY

28.

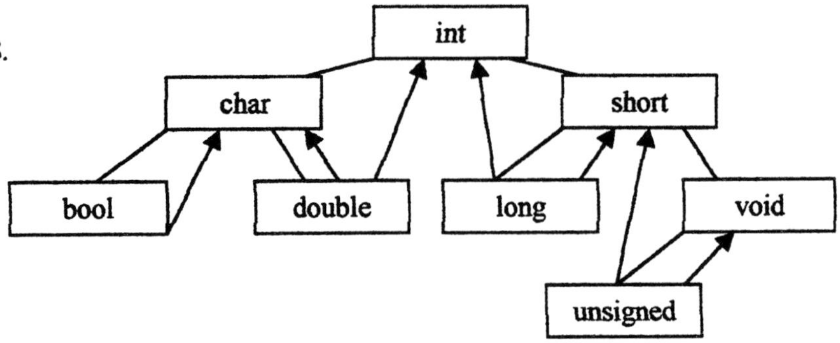

29.

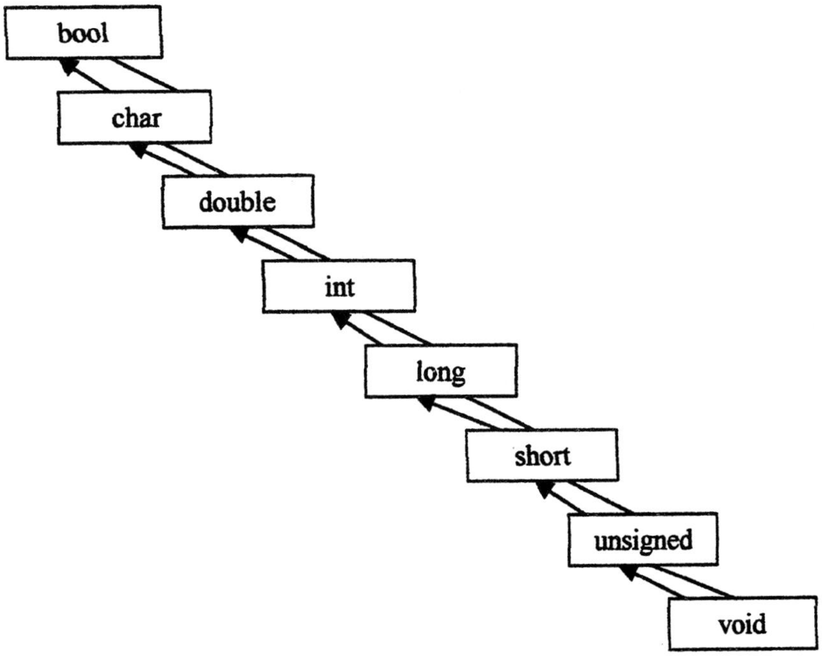

30. No null left links: fully threaded BST is same as right-threaded BST. See #6

31.

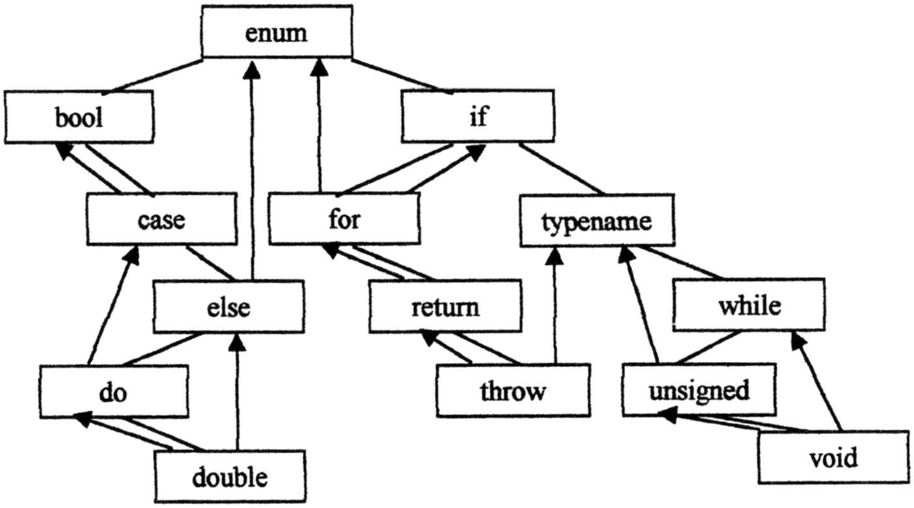

32. Algorithm to fully-thread a BST:

Perform an inorder traversal of the BST.

- When a node is visited, set Pred = the current node.
- Whenever a node x with a null right pointer is encountered, replace this right link with a thread to the inorder successor of x.
- Whenever a node x with a null left pointer is encountered, replace this left link with a thread to Pred.

33. Algorithm to insert a node into a fully threaded BST:

```
1.  Node* temp = new Node.
2.  temp->data = item
3.  temp->rightThread = false;
4.  temp->leftThread = false

5.  If (BST == 0)
        BST = temp
        temp->rightThread = false
        temp->leftThread = false

6.  done = false
7.  root = BST.

8.  While (!done)

        If (temp->data < root->data )
            If (root->left == 0)
                (i)   root->left = temp;
                (ii)  temp->right = root;

                (iii) temp->rightThread = true.

                (iv)  temp->left = null
                (v)   temp->leftThread = false

                (vi)  done = true

            Else if (root->leftThread)

                (i)   temp->left = root->left
                (ii)  temp->leftThread = true

                (iii) temp->rightThread = true;
                (iv)  temp->right = root.

                (v)   root->leftThread = false;
                (vi)  root->left = temp.

                (vii) done = true

            Else
                root = root->left

        Else if (temp->data > root->data)
```

If (!root->right != 0)

(i) root->right = temp;
(ii) temp->right = null

(iii) temp->left = null

(iv) temp->leftThread = true
(v) temp->left = root.

(vi) done = true

Else if root->rightThread then

(i) temp->right = root->right

(ii) temp->rightThread = true

(iii) root->right = temp
(iv) root->rightThread = false.

(iii) temp->leftThread = true
(iv) temp->left = Root.

(vi) done = true

Else
root = root->left

Else display a message that item is already in the list.

33. Algorithm to find parent of node n in a fully-threaded BST.

1. Node* ptr = n.

2. While (ptr != 0 && !ptr->leftThread)

   ptr = ptr->left

3. If (ptr != 0 && ptr->left->right == n)

   Parent = ptr->left

```
Else

  a. ptr = n.

  b. While (ptr  != 0  &&  !ptr->rightThread)

           ptr = ptr->right
  c. If (ptr == 0)
           Parent = null    // n is root node
     Else
          Parent = ptr->right
```

13.2 Exercises

1.

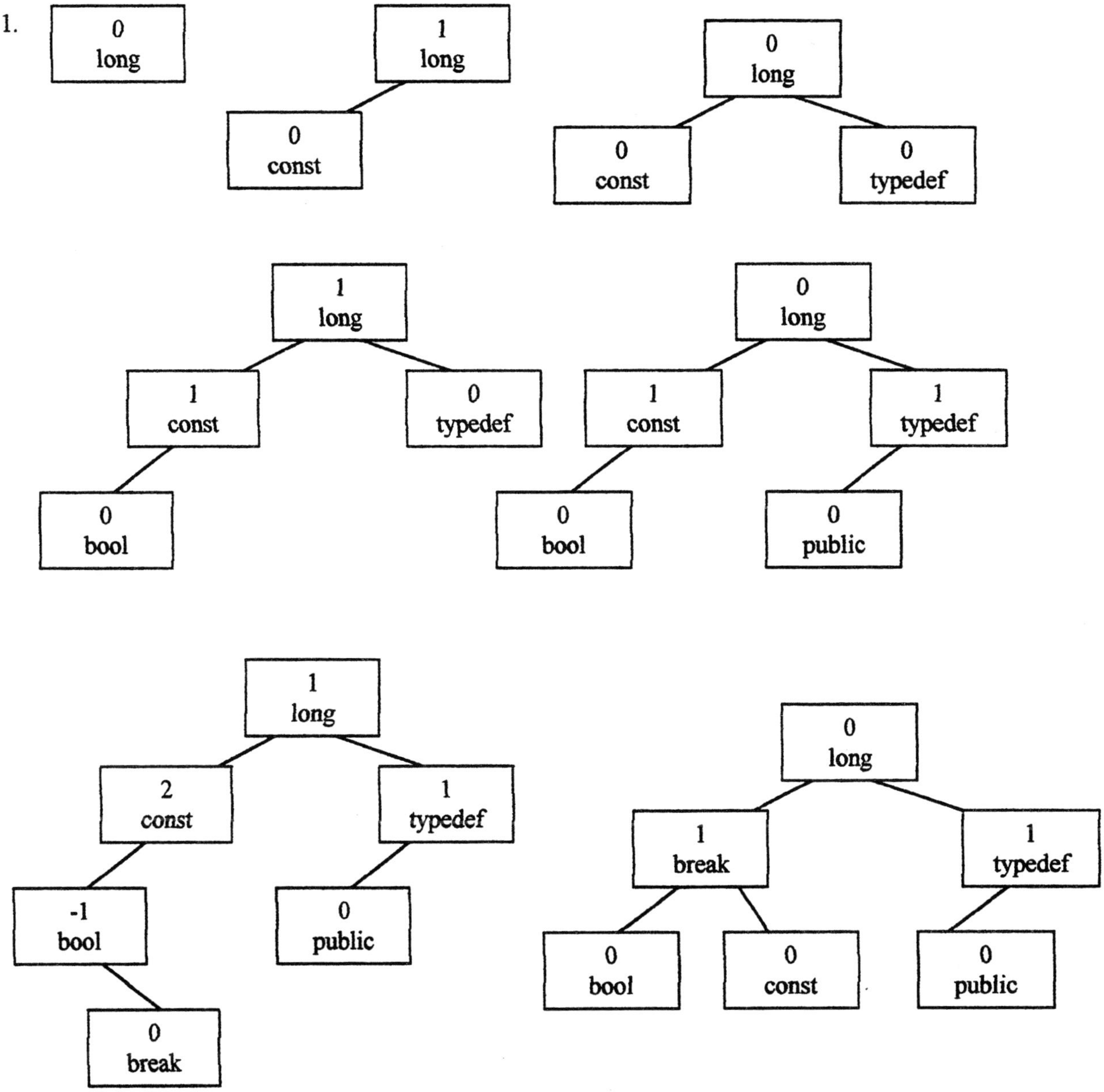

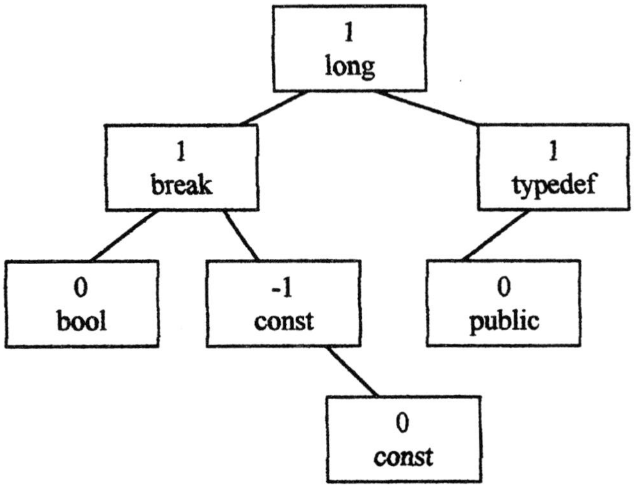
1
long
1
break
1
typedef
0
bool
-1
const
0
public
0
const

2.

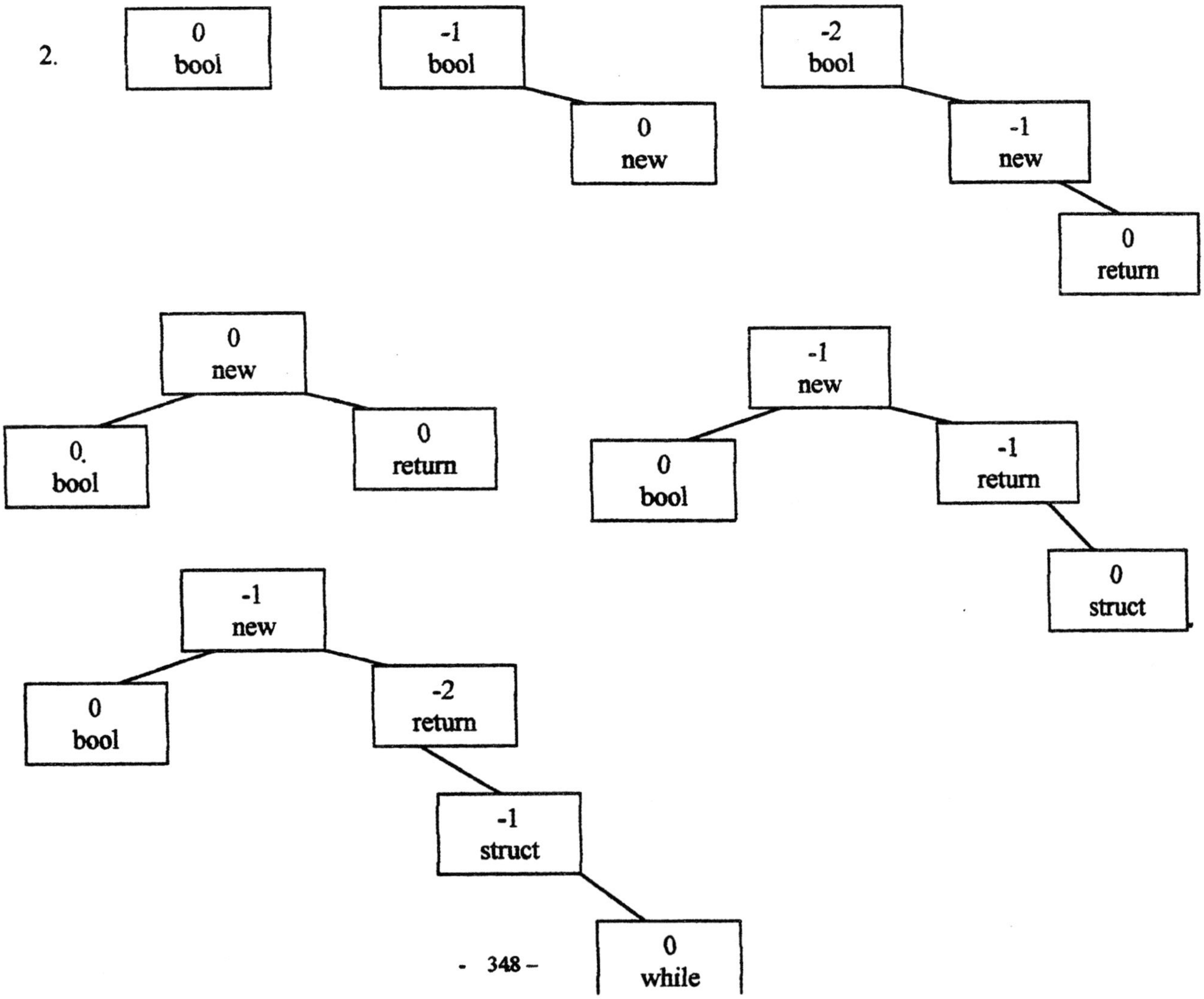
0
bool
-1
bool
0
new
-2
bool
-1
new
0
return
0
new
0
bool
0
return
-1
new
0
bool
-1
return
0
struct
-1
new
0
bool
-2
return
-1
struct
0
while

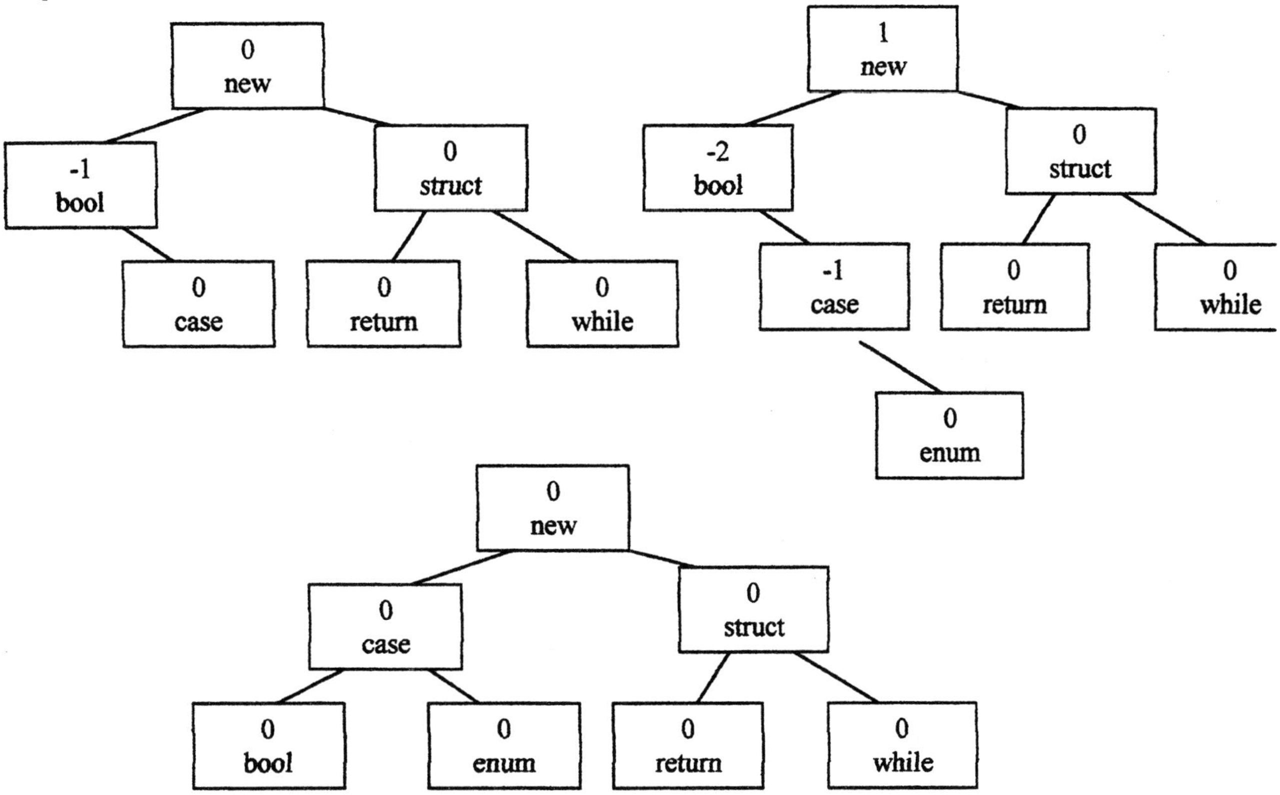
0
new
-1
bool
0
struct
0
case
0
return
0
while
1
new
-2
bool
0
struct
-1
case
0
return
0
while
0
enum
0
new
0
case
0
struct
0
bool
0
enum
0
return
0
while

3.

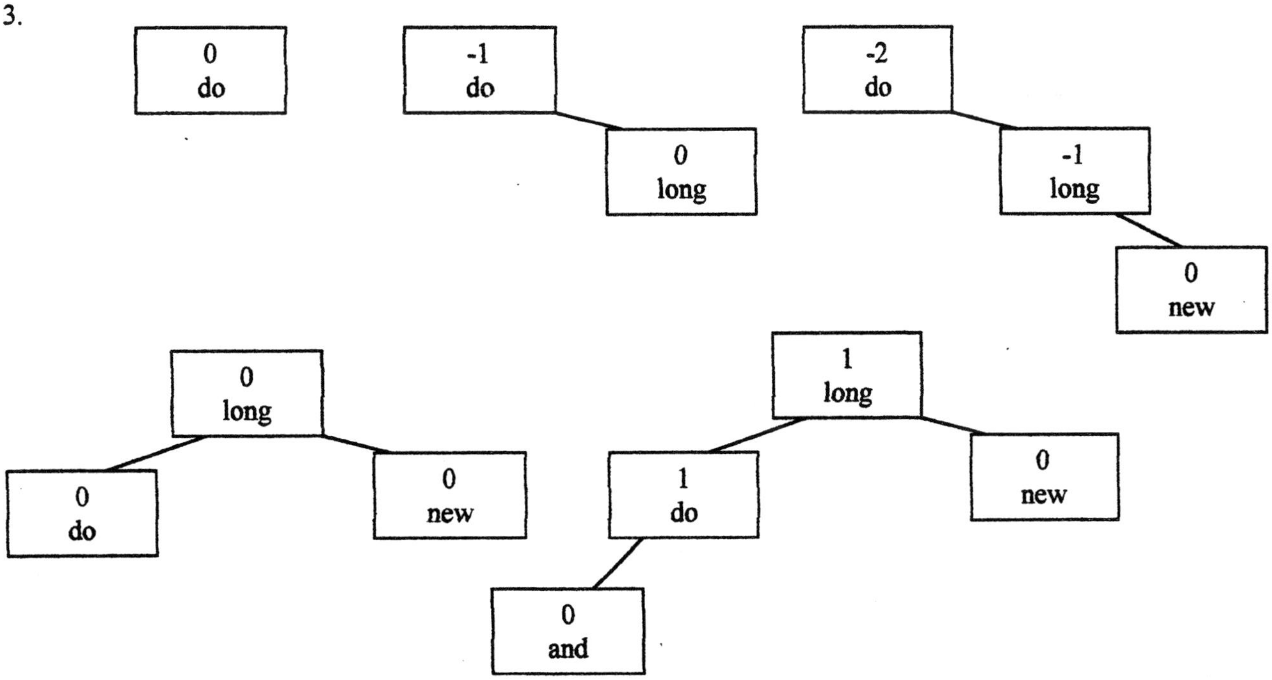
0
do
-1
do
0
long
-2
do
-1
long
0
new
0
long
0
do
0
new
1
long
1
do
0
new
0
and

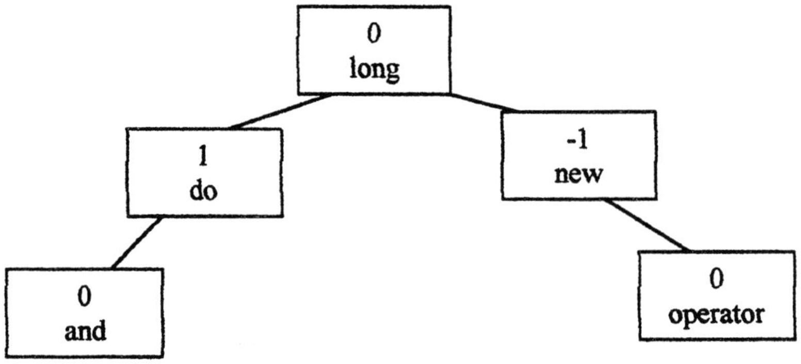
0
long
1
do
-1
new
0
and
0
operator

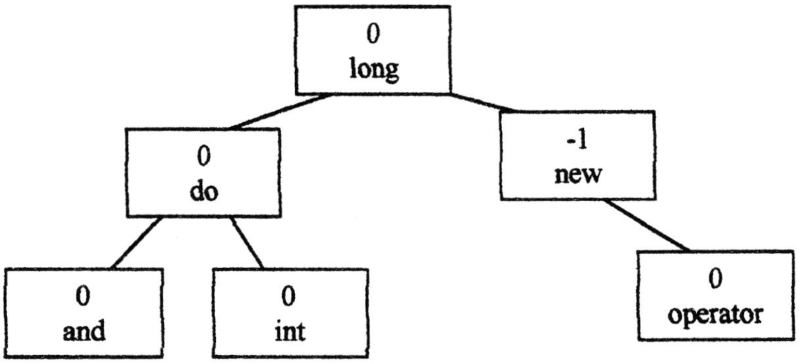
0
long
0
do
-1
new
0
and
0
int
0
operator

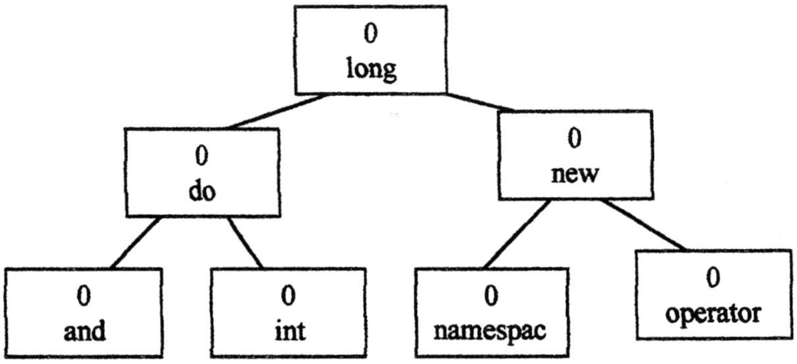
0
long
0
do
0
new
0
and
0
int
0
namespac
0
operator

4.

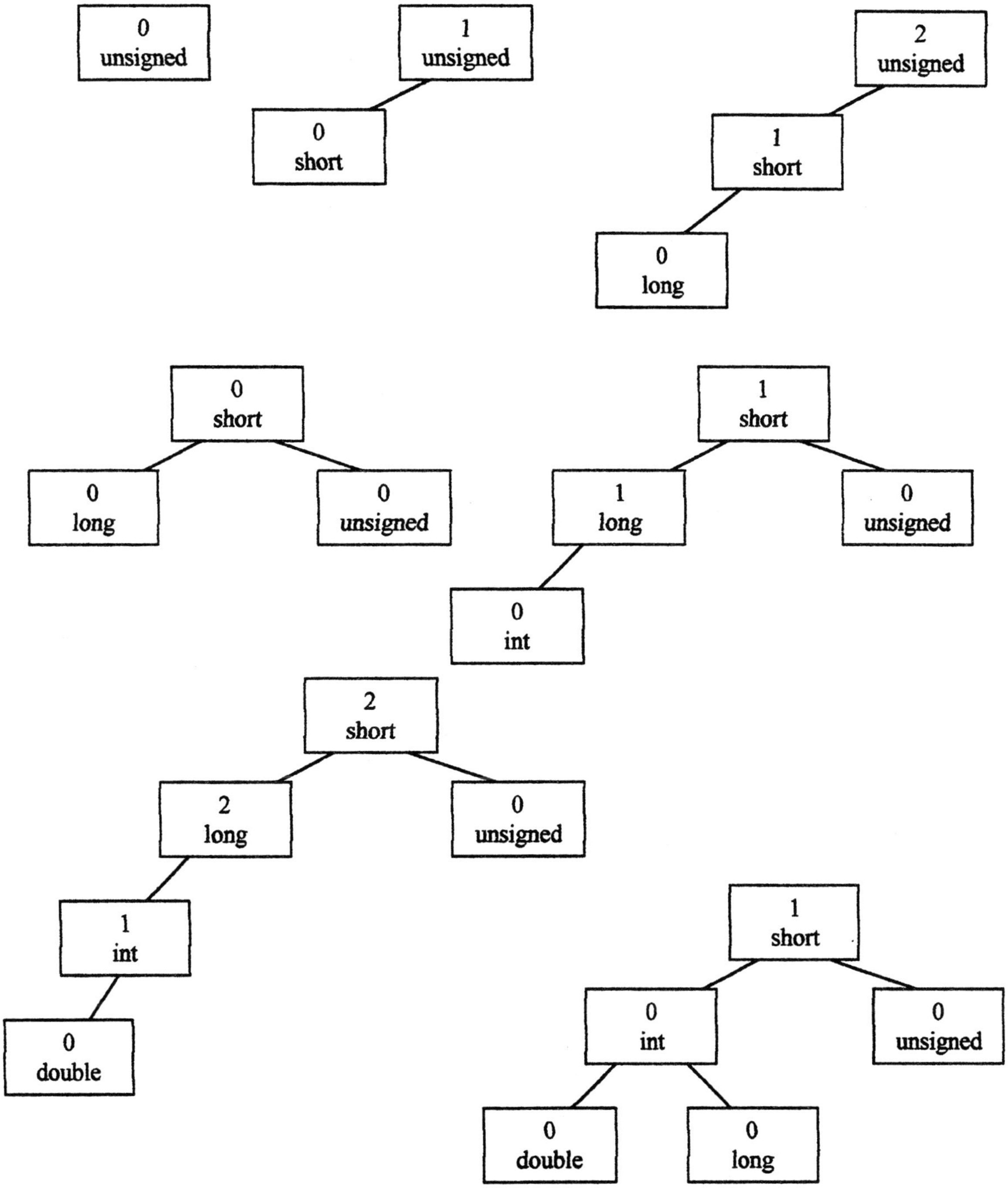
0
unsigned
1
unsigned
0
short
2
unsigned
1
short
0
long
0
short
0
long
0
unsigned
1
short
1
long
0
unsigned
0
int
2
short
2
long
0
unsigned
1
int
0
double
1
short
0
int
0
unsigned
0
double
0
long

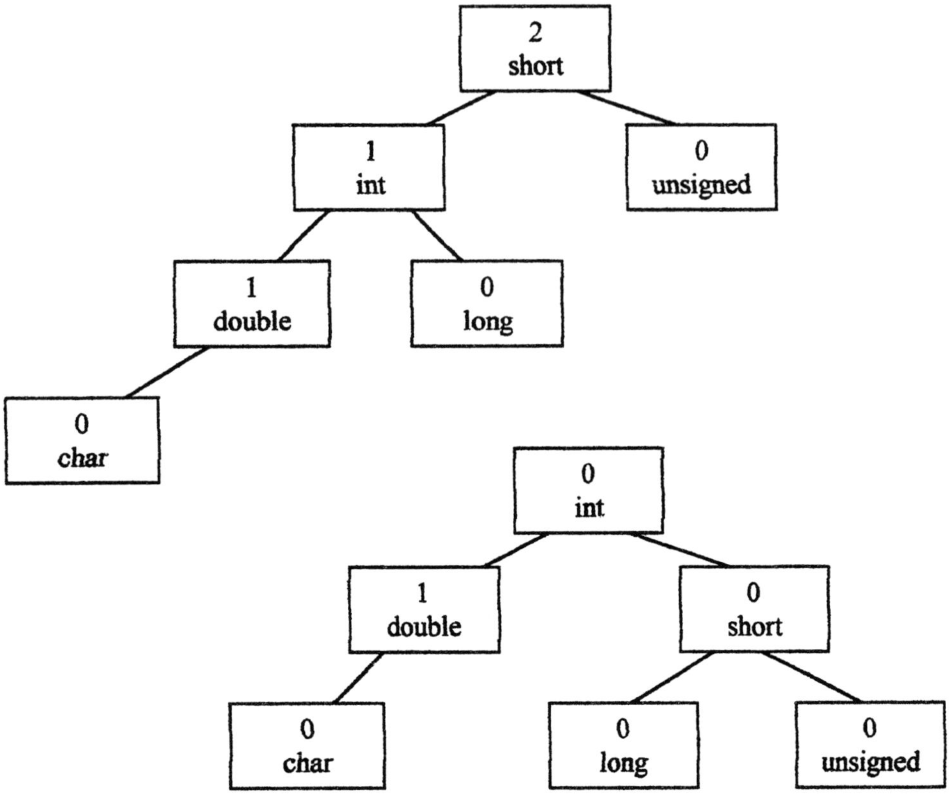
2
short
1
int
0
unsigned
1
double
0
long
0
char
0
int
1
double
0
short
0
char
0
long
0
unsigned

5.

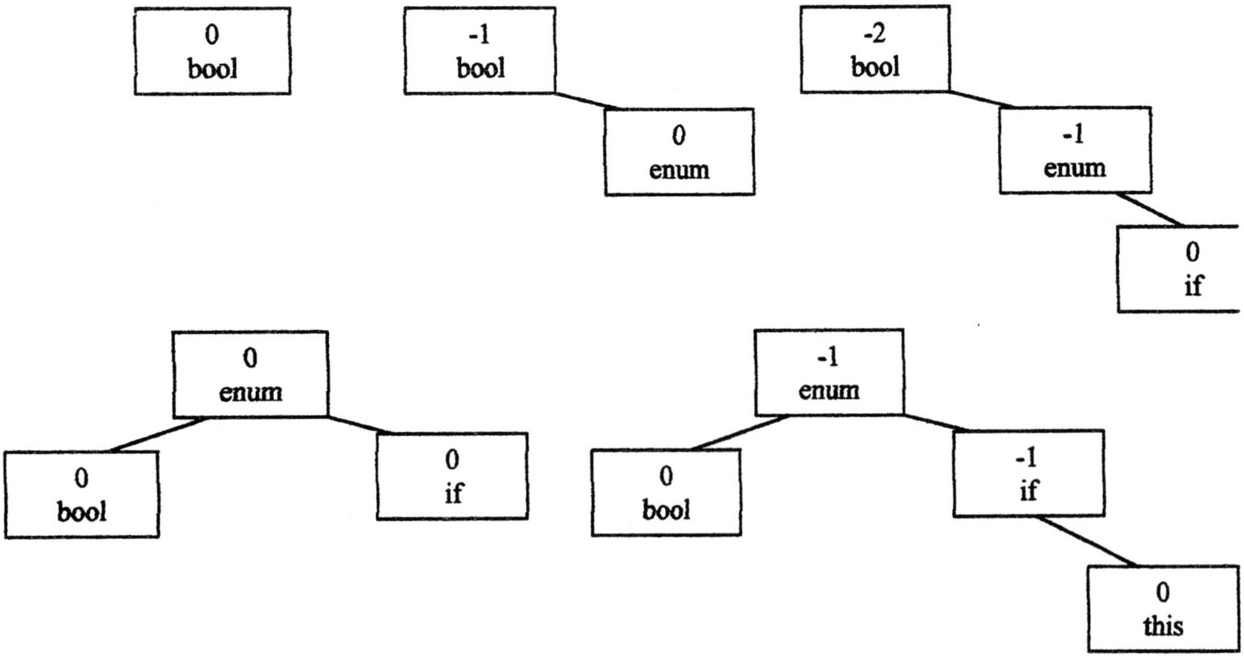
0
bool
-1
bool
0
enum
-2
bool
-1
enum
0
if
0
enum
0
bool
0
if
-1
enum
0
bool
-1
if
0
this

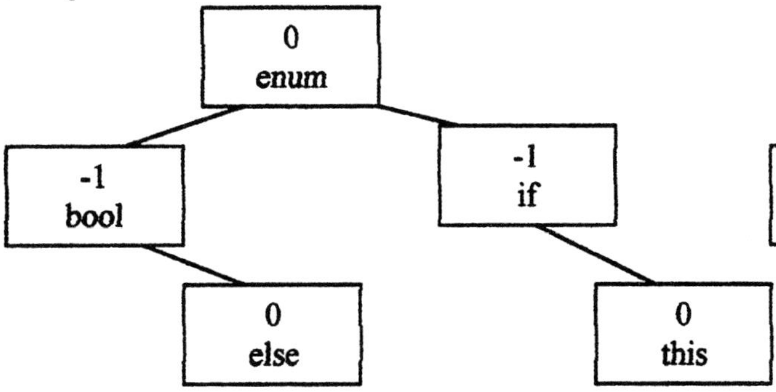
0
enum
-1
bool
-1
if
0
else
0
this

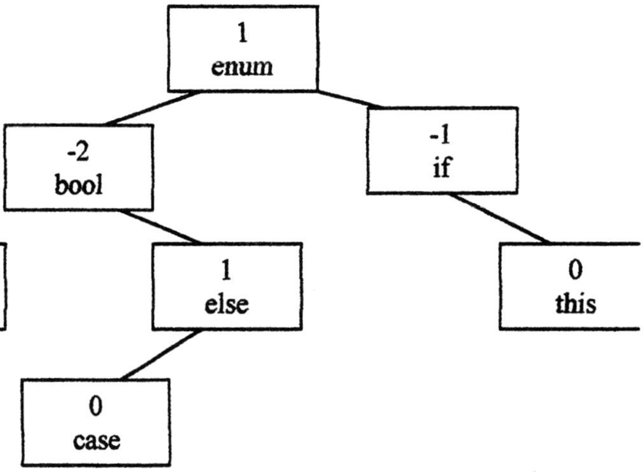
1
enum
-2
bool
-1
if
1
else
0
this
0
case

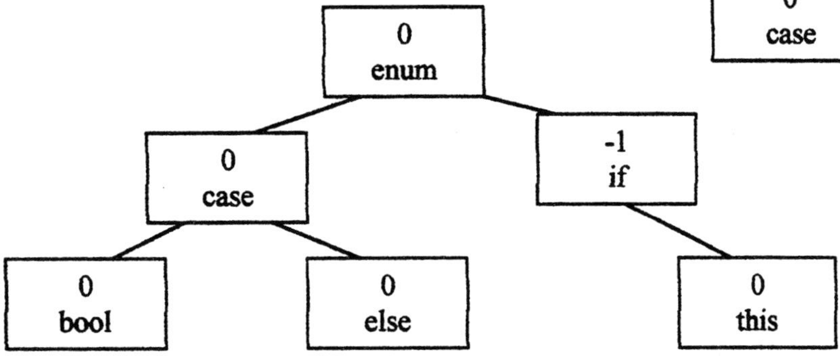
0
enum
0
case
-1
if
0
bool
0
else
0
this

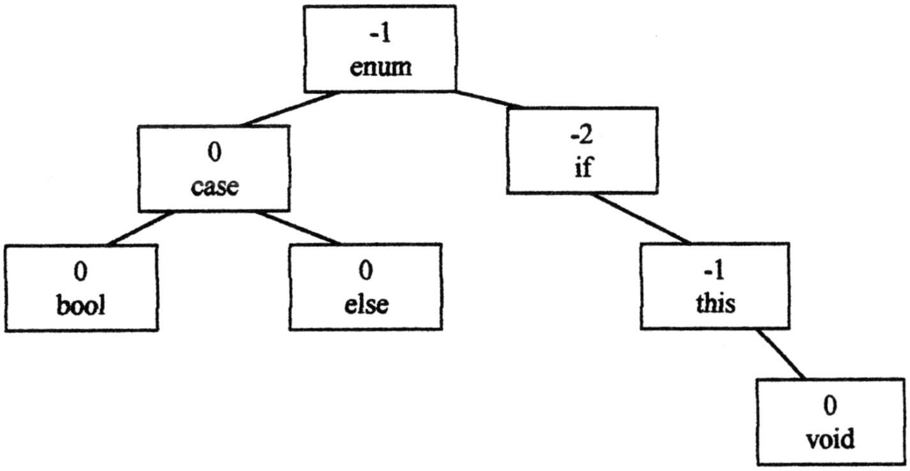
-1
enum
0
case
-2
if
0
bool
0
else
-1
this
0
void

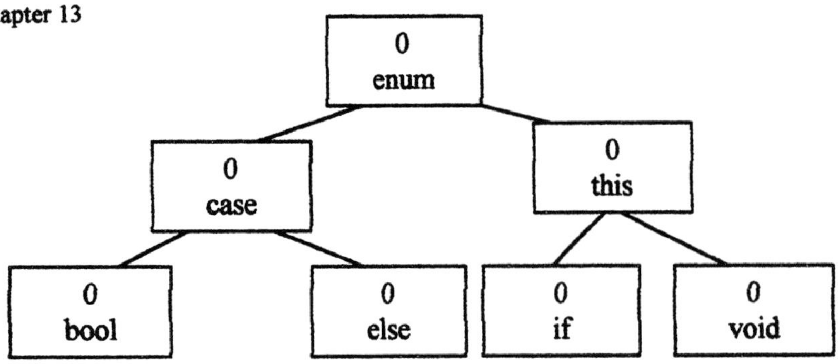
0
enum
0
case
0
this
0
bool
0
else
0
if
0
void

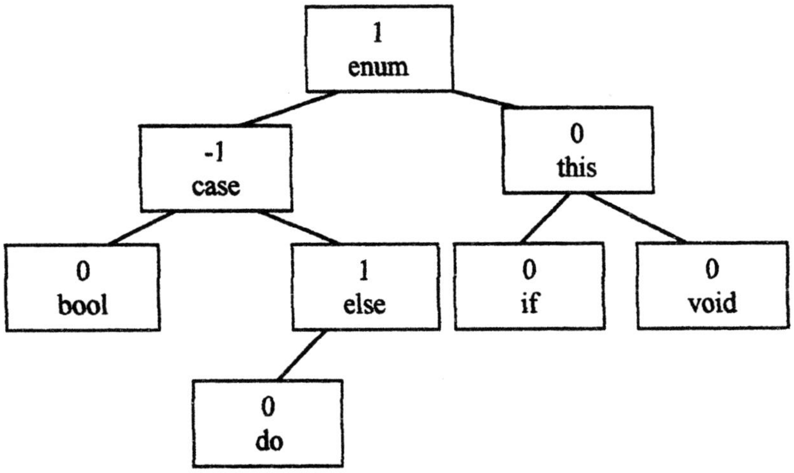
1
enum
-1
case
0
this
0
bool
1
else
0
if
0
void
0
do

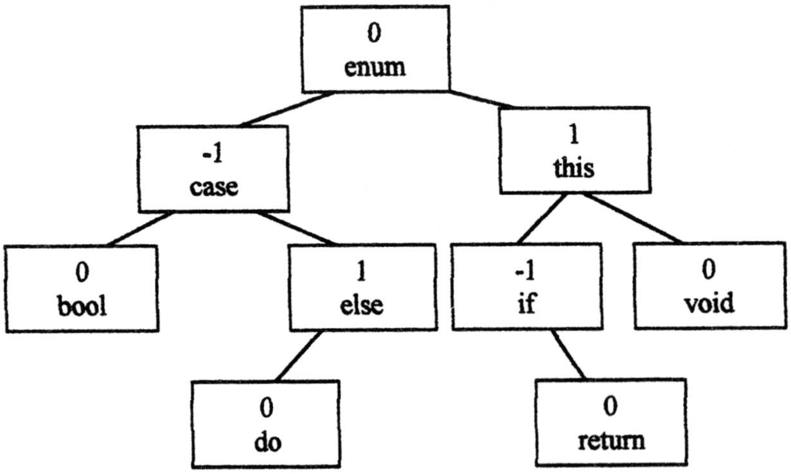
0
enum
-1
case
1
this
0
bool
1
else
-1
if
0
void
0
do
0
return

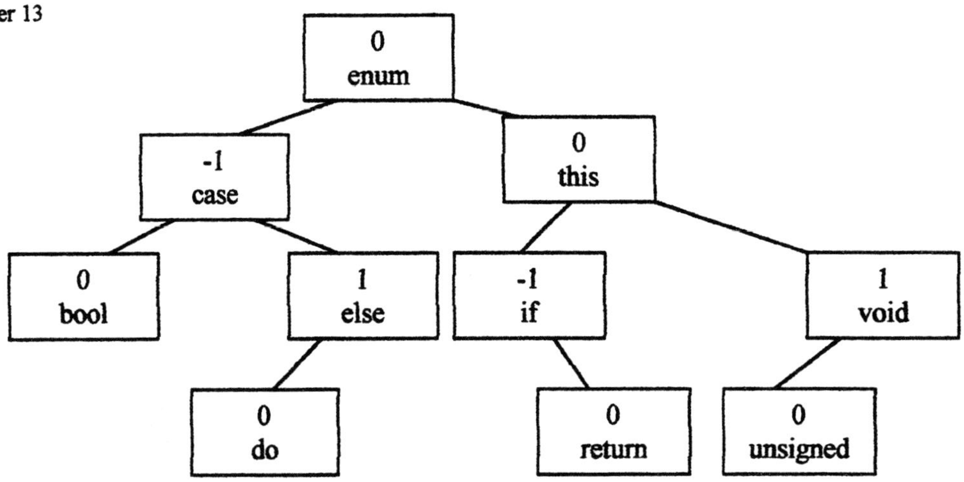
0
enum
-1
case
0
this
0
bool
1
else
-1
if
1
void
0
do
0
return
0
unsigned

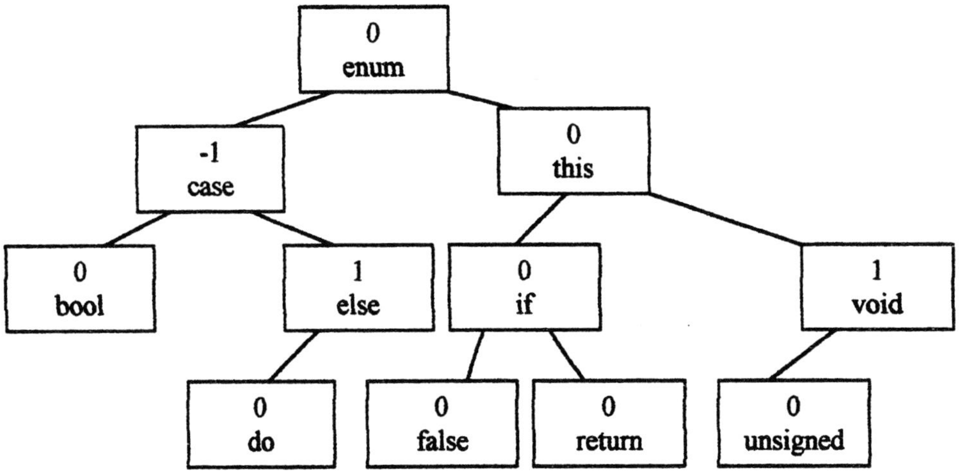
0
enum
-1
case
0
this
0
bool
1
else
0
if
1
void
0
do
0
false
0
return
0
unsigned

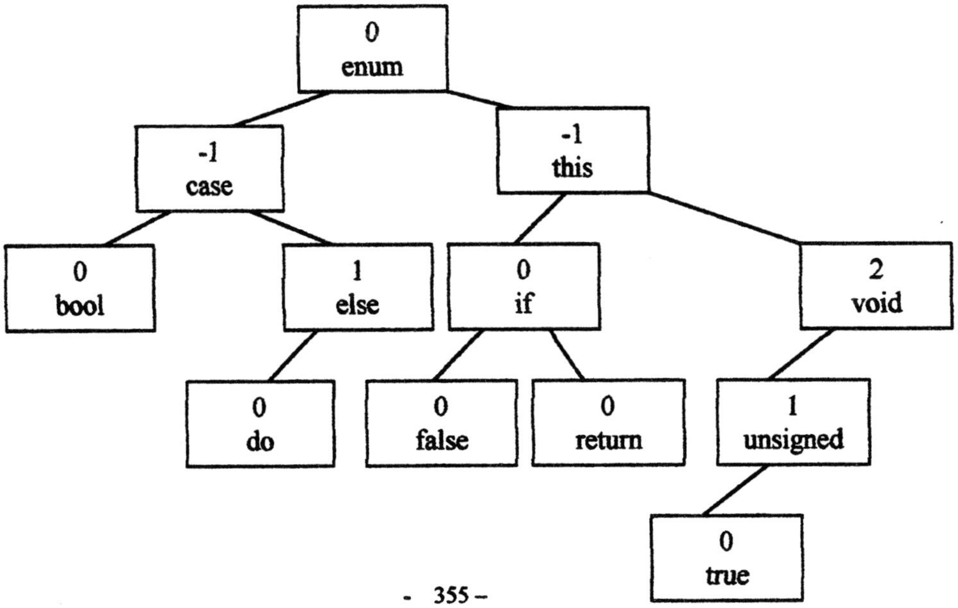
0
enum
-1
case
-1
this
0
bool
1
else
0
if
2
void
0
do
0
false
0
return
1
unsigned
0
true

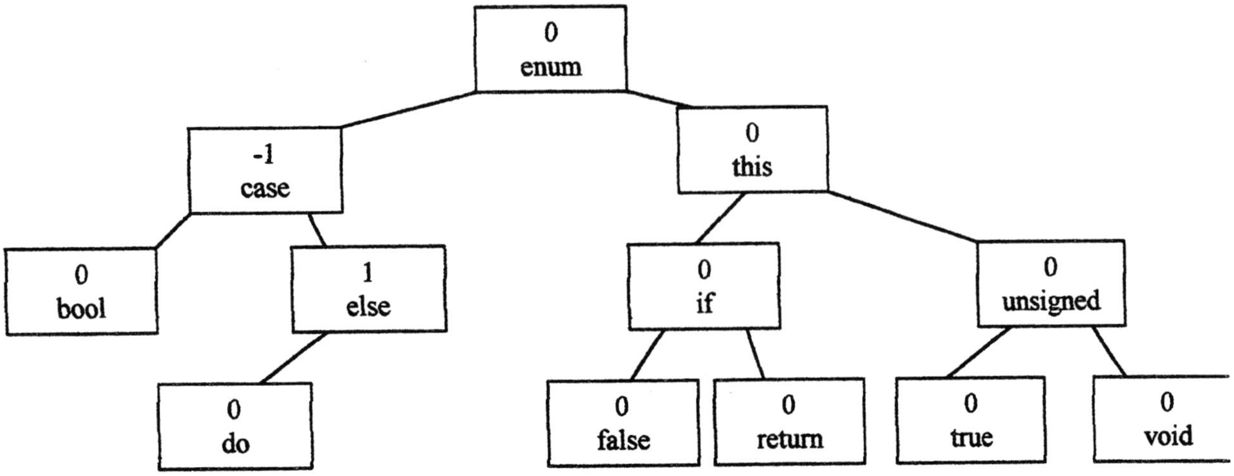
0
enum
-1
case
0
this
0
bool
1
else
0
if
0
unsigned
0
do
0
false
0
return
0
true
0
void

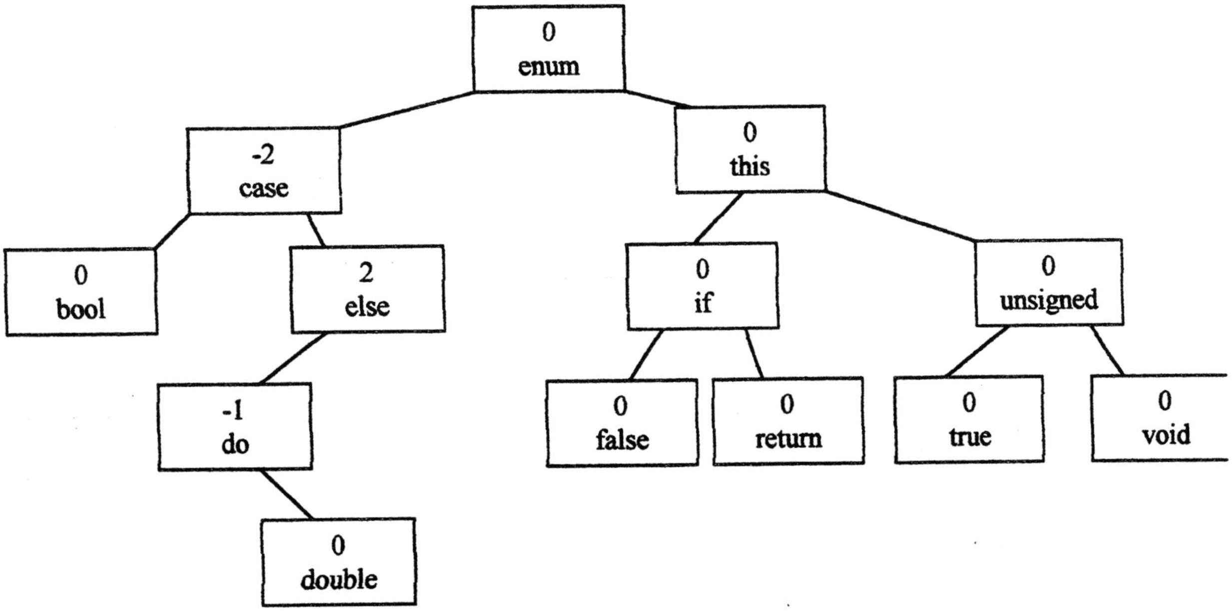
0
enum
-2
case
0
this
0
bool
2
else
0
if
0
unsigned
-1
do
0
false
0
return
0
true
0
void
0
double

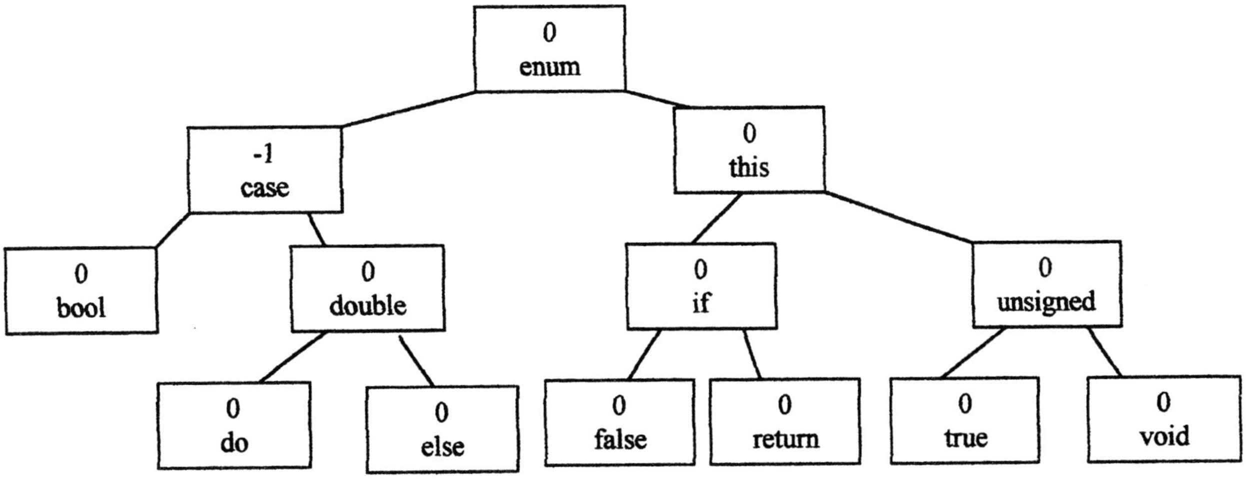
0
enum
-1
case
0
this
0
bool
0
double
0
if
0
unsigned
0
do
0
else
0
false
0
return
0
true
0
void

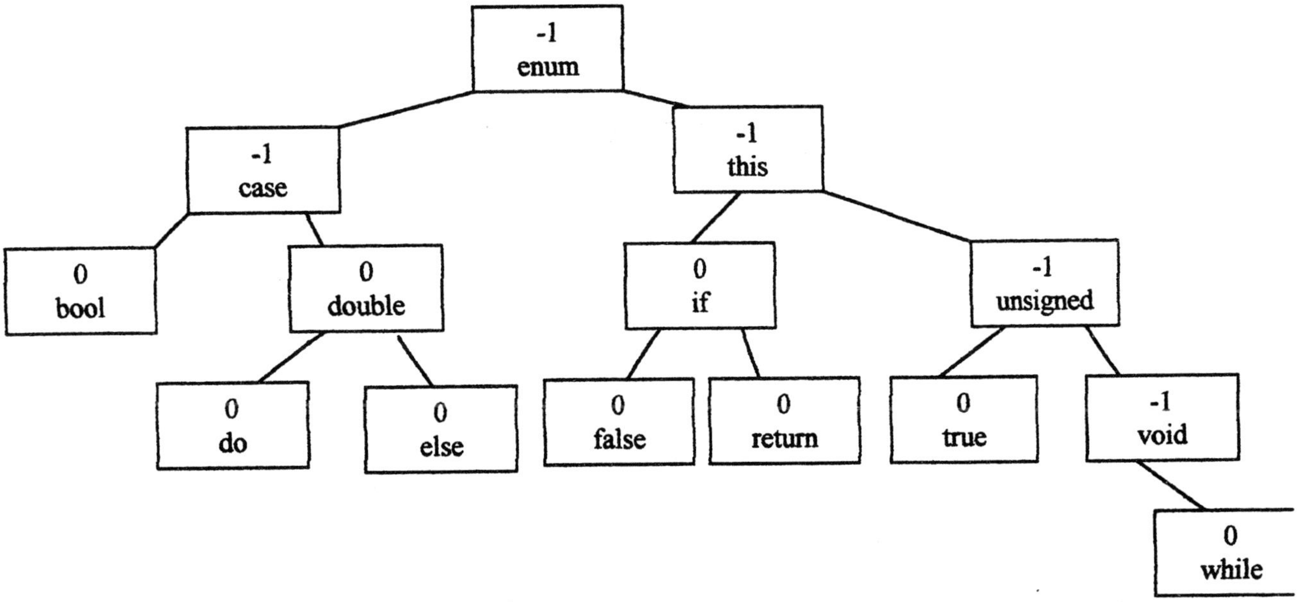
-1
enum
-1
case
-1
this
0
bool
0
double
0
if
-1
unsigned
0
do
0
else
0
false
0
return
0
true
-1
void
0
while

6.

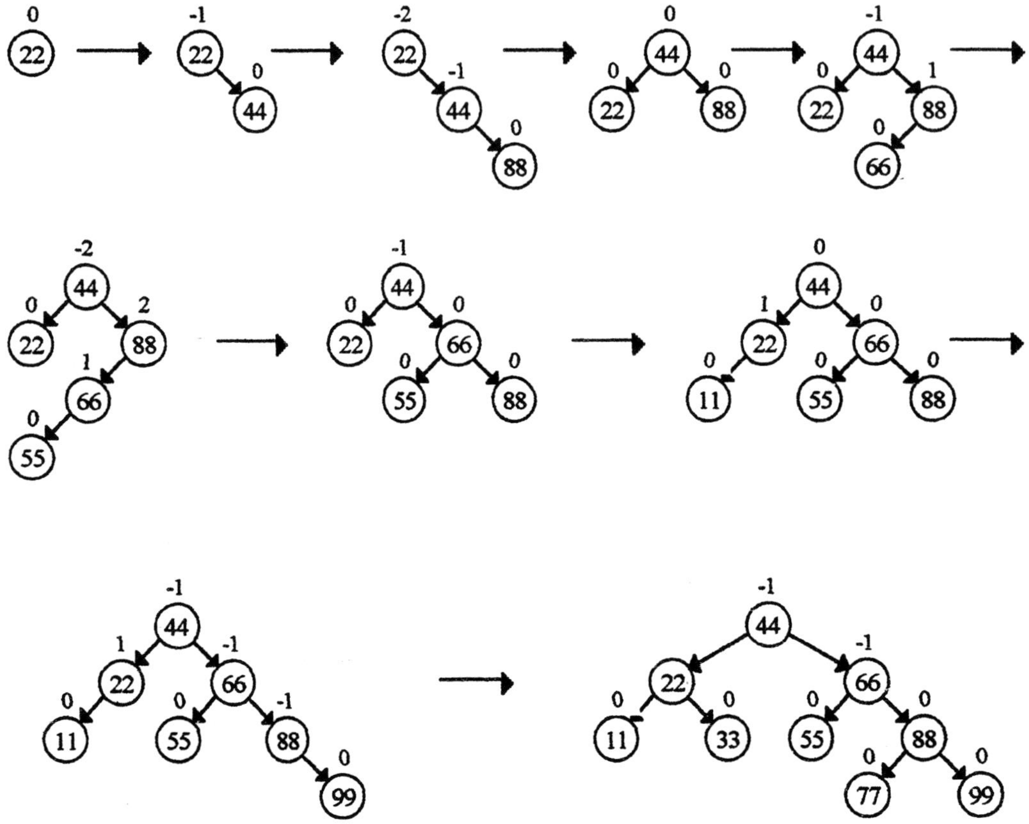
0
22
-1
22
0
44
-2
22
-1
44
0
88
0
44
0
22
0
88
-1
44
0
22
1
88
0
66
-2
44
0
22
2
88
1
66
0
55
-1
44
0
22
0
66
0
55
0
88
0
44
1
22
0
66
0
11
0
55
0
88
-1
44
1
22
-1
66
0
11
0
55
-1
88
0
99
-1
44
22
-1
66
0
11
0
33
0
55
0
88
0
77
0
99

7.

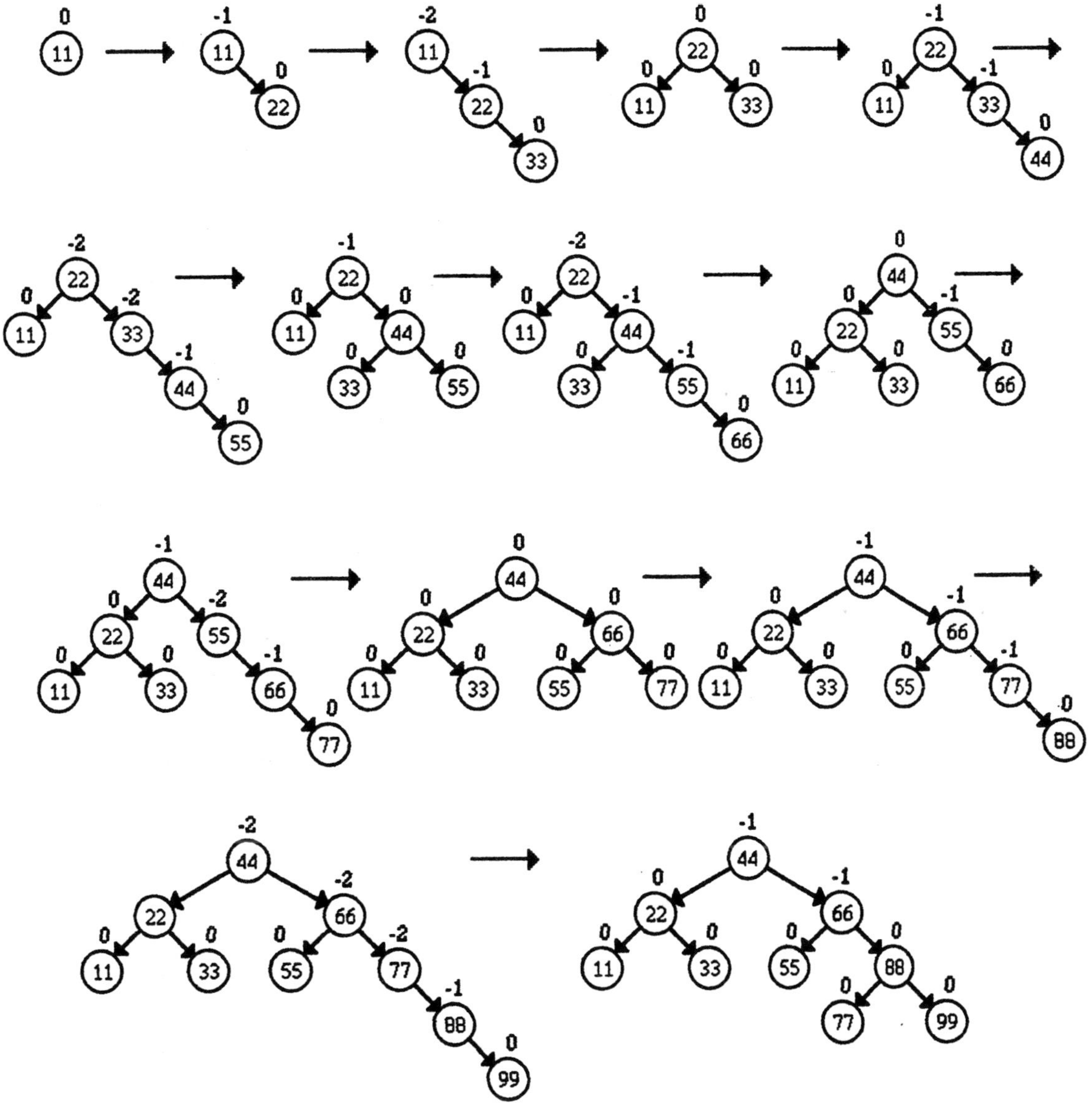
0
11
-1
11
0
22
-2
11
-1
22
0
33
0
22
0
11
0
33
-1
22
0
11
-1
33
0
44
-2
22
0
11
-2
33
-1
44
0
55
-1
22
0
11
0
44
0
33
0
55
-2
22
0
11
-1
44
0
33
-1
55
0
66
0
44
0
22
-1
55
0
11
0
33
0
66
-1
44
0
22
-2
55
0
11
0
33
-1
66
0
77
0
44
0
22
0
66
0
11
0
33
0
55
0
77
-1
44
0
22
-1
66
0
11
0
33
0
55
-1
77
0
88
-2
44
0
22
-2
66
0
11
0
33
0
55
-2
77
-1
88
0
99
-1
44
0
22
-1
66
0
11
0
33
0
55
0
88
0
77
0
99

8.

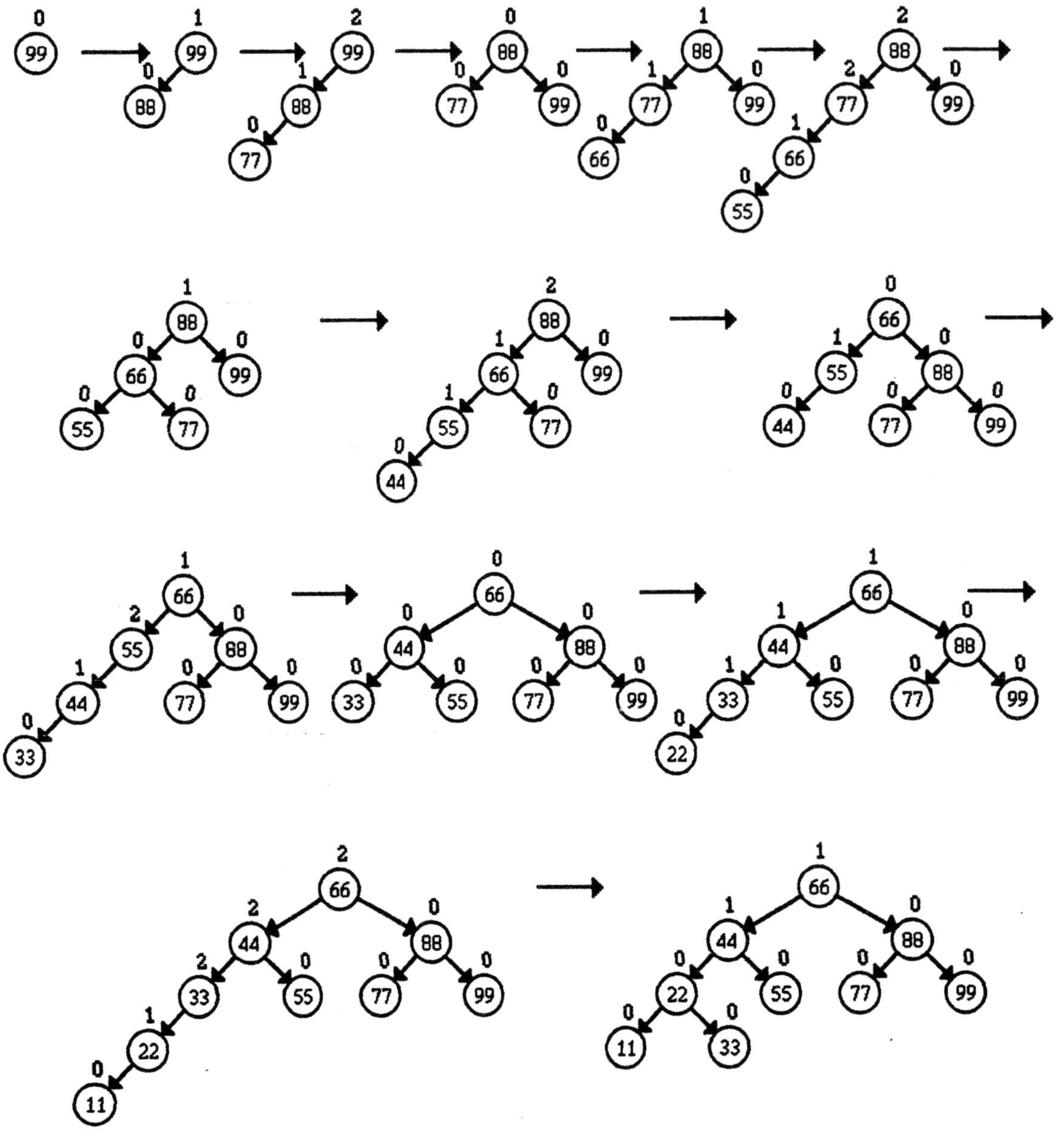

9.

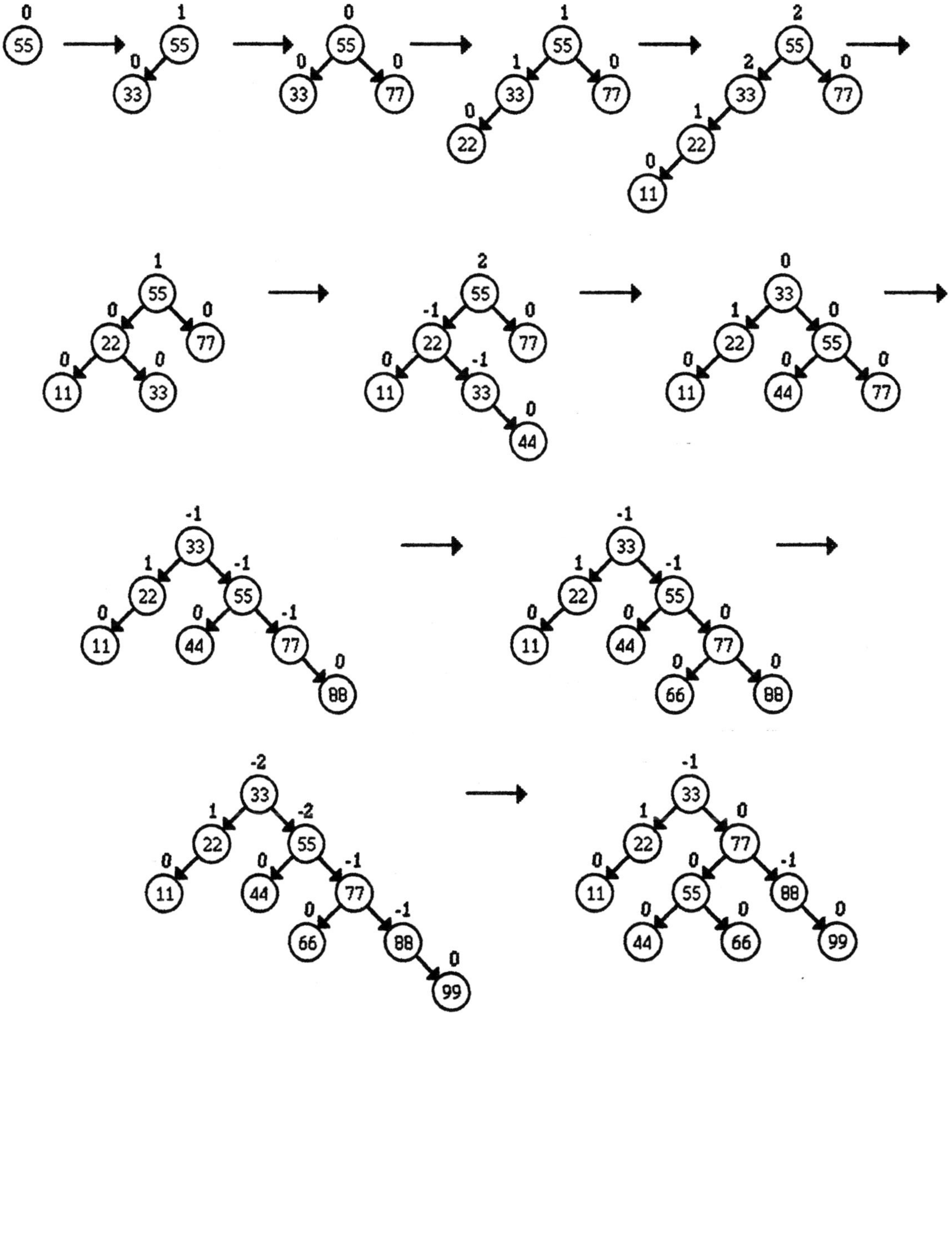
0 55
1 55 0 33
0 55 0 33 0 77
1 55 1 33 0 77 0 22
2 55 2 33 0 77 1 22 0 11
1 55 0 22 0 77 0 11 0 33
2 55 -1 22 0 77 0 11 -1 33 0 44
0 33 1 22 0 55 0 11 0 44 0 77
-1 33 1 22 -1 55 0 11 0 44 -1 77 0 88
-1 33 1 22 -1 55 0 11 0 44 0 77 0 66 0 88
-2 33 1 22 -2 55 0 11 0 44 -1 77 0 66 -1 88 0 99
-1 33 1 22 0 77 0 11 0 55 -1 88 0 44 0 66 0 99

10.

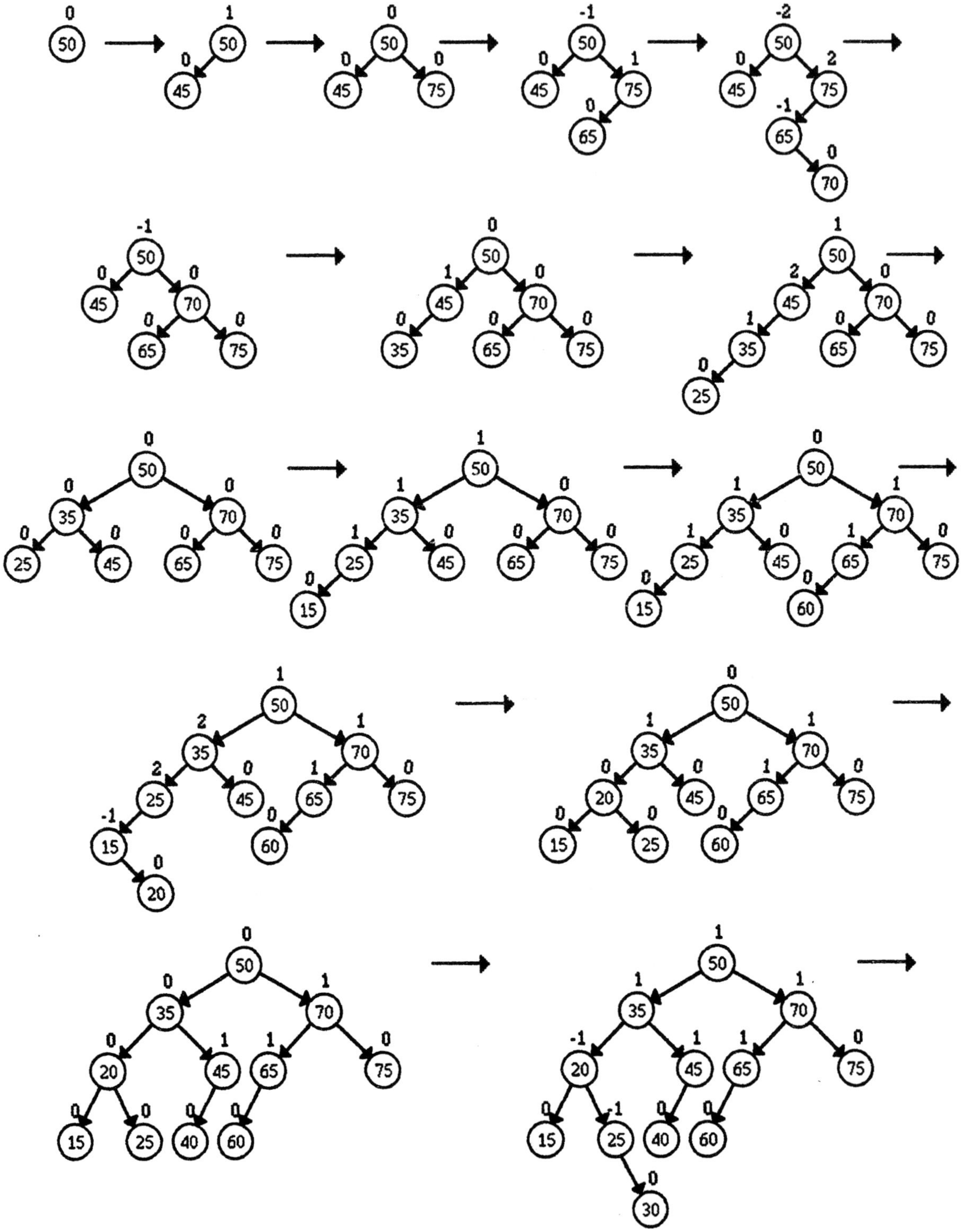

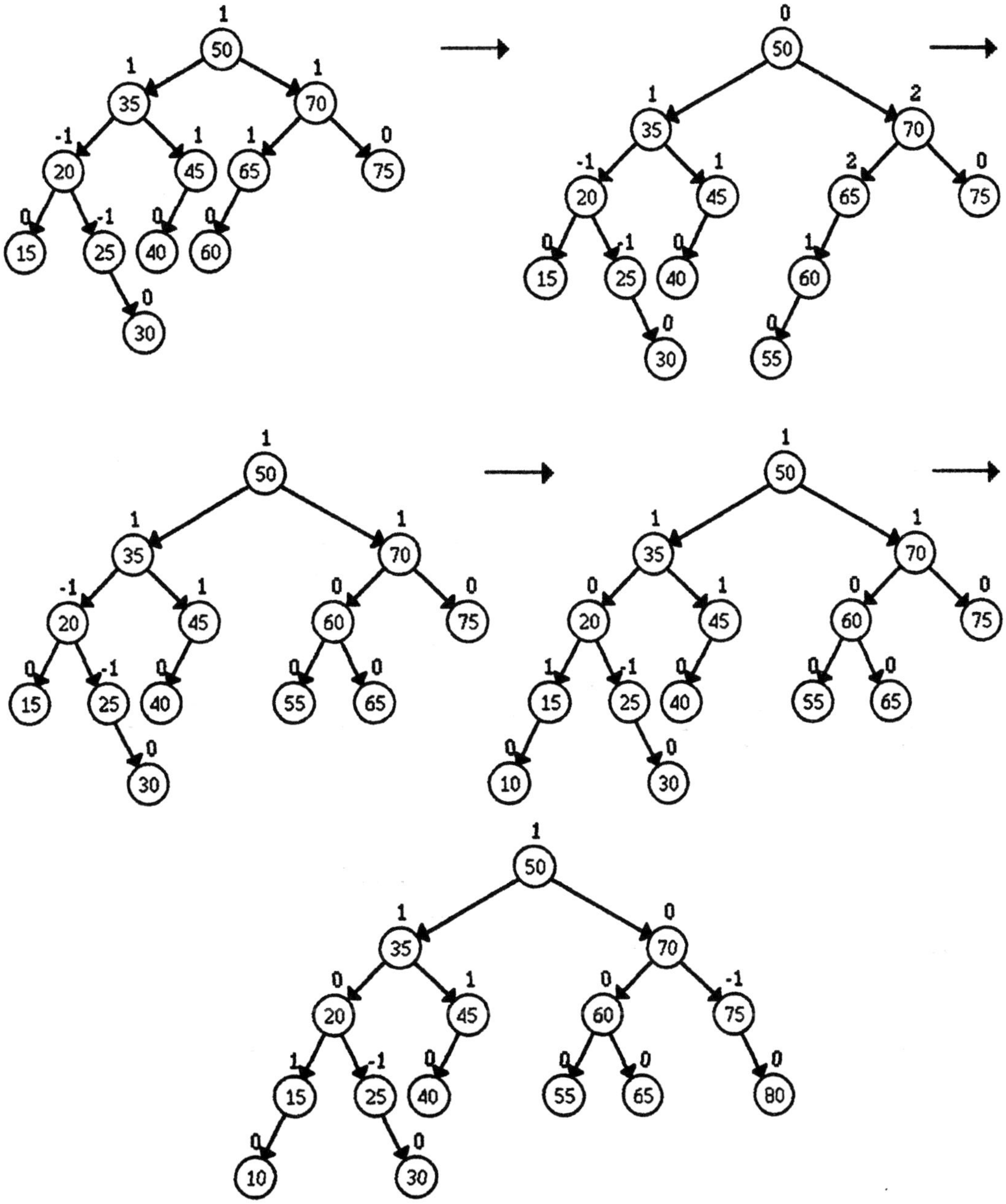
50
35 70
20 45 65 75
15 25 40 60
30
50
35 70
20 45 65 75
15 25 40 60
30 55
50
35 70
20 45 60 75
15 25 40 55 65
30
50
35 70
20 45 60 75
15 25 40 55 65
10 30
50
35 70
20 45 60 75
15 25 40 55 65 80
10 30

11.

Balanced Subtree Before Insertion

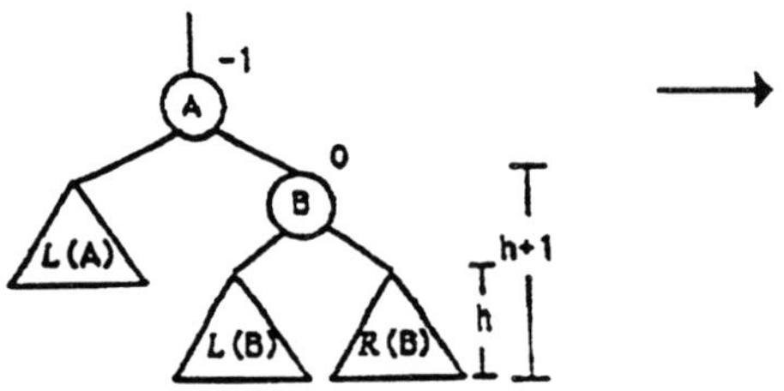

Unbalanced Subtree After Insertion

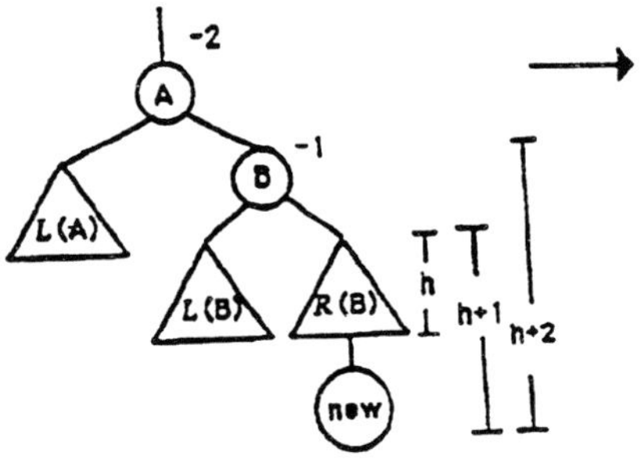

Balanced Subtree After Simple Left Rotation

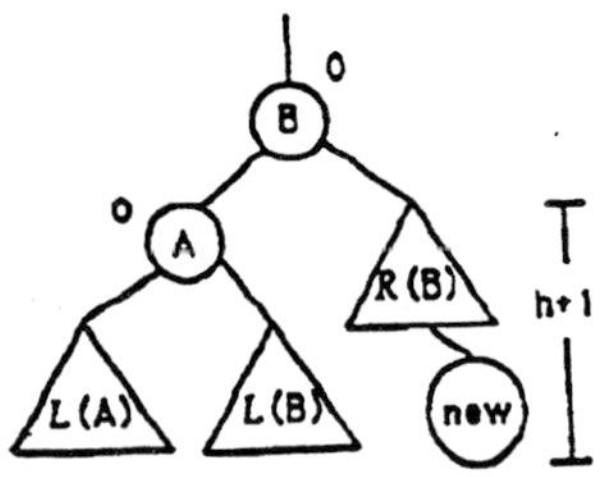

13.

Balanced Subtree Before Insertion

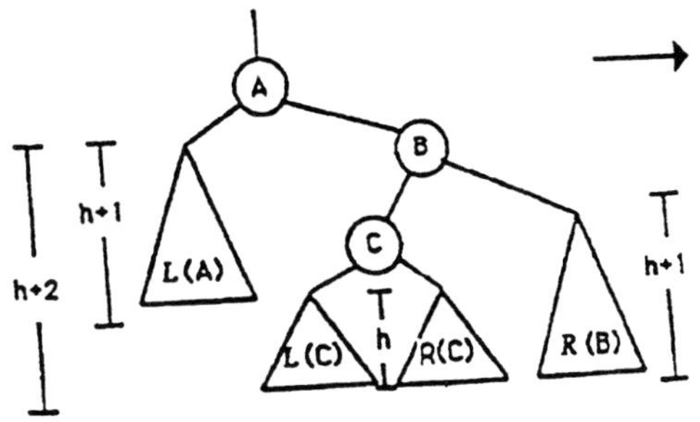

Unbalanced Subtree After Insertion

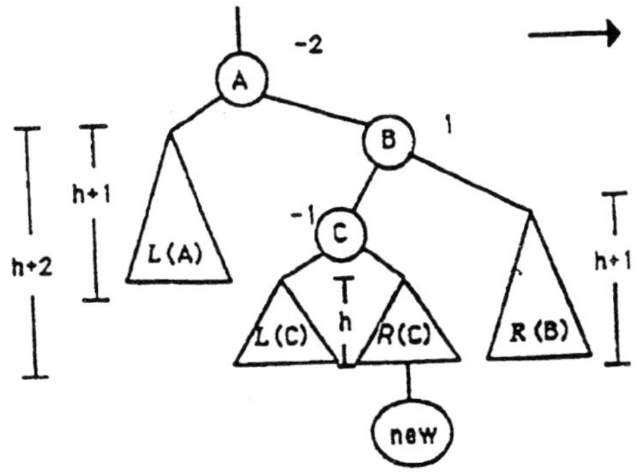

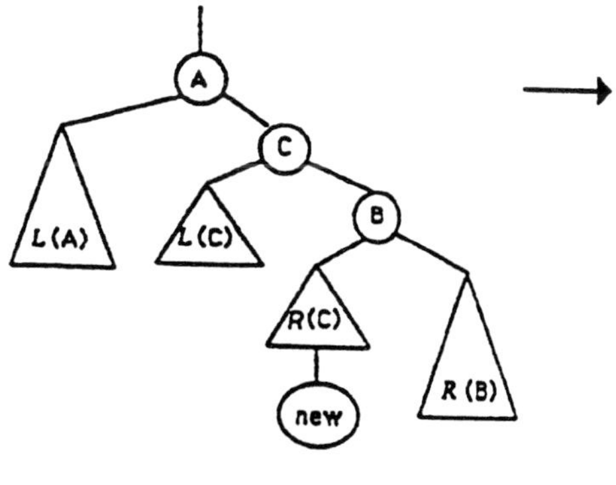

Balanced Subtree After Right - Left Rotation

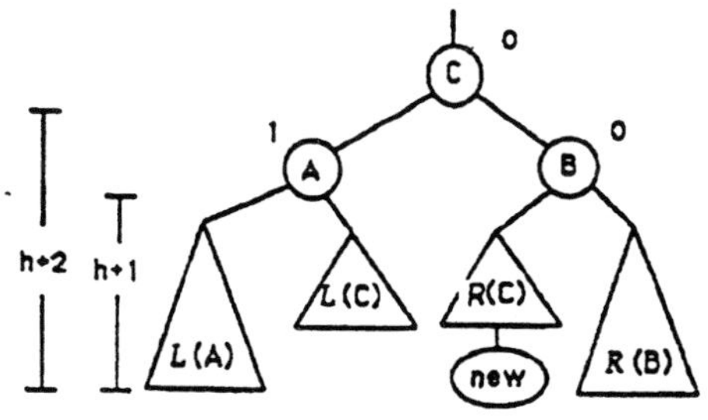

14. /* AVLtree class is a good example of the delineation of public interface methods and private utility methods. Users of AVL trees should be able to modify the tree as needed without having to worry about right, left, left-right or right-left rotations. Make these latter methods private. */

```
template<typename ElementType>
class AVLtree
{
   public:
     AVLtree();
     AVLtree(const AVLtree&); // copy constructor
     ~AVLtree();

     void insert(ElementType);

     void traverse();

   private:

     class AVLnode
     {
       public:
         ElementType data;
         short int balanceFactor;
         AVLNode*  left;
         AVLNode*  right;

         AVLNode()
         {
              balanceFactor = 0;
              left = right = 0;
         }

       AVLNode(ElementType item)
         {
              data = item;
              balanceFactor = 0;
              left = right = 0;
         }
       };

   void rightRotate(AVLNode*);
   void left-rightRotate(AVLNode*);
   void right-leftRotate(AVLNode*);
   void leftRotate(AVLNode*);
   };
```

13.3 Exercises

1.

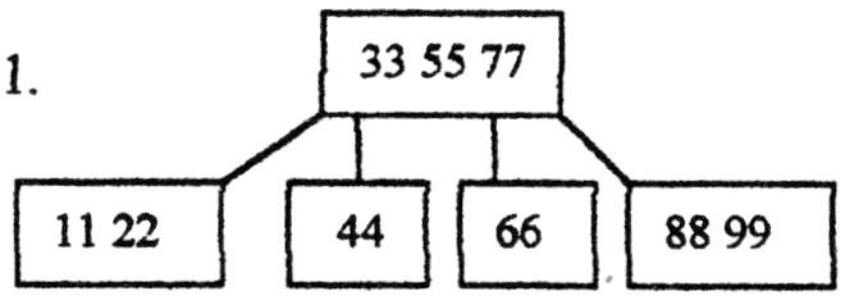

2.

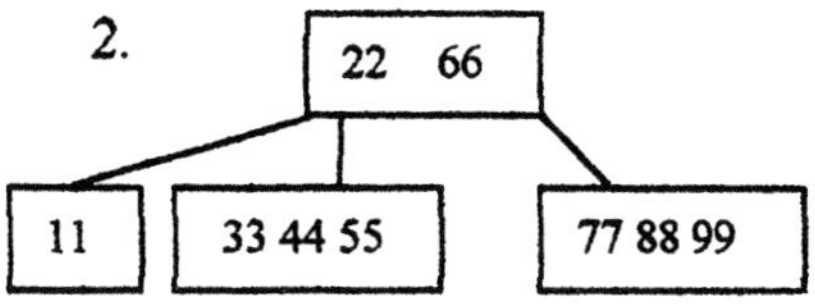

3

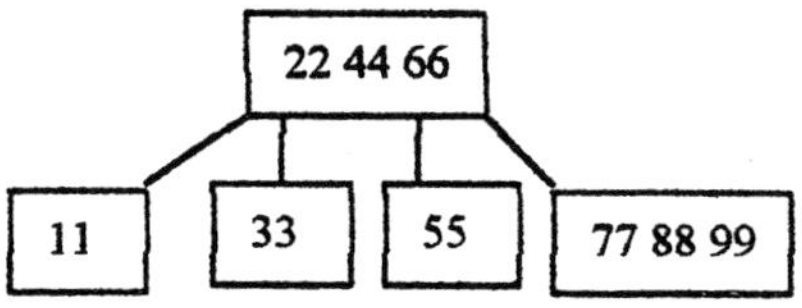

4.

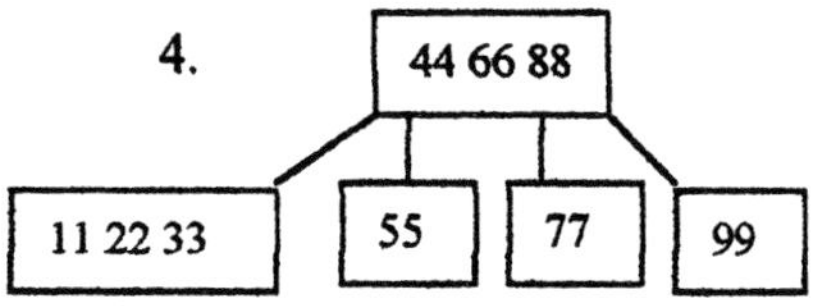

5.

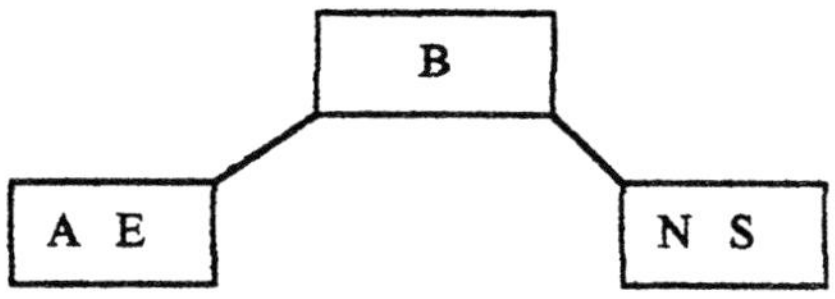

6.

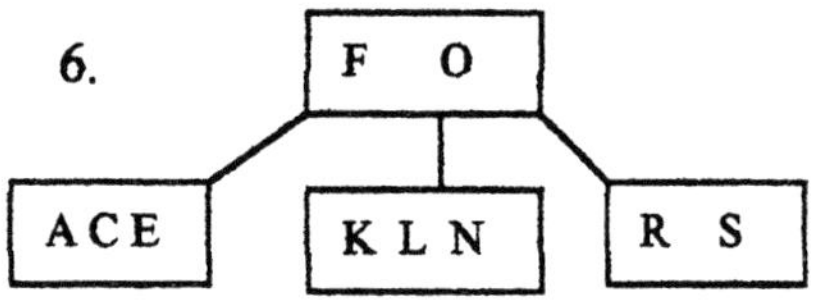

7.

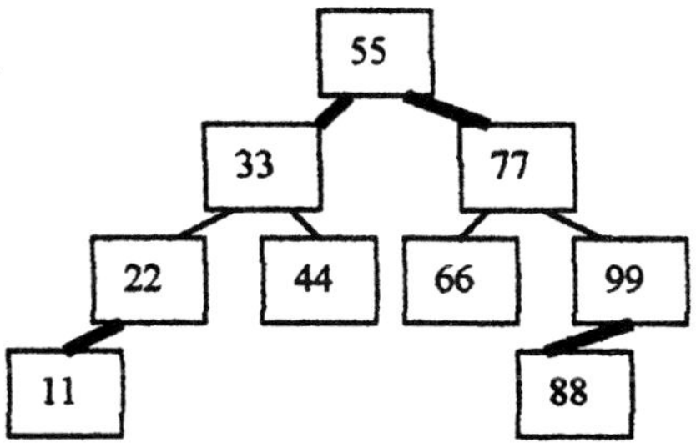

8.

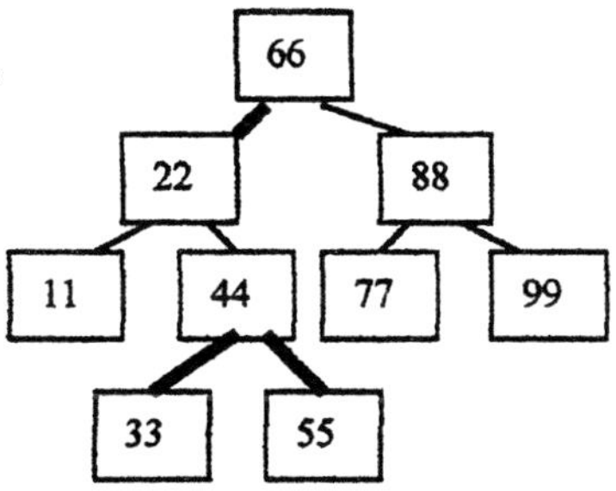

9.

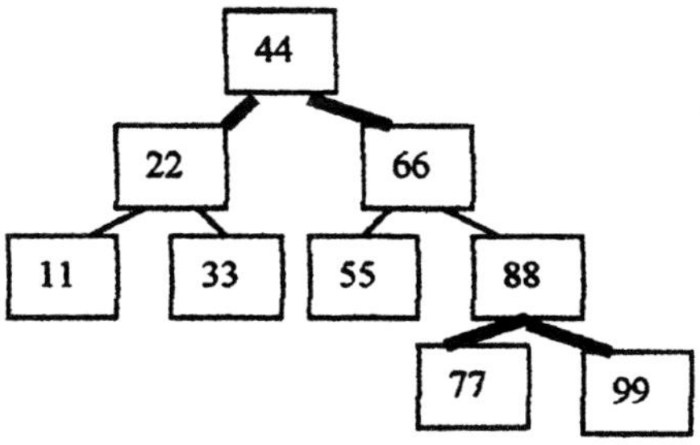

10.

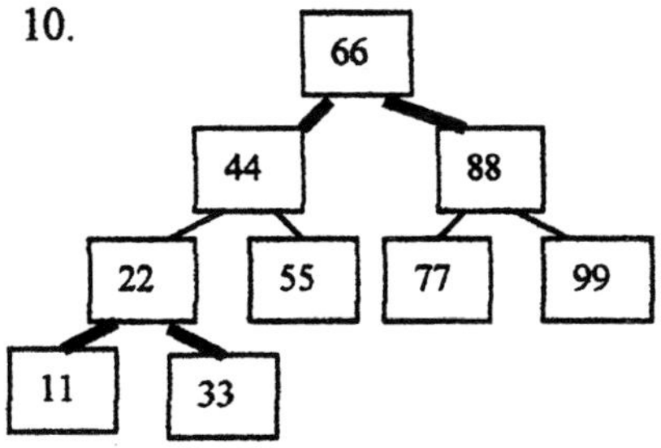

11.

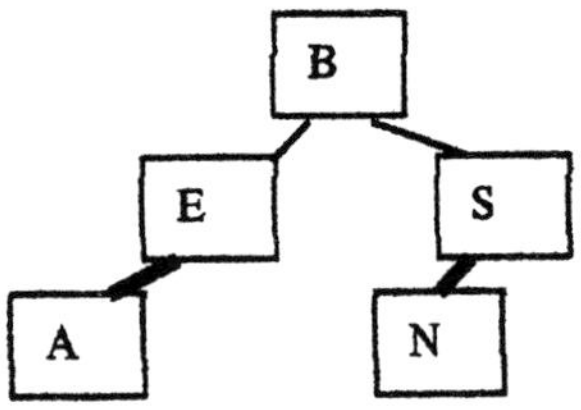

12.

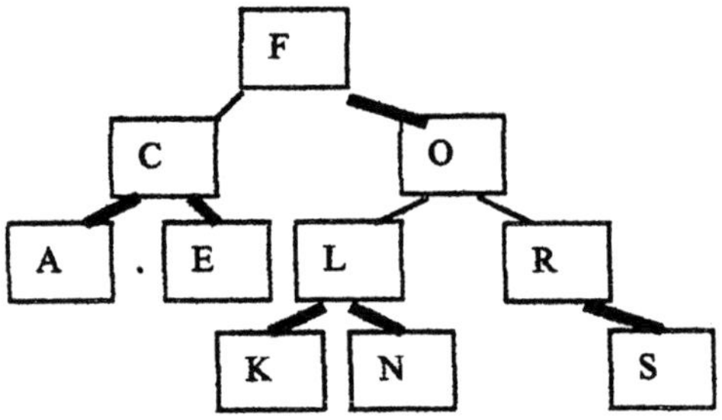

13.

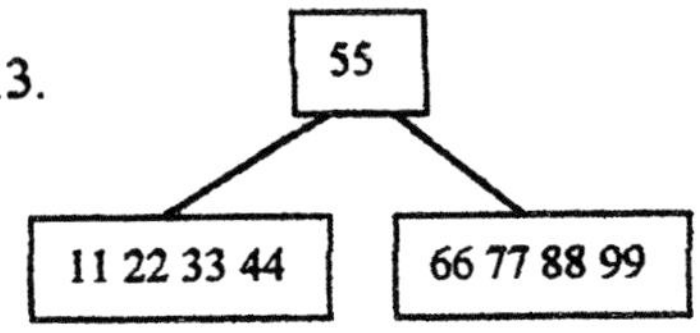

14.

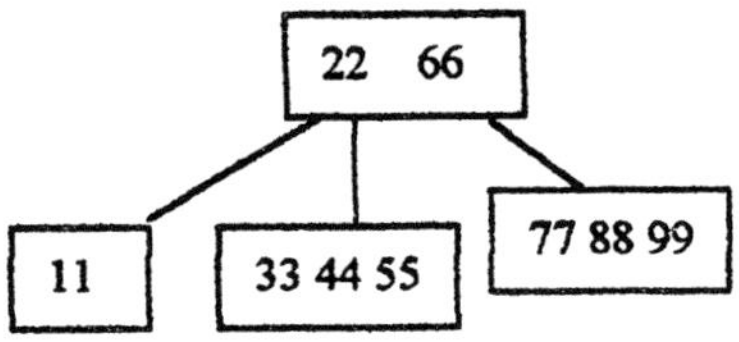

15.

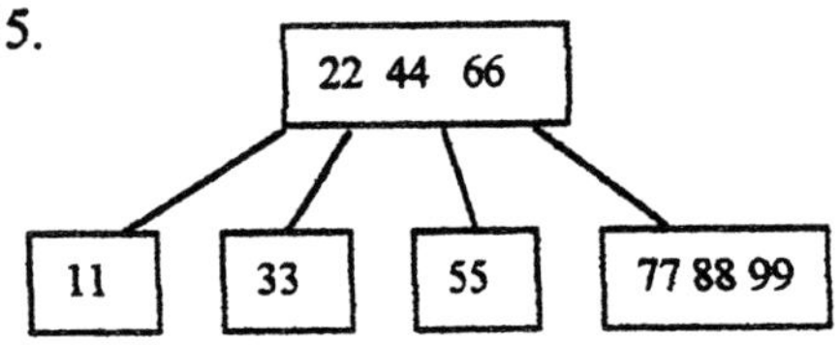

16.

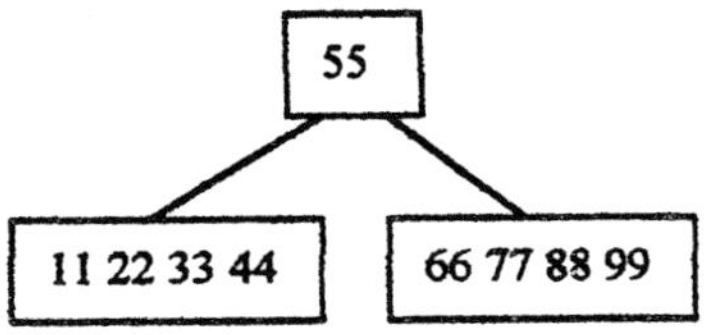

17.

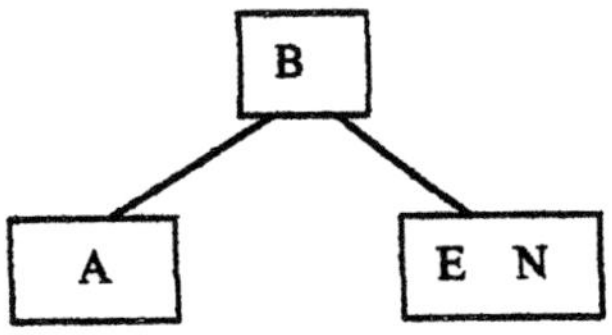

18.

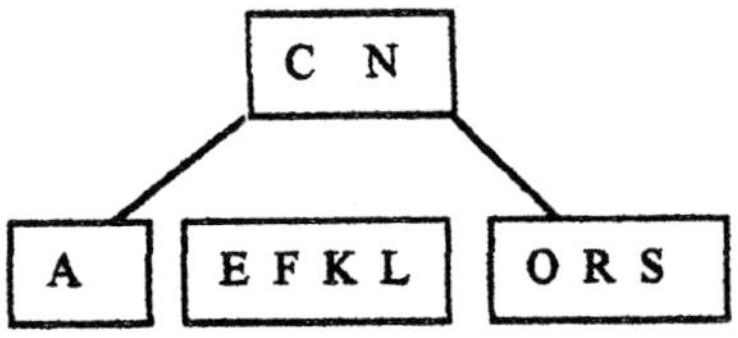

19.

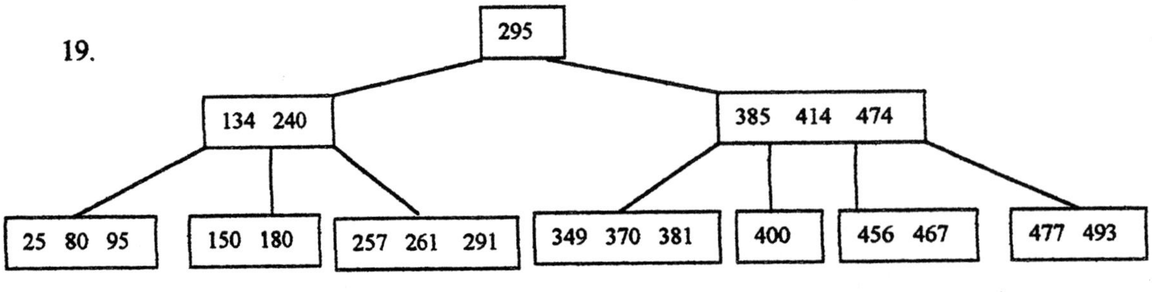

20.

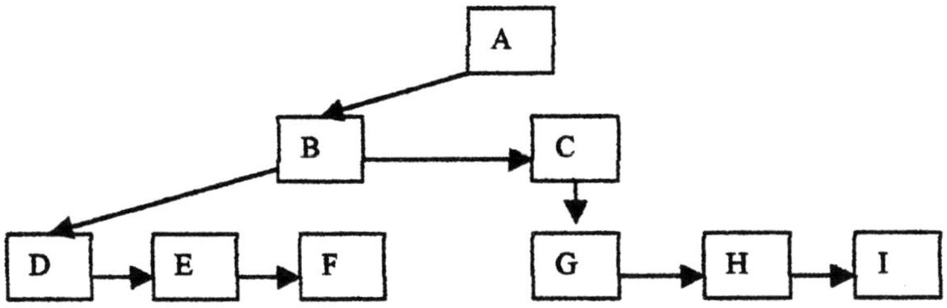

21.

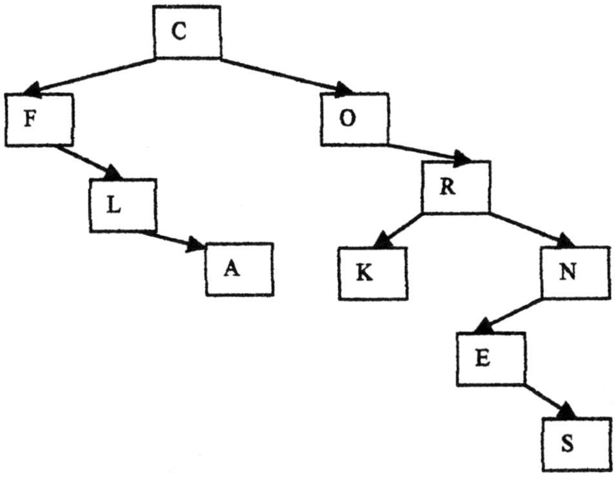

22. An algorithm to delete a node from an AVL tree must deal with the rebalancing that may be necessary after an element is removed. Recall that balance factors were tracked as insertion were made into an AVL tree, and that factors other than 0, -1 or 1 caused a rotation to be performed in order to balance the tree. The same technique is used upon deletion. The following cases are considered for deletion:
    - deletion of a leaf node
        - recalculate balance factors
        - perform appropriate rotations as needed
    - deletion of an internal node with one child
        - replace node with child
        - recalculate balance factors
        - perform appropriate rotations as needed
    - deletion of an internal node with two children
        - if node->balanceFactor < 0 // left subtree smaller
            - replace with right child
        - else // trees equal or right smaller
            - replace with left child
        - recalculate balance factors
        - perform appropriate rotations as needed

23. An algorithm to delete a node from a 2-3-4 tree must deal with the rebalancing that may be necessary after an element is removed. Recall that insertion sometimes results in a splitting of a node and that split may propogate up or down the tree, depending on whether one is performing a top-down insertion or a bottom-in insertion. In a like manner, deleting an element from a 2-3-4 tree may cause perturbations elsewhere in the tree. There are two main considerations: deletion of a 2-node necessitates the replacement of that value with one from its child nodes; deletion of a 3- or 4-node element may necessitate the merging of child nodes (because in effect the elements of a 3- or 4-node serve as separator values for their children). Note that in the latter case, a merge may result in overflow. In which case, we actually need a merge-split operation: merge sibling nodes (causing overflow) and then split resulting node.

To streamline the deletion process, we reduce the deletion of an arbitrary element to the deletion of an element that is in a leaf node. If the element to be deleted is in a 3-node or 4-node leaf, then after deletion, we have a 2-node or 3-node leaf. No restructuring is then required. To avoid propogation of restructuring, we need to ensure that the element to be deleted in a 3-node or 4-node leaf before deletion. That is, restructuring is done as we search for the element to be deleted.

The restructuring process rests on the search for the item to be deleted as progressing through only 3-node and 4-nodes. If we move through a 2-node, then restructuring is required. The following steps detail the process. Assume that we are at node p and will next move to node q, where q is a child of p.

- If p is a leaf, the element to be deleted is either in node p or not in the tree.
  Delete. No restructuring needed.
- q is a 3-node or 4-node.
  Move to q.
- q is a 2-node (children x & y) and its nearest sibling r is also a 2-node (children v & w).
  - if p is a 2-node with children (q & r), merge q, p and r into a 4-node with children x, y, v and w.
  - if p is a 3-node (or 4-node), q, p and r are merged into a 4-node with children x, y, v and w (as before) but this 4-node is a child of the 2-node (or 3-node) containing the remaining elements of p's original node.
- q is a 2-node and its nearest sibling r is a 3-node (or 4-node). Transform q into a 3-node by taking the appropriate separator out of p and one of its children out of r.

24. Algorithm to delete a node from a red-black tree must deal with the rebalancing that may be necessary after an element is removed. As explored in detail above, restructuring may be confined if one ensures that the node to be deleted is a leaf node, in this case one with a red link from its parent. Again, rebalancing is done as we search for the element to be deleted. As in #23, the insertion transformations (rotations) are performed in reverse. However, here the cost is cheaper since color changes take care of most transformations.

25. **/* red-black tree template */**

```
template <typename ElementType>
class redBlack
{
  public:

     redBlack();
     redBlack(const redBlack&);
     ~redBlack();

     void insert(ElementType);
     void delete(ElementType);
     void traverse();

   private:
     class RBnode
     {
        public:
          ElementType    data;
          bool           Red;
          RBnode*        right;
          Rbnode*        left;

        RBnode()
        {
          Red = false;
          left = right = 0;
        }

        RBnode(ElementType item)
        {
          data = item;
          left = right = 0;
          Red = false;
        }
     };

     void rotateRight(RBnode*);
     void rotateLeft(RBnode*);
     void rotateRightLeft(RBnode*);
     void rotateLeftRight(RBnode*);
 };
```

26. /* By definition, each node in a B tree of order m has at most m-1 data items and m links. To avoid defining a class template for each value of m, we use an array of pointers to represent the links. As noted in the text, carrying all these links is tremendous overhead*/

```
template <typename ElementType>
class B
{
  public:

     B();
     B(const B&);
     ~B();

     void insert(ElementType);
     void delete(ElementType);
     void traverse();
   private:
     class Bnode
     {
        public:
          ElementType    data;

          const int m = some_value;
          Bnode*         link[m];

        Bnode()
        {
          for (int index = 0; index < m; index++)
               link[index] = 0;
        }

        Bnode(ElementType item)
        {
          data = item;
          for (int index = 0; index < m; index++)
               link[index] = 0;
        }
     };
     void merge(Bnode*);
     void split(Bnode*);
};
```

27. The representation of general search trees as binary trees does not change the implementation of binary trees, just its interpretation. See chapter 10 for description of binary tree implementations. This chapter has concentrated on balancing which is not strictly necessary here.

Programming Problems

All these problems are drivers for tree functions and tree classes.

In each driver, one needs to construct a tree, traverse and/or modify it. For destructive actions, one needs to check that tree properties are preserved. One way to do this is to construct 2 tree objects, making the two trees identical. Alter one tree but not the other and compare the results. Then, undo the modifications made to the altered tree and compare it to the unaltered version. The two should be the same.

Drivers developed for chapter 10 can be modified for reuse here. Specifically, see programming problems 14 - 17 & 21 - 24 from chapter 10.

Chapter Fourteen: Graphs

14.1 Exercises

1. Adj: $\begin{bmatrix} 1101 \\ 1110 \\ 0111 \\ 1011 \end{bmatrix}$ Data: $\begin{bmatrix} 1 \\ 2 \\ 3 \\ 4 \end{bmatrix}$

2. Adj: $\begin{bmatrix} 1000 \\ 0100 \\ 0010 \\ 0001 \end{bmatrix}$ Data: $\begin{bmatrix} 16 \\ 22 \\ 40 \\ 57 \end{bmatrix}$

3. Adj: $\begin{bmatrix} 01000 \\ 00100 \\ 00010 \\ 00001 \\ 00000 \end{bmatrix}$ Data: $\begin{bmatrix} \text{B} \\ \text{BE} \\ \text{BEA} \\ \text{BEAR} \\ \text{BEARD} \end{bmatrix}$

4. Adj: $\begin{bmatrix} 011101 \\ 001000 \\ 010000 \\ 101010 \\ 011000 \\ 111010 \end{bmatrix}$ Data: $\begin{bmatrix} \text{cat} \\ \text{zebra} \\ \text{horse} \\ \text{rat} \\ \text{bear} \\ \text{dog} \end{bmatrix}$

5.

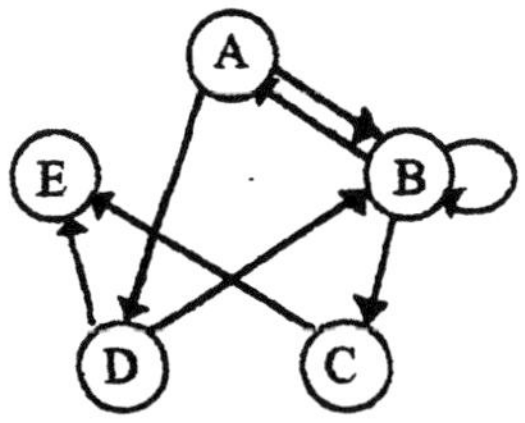

6.

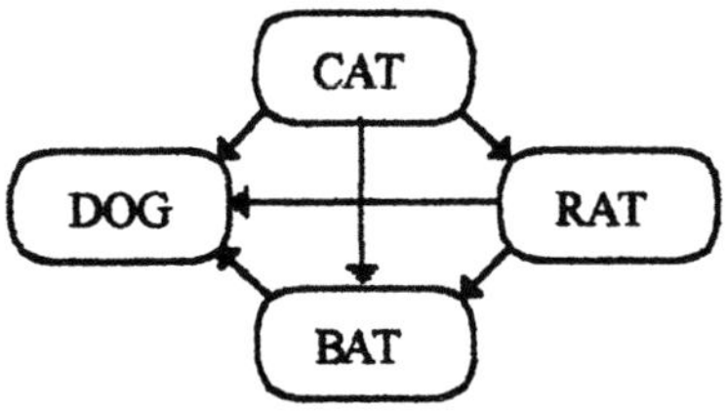

7.

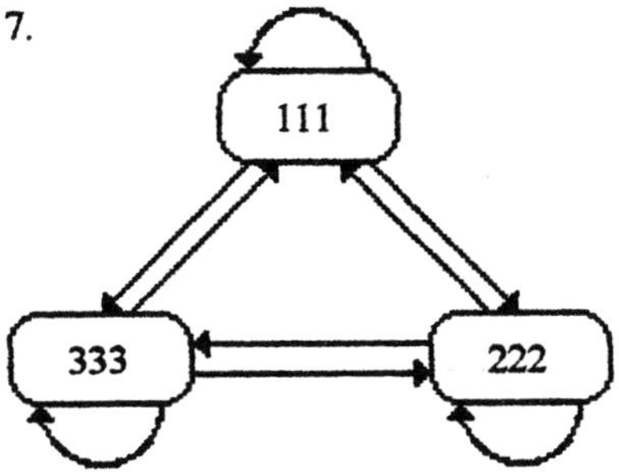

8.

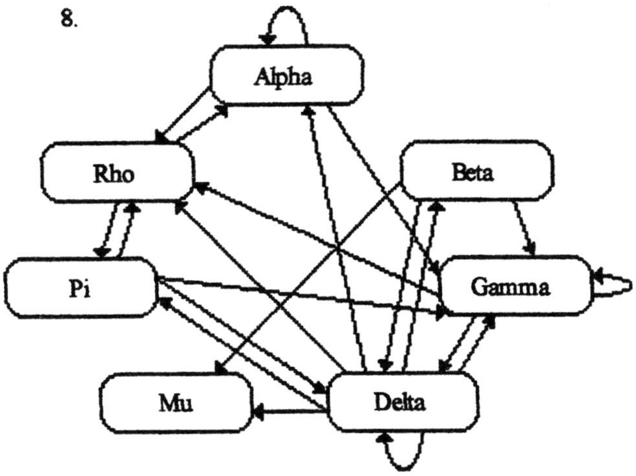

In the diagrams for Exercises 9-24, a dot in a node with no arrow emanating from it represents a null pointer.

9.

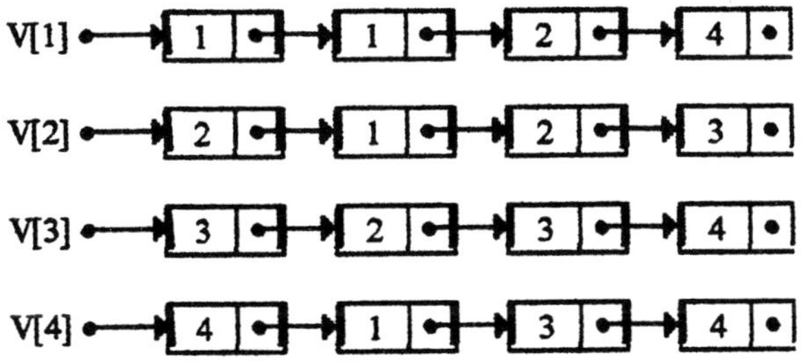

10.

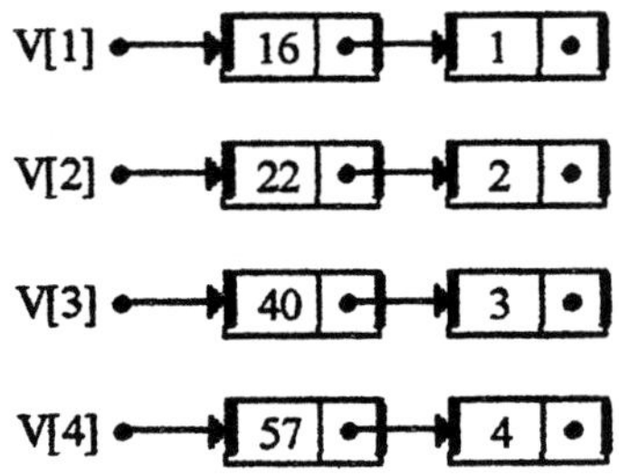
V[1]
16
1
V[2]
22
2
V[3]
40
3
V[4]
57
4

11.

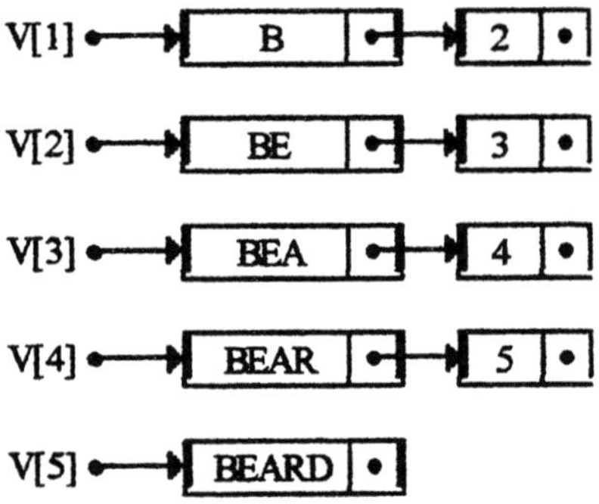
V[1]
B
2
V[2]
BE
3
V[3]
BEA
4
V[4]
BEAR
5
V[5]
BEARD

12.

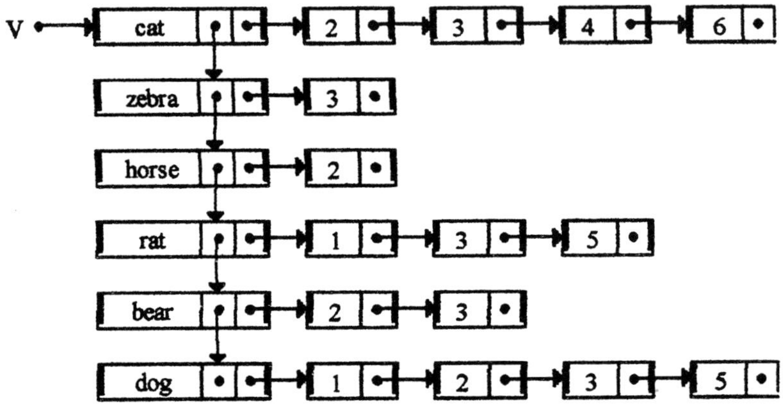
V
cat
2
3
4
6
zebra
3
horse
2
rat
1
3
5
bear
2
3
dog
1
2
3
5

13.

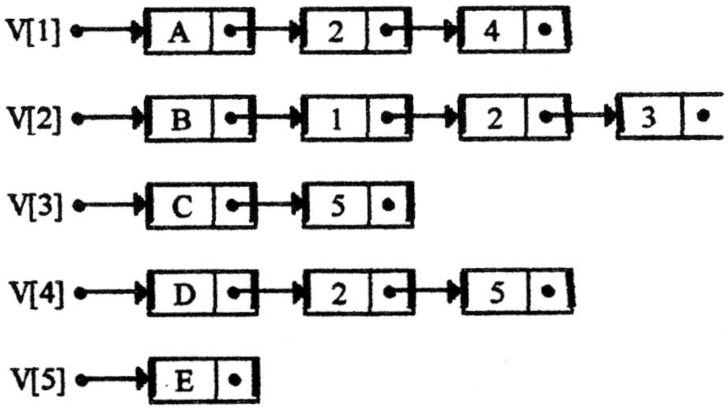
V[1]
A
2
4
V[2]
B
1
2
3
V[3]
C
5
V[4]
D
2
5
V[5]
E

14.

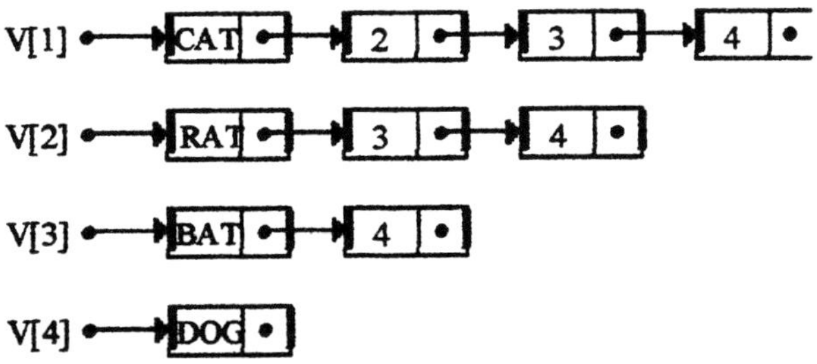
V[1]
CAT
2
3
4
V[2]
RAT
3
4
V[3]
BAT
4
V[4]
DOG

15.

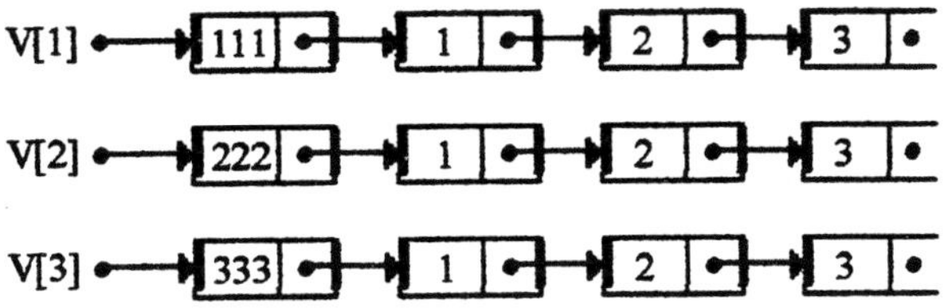
V[1]
111
1
2
3
V[2]
222
1
2
3
V[3]
333
1
2
3

16.

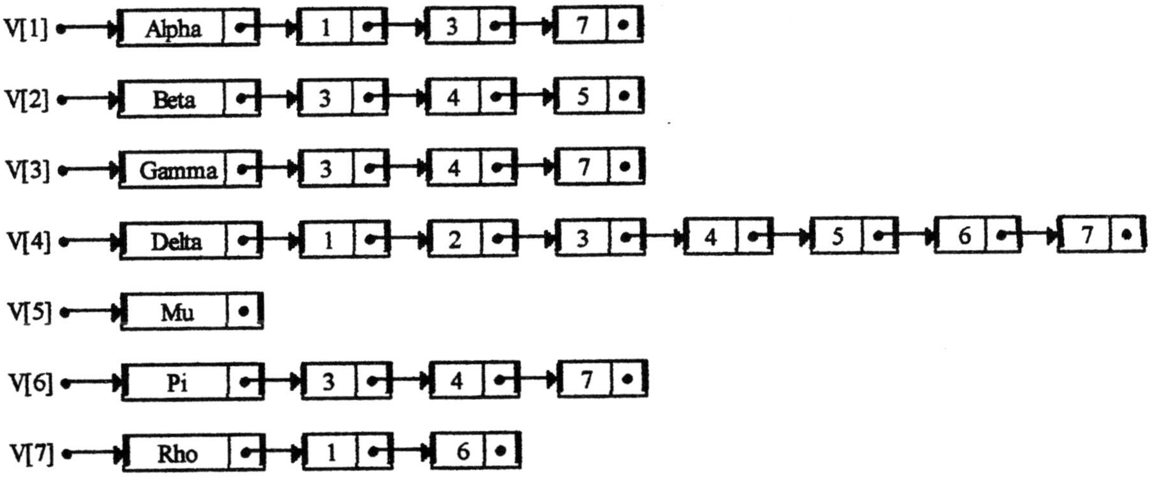
V[1]
Alpha
1
3
7
V[2]
Beta
3
4
5
V[3]
Gamma
3
4
7
V[4]
Delta
1
2
3
4
5
6
7
V[5]
Mu
V[6]
Pi
3
4
7
V[7]
Rho
1
6

17. 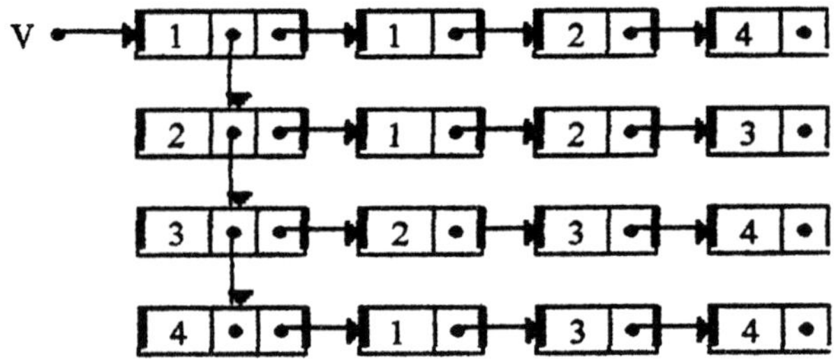
V
1
1
2
4
2
1
2
3
3
2
3
4
4
1
3
4

18. 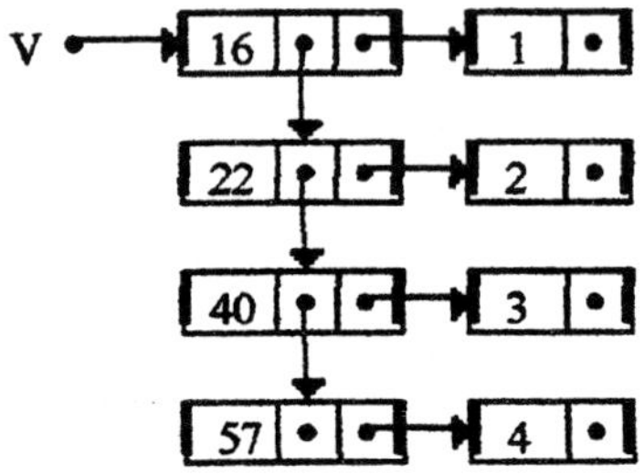
V
16
1
22
2
40
3
57
4

19. 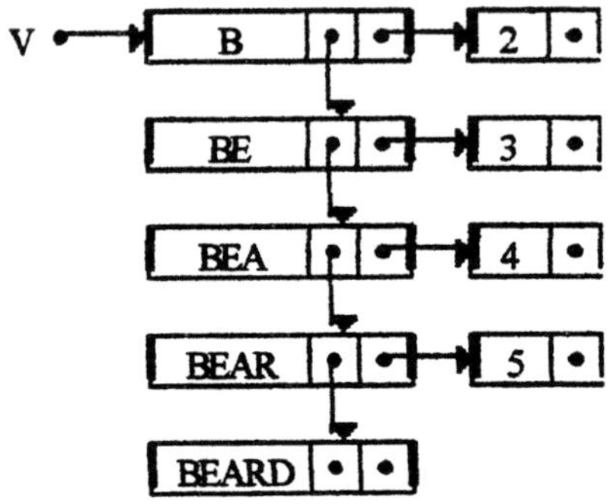
V
B
2
BE
3
BEA
4
BEAR
5
BEARD

20. 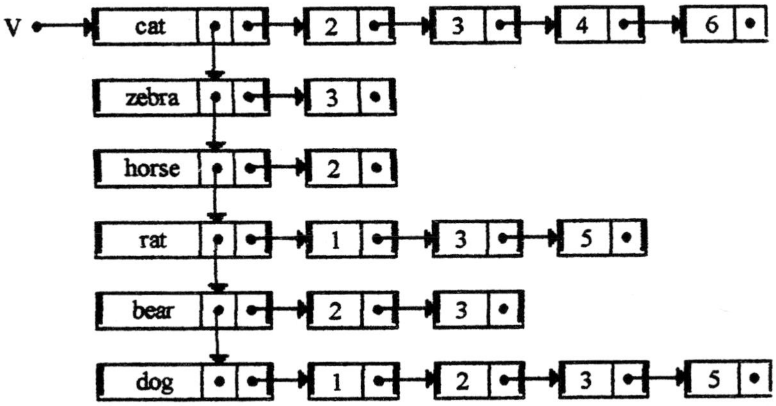
V
cat
2
3
4
6
zebra
3
horse
2
rat
1
3
5
bear
2
3
dog
1
2
3
5

21.

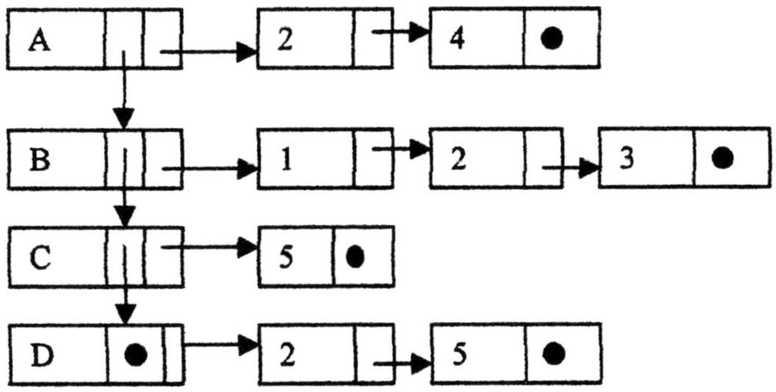

22.

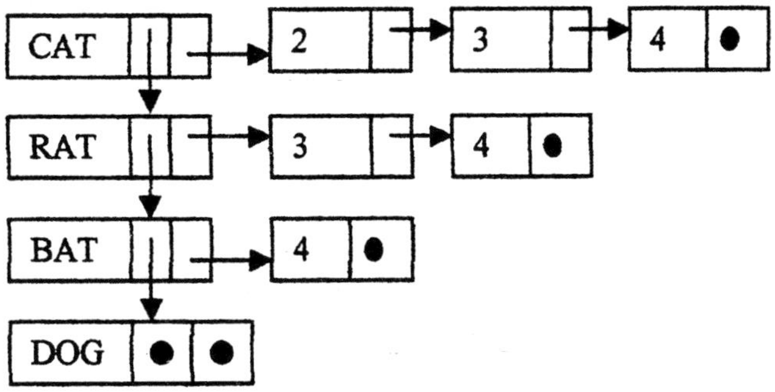

23.

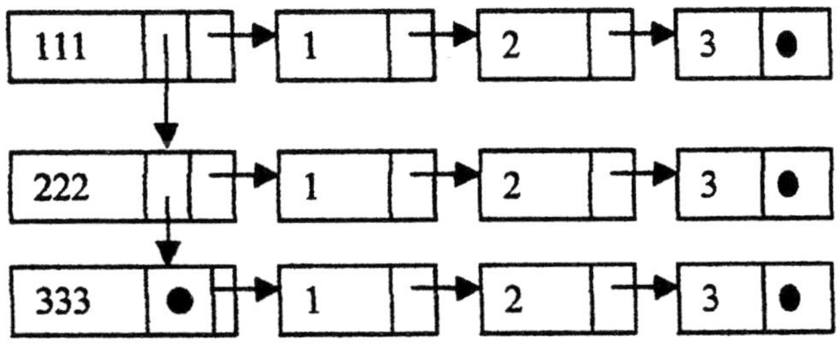

24.

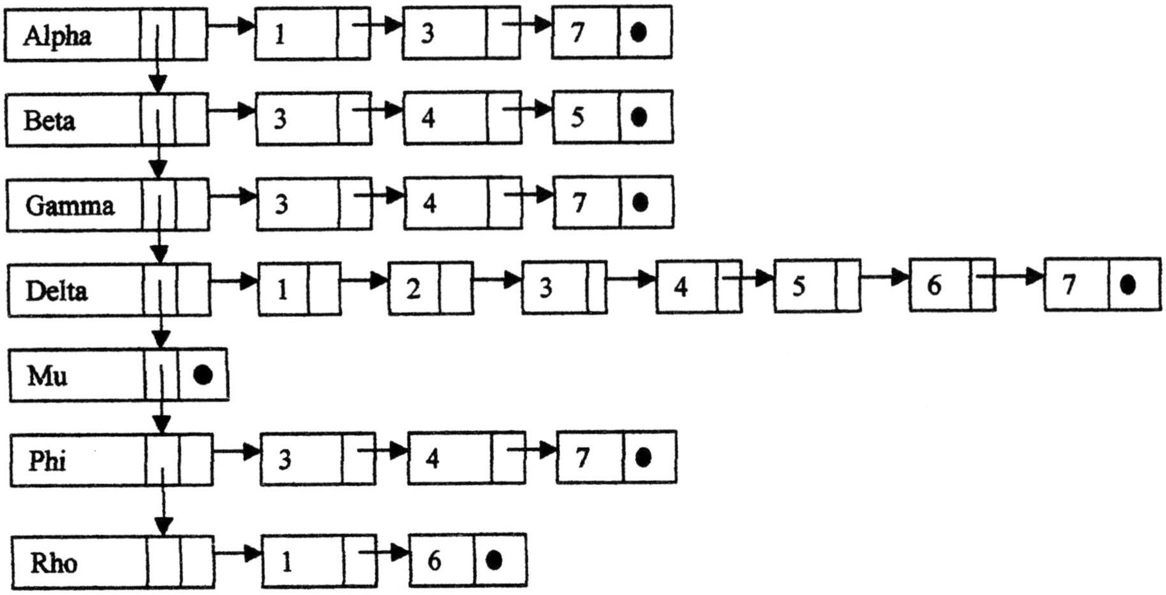

25.

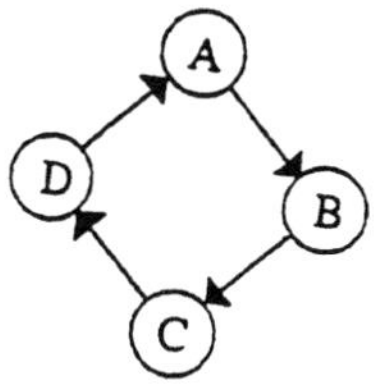

26.

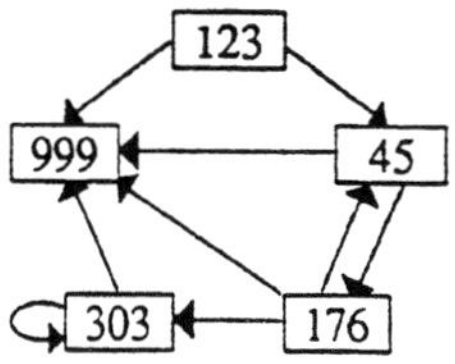

27.

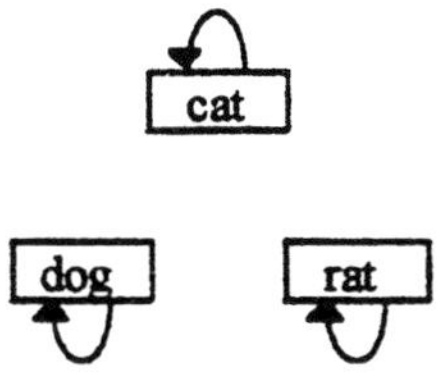

28.

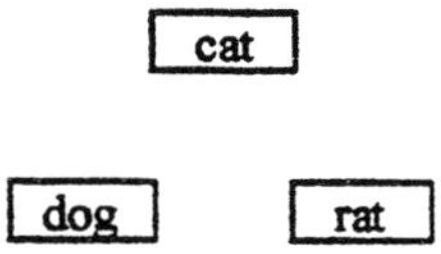

29.

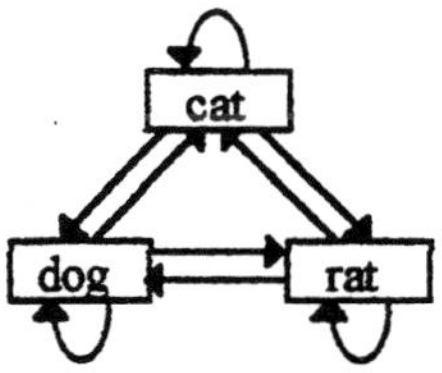

30.

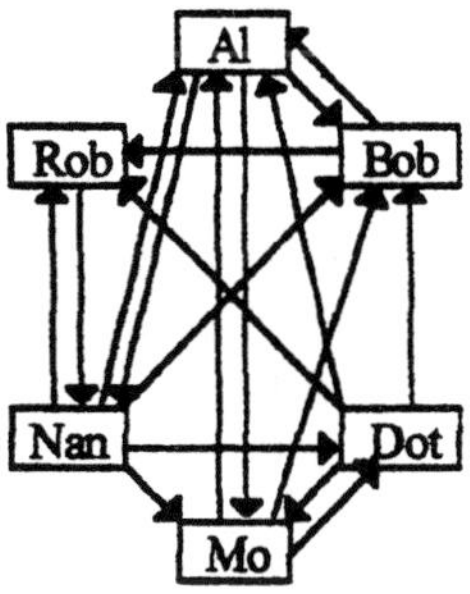

14.2 Exercises

1.

Step	v	w	Visit
1.	1		1
2.	1	2	
1.	2		2
2.	2	3	
1.	3		3
2.	3	4	
1.	4		4
2.	4		

2.

Step	v	w	Visit
1.	2		2
2.	2	3	
1.	3		3
2.	3	4	
1.	4		4
2.	4	1	
1.	1		1
2.	1		

3.

Step	v	Visit	Queue
1,2		1	1
3a	1		
3b	1	2 4	2 4
3a	2		4
3b	2	3	4 3
3a	4		3
3b	4		3
3a	3		
3b	3		

4.

Step	v	Visit	Queue
1,2		2	2
3a	2		
3b	2	1 3	1 3
3a	1		3
3b	1	4	3 4
3a	3		4
3b	3		4
3a	4		
3b	4		

5.

Step	v	Distance	Queue	Labels for 1	2	3	4
1,2,3		0	2		0		
4	2	0	1 3	1	0	1	
4	1	1	3 4	1	0	1	2

5 Distance = 2
6 P[2]=4, P[1]=1, P[0]=2

6.

Step	v	w	Visit
1.	cat		cat
2.	cat	zebra	
1.	zebra		zebra
2.	zebra	horse	
1.	horse		horse
2.	horse		
1.	rat		rat
2.	rat	bear	
1.	bear		bear
2.	bear		
1.	dog		dog
2.	dog		

7.

Step	v	w	Visit
1.	zebra		zebra
2.	zebra	horse	
1.	horse		horse
2.	horse		

8.

Step	v	Visit	Queue
1,2		cat	cat
3a	cat		
3b	cat	zebra, rat, dog	zebra rat dog
3a	zebra		rat dog
3b	zebra	horse	rat dog horse
3a	rat		dog horse
3b	rat	bear	dog horse bear
3a	dog		horse bear
3b	dog		horse bear
3a	horse		bear
3b	horse		bear
3a	bear		
3b	bear		

9.

Step	v	Visit	Queue
1,2		zebra	zebra
3a	zebra		
3b	zebra	horse	horse
3a	horse		
3b	horse		

10.

Step	v	Distance	Queue	Labels for cat	zebra	horse	rat	bear	dog
1,2,3		0	rat				0		
4	rat	0	cat horse bear	1		1	0	1	
4	cat	1	zebra dog	1	2	1	0	1	2

5 Distance = 2

7 P[2]=dog, P[1]=cat, P[0]=rat

11.

Step	v	w	Visit
1.	A		A
2.	A	B	
1.	B		B
2.	B	C	
1.	C		C
2.	C	E	
1.	E		E
2.	E	F	
1.	F		F
2.	F	J	
1.	J		J
2.	J	K	
1.	K		K
2.	K	I	
1.	I		I
2.	I		
1.	G		G
2.	G	H	
1.	H		H
2.	H		
1.	D		D
2.	D		

12.

Step	v	w	Visit
1.	F		F
2.	F	J	
1.	J		J
2.	J	K	
1.	K		K
2.	K	I	
1.	I		I
2.	I		

13.

Step	v	Visit	Queue
1,2		A	A
3a	A		
3b	A	BD	BD
3a	B		D
3b	B	C	DC
3a	D		C
3b	D		C
3a	C		
3b	C	EF	EF
3a	E		F
3b	E	GI	FGI
3a	F		GI
3b	F	J	GIJ
3a	G		IJ
3b	G	H	IJH
3a	I		JH
3b	I		JH
3a	J		H
3b	J	K	HK
3a	H		K
3b	H		K
3a	K		
3b	K		

14.

Step	v	Visit	Queue
1,2		F	F
3a	F		
3b	F	J	J
3a	J		
3b	J	K	K
3a	K		
3b	K	I	I
3a	I		
3b	I		

15.

Step	v	Distance	Queue	Labels for A	B	C	D	E	F	G	H	I	J	K
1,2,3		0	A	0										
4	A	0	BD	0	1		1							
4	B	1	DC	0	1	2	1							
4	D	1	C	0	1	2	1							
4	C	2	EF	0	1	2	1	3	3					

5 Distance = 3

6 P[3]=E, P[2]=C, P[1]=B, P[0]=A

16.

Step	v	Distance	Queue	A	B	C	D	E	F	G	H	I	J	K
1,2,3		0	A	0										
4	A	0	BD	0	1		1							
4	B	1	DC	0	1	2	1							
4	D	1	C	0	1	2	1							
4	C	2	EF	0	1	2	1	3	3					
4	E	3	FGI	0	1	2	1	3	3	4		4		
4	F	3	GIJ	0	1	2	1	3	3	4		4	5	
4	G	4	IJH	0	1	2	1	3	3	4	5	4	5	

(Label columns: Labels for A B C D E F G H I J K)

5 Distance = 5

6 P[5]=H, P[4]=G, P[3]=E, P[2]=C, P[1]=B, P[0]=A

17.

Step	v	Distance	Queue	A	B	C	D	E	F	G	H	I	J	K
1,2,3		0	G							0				
4	G	0	HI							0	1	1		
4	H	1	IAE	2				2		0	1	1		
4	I	1	AEJ	2				2		0	1	1	2	
4	A	2	EJBD	2	3		3	2		0	1	1	2	
4	E	2	JBDF	2	3		3	2	3	0	1	1	2	
4	J	2	BDFK	2	3		3	2	3	0	1	1	2	3
4	B	3	DFKC	2	3	4	3	2	3	0	1	1	2	3

(Label columns: Labels A B C D E F G H I J K)

5 Distance = 4

6 P[4]=C, P[3]=B, P[2]=A, P[1]=H, P[0]=G

18.

Step	v	Distance	Queue	A	B	C	D	E	F	G	H	I	J	K
1,2,3		0	J										0	
4	J	0	K										0	1
4	K	1	I									2	0	1

(Label columns: Labels for A B C D E F G H I J K)

5 Distance = 2

6 P[2]=I, P[1]=K, P[0]=J

19.

Step	v	Distance	Queue	A	B	C	D	E	F	G	H	I	J	K
1,2,3		0	J										0	
4	J	0	K										0	1
4	K	1	I									2	0	1
4	I	2	EMPTY											

(Label columns: Labels for A B C D E F G H I J K)

5 No such path.

20. /* BFS for digraph class template. */

```
#include "QueueT.h"       // or could use STL

void Digraph<DataType>::BFS(int start)
{
    // process v[start].data here

    Queue<VertexInfo>   Q;
    Q.addq(v[start]);

    while (!Q.empty())
    {
        VertexInfo      v = Q.removeq();

        for (list<int>::iterator
                    it = v[start].adjacencyList.begin();
                    it != v[start].adjacencyList.end();
                    it++)

            if (unvisited[*it]}
            {
                // process *it here

                Q.addq(*it);
            }
    }
    return;
}
```

21. /* find reachability matrix. Use matrix multiplication and addition developed previously */

```
#include "Matrix.h"

Matrix findReachM(Matrix G)
{

     Matrix I = Matrix(G.size());

     I.initialize();             //set I to identity matrix

     Matrix A = G;
     Matrix Aprod = A;
     Matrix R = I + G;
```

```
    for (int index = 2; index < G.size(); index++)
    {
            R += A*Aprod;
            Aprod *= A;
    }
    return R;
}
```

22. This approach is a simple modification of #21. Use boolean values to represent edges (paths) rather than 0s and 1s. Use && instead of multiplication and || instead of addition.

23. The reachability matrix is:

$$R = \begin{bmatrix} 0\,1\,1\,1\,1 \\ 0\,1\,1\,1\,0 \\ 0\,1\,1\,1\,0 \\ 0\,0\,0\,1\,0 \\ 0\,0\,0\,0\,0 \end{bmatrix}$$

24. This exercise is a straight-forward implementation of the algorithm given in #23.

14.3 Exercises

1. Adj: $\begin{bmatrix} 0111 \\ 1011 \\ 1101 \\ 1110 \end{bmatrix}$ Data: $\begin{bmatrix} 1 \\ 2 \\ 3 \\ 4 \end{bmatrix}$

2. Adj: $\begin{bmatrix} 0100 \\ 1010 \\ 0101 \\ 0010 \end{bmatrix}$ Data: $\begin{bmatrix} 16 \\ 22 \\ 40 \\ 57 \end{bmatrix}$

3 Adj: $\begin{bmatrix} 01001 \\ 10100 \\ 01010 \\ 00101 \\ 10010 \end{bmatrix}$ Data: $\begin{bmatrix} \text{B} \\ \text{BE} \\ \text{BEA} \\ \text{BEAR} \\ \text{BEARD} \end{bmatrix}$

4. Adj:

$$\begin{bmatrix} 0110000 \\ 1000100 \\ 1000100 \\ 0000011 \\ 0110000 \\ 0001001 \\ 0001010 \end{bmatrix}$$

Data: $\begin{bmatrix} \text{moose} \\ \text{zebra} \\ \text{horse} \\ \text{rat} \\ \text{bear} \\ \text{dog} \\ \text{cow} \end{bmatrix}$

5.

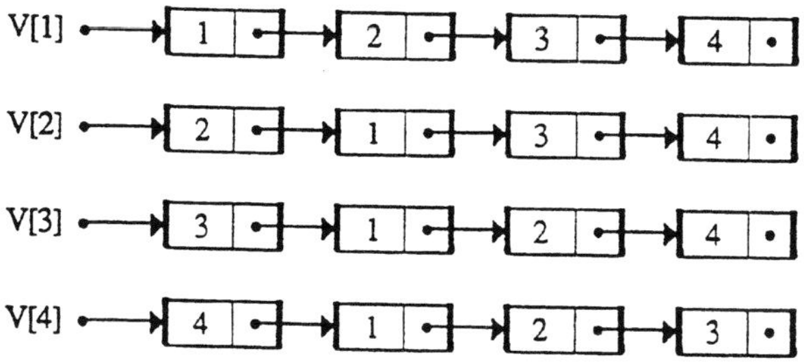
V[1] 1 2 3 4
V[2] 2 1 3 4
V[3] 3 1 2 4
V[4] 4 1 2 3

6.

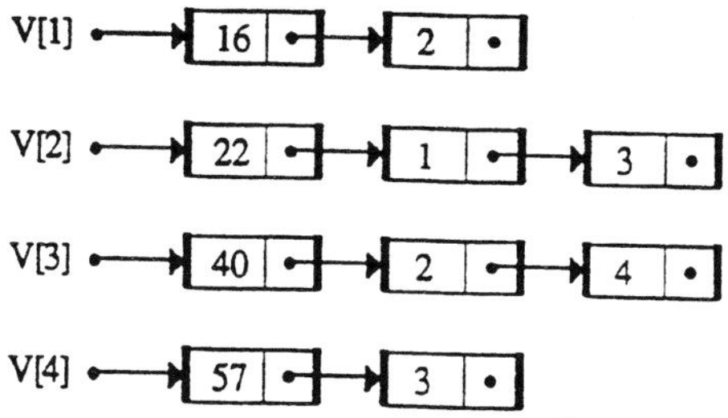
V[1] 16 2
V[2] 22 1 3
V[3] 40 2 4
V[4] 57 3

7.

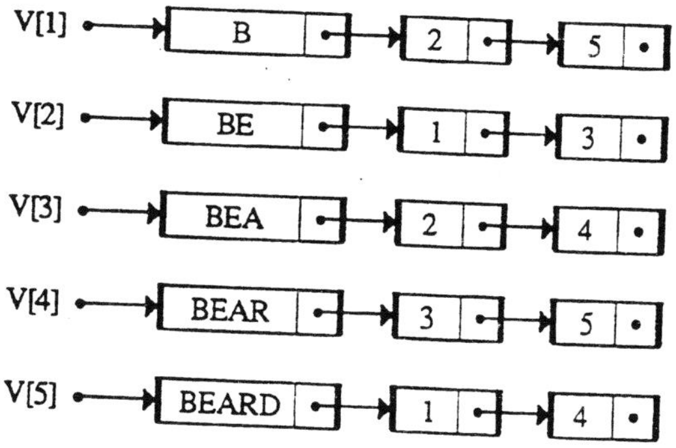
V[1] B 2 5
V[2] BE 1 3
V[3] BEA 2 4
V[4] BEAR 3 5
V[5] BEARD 1 4

8.

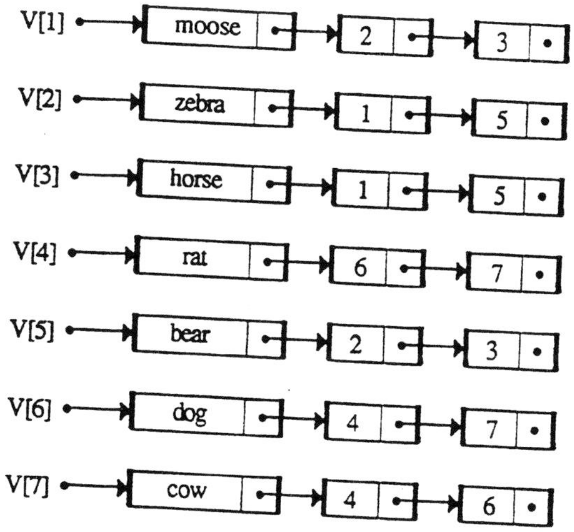
V[1] moose 2 3
V[2] zebra 1 5
V[3] horse 1 5
V[4] rat 6 7
V[5] bear 2 3
V[6] dog 4 7
V[7] cow 4 6

9.

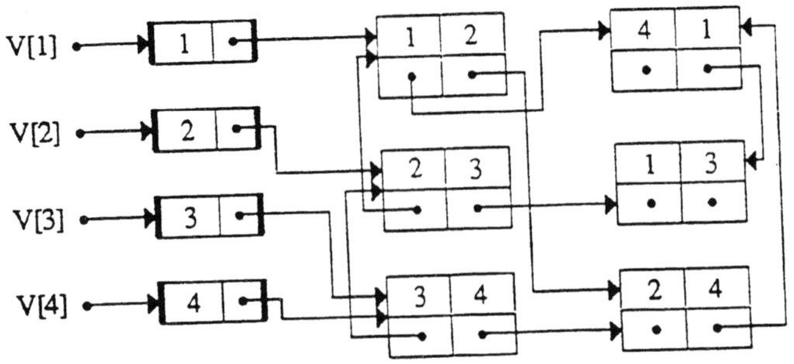
V[1]
1
V[2]
2
V[3]
3
V[4]
4
1 2
2 3
3 4
4 1
1 3
2 4

10.

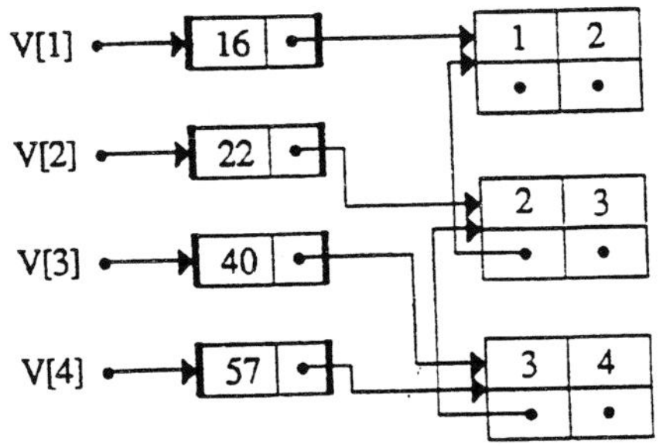
V[1]
16
V[2]
22
V[3]
40
V[4]
57
1 2
2 3
3 4

11.

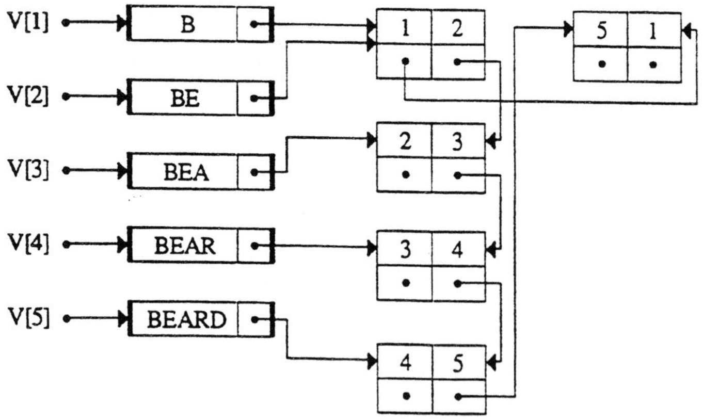
V[1]
B
V[2]
BE
V[3]
BEA
V[4]
BEAR
V[5]
BEARD
1 2
2 3
3 4
4 5
5 1

12.

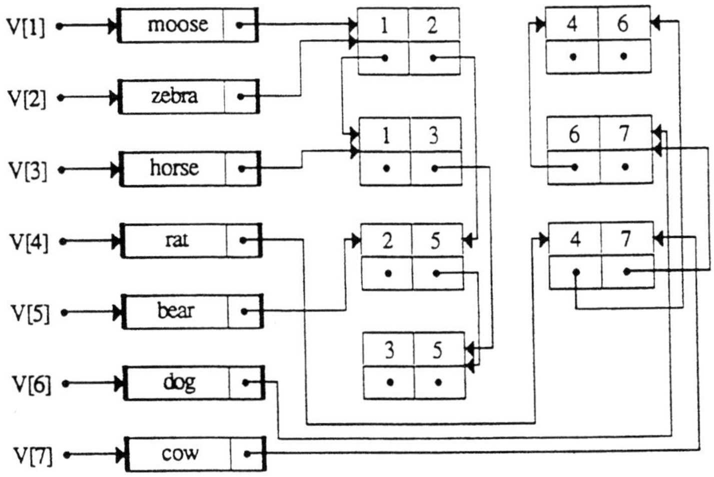
V[1]
V[2]
V[3]
V[4]
V[5]
V[6]
V[7]
moose
zebra
horse
rat
bear
dog
cow
1 2
1 3
2 5
3 5
4 6
6 7
4 7

13.

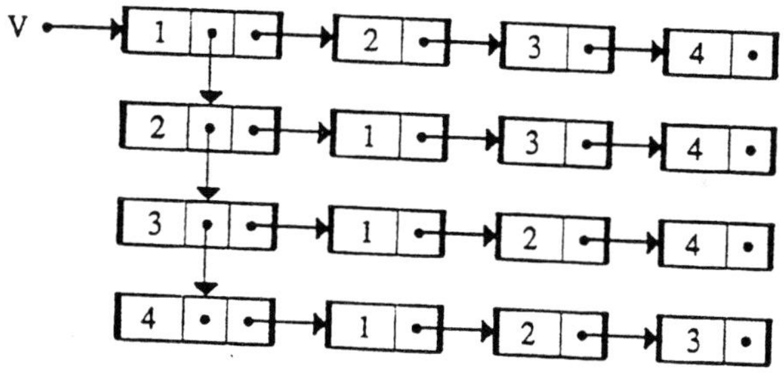
V
1
2
3
4
2
1
3
4
3
1
2
4
4
1
2
3

14.

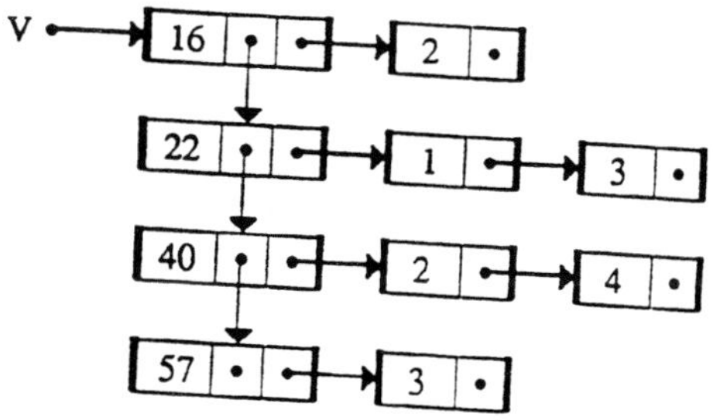
V
16
2
22
1
3
40
2
4
57
3

15.

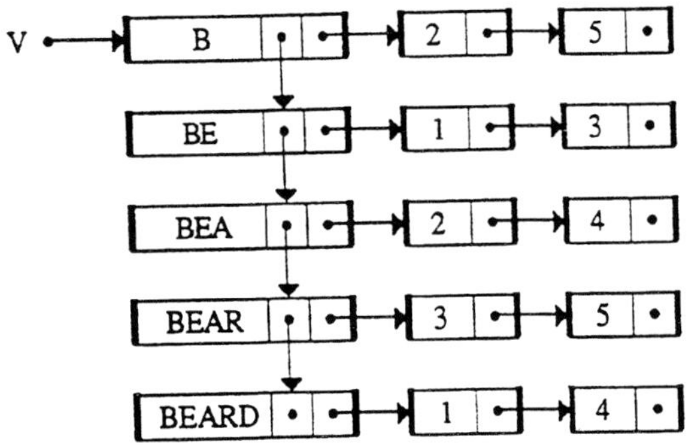
V
B
2
5
BE
1
3
BEA
2
4
BEAR
3
5
BEARD
1
4

16.

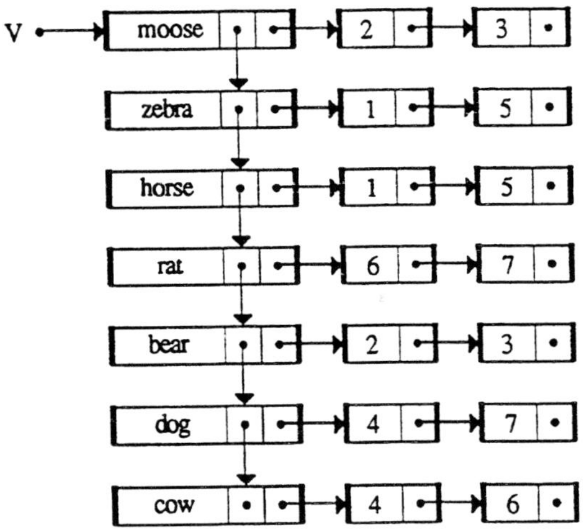
V
moose
2
3
zebra
1
5
horse
1
5
rat
6
7
bear
2
3
dog
4
7
cow
4
6

17.

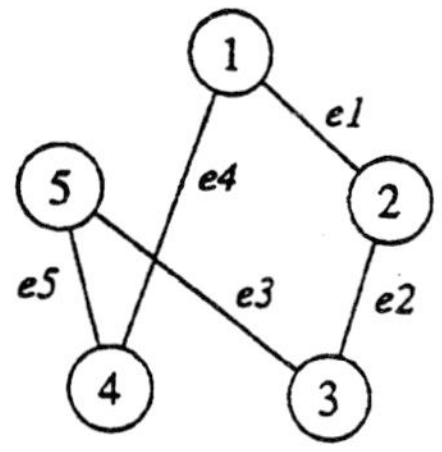
1
2
3
4
5
e1
e2
e3
e4
e5

18.

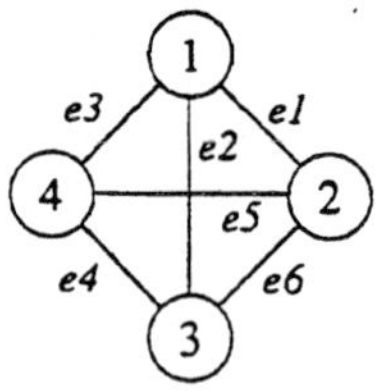
1
2
3
4
e1
e2
e3
e4
e5
e6

19.

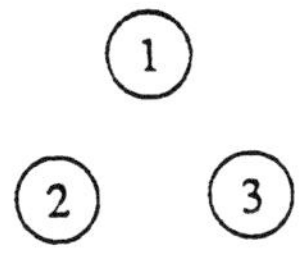

20.

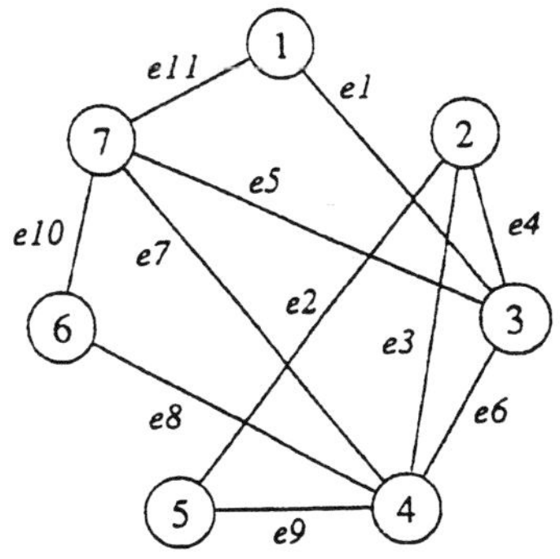

21.

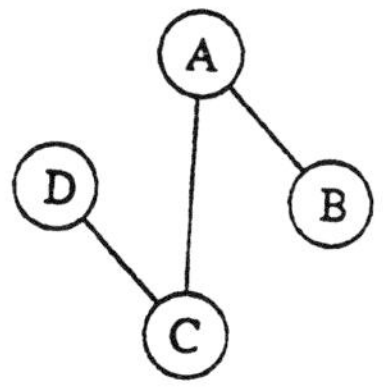

22.

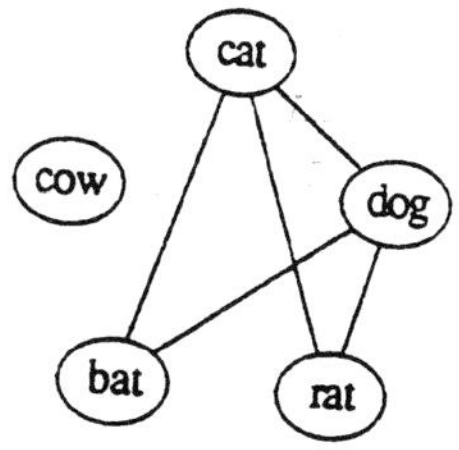

23.

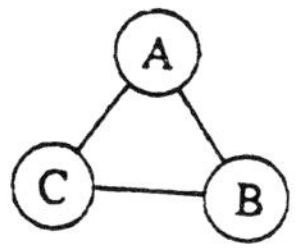

24.

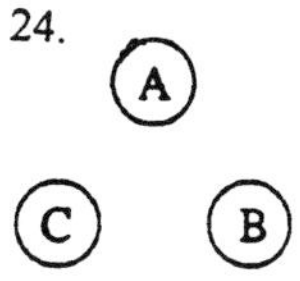

25.

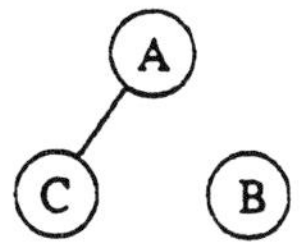

26.

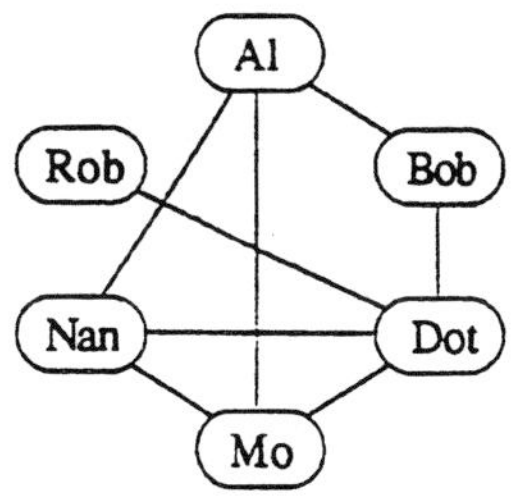

27.

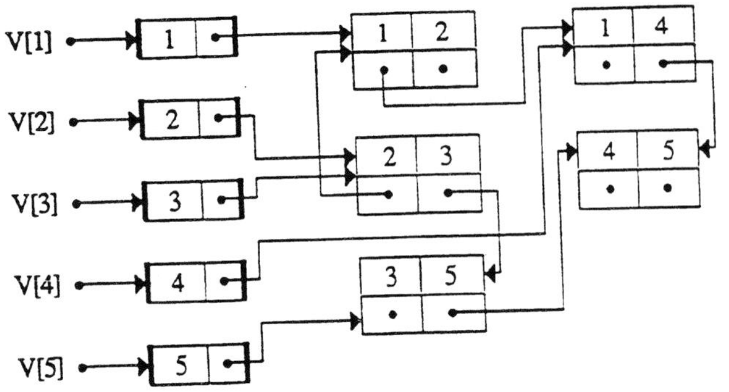
V[1]
V[2]
V[3]
V[4]
V[5]
1
2
3
4
5
1 2
2 3
3 5
1 4
4 5

28.

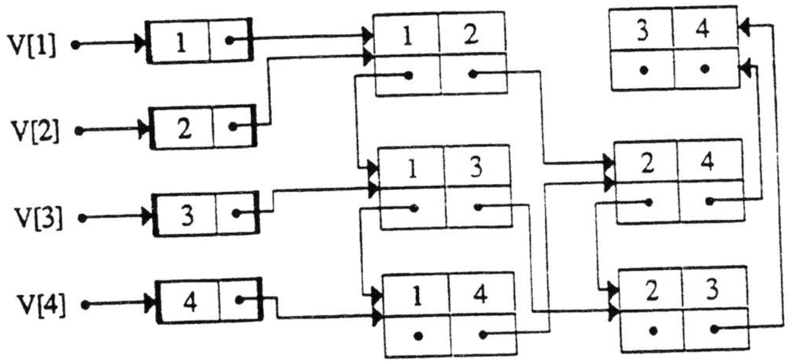
V[1]
V[2]
V[3]
V[4]
1
2
3
4
1 2
1 3
1 4
3 4
2 4
2 3

29.

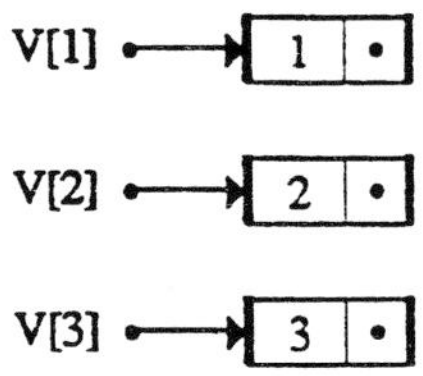
V[1]
V[2]
V[3]
1
2
3

30.

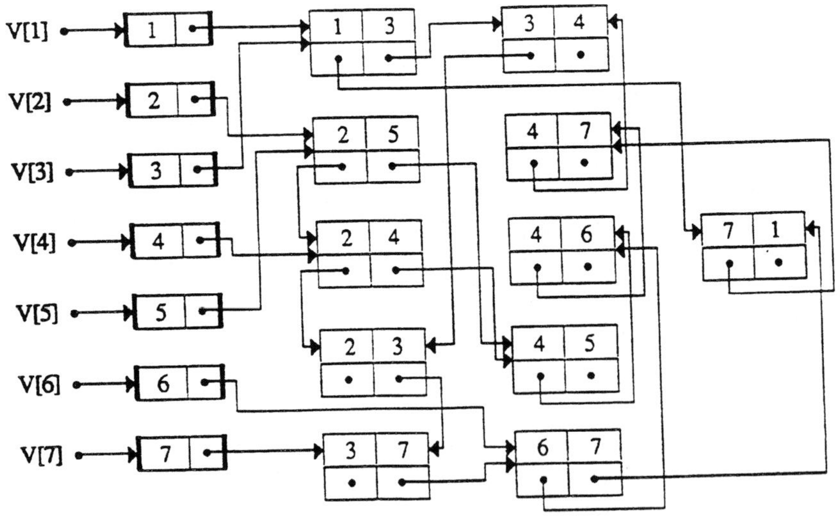
V[1]
V[2]
V[3]
V[4]
V[5]
V[6]
V[7]
1
2
3
4
5
6
7
1 3
2 5
2 4
2 3
3 7
3 4
4 7
4 6
4 5
6 7
7 1

33. Algorithm to insert a new vertex and its connecting edges into a graph:

1. Get a new head node.

2. Search the array V to find the first V[k] = null and set V[k] to point to this new head node. // Assume V is initialized to null

3. Set the data field of the head node to the given item.

4. Repeat the following for each vertex number adjacent to the new vertex, as entered by the user:

    a. Add a new node to the new vertex list, having the number of the adjacent vertex.

    b. Add a new node to the adjacent vertex list, having the number of the new vertex.

34. Algorithm to search for a vertex containing a given data item:

Simply search the V array for a head node containing the data item.

35. Algorithm to delete a given data item and all edges incident to it:

1. Read the data item.

2. Search the V array for the head node containing the data item // assume found at location k.

3. ptr = V[k]->Next.

4. While (ptr != 0)

    a. Search the V[ptr->Vertex] list for the node whose data item is the given data item and delete this node from the list.

    b. Set ptr = ptr->Next.

5. Delete the entire list at V[k], setting V[k] to null.

36. Algorithm to find all vertices adjacent to a given vertex:

    1. Read the data item of a vertex.

    2. Search the V array for the head node containing the data item.
       Assume found at location k.

    3. ptr = V[k]->Next.

    4. While (ptr != 0)
       a. An adjacent vertex is V[ptr->Vertex->Data.
       b. ptr = ptr->Next.

37. One method of determining if a graph (with adjacency matrix A) has a cycle follows:

    1. Multiply A times itself (producing matrix A^2).

    2. Set i = 2 and done = false.

    3. While (!done)

       a. Multiply A times itself.
       b. If the diagonal of A has a non-zero entry, or i = number of vertices in graph
          done = true
          Else
          i = i + 1.

    4. If i = number of vertices in the graph, then the graph has no cycle.

38. To easily determine if the addition of an edge will form a cycle, one need only to test if both endpoints of the edge lie in the spanning tree already constructed. If so, discard the edge because it will form a cycle if added. If not, add it to the spanning tree. One is done when (n-1) edges have been added to the spanning tree.

39. Kruskal's algorithm is a simple modification of the above algorithm where one selects at each step the cheapest possible candidate edge. The most efficient implementation of this algorithm uses (min) heaps (O nlogn) to order the edges so that the selection cost is minimal.

Programming Problems

1. - 4. These problems are all drivers for graphical functions that are essentially scans of 2D structures (graphs).

In each, one needs to construct a graph and then apply the noted function.

Results need to be confirmed, i.e. make sure modifications are made and that non-destructive manipulations do not change the graph object manipulated.

A standard method of confirmation is to construct 2 graph objects, making the two graphs identical. Run the function on one graph but not the other and compare the results. Then, undo the modifications made to the altered graph and compare it to the unaltered version. The two should be the same.

See the driver for #7 - #13.

5 - 6. These two problems deal with an alteration of the private data representation of the class template Digraph. One needs to replace the adjacency-list representation with first adjacency-matrix representation and then linked adjacency-list representation.

These exercises involved then a rewrite of the class template implementation but should NOT affect the interface at all.

7 - 13. These problems are all drivers for graphical functions.

Note that some of these functions are non-destructive scans (#10 - #13) while the others are destructive.

The strategy used for the drivers in 1-4 can be used for 10 - 13.

For the remaining, additional testing needs to be done to insure that alteration of the graph has preserved intended properties of the graph (e.g. vertex-insertion may create cycles but it should not disconnect the graph).

```
#include "Graph.h"
#include <iostream>

using namespace std;

int main()
{
     int numVertices, numEdges;

     cout << "Enter the number of vertices, followed by
               the number of edges in the graph"  << endl;
     cin >> numVertices >> numEdges;

     Graph<char>    g;
     g.read(cin, numVertices, numEdges);

     Graph<char>    backup = g;

     bool one_piece = g.Connected();

     g.search();              // item not found
     g.cycle();
     g.adjacent();
     g.SpanningT();

     g.insert();              // insert item

     g.search();              // item found
     g.cycle();
     g.adjacent();
     g.SpanningT();

     if (one_piece == g.Connected)
          cout << "Insertion ok, graph still connected"
               << endl;
     else if (one_piece)
          cout << "Problem, insertion disconnected
               the graph" << endl;

     g.delete();

     if (g == backup)
          cout << "OK, graph back in original state"
               << endl;
     else
          cout << "Problem with insert or delete" << endl;
     return 0;
}
```

14 -16. Like 5 & 6, these problems involve an alteration of the private data representation of a class template. One needs to replace the edge-list representation of the class template Graph with first adjacency-matrix representation, then adjacency-list representation and finally linked adjacency-list representation.

These exercises involved then a rewrite of the class template implementation but should NOT affect the interface at all.

17. This programming project brings together the graph construction functionality discussed in the text with the functions exercised above. A user-interface needs to layered on top. #a and #b involve altering the graph while #c and #d involve retrieving information from the graph via a scan. One design issue that involves the user interface and the ease with which the graph is constructed is how to represent what jobs a person is qualified for. Presumably, one could simply enumerate after inserting a new applicant. When inserting a new job position, however, one needs to scan the graph, and for each person-vertex, query the user as to whether this person is qualified for the newly added job.